2

STORY & ART BY MOTORO MASE

IKIGAMI

THE ULTIMATE LIMIT

IKIGAMI
THE ULTIMATE LIMIT

VIZ Signature Edition

STORY AND ART BY Motoro Mase

Translation/John Werry
English Adaptation/Kristina Blachere
Touch-up Art & Lettering/Freeman Wong
Design/Amy Martin
Editors/Joel Enos and Rich Amtower

Editor in Chief, Books/Alvin Lu
Editor in Chief, Magazines/Marc Weidenbaum
VP, Publishing Licensing/Rika Inouye
VP, Sales & Product Marketing/Gonzalo Ferreyra
VP, Creative/Linda Espinosa
Publisher/Hyoe Narita

IKIGAMI 2 by Motoro MASE
© 2006 Motoro MASE
All rights reserved. Original Japanese edition
published in 2006 by Shogakukan Inc., Tokyo.

Printed in the U.S.A.

Published by VIZ Media, LLC
P.O. Box 77010
San Francisco, CA 94107

VIZ Signature Edition
10 9 8 7 6 5 4 3 2 1
First printing, August 2009

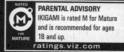

www.viz.com

store.viz.com

IKIGAMI

THE ULTIMATE LIMIT

VOL. 2 STORY & ART BY MOTORO MASE

IKIGAMI
THE ULTIMATE LIMIT

CONTENTS

Episode 3 The Pure Love Drug Act 1

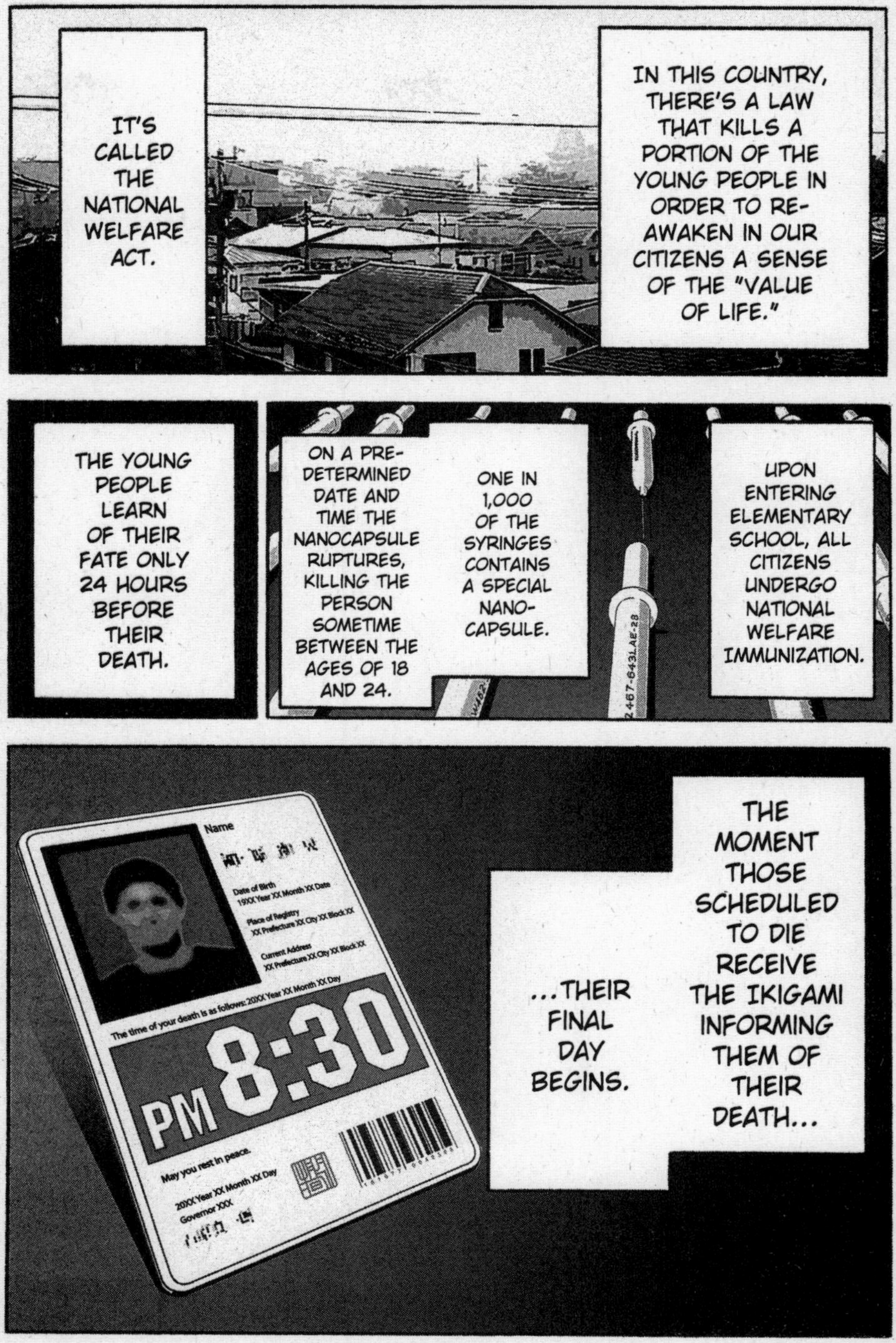
IN THIS COUNTRY, THERE'S A LAW THAT KILLS A PORTION OF THE YOUNG PEOPLE IN ORDER TO RE-AWAKEN IN OUR CITIZENS A SENSE OF THE "VALUE OF LIFE."
IT'S CALLED THE NATIONAL WELFARE ACT.
UPON ENTERING ELEMENTARY SCHOOL, ALL CITIZENS UNDERGO NATIONAL WELFARE IMMUNIZATION.
2467-643LAE-28
ONE IN 1,000 OF THE SYRINGES CONTAINS A SPECIAL NANO-CAPSULE.
ON A PRE-DETERMINED DATE AND TIME THE NANOCAPSULE RUPTURES, KILLING THE PERSON SOMETIME BETWEEN THE AGES OF 18 AND 24.
THE YOUNG PEOPLE LEARN OF THEIR FATE ONLY 24 HOURS BEFORE THEIR DEATH.
THE MOMENT THOSE SCHEDULED TO DIE RECEIVE THE IKIGAMI INFORMING THEM OF THEIR DEATH...
...THEIR FINAL DAY BEGINS.
Name
Date of Birth
19XX Year XX Month XX Date
Place of Registry
XX Prefecture XX City XX Block XX
Current Address
XX Prefecture XX City XX Block XX
The time of your death is as follows: 20XX Year XX Month XX Day
PM 8:30
May you rest in peace.
20XX Year XX Month XX Day
Governor XXX

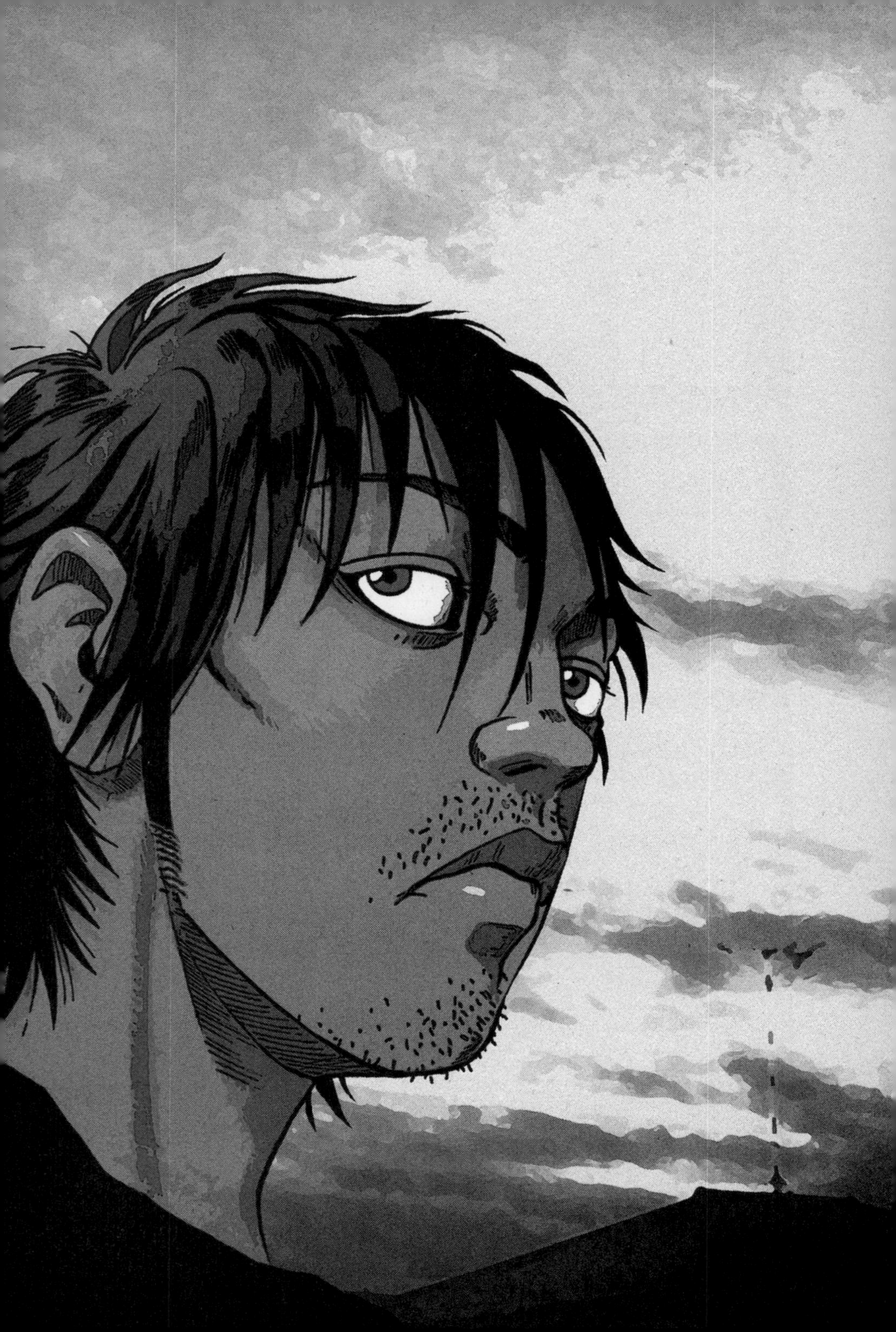

Episode 3 The Pure Love Drug Act 1

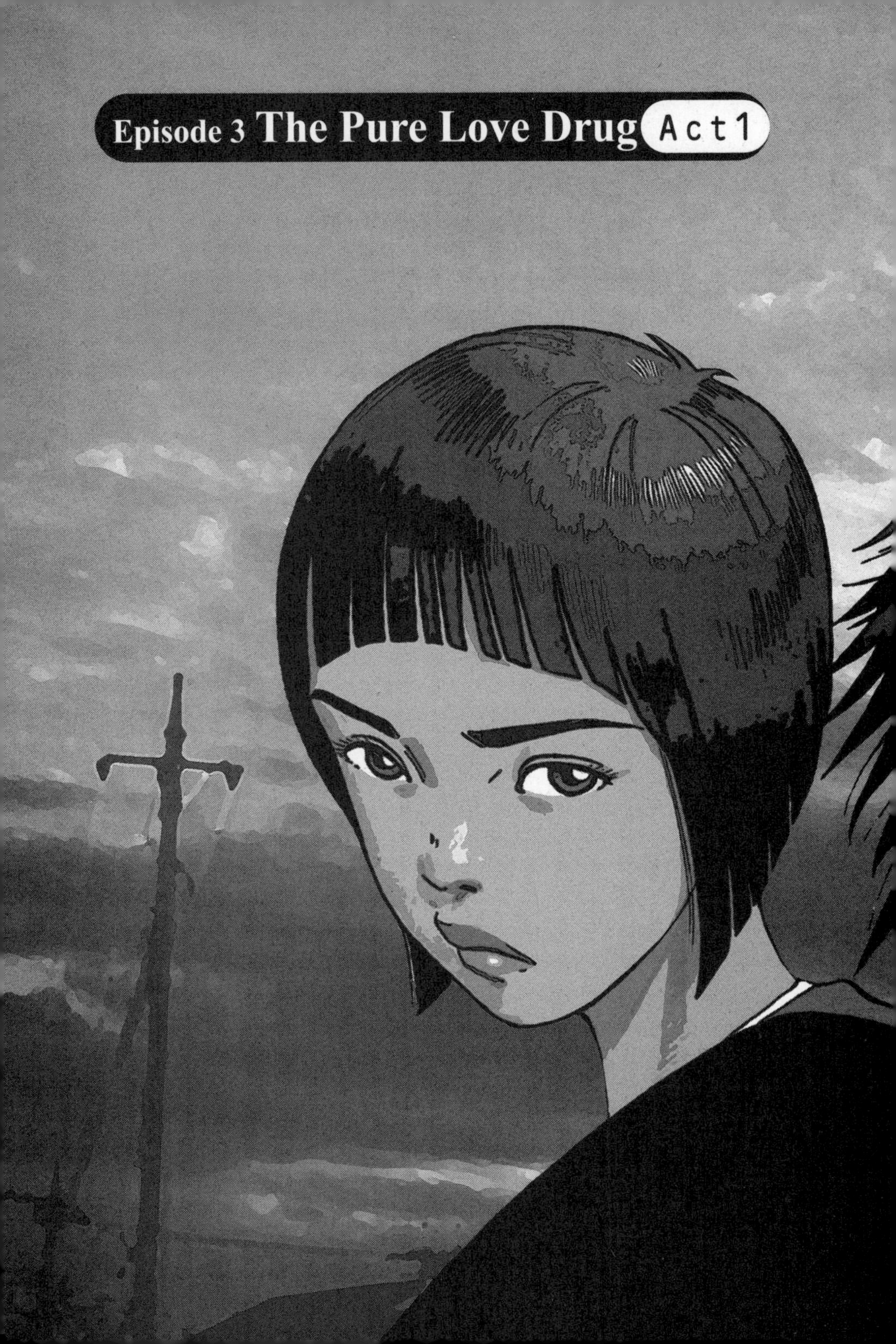

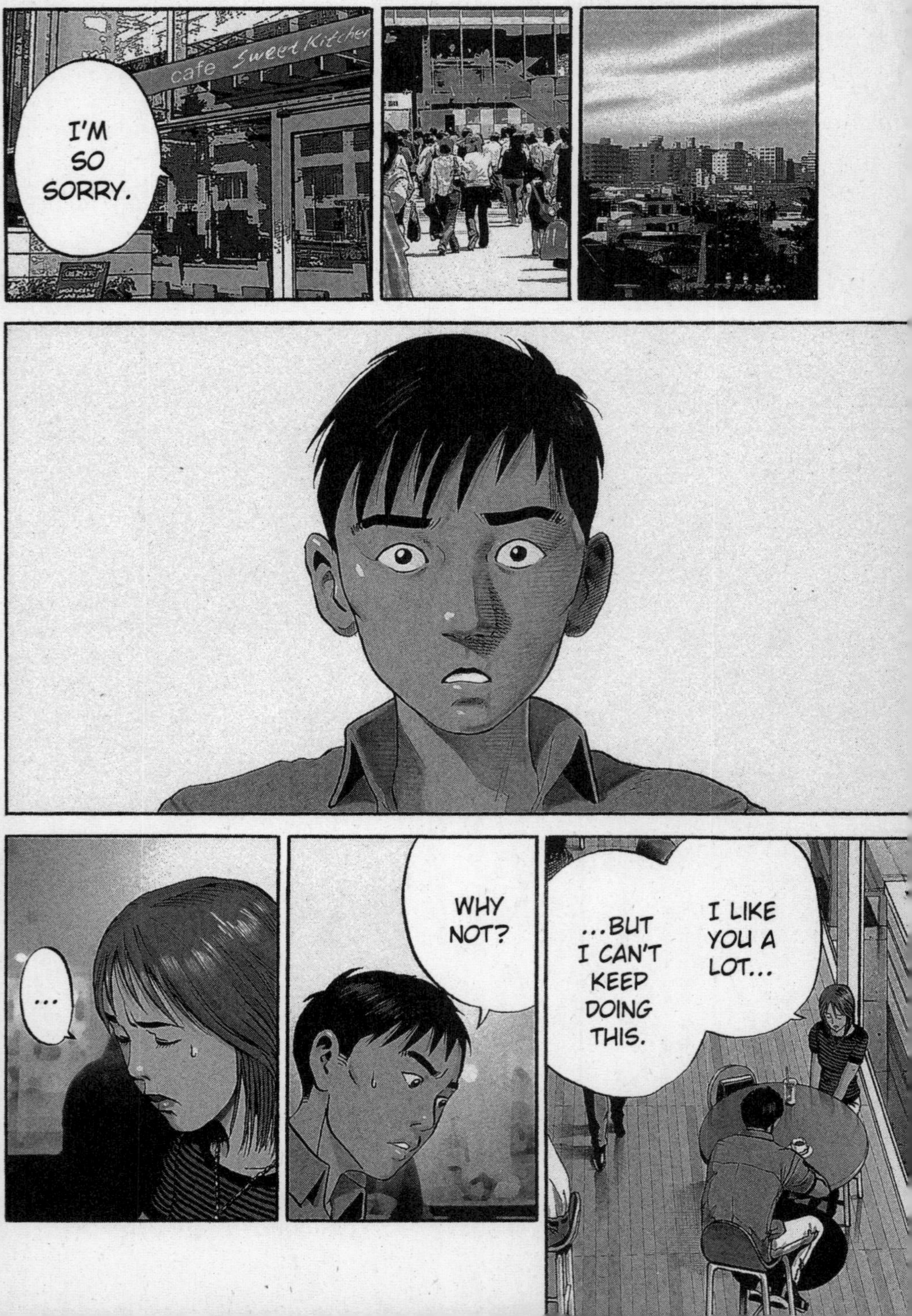

I'M SO SORRY.
I LIKE YOU A LOT...
...BUT I CAN'T KEEP DOING THIS.
WHY NOT?
...

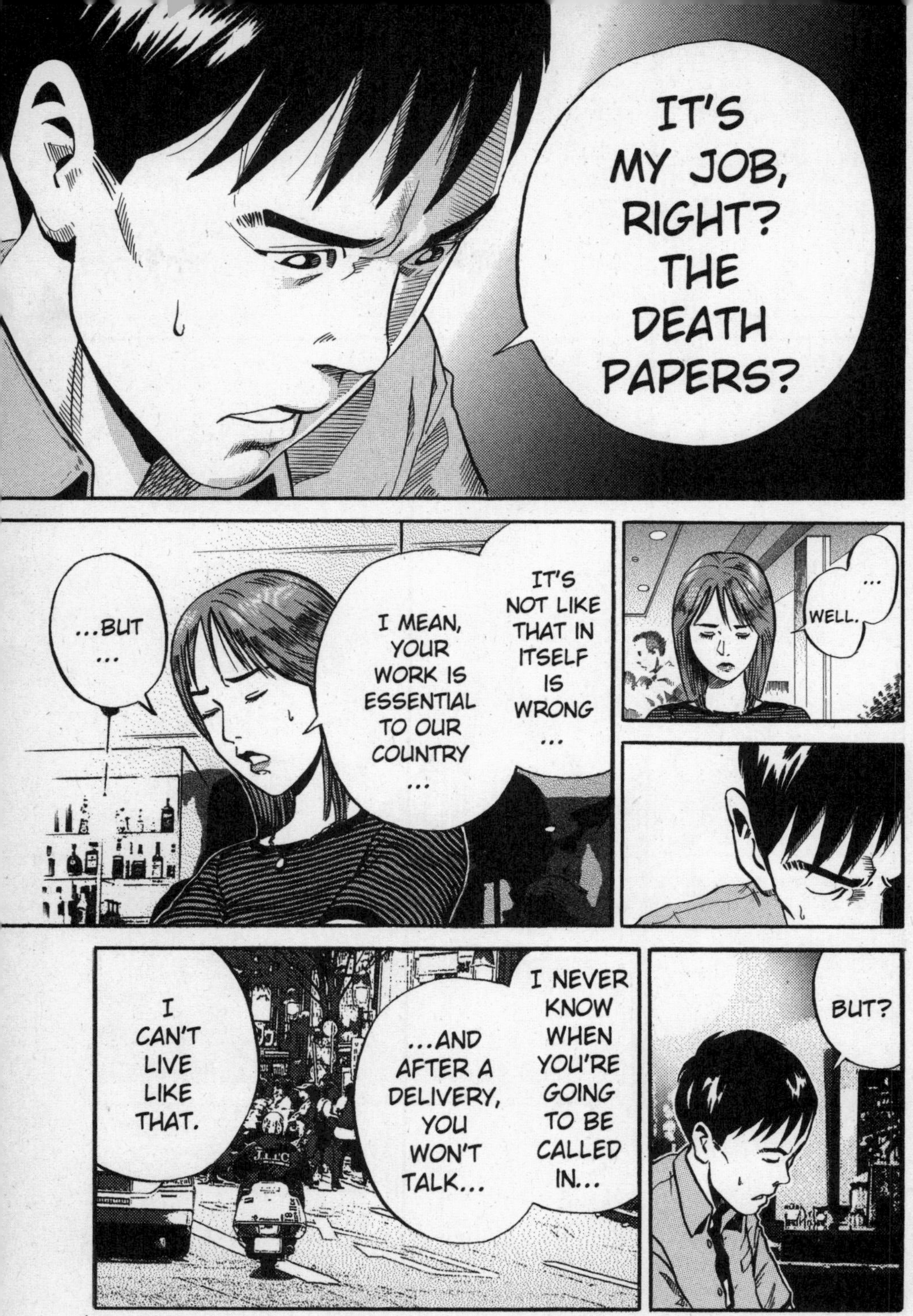
IT'S MY JOB, RIGHT? THE DEATH PAPERS?
... WELL.
IT'S NOT LIKE THAT IN ITSELF IS WRONG ...
I MEAN, YOUR WORK IS ESSENTIAL TO OUR COUNTRY ...
...BUT ...
BUT?
I NEVER KNOW WHEN YOU'RE GOING TO BE CALLED IN...
...AND AFTER A DELIVERY, YOU WON'T TALK...
I CAN'T LIVE LIKE THAT.

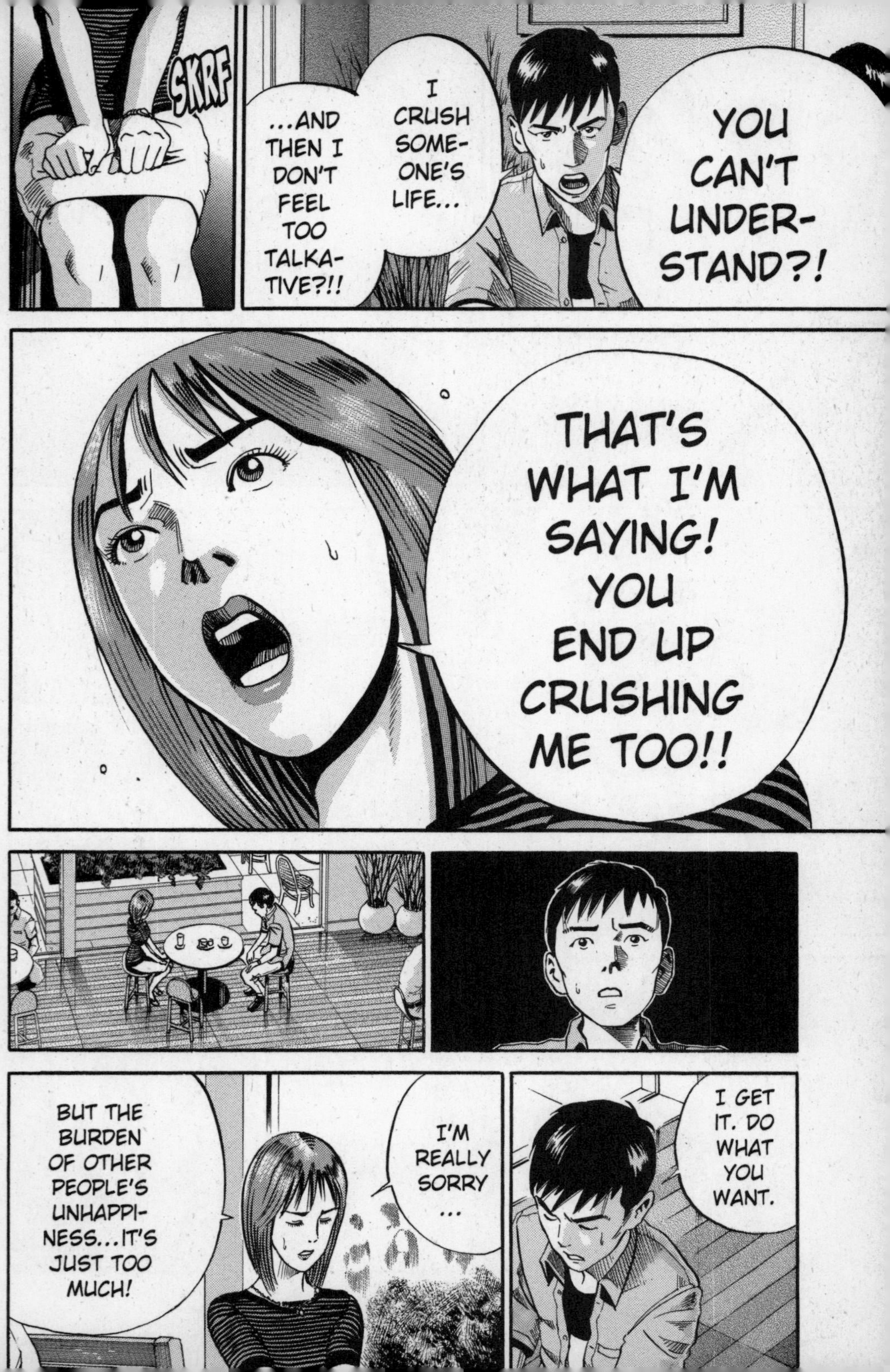
YOU CAN'T UNDER-STAND?!
I CRUSH SOME-ONE'S LIFE...
...AND THEN I DON'T FEEL TOO TALKA-TIVE?!!
SKRF
THAT'S WHAT I'M SAYING! YOU END UP CRUSHING ME TOO!!
I GET IT. DO WHAT YOU WANT.
I'M REALLY SORRY ...
BUT THE BURDEN OF OTHER PEOPLE'S UNHAPPI-NESS...IT'S JUST TOO MUCH!

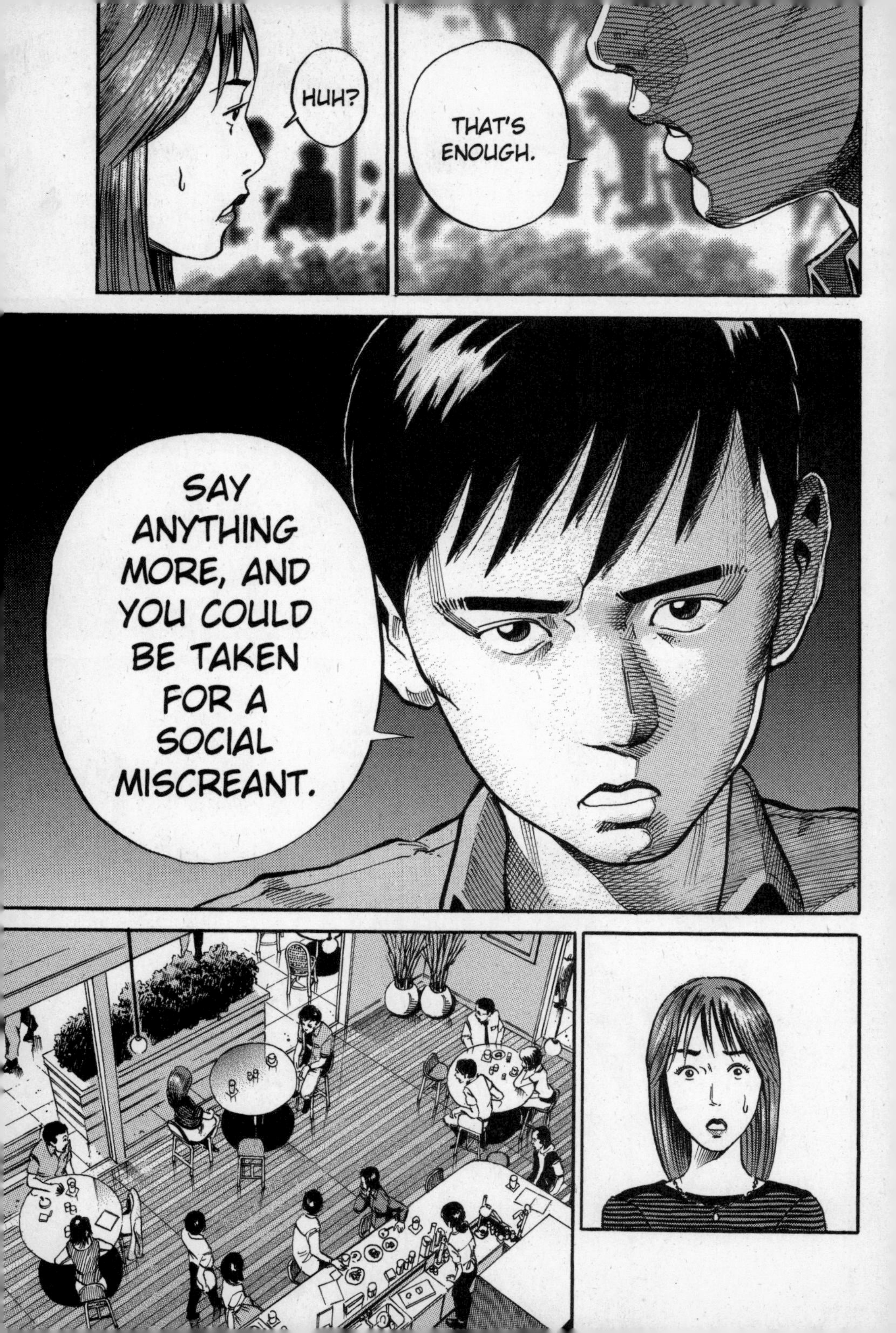
THAT'S ENOUGH.
HUH?
SAY ANYTHING MORE, AND YOU COULD BE TAKEN FOR A SOCIAL MISCREANT.

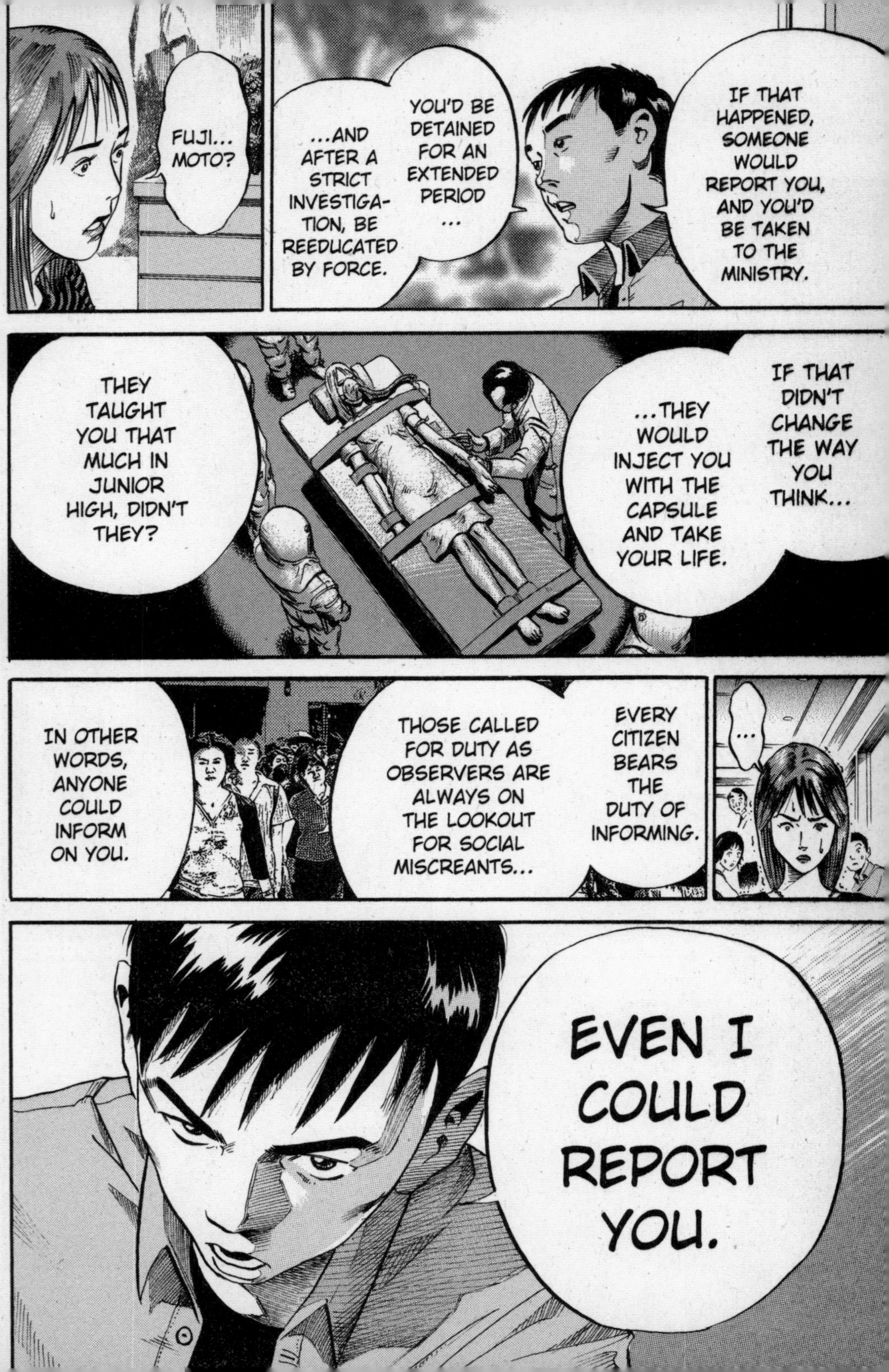

IF THAT HAPPENED, SOMEONE WOULD REPORT YOU, AND YOU'D BE TAKEN TO THE MINISTRY.
YOU'D BE DETAINED FOR AN EXTENDED PERIOD ...
...AND AFTER A STRICT INVESTIGATION, BE REEDUCATED BY FORCE.
FUJI... MOTO?
IF THAT DIDN'T CHANGE THE WAY YOU THINK...
...THEY WOULD INJECT YOU WITH THE CAPSULE AND TAKE YOUR LIFE.
THEY TAUGHT YOU THAT MUCH IN JUNIOR HIGH, DIDN'T THEY?
...
EVERY CITIZEN BEARS THE DUTY OF INFORMING.
THOSE CALLED FOR DUTY AS OBSERVERS ARE ALWAYS ON THE LOOKOUT FOR SOCIAL MISCREANTS...
IN OTHER WORDS, ANYONE COULD INFORM ON YOU.
EVEN I COULD REPORT YOU.

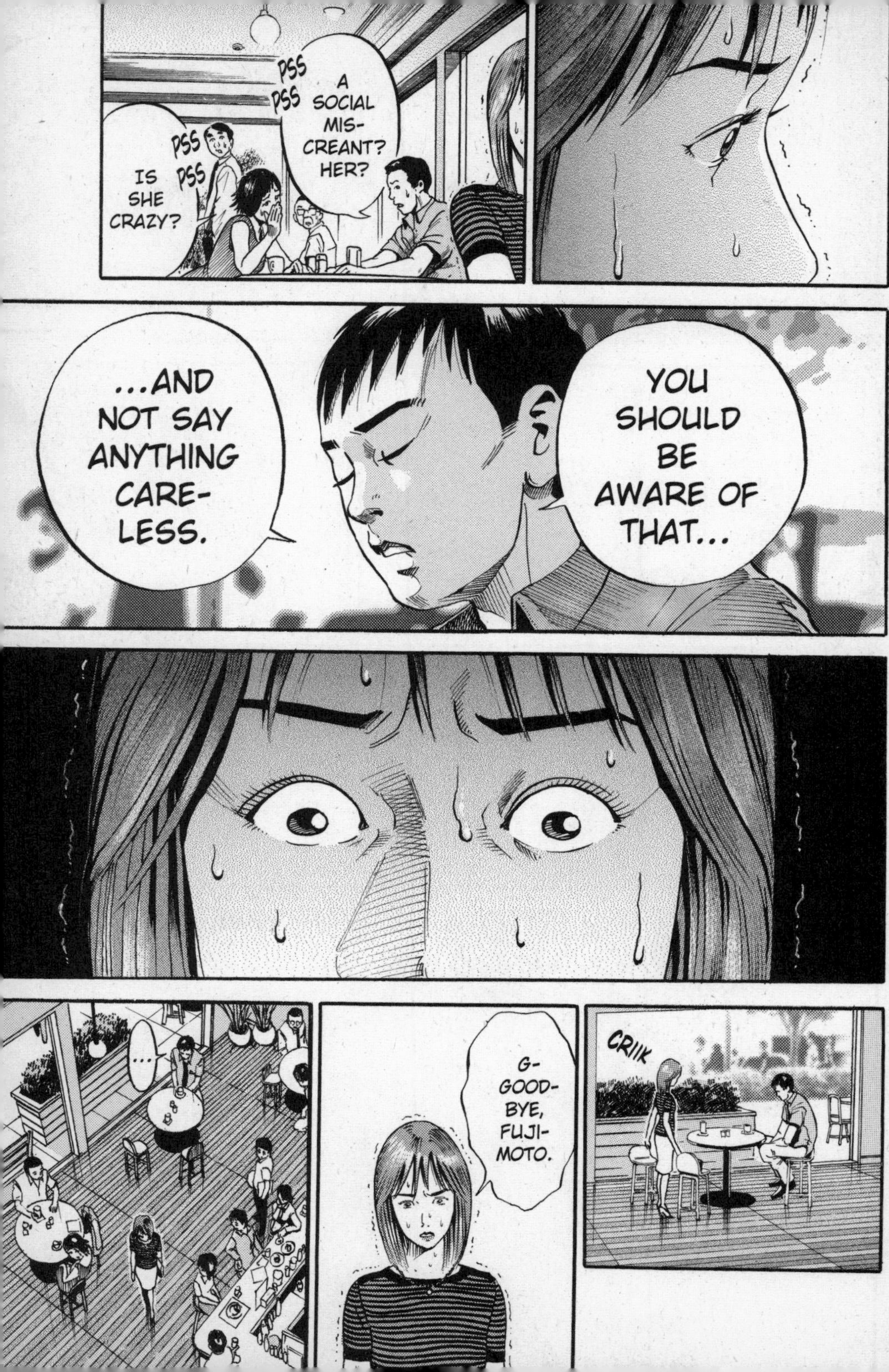
PSS PSS
A SOCIAL MIS-CREANT? HER?
PSS PSS
IS SHE CRAZY?
YOU SHOULD BE AWARE OF THAT...
...AND NOT SAY ANYTHING CARE-LESS.
CRIIK
G-GOODBYE, FUJI-MOTO.
...

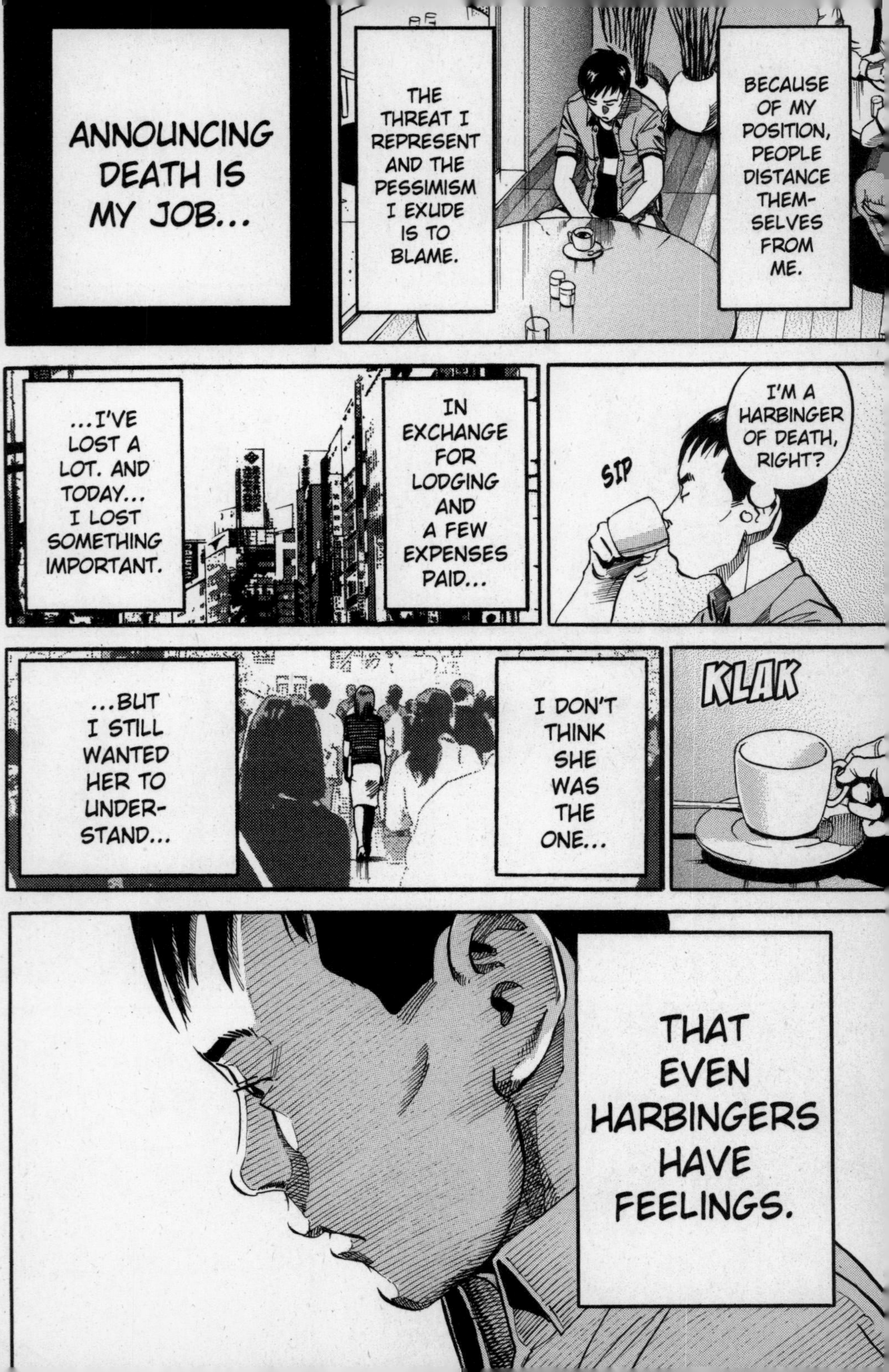
BECAUSE OF MY POSITION, PEOPLE DISTANCE THEM-SELVES FROM ME.
THE THREAT I REPRESENT AND THE PESSIMISM I EXUDE IS TO BLAME.
ANNOUNCING DEATH IS MY JOB...
I'M A HARBINGER OF DEATH, RIGHT?
SIP
IN EXCHANGE FOR LODGING AND A FEW EXPENSES PAID...
...I'VE LOST A LOT. AND TODAY... I LOST SOMETHING IMPORTANT.
KLAK
I DON'T THINK SHE WAS THE ONE...
...BUT I STILL WANTED HER TO UNDER-STAND...
THAT EVEN HARBINGERS HAVE FEELINGS.

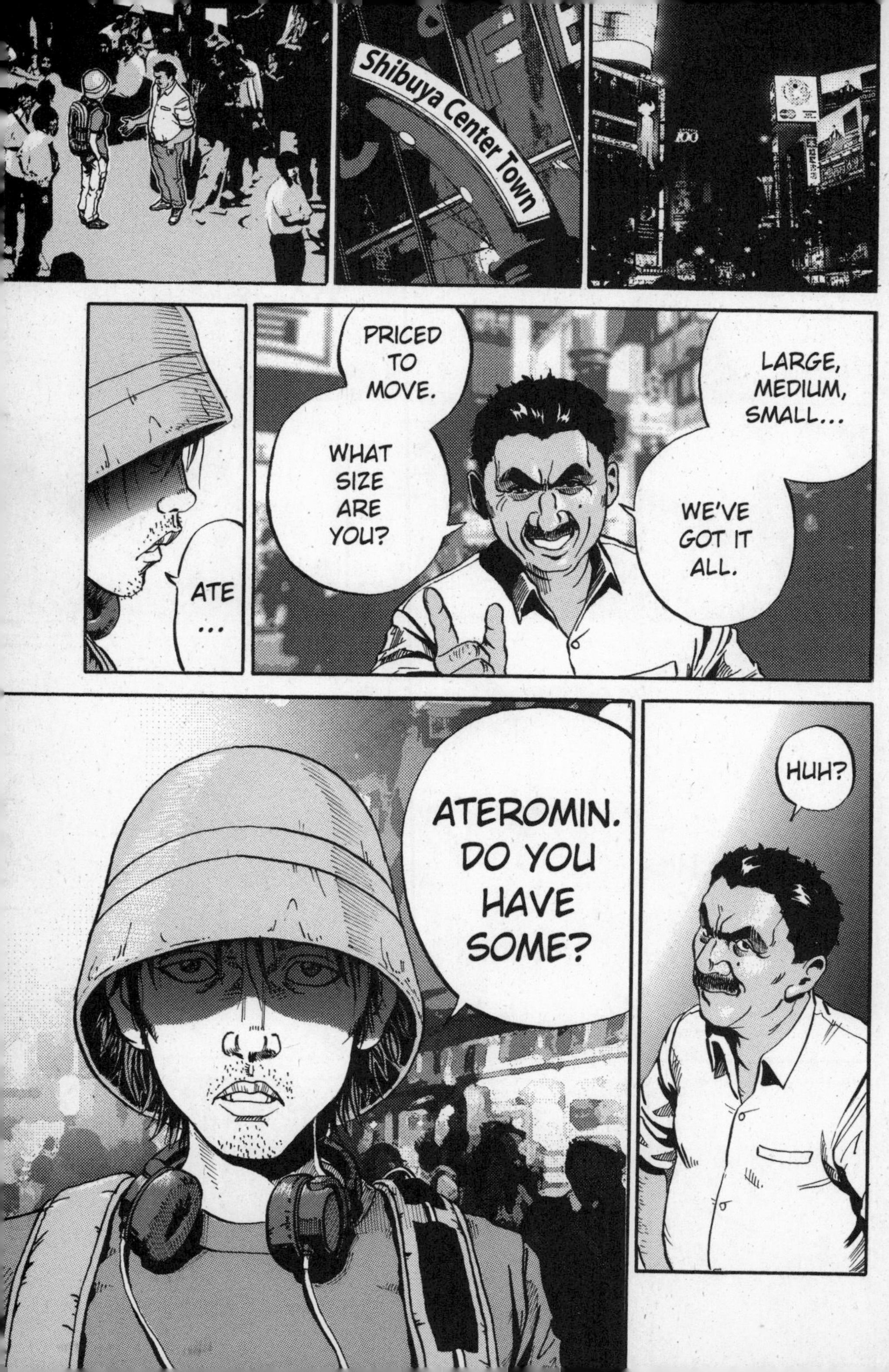
Shibuya Center Town
LARGE, MEDIUM, SMALL...
WE'VE GOT IT ALL.
PRICED TO MOVE.
WHAT SIZE ARE YOU?
ATE ...
HUH?
ATEROMIN. DO YOU HAVE SOME?

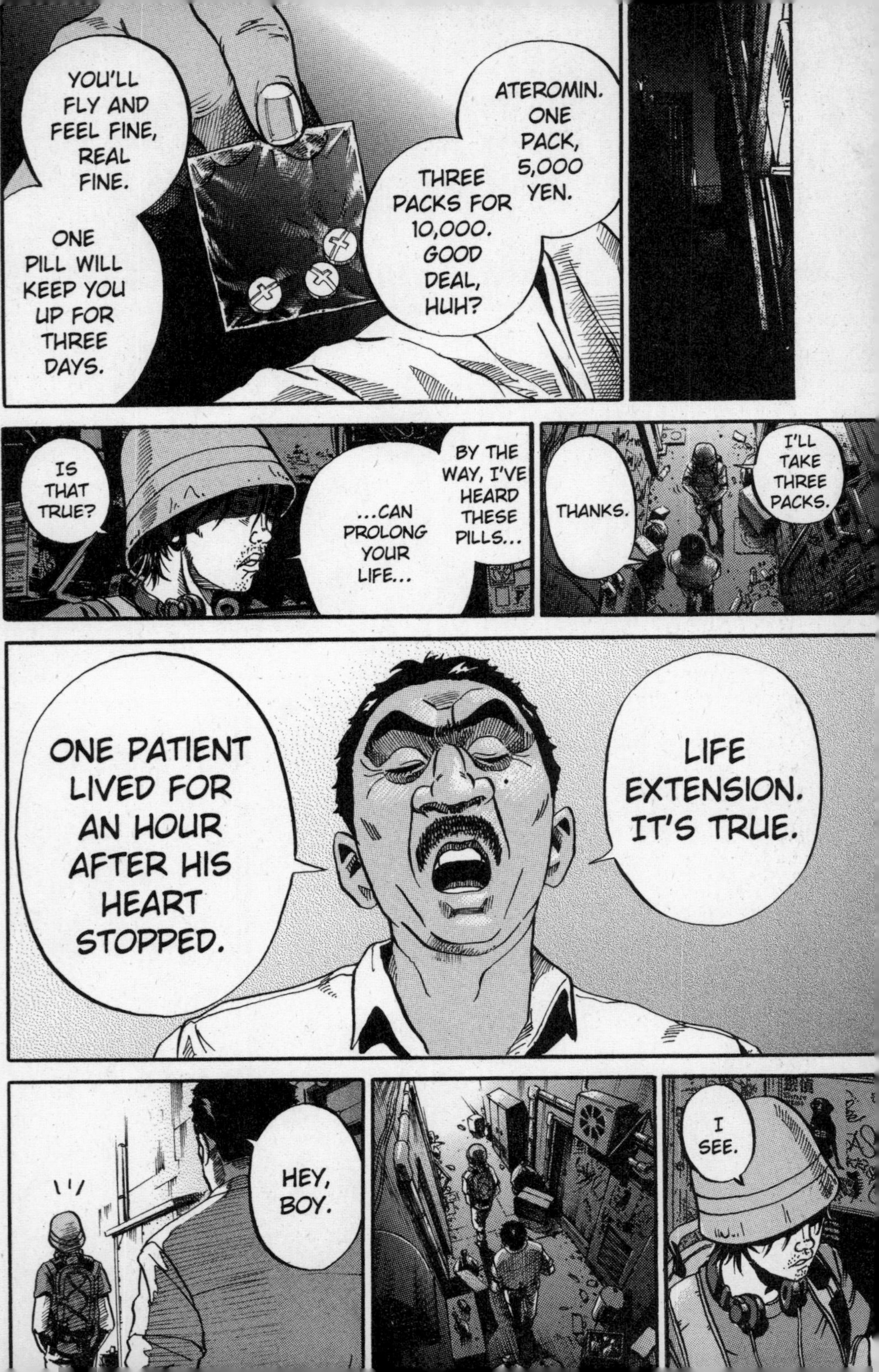
ATEROMIN. ONE PACK, 5,000 YEN.
THREE PACKS FOR 10,000. GOOD DEAL, HUH?
YOU'LL FLY AND FEEL FINE, REAL FINE.
ONE PILL WILL KEEP YOU UP FOR THREE DAYS.
I'LL TAKE THREE PACKS.
THANKS.
BY THE WAY, I'VE HEARD THESE PILLS...
...CAN PROLONG YOUR LIFE...
IS THAT TRUE?
LIFE EXTENSION. IT'S TRUE.
ONE PATIENT LIVED FOR AN HOUR AFTER HIS HEART STOPPED.
I SEE.
HEY, BOY.

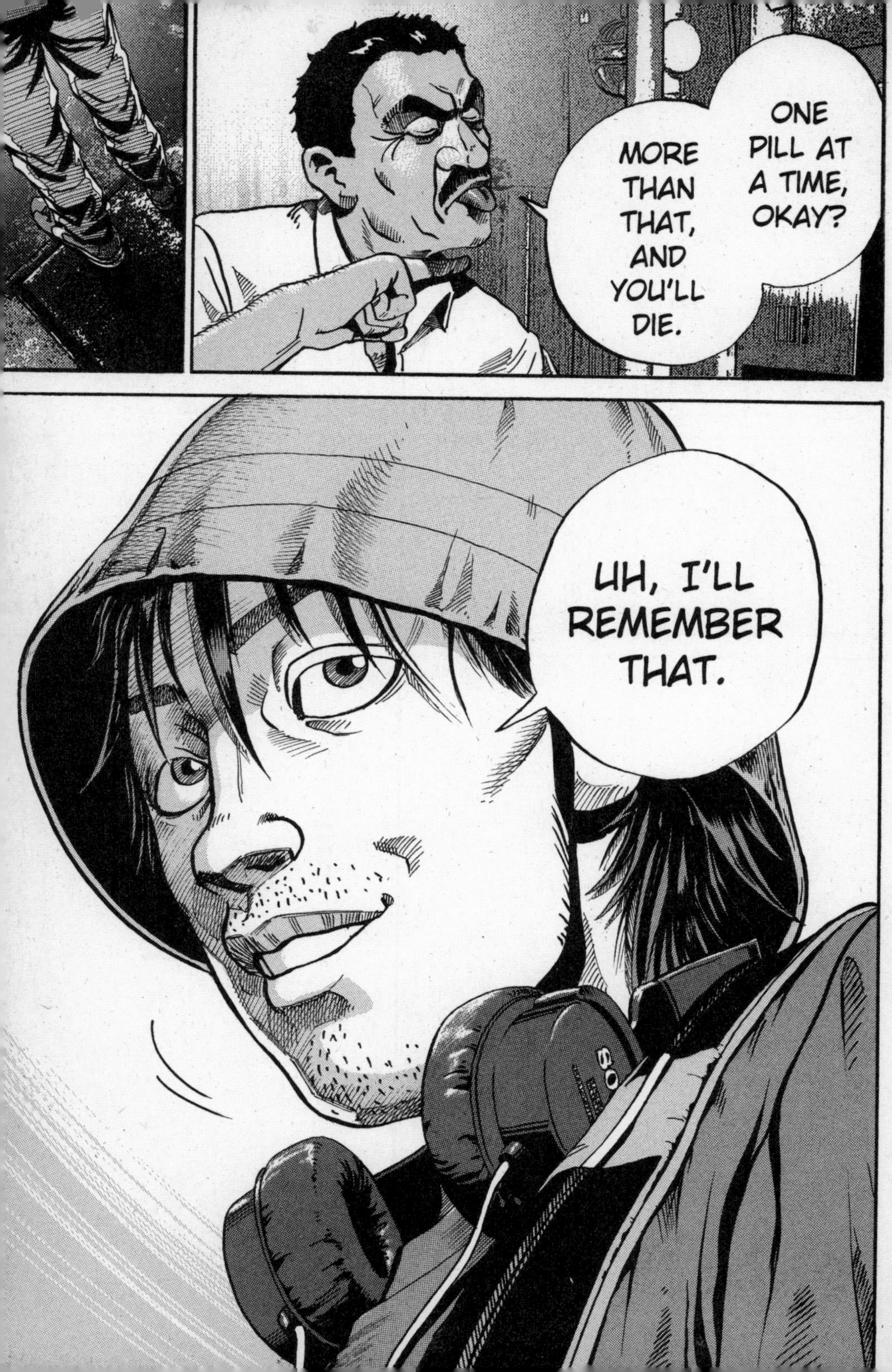
ONE PILL AT A TIME, OKAY?
MORE THAN THAT, AND YOU'LL DIE.
UH, I'LL REMEMBER THAT.

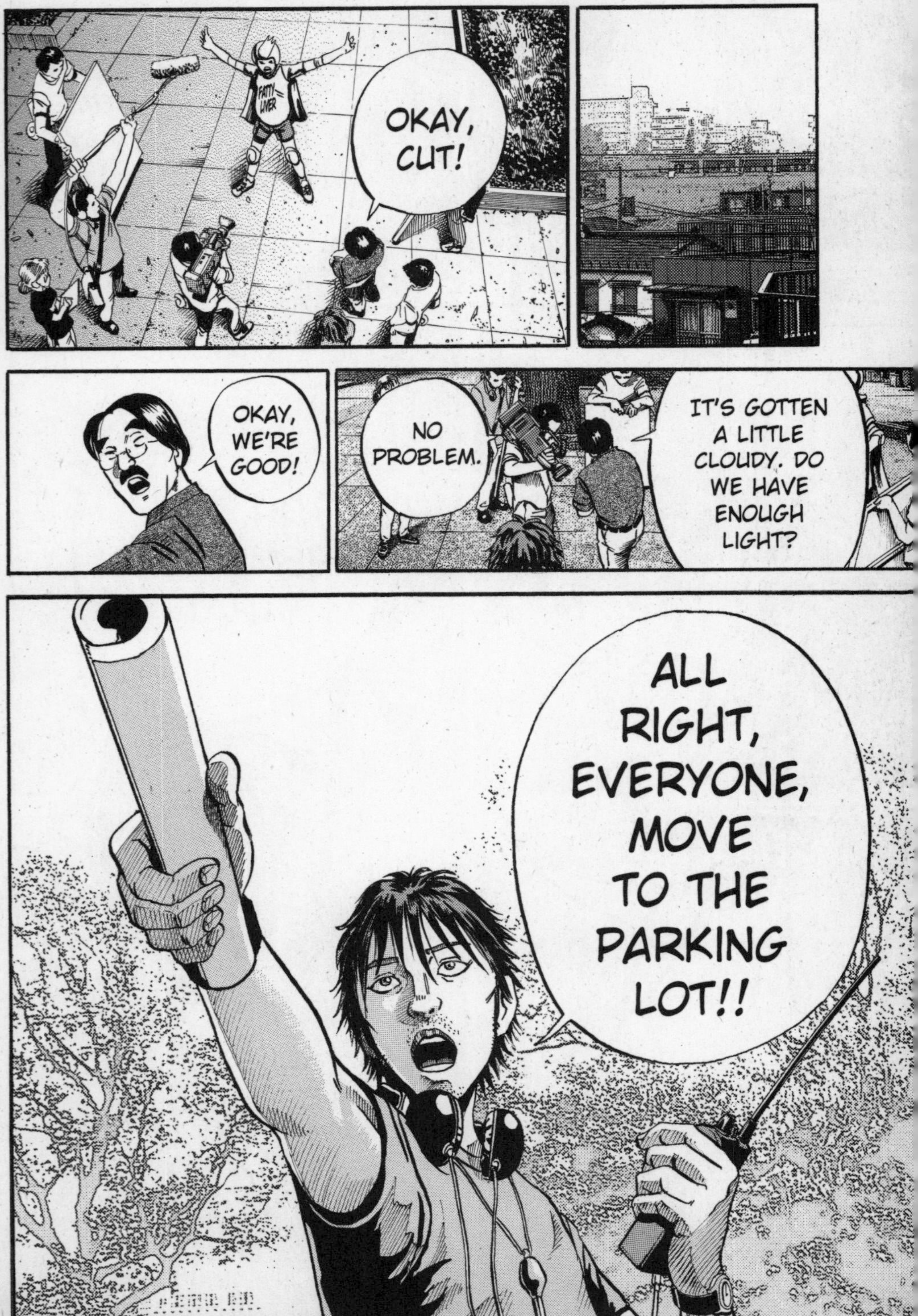
FATTY LIVER
OKAY, CUT!
IT'S GOTTEN A LITTLE CLOUDY. DO WE HAVE ENOUGH LIGHT?
NO PROBLEM.
OKAY, WE'RE GOOD!
ALL RIGHT, EVERYONE, MOVE TO THE PARKING LOT!!

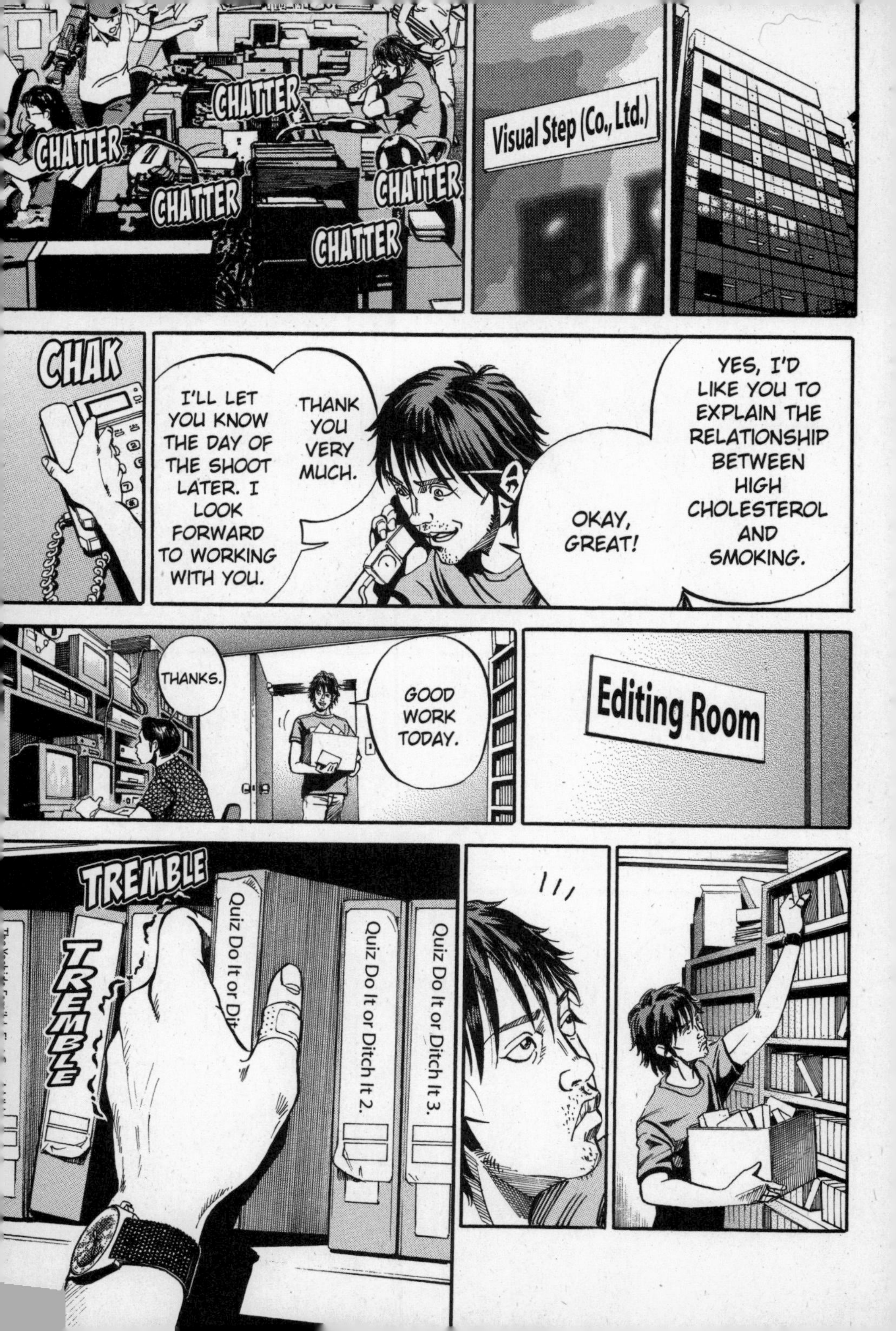
Visual Step (Co., Ltd.)
CHATTER
CHATTER
CHATTER
CHATTER
CHATTER
YES, I'D LIKE YOU TO EXPLAIN THE RELATIONSHIP BETWEEN HIGH CHOLESTEROL AND SMOKING.
OKAY, GREAT!
THANK YOU VERY MUCH.
I'LL LET YOU KNOW THE DAY OF THE SHOOT LATER. I LOOK FORWARD TO WORKING WITH YOU.
CHAK
Editing Room
GOOD WORK TODAY.
THANKS.
TREMBLE
TREMBLE
Quiz Do It or Ditch It 3.
Quiz Do It or Ditch It 2.
Quiz Do It or Dit

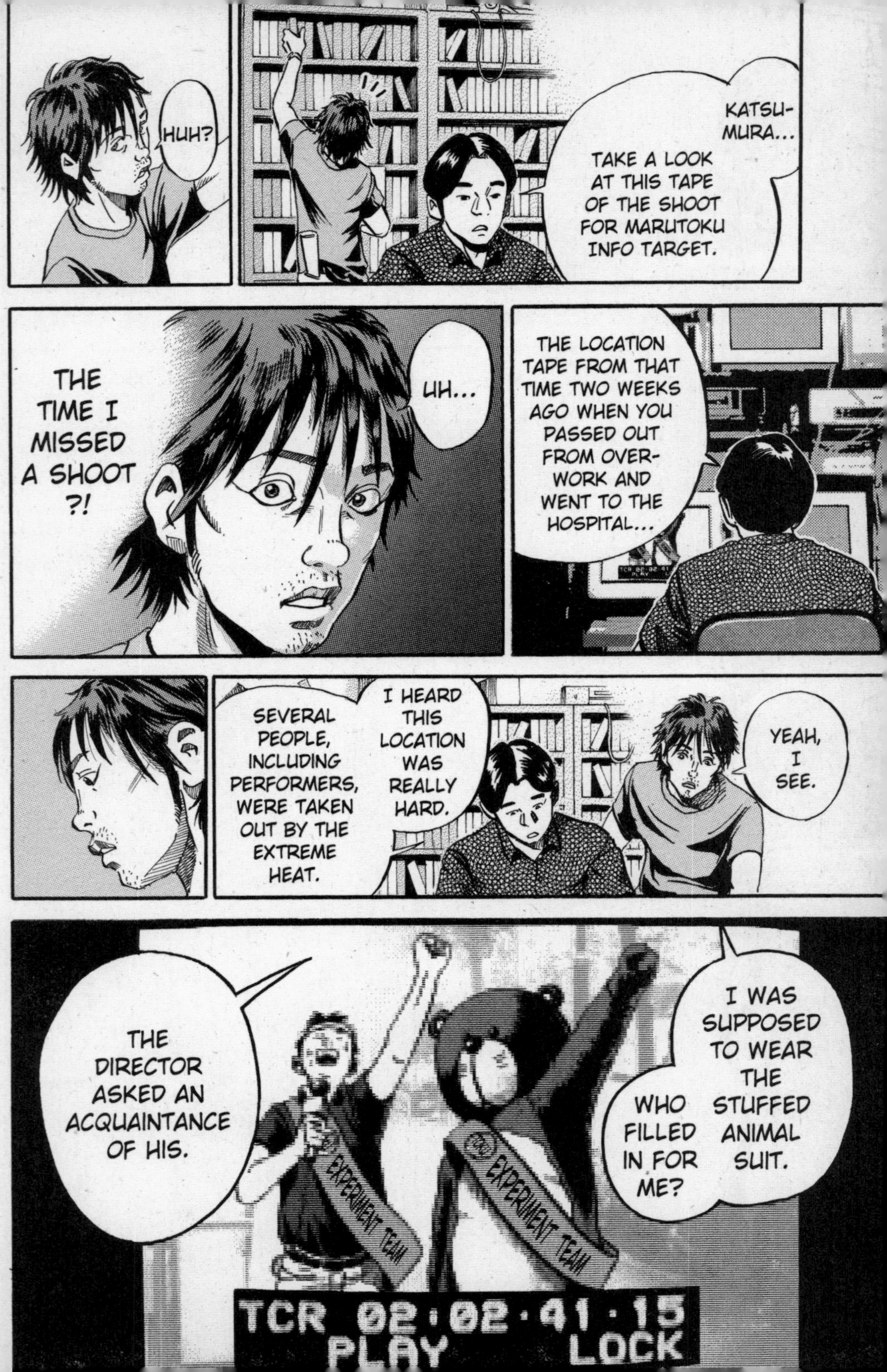
KATSU-MURA... TAKE A LOOK AT THIS TAPE OF THE SHOOT FOR MARUTOKU INFO TARGET.
HUH?
THE LOCATION TAPE FROM THAT TIME TWO WEEKS AGO WHEN YOU PASSED OUT FROM OVER-WORK AND WENT TO THE HOSPITAL...
UH...
THE TIME I MISSED A SHOOT ?!
YEAH, I SEE.
I HEARD THIS LOCATION WAS REALLY HARD.
SEVERAL PEOPLE, INCLUDING PERFORMERS, WERE TAKEN OUT BY THE EXTREME HEAT.
I WAS SUPPOSED TO WEAR THE STUFFED ANIMAL SUIT.
WHO FILLED IN FOR ME?
THE DIRECTOR ASKED AN ACQUAINTANCE OF HIS.
EXPERIMENT TEAM
EXPERIMENT TEAM
TCR 02·02·41·15
PLAY LOCK

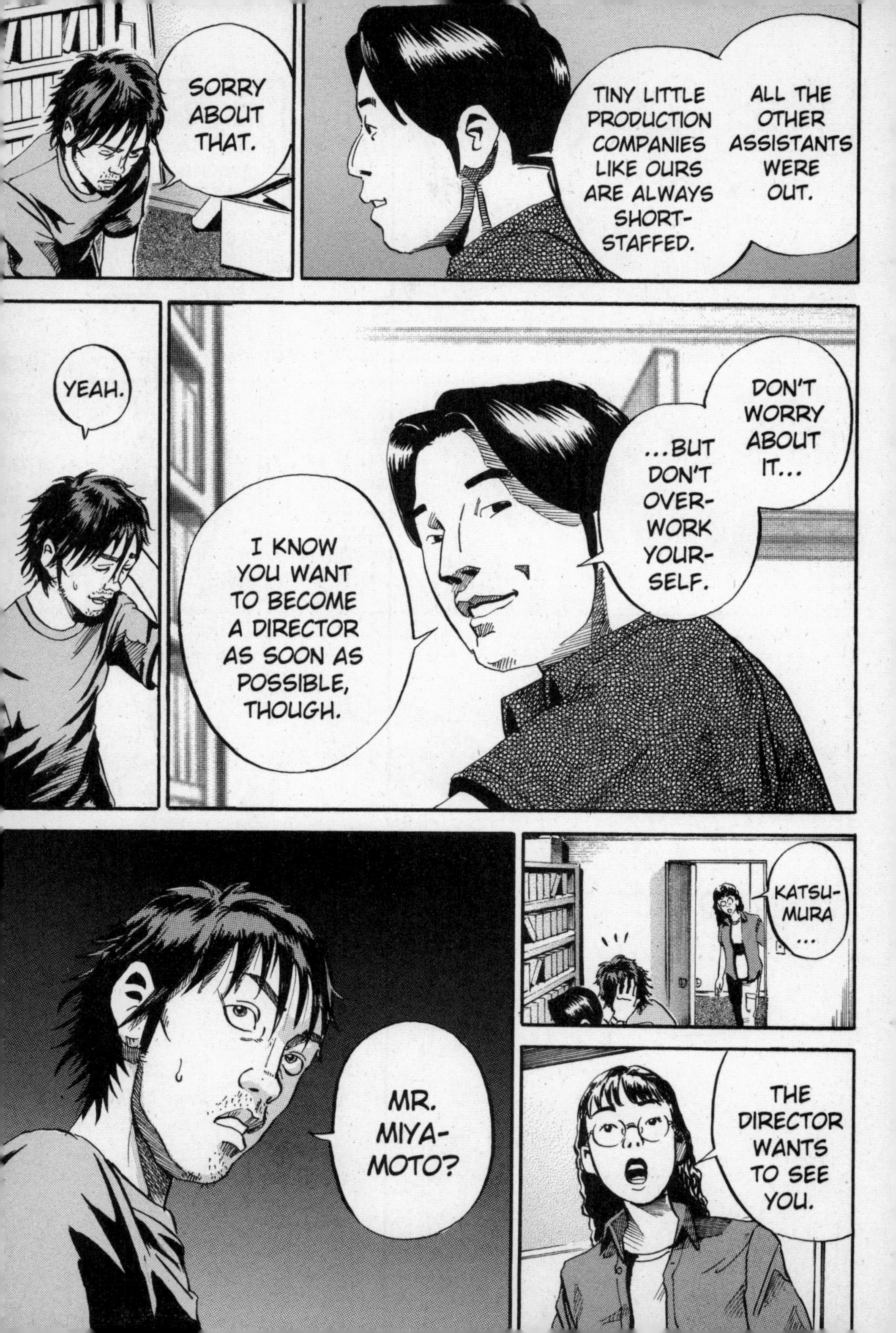
ALL THE OTHER ASSISTANTS WERE OUT.
TINY LITTLE PRODUCTION COMPANIES LIKE OURS ARE ALWAYS SHORT-STAFFED.
SORRY ABOUT THAT.
DON'T WORRY ABOUT IT...
...BUT DON'T OVER-WORK YOUR-SELF.
I KNOW YOU WANT TO BECOME A DIRECTOR AS SOON AS POSSIBLE, THOUGH.
YEAH.
KATSU-MURA...
THE DIRECTOR WANTS TO SEE YOU.
MR. MIYA-MOTO?

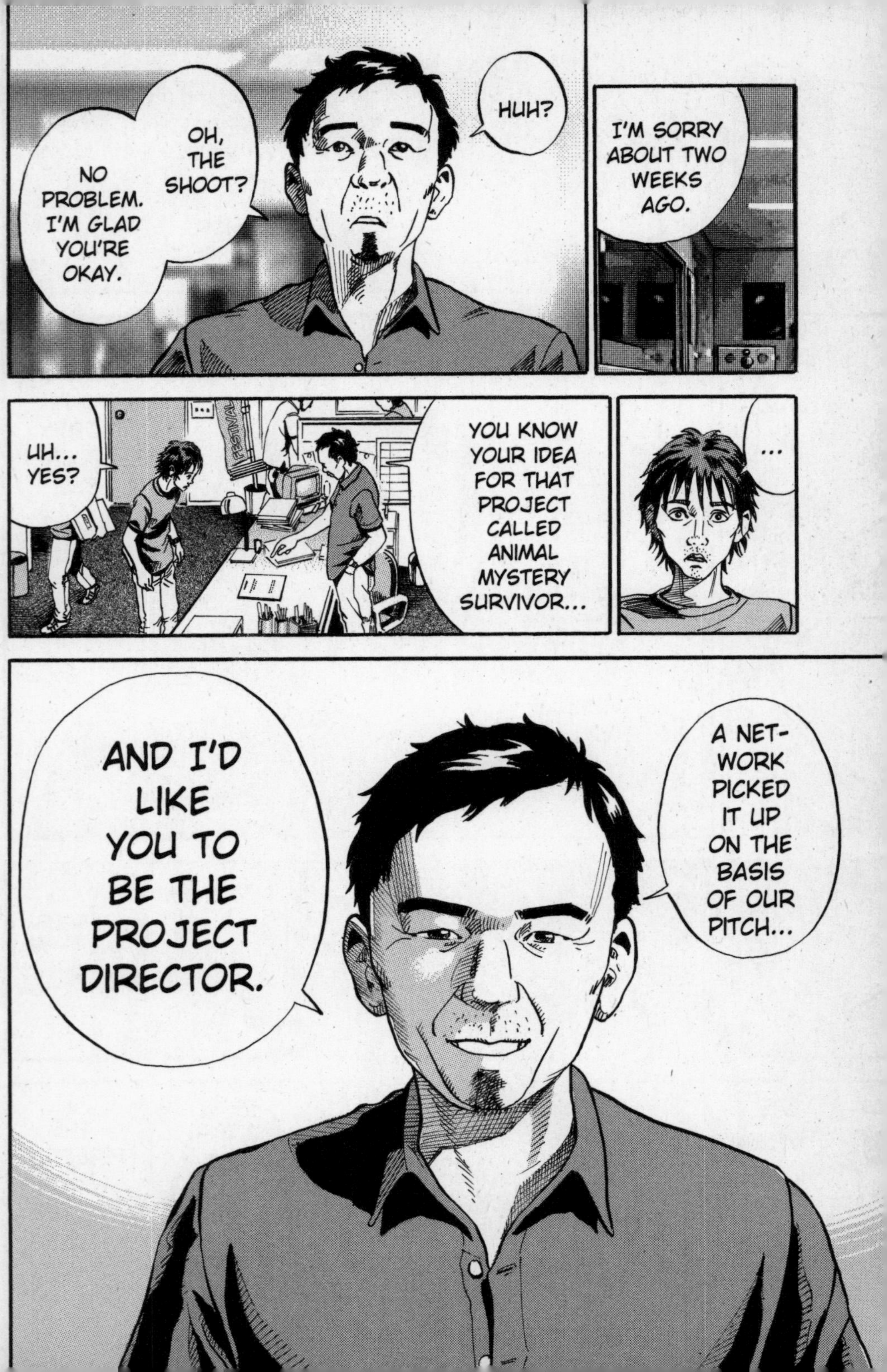
I'M SORRY ABOUT TWO WEEKS AGO.
HUH?
OH, THE SHOOT?
NO PROBLEM. I'M GLAD YOU'RE OKAY.
...
YOU KNOW YOUR IDEA FOR THAT PROJECT CALLED ANIMAL MYSTERY SURVIVOR...
UH... YES?
A NET-WORK PICKED IT UP ON THE BASIS OF OUR PITCH...
AND I'D LIKE YOU TO BE THE PROJECT DIRECTOR.

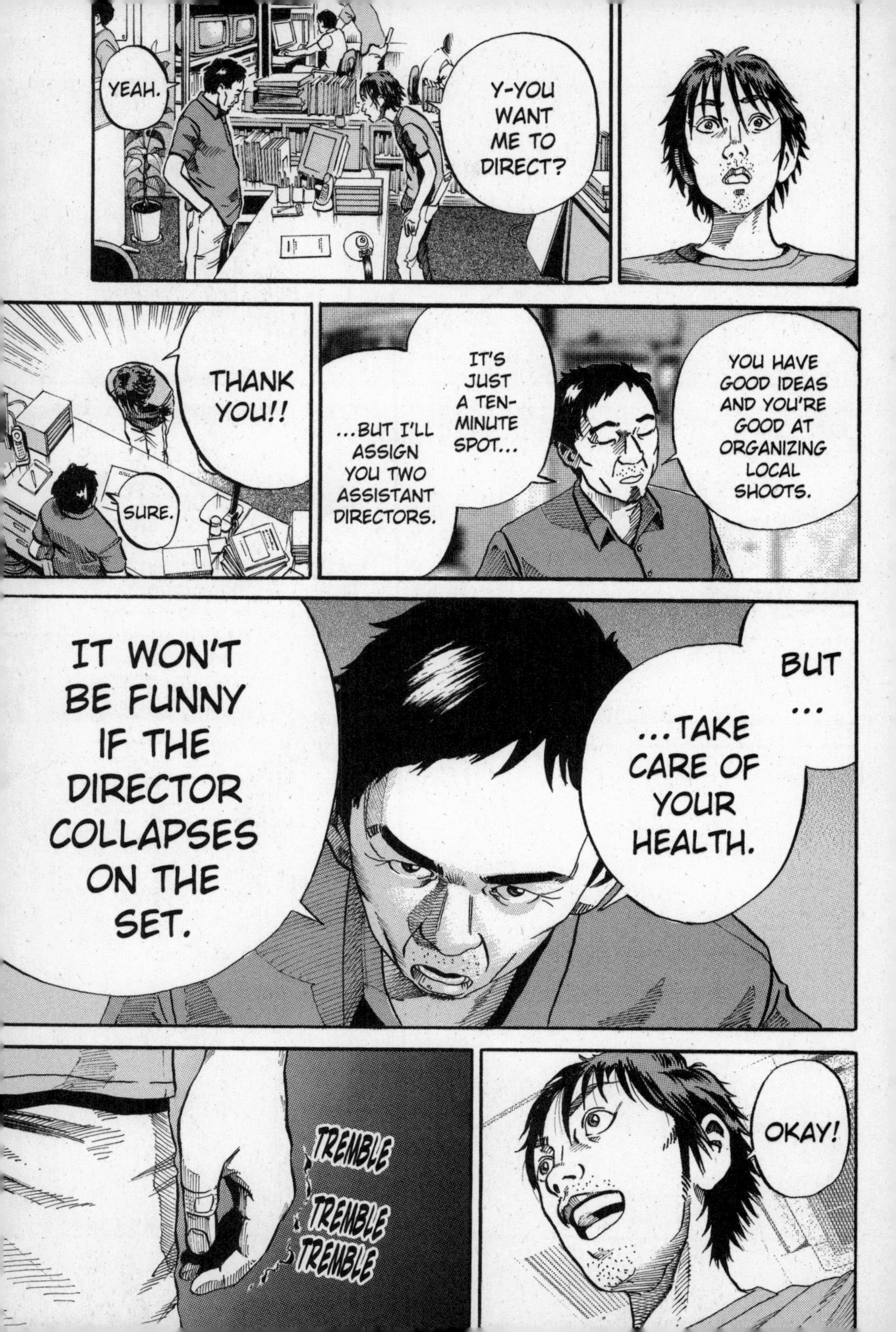
Y-YOU WANT ME TO DIRECT?
YEAH.
YOU HAVE GOOD IDEAS AND YOU'RE GOOD AT ORGANIZING LOCAL SHOOTS.
IT'S JUST A TEN-MINUTE SPOT...
...BUT I'LL ASSIGN YOU TWO ASSISTANT DIRECTORS.
THANK YOU!!
SURE.
BUT ...
...TAKE CARE OF YOUR HEALTH.
IT WON'T BE FUNNY IF THE DIRECTOR COLLAPSES ON THE SET.
OKAY!
TREMBLE
TREMBLE
TREMBLE

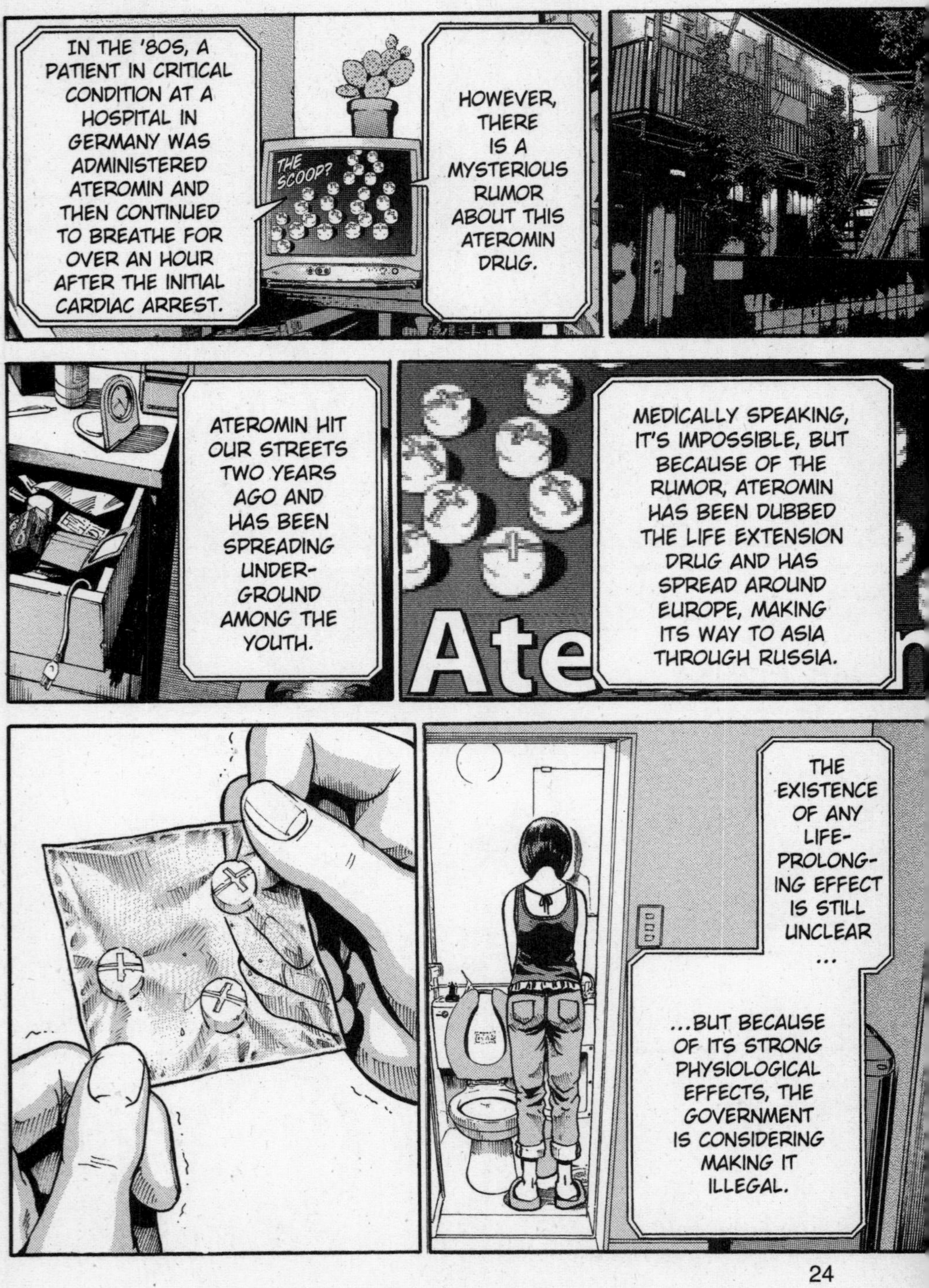
HOWEVER, THERE IS A MYSTERIOUS RUMOR ABOUT THIS ATEROMIN DRUG.
THE SCOOP?
IN THE '80S, A PATIENT IN CRITICAL CONDITION AT A HOSPITAL IN GERMANY WAS ADMINISTERED ATEROMIN AND THEN CONTINUED TO BREATHE FOR OVER AN HOUR AFTER THE INITIAL CARDIAC ARREST.
MEDICALLY SPEAKING, IT'S IMPOSSIBLE, BUT BECAUSE OF THE RUMOR, ATEROMIN HAS BEEN DUBBED THE LIFE EXTENSION DRUG AND HAS SPREAD AROUND EUROPE, MAKING ITS WAY TO ASIA THROUGH RUSSIA.
Ate
ATEROMIN HIT OUR STREETS TWO YEARS AGO AND HAS BEEN SPREADING UNDER-GROUND AMONG THE YOUTH.
THE EXISTENCE OF ANY LIFE-PROLONG-ING EFFECT IS STILL UNCLEAR ...
...BUT BECAUSE OF ITS STRONG PHYSIOLOGICAL EFFECTS, THE GOVERNMENT IS CONSIDERING MAKING IT ILLEGAL.

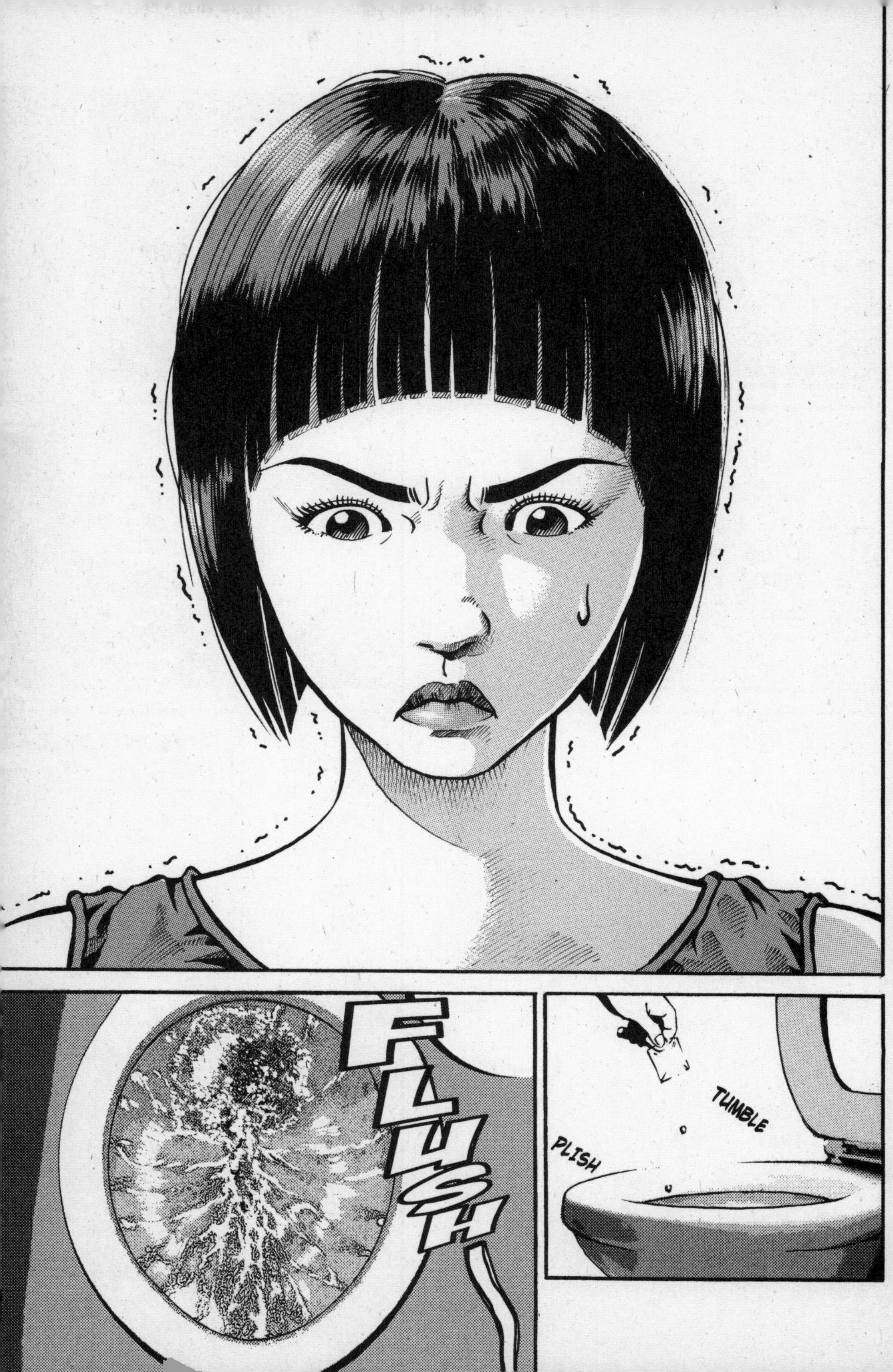
TUMBLE
PLISH
FLUSH

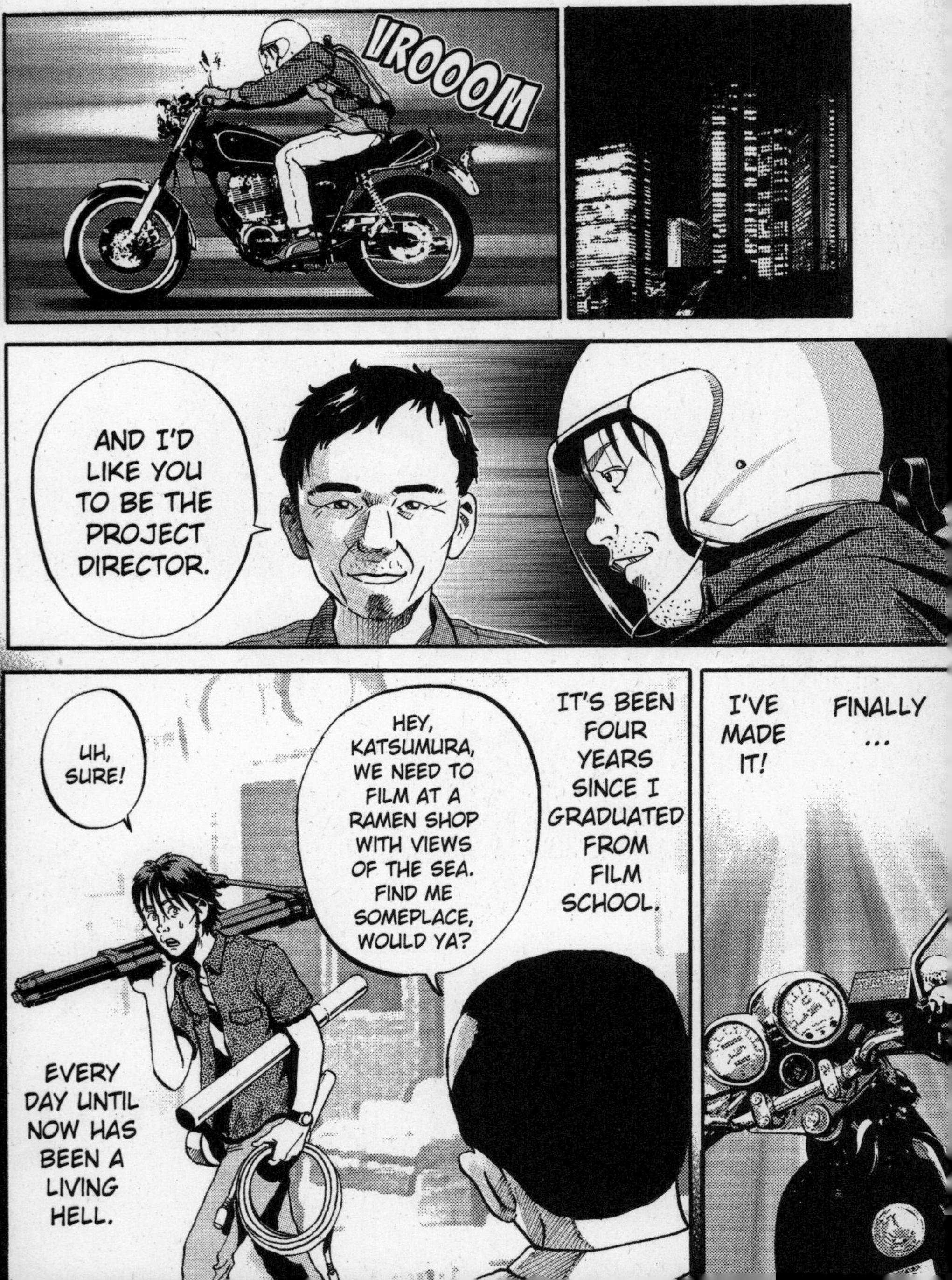
VROOOM
AND I'D LIKE YOU TO BE THE PROJECT DIRECTOR.
FINALLY ...
I'VE MADE IT!
IT'S BEEN FOUR YEARS SINCE I GRADUATED FROM FILM SCHOOL.
HEY, KATSUMURA, WE NEED TO FILM AT A RAMEN SHOP WITH VIEWS OF THE SEA. FIND ME SOMEPLACE, WOULD YA?
UH, SURE!
EVERY DAY UNTIL NOW HAS BEEN A LIVING HELL.

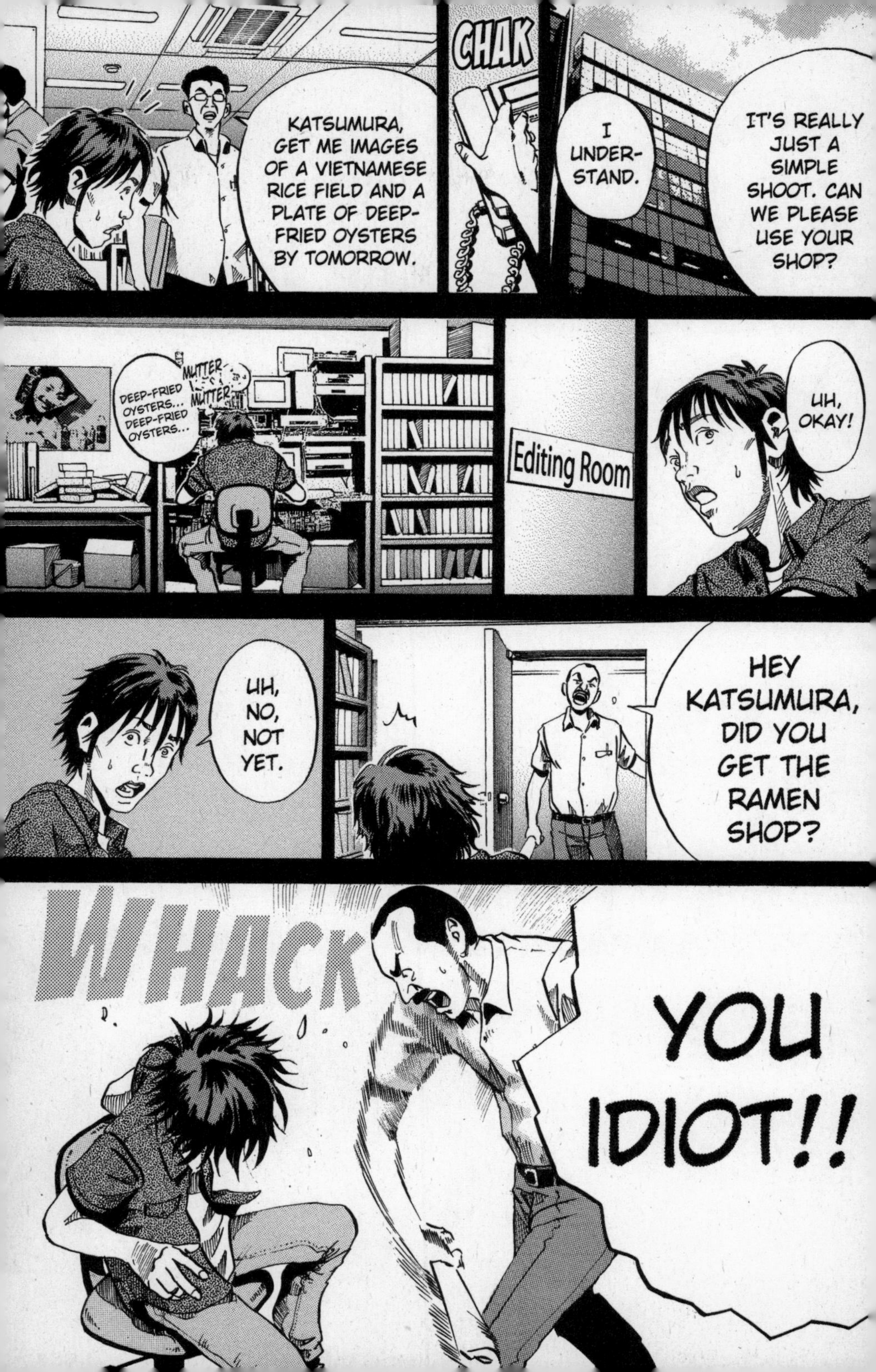
IT'S REALLY JUST A SIMPLE SHOOT. CAN WE PLEASE USE YOUR SHOP?
I UNDER-STAND.
CHAK
KATSUMURA, GET ME IMAGES OF A VIETNAMESE RICE FIELD AND A PLATE OF DEEP-FRIED OYSTERS BY TOMORROW.
UH, OKAY!
Editing Room
MUTTER MUTTER
DEEP-FRIED OYSTERS... DEEP-FRIED OYSTERS...
HEY KATSUMURA, DID YOU GET THE RAMEN SHOP?
UH, NO, NOT YET.
WHACK
YOU IDIOT!!

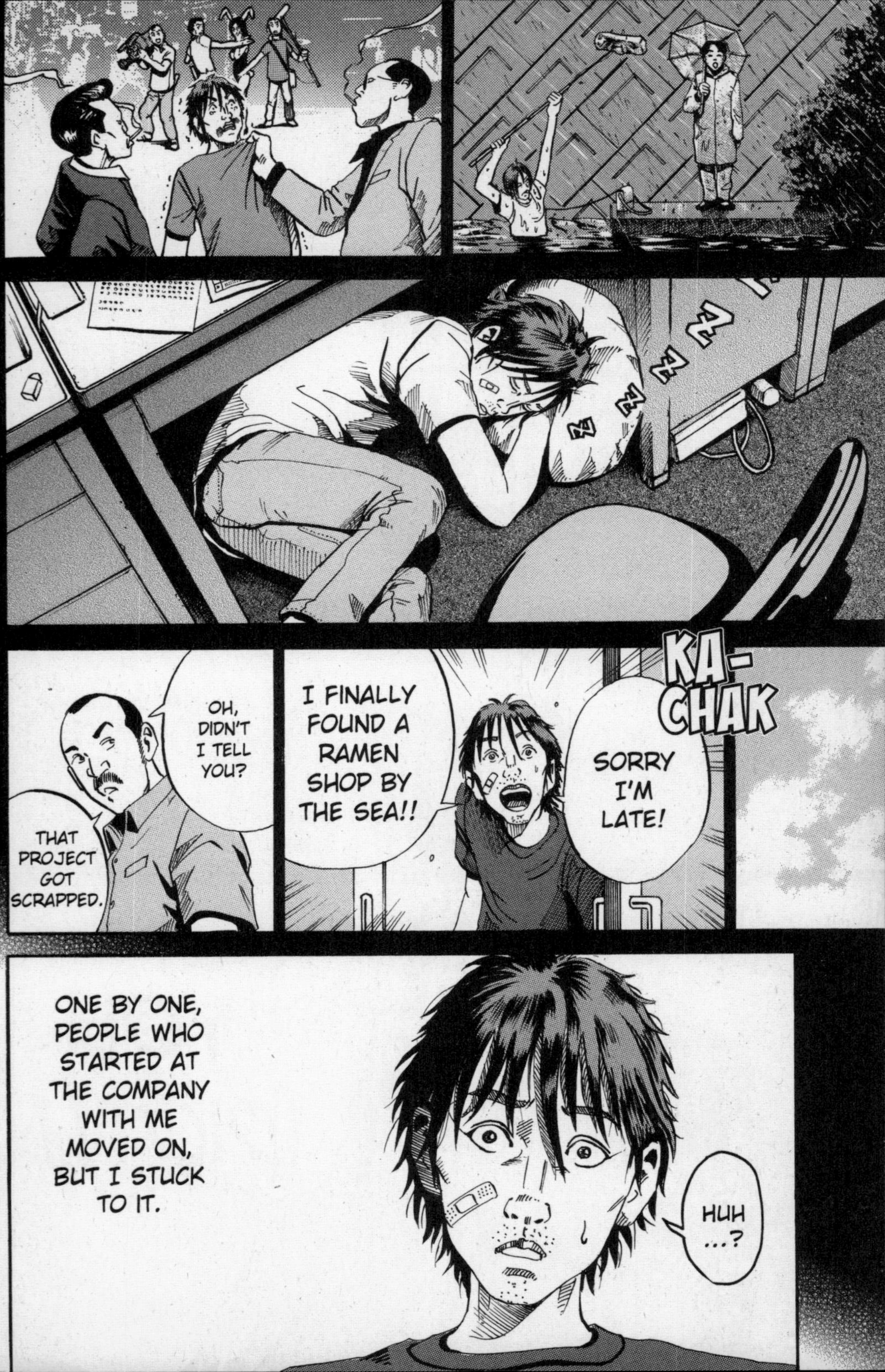
KA-CHAK
SORRY I'M LATE!
I FINALLY FOUND A RAMEN SHOP BY THE SEA!!
OH, DIDN'T I TELL YOU?
THAT PROJECT GOT SCRAPPED.
ONE BY ONE, PEOPLE WHO STARTED AT THE COMPANY WITH ME MOVED ON, BUT I STUCK TO IT.
HUH ...?

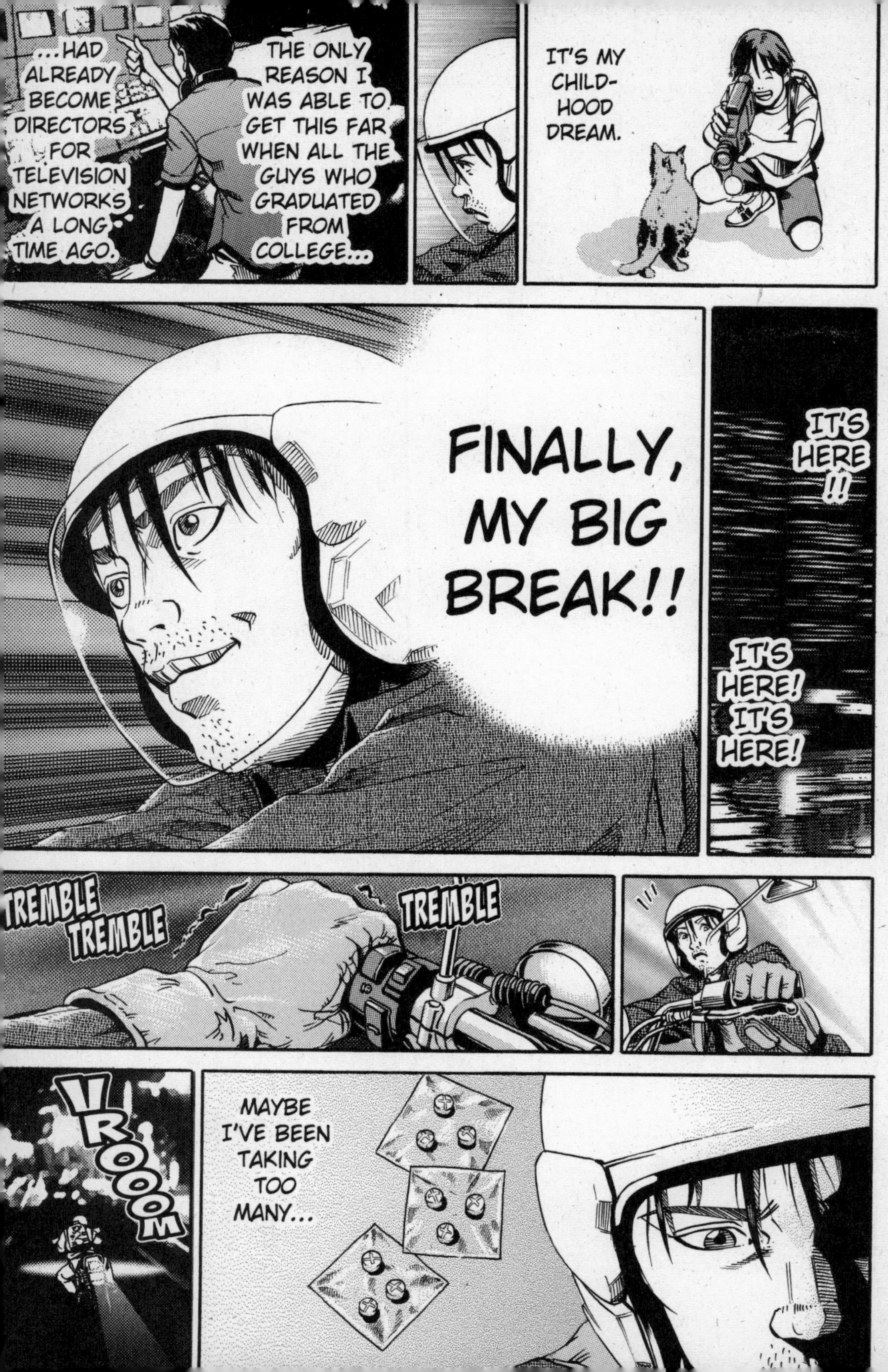
IT'S MY CHILDHOOD DREAM.
THE ONLY REASON I WAS ABLE TO GET THIS FAR WHEN ALL THE GUYS WHO GRADUATED FROM COLLEGE...
...HAD ALREADY BECOME DIRECTORS FOR TELEVISION NETWORKS A LONG TIME AGO.
IT'S HERE!!
IT'S HERE! IT'S HERE!
FINALLY, MY BIG BREAK!!
TREMBLE
TREMBLE TREMBLE
MAYBE I'VE BEEN TAKING TOO MANY...
VROOOOM

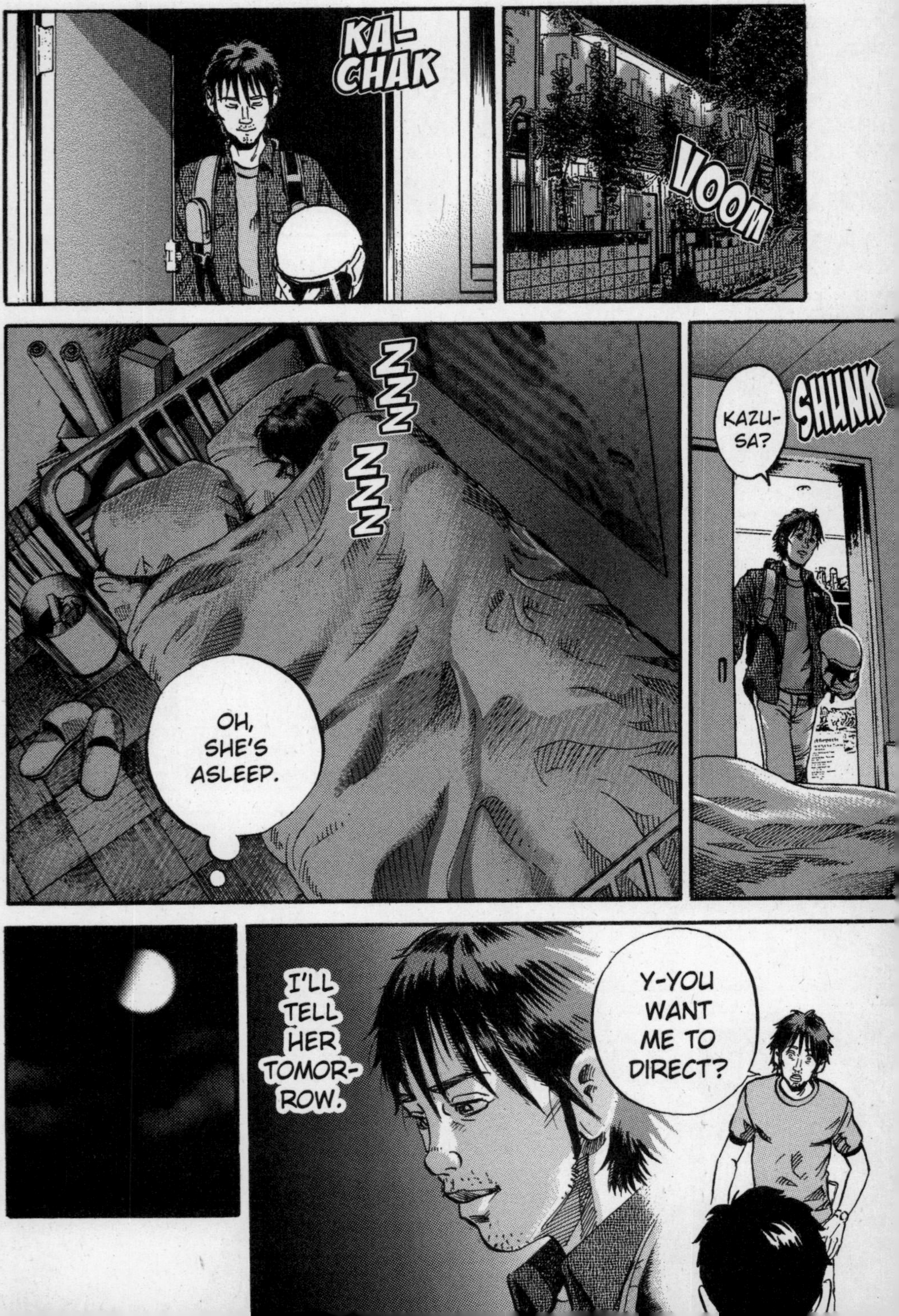
VOOM
KA-CHAK
SHUNK
KAZUSA?
ZZZ ZZZ
OH, SHE'S ASLEEP.
Y-YOU WANT ME TO DIRECT?
I'LL TELL HER TOMORROW.

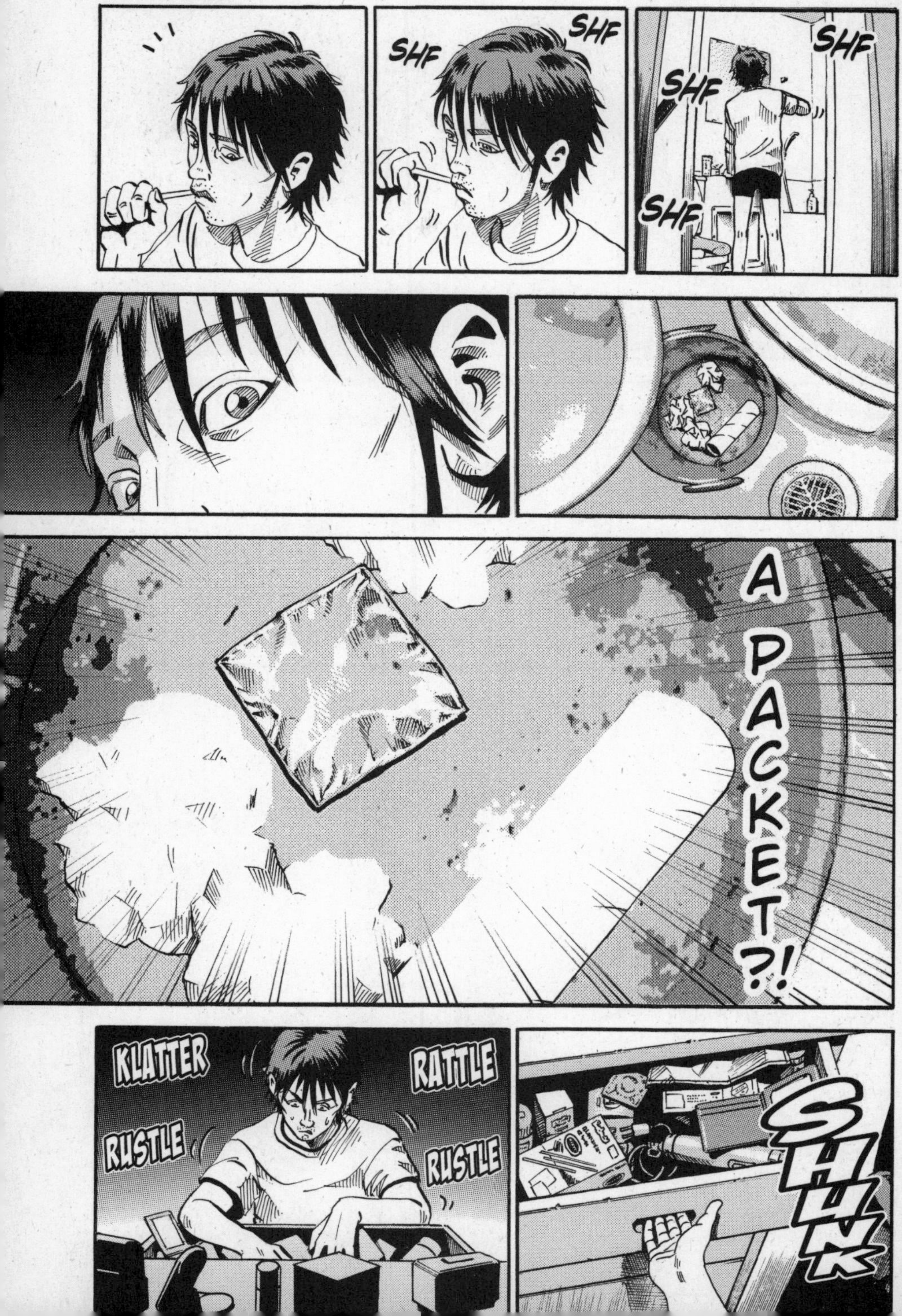
SHF
SHF
SHF
SHF
SHF
A PACKET?!
SHUNK
RATTLE
KLATTER
RUSTLE
RUSTLE

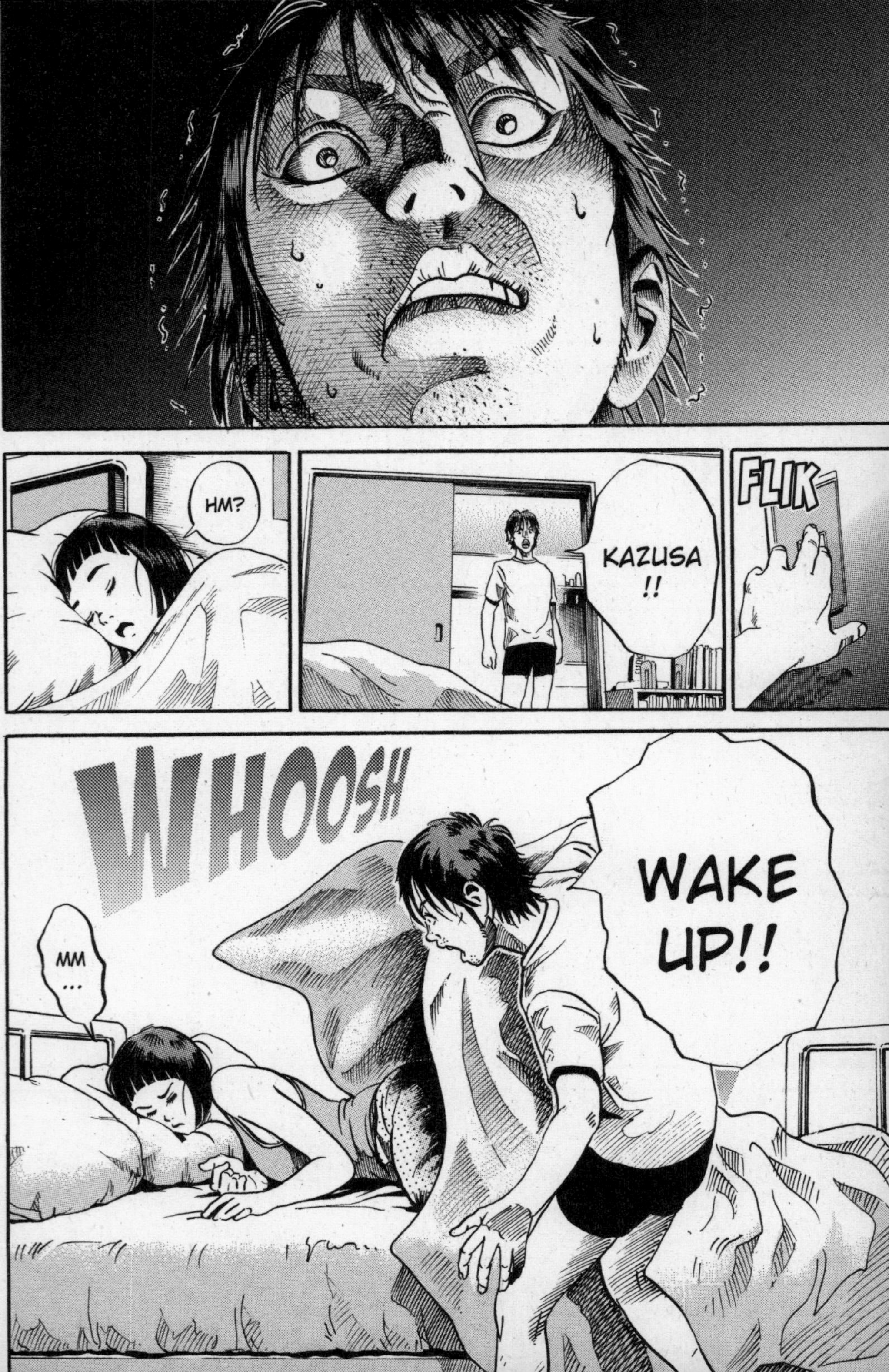
FLIK
KAZUSA !!
HM?
WAKE UP!!
WHOOSH
MM ...

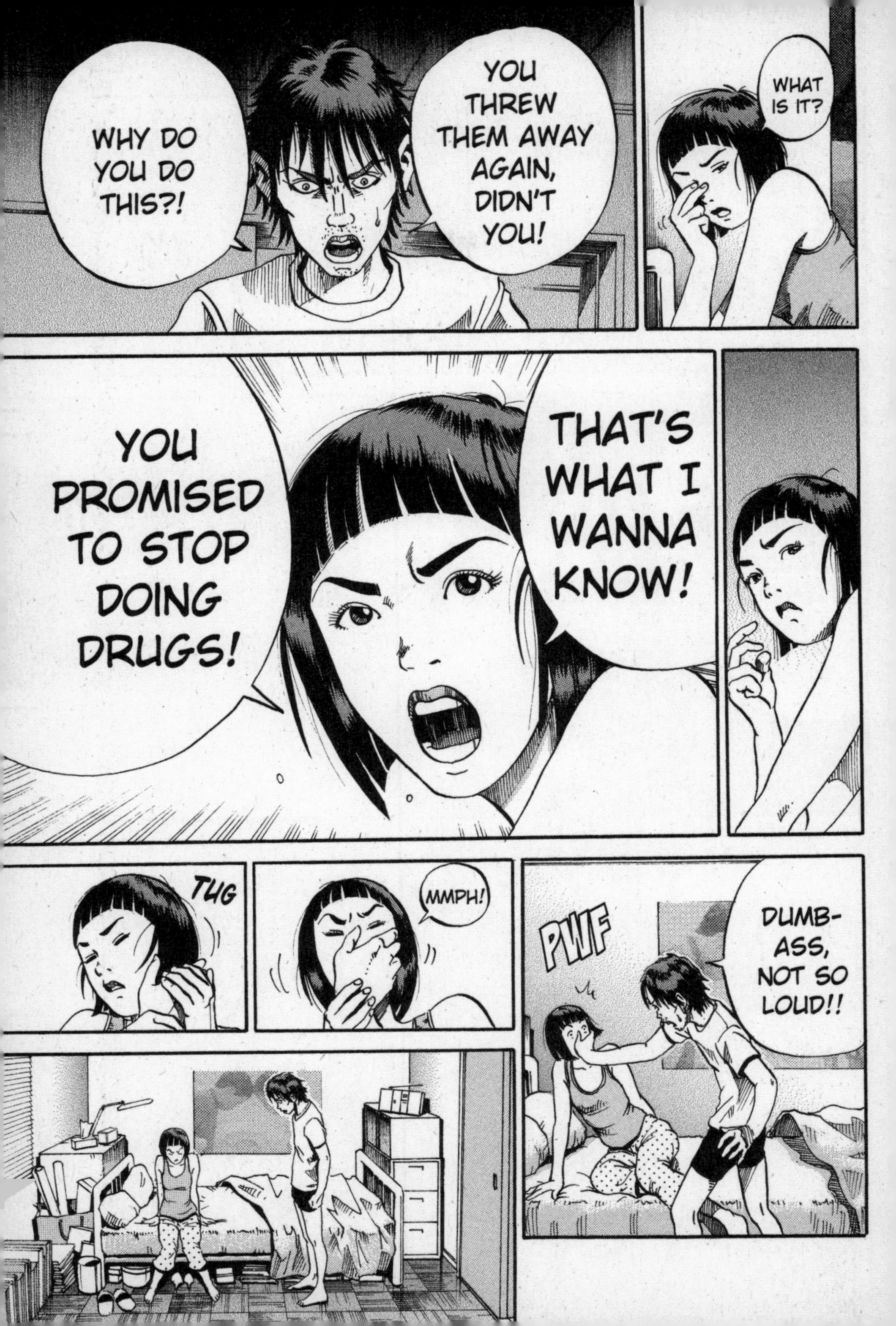
WHAT IS IT?
YOU THREW THEM AWAY AGAIN, DIDN'T YOU!
WHY DO YOU DO THIS?!
THAT'S WHAT I WANNA KNOW!
YOU PROMISED TO STOP DOING DRUGS!
DUMB-ASS, NOT SO LOUD!!
PWF
MMPH!
TUG

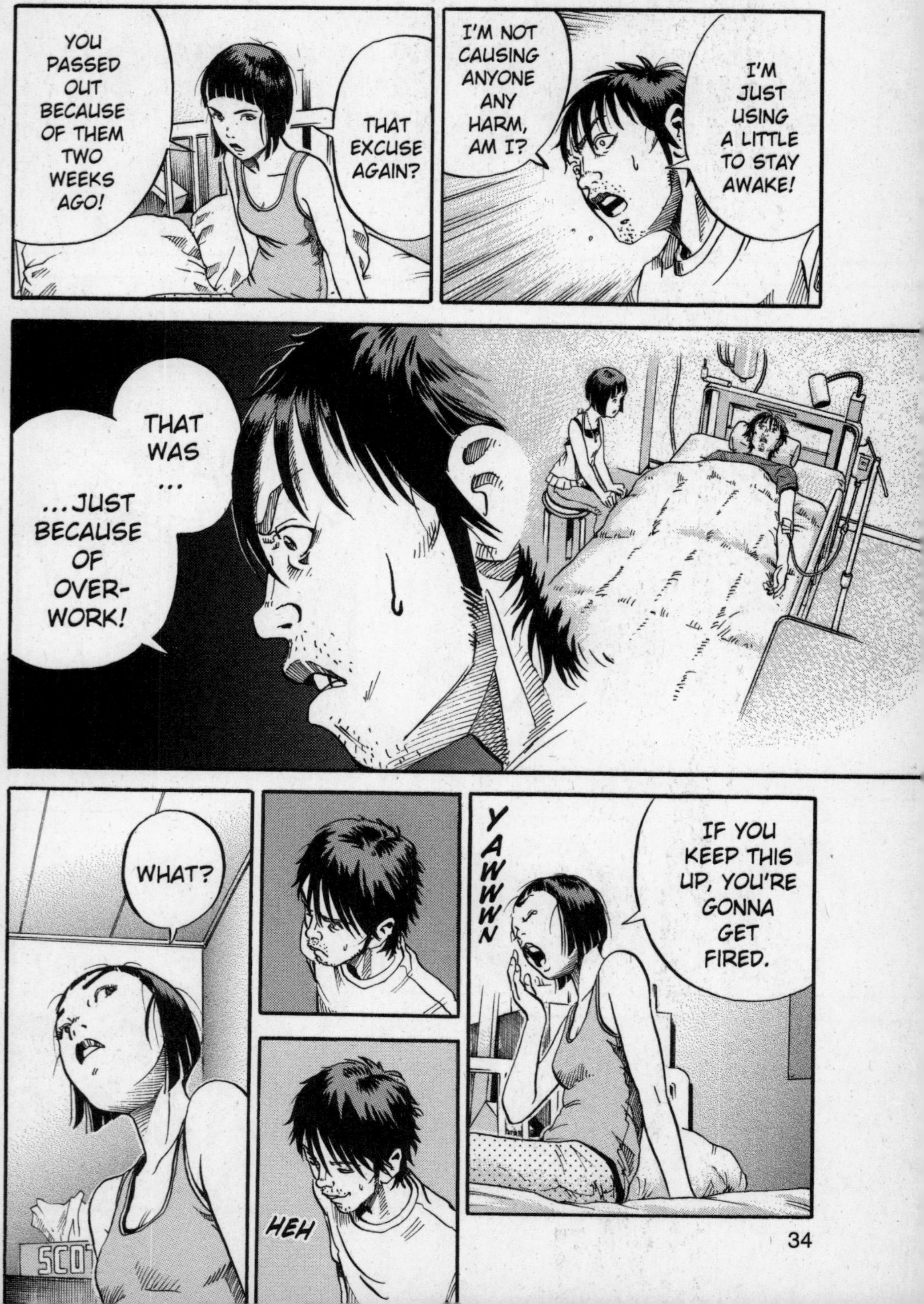
I'M NOT CAUSING ANYONE ANY HARM, AM I?
I'M JUST USING A LITTLE TO STAY AWAKE!
THAT EXCUSE AGAIN?
YOU PASSED OUT BECAUSE OF THEM TWO WEEKS AGO!
THAT WAS...
...JUST BECAUSE OF OVER-WORK!
IF YOU KEEP THIS UP, YOU'RE GONNA GET FIRED.
YAWWWN
HEH
WHAT?

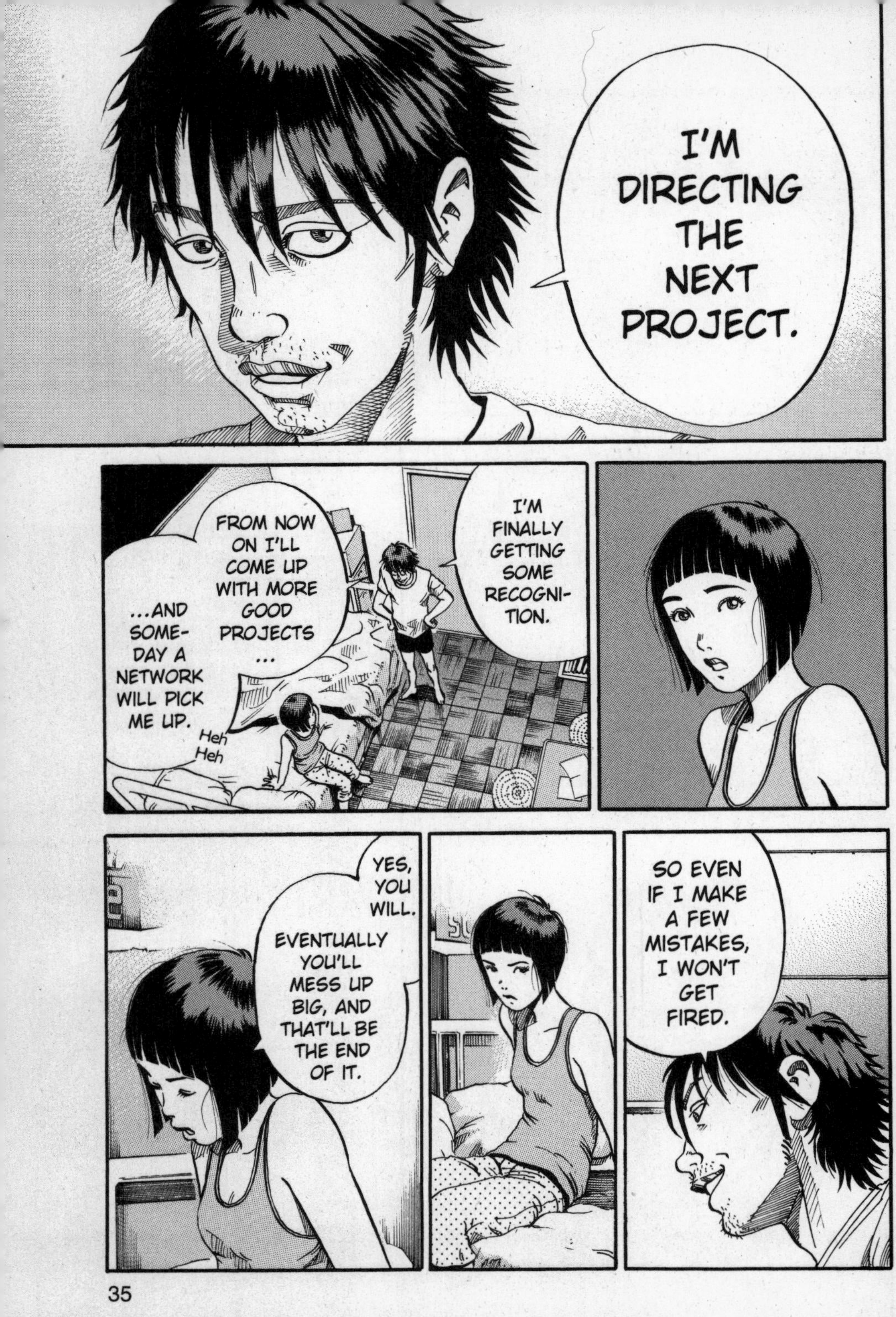
I'M DIRECTING THE NEXT PROJECT.
I'M FINALLY GETTING SOME RECOGNITION.
FROM NOW ON I'LL COME UP WITH MORE GOOD PROJECTS ...
...AND SOMEDAY A NETWORK WILL PICK ME UP.
Heh Heh
SO EVEN IF I MAKE A FEW MISTAKES, I WON'T GET FIRED.
YES, YOU WILL.
EVENTUALLY YOU'LL MESS UP BIG, AND THAT'LL BE THE END OF IT.

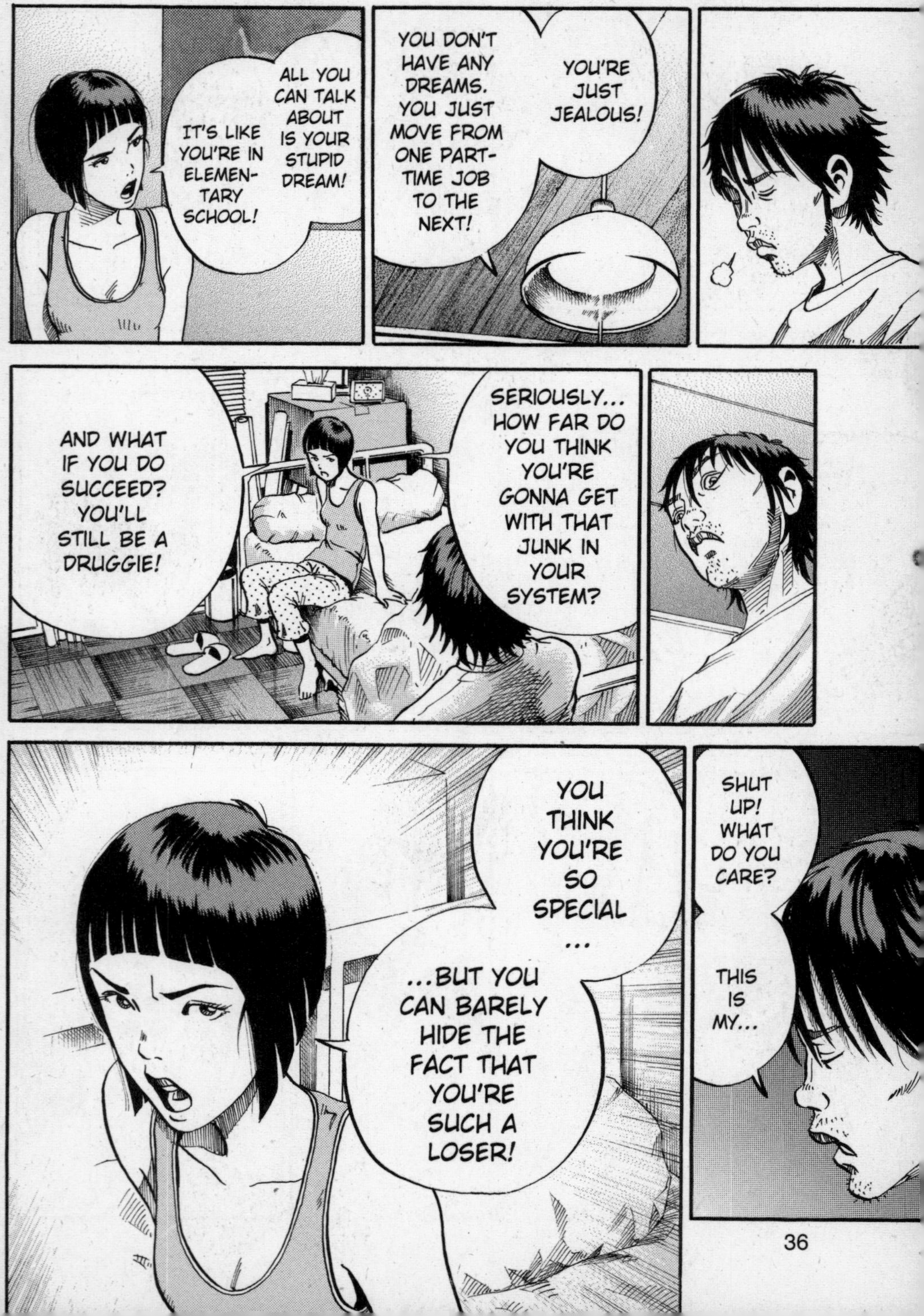
YOU'RE JUST JEALOUS!
YOU DON'T HAVE ANY DREAMS. YOU JUST MOVE FROM ONE PART-TIME JOB TO THE NEXT!
ALL YOU CAN TALK ABOUT IS YOUR STUPID DREAM!
IT'S LIKE YOU'RE IN ELEMENTARY SCHOOL!
SERIOUSLY... HOW FAR DO YOU THINK YOU'RE GONNA GET WITH THAT JUNK IN YOUR SYSTEM?
AND WHAT IF YOU DO SUCCEED? YOU'LL STILL BE A DRUGGIE!
SHUT UP! WHAT DO YOU CARE?
THIS IS MY...
YOU THINK YOU'RE SO SPECIAL...
...BUT YOU CAN BARELY HIDE THE FACT THAT YOU'RE SUCH A LOSER!

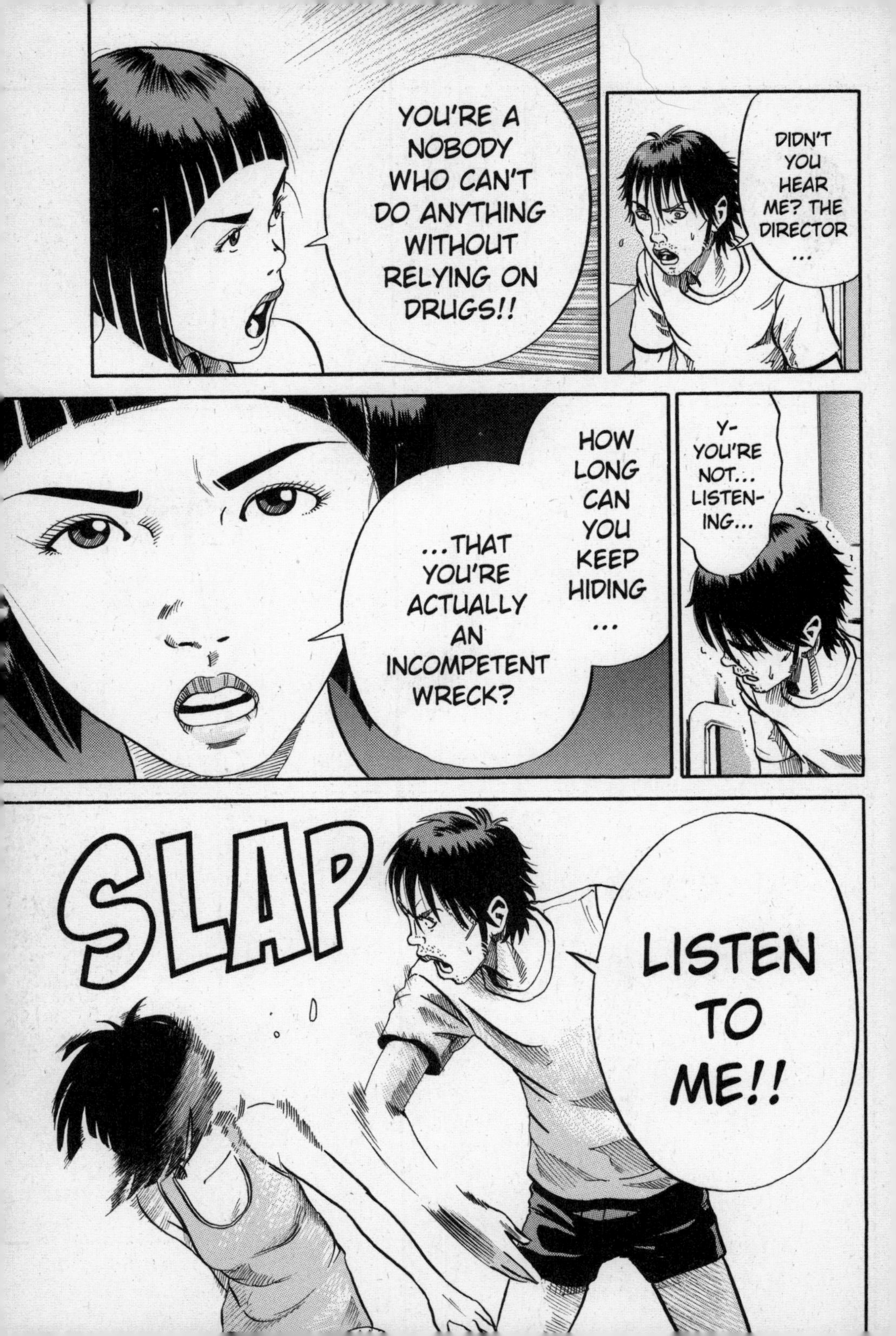
DIDN'T YOU HEAR ME? THE DIRECTOR ...
YOU'RE A NOBODY WHO CAN'T DO ANYTHING WITHOUT RELYING ON DRUGS!!
Y-YOU'RE NOT... LISTEN-ING...
HOW LONG CAN YOU KEEP HIDING ...
...THAT YOU'RE ACTUALLY AN INCOMPETENT WRECK?
LISTEN TO ME!!
SLAP

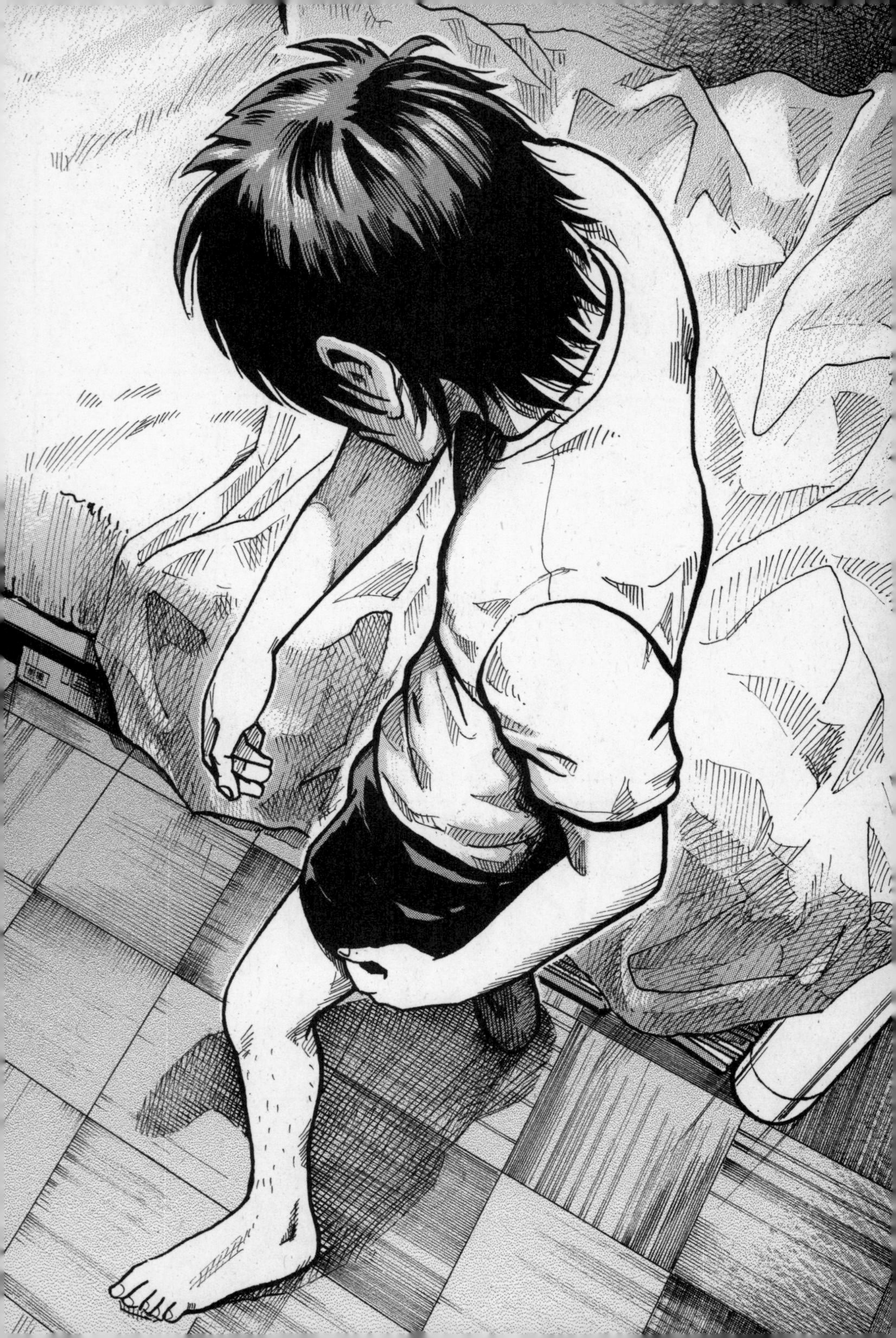

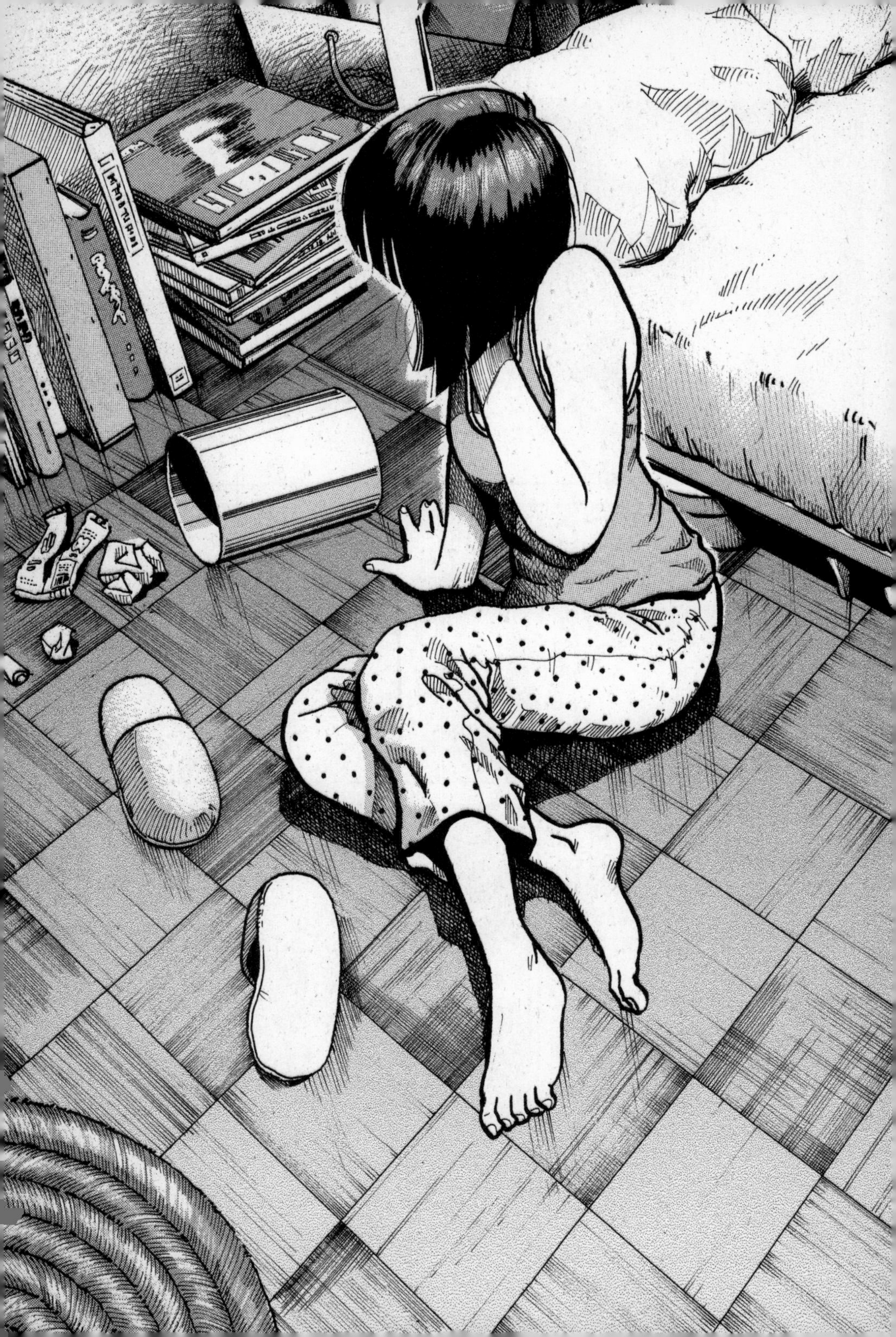

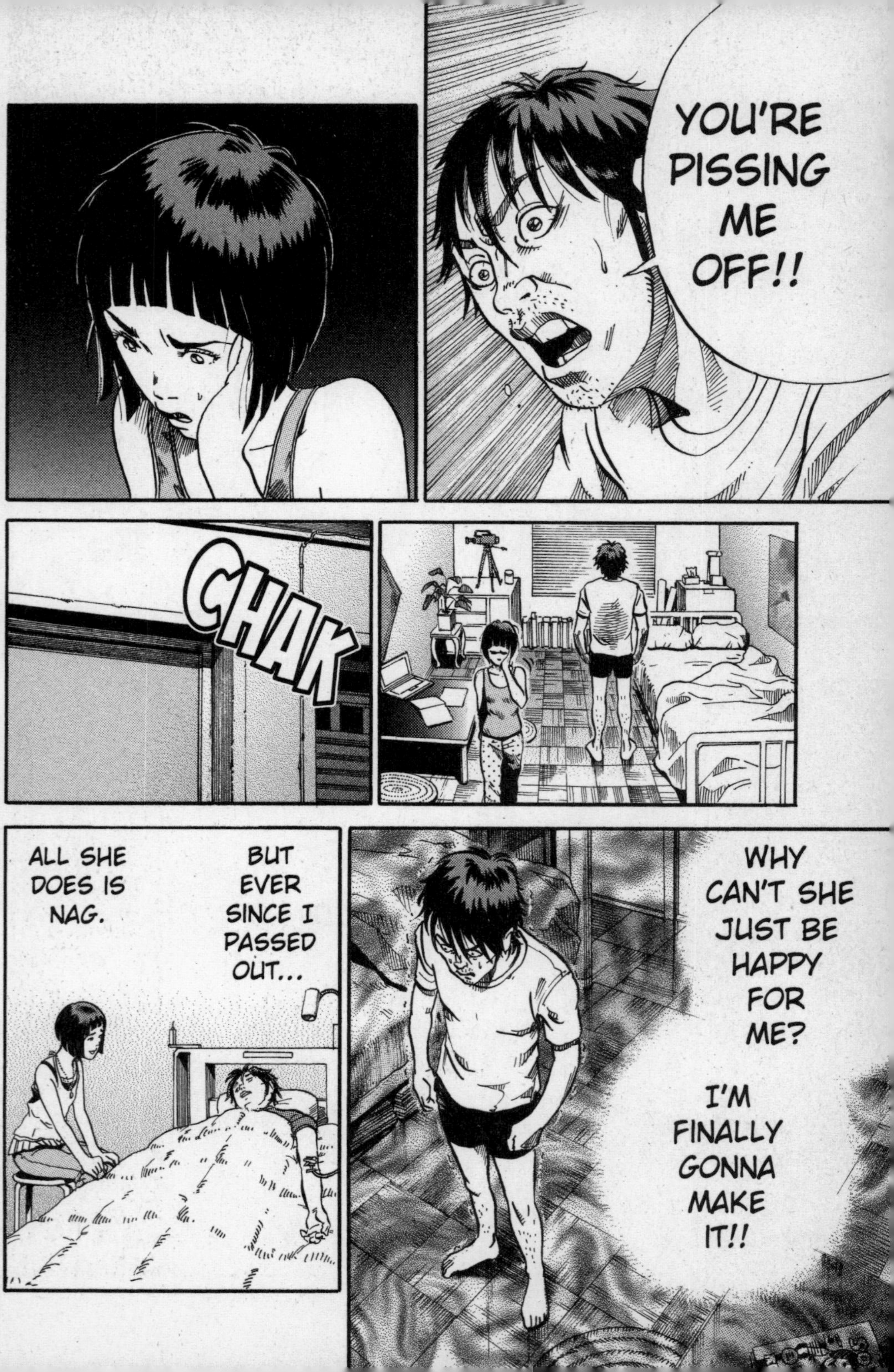
YOU'RE PISSING ME OFF!!
CHAK
WHY CAN'T SHE JUST BE HAPPY FOR ME?
I'M FINALLY GONNA MAKE IT!!
ALL SHE DOES IS NAG.
BUT EVER SINCE I PASSED OUT...

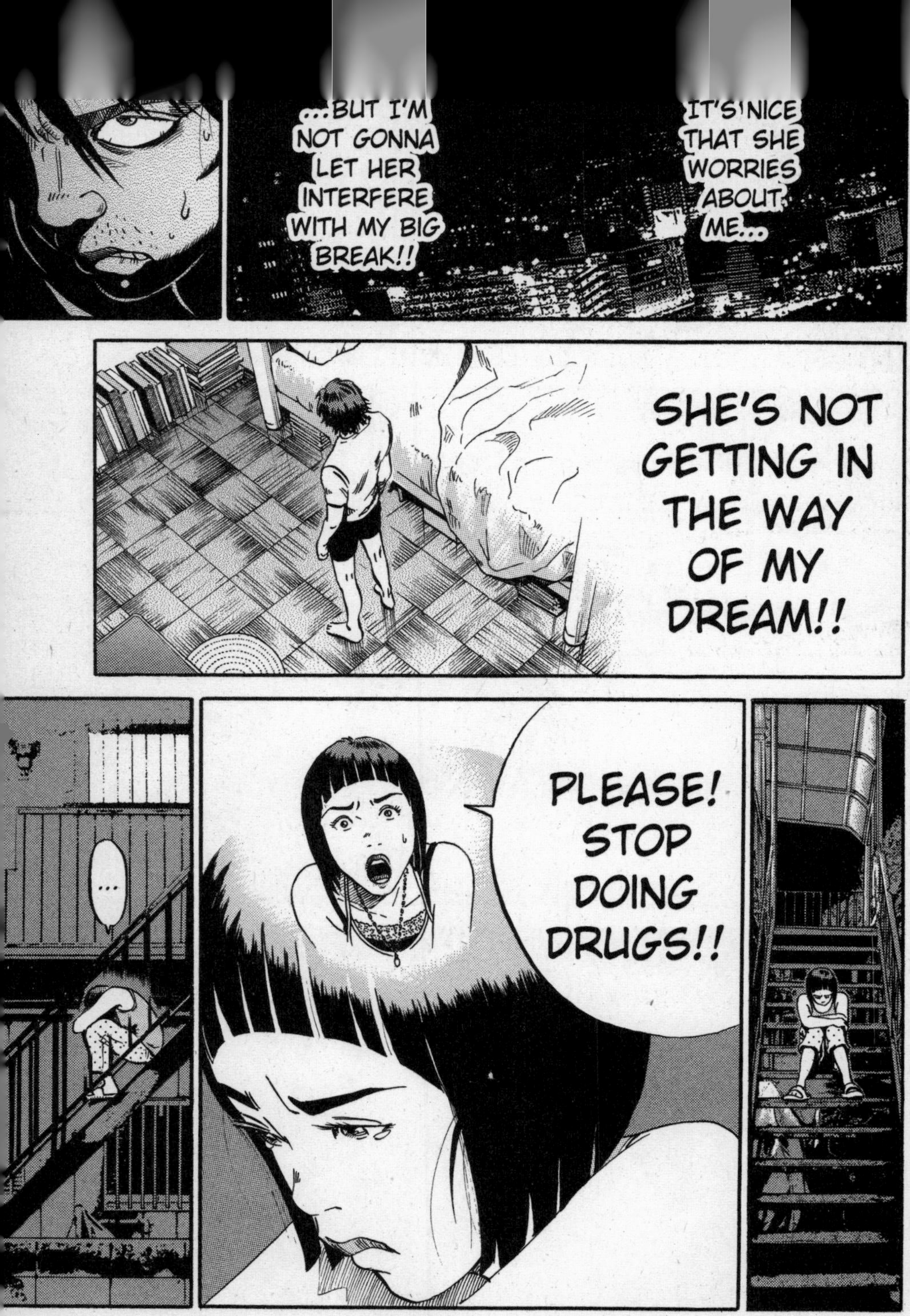
IT'S NICE THAT SHE WORRIES ABOUT ME...
...BUT I'M NOT GONNA LET HER INTERFERE WITH MY BIG BREAK!!
SHE'S NOT GETTING IN THE WAY OF MY DREAM!!
PLEASE! STOP DOING DRUGS!!
...

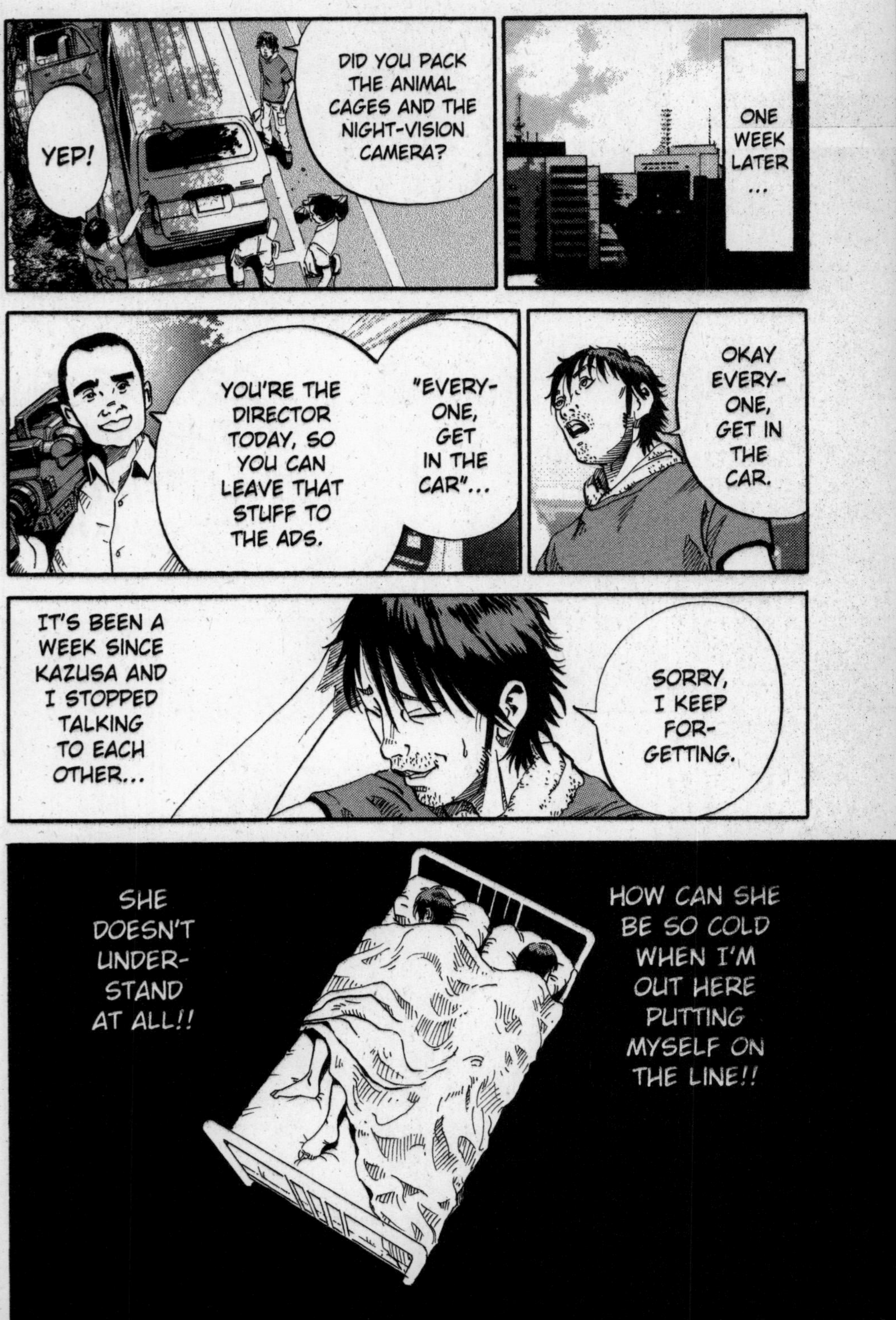
ONE WEEK LATER...
DID YOU PACK THE ANIMAL CAGES AND THE NIGHT-VISION CAMERA?
YEP!
OKAY EVERY-ONE, GET IN THE CAR.
"EVERY-ONE, GET IN THE CAR"...
YOU'RE THE DIRECTOR TODAY, SO YOU CAN LEAVE THAT STUFF TO THE ADS.
SORRY, I KEEP FOR-GETTING.
IT'S BEEN A WEEK SINCE KAZUSA AND I STOPPED TALKING TO EACH OTHER...
HOW CAN SHE BE SO COLD WHEN I'M OUT HERE PUTTING MYSELF ON THE LINE!!
SHE DOESN'T UNDER-STAND AT ALL!!

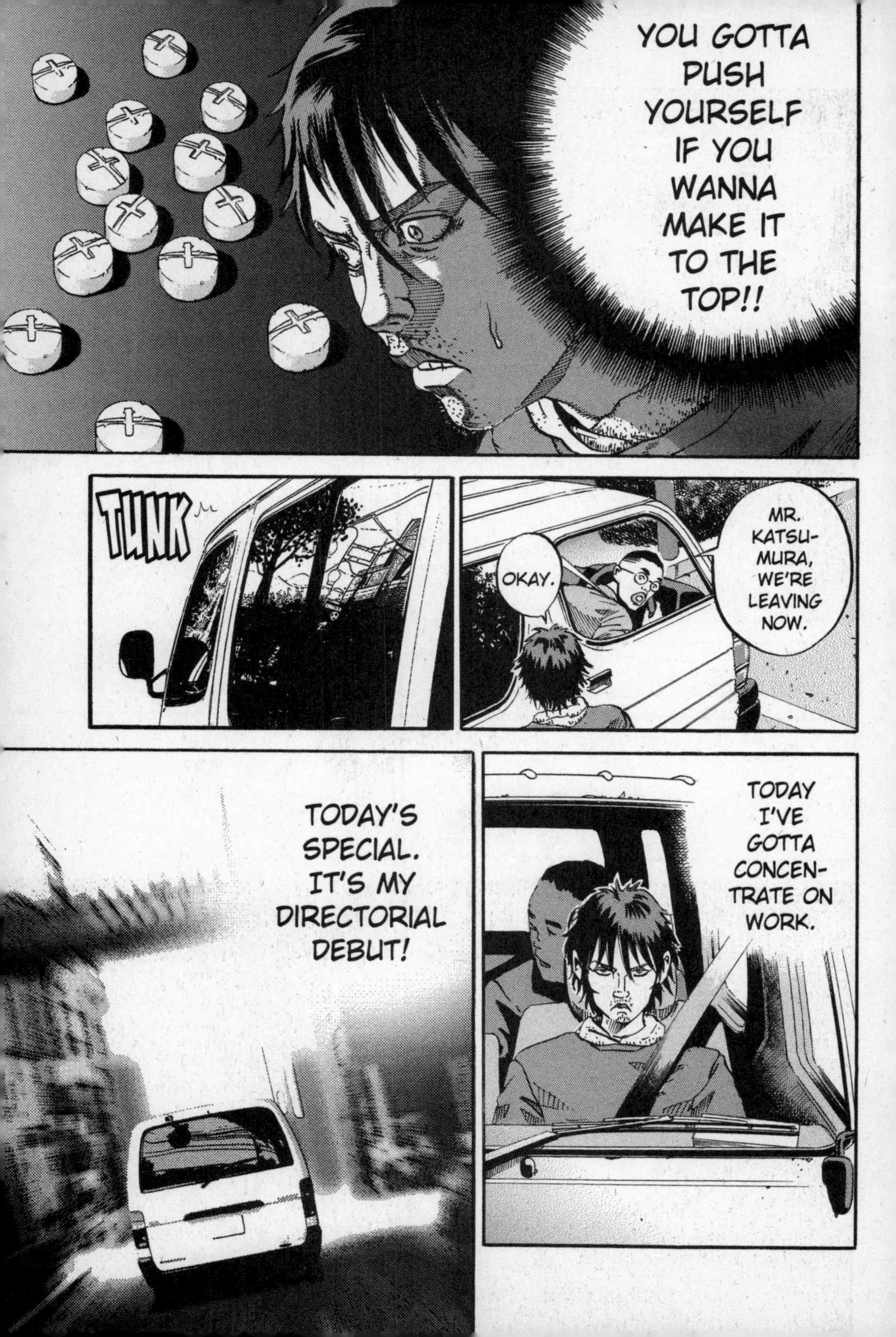
YOU GOTTA PUSH YOURSELF IF YOU WANNA MAKE IT TO THE TOP!!
MR. KATSUMURA, WE'RE LEAVING NOW.
OKAY.
TUNK
TODAY I'VE GOTTA CONCENTRATE ON WORK.
TODAY'S SPECIAL. IT'S MY DIRECTORIAL DEBUT!

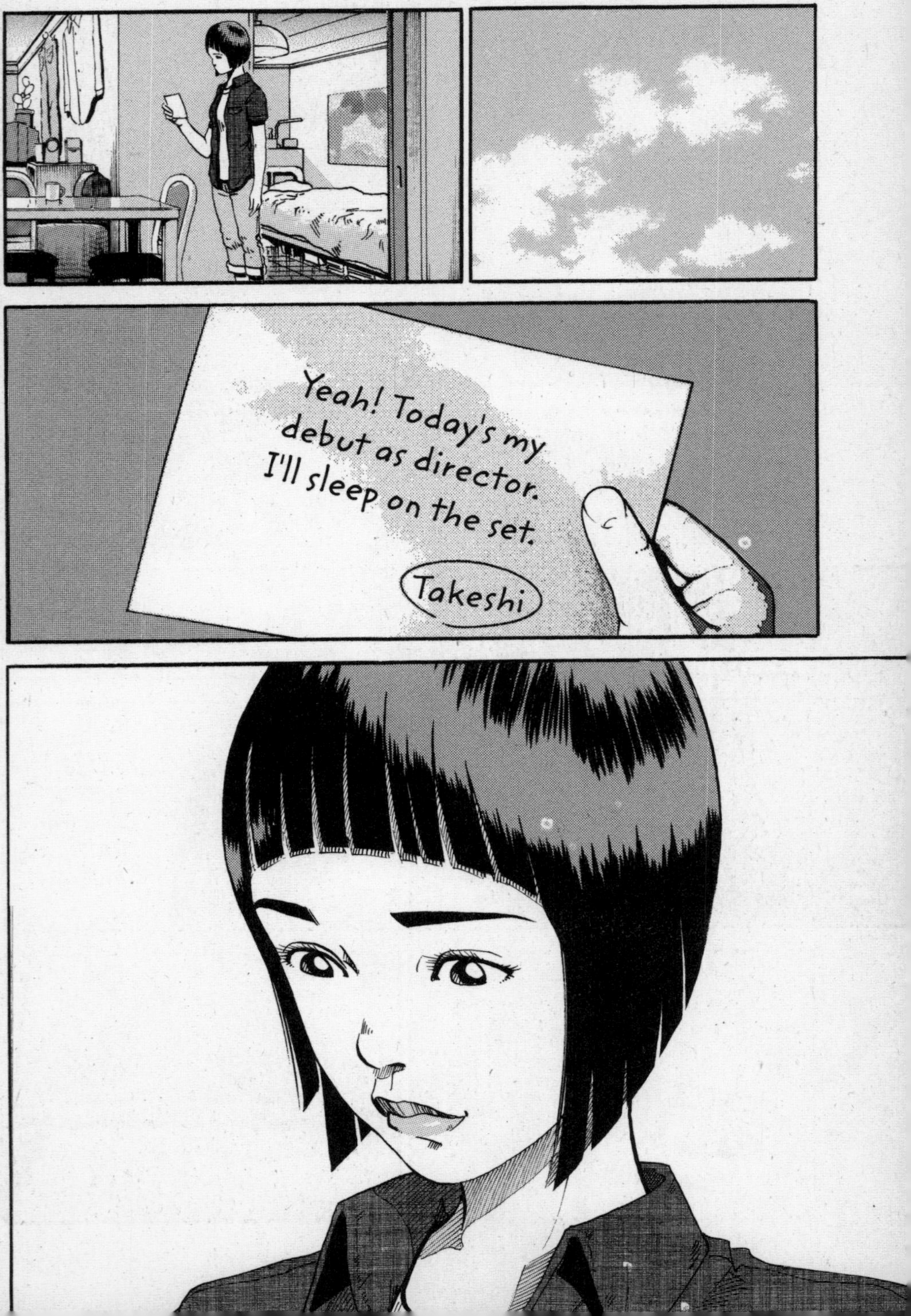
Yeah! Today's my debut as director. I'll sleep on the set.
Takeshi

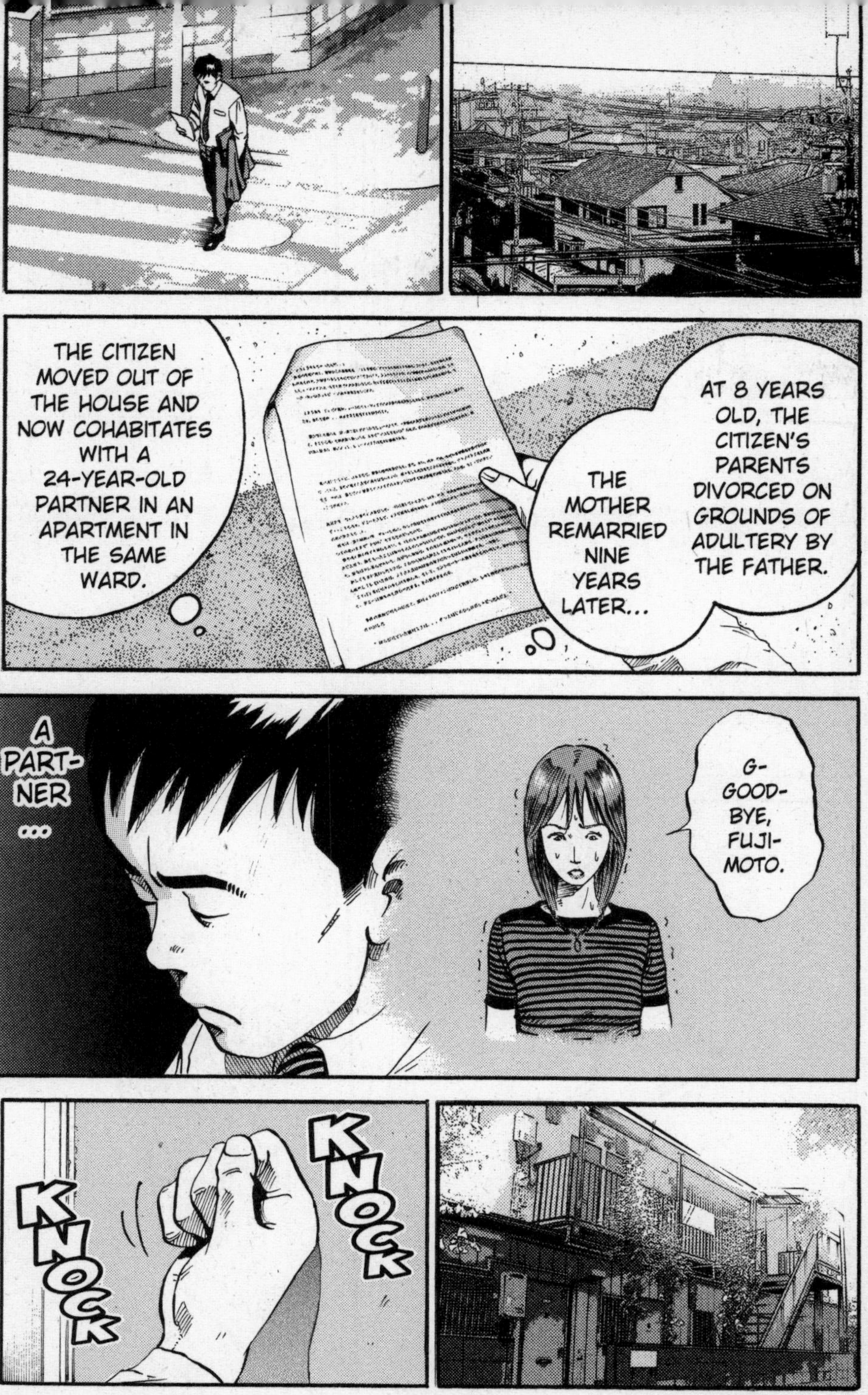
AT 8 YEARS OLD, THE CITIZEN'S PARENTS DIVORCED ON GROUNDS OF ADULTERY BY THE FATHER.
THE MOTHER REMARRIED NINE YEARS LATER...
THE CITIZEN MOVED OUT OF THE HOUSE AND NOW COHABITATES WITH A 24-YEAR-OLD PARTNER IN AN APARTMENT IN THE SAME WARD.
G-GOODBYE, FUJIMOTO.
A PARTNER...
KNOCK
KNOCK

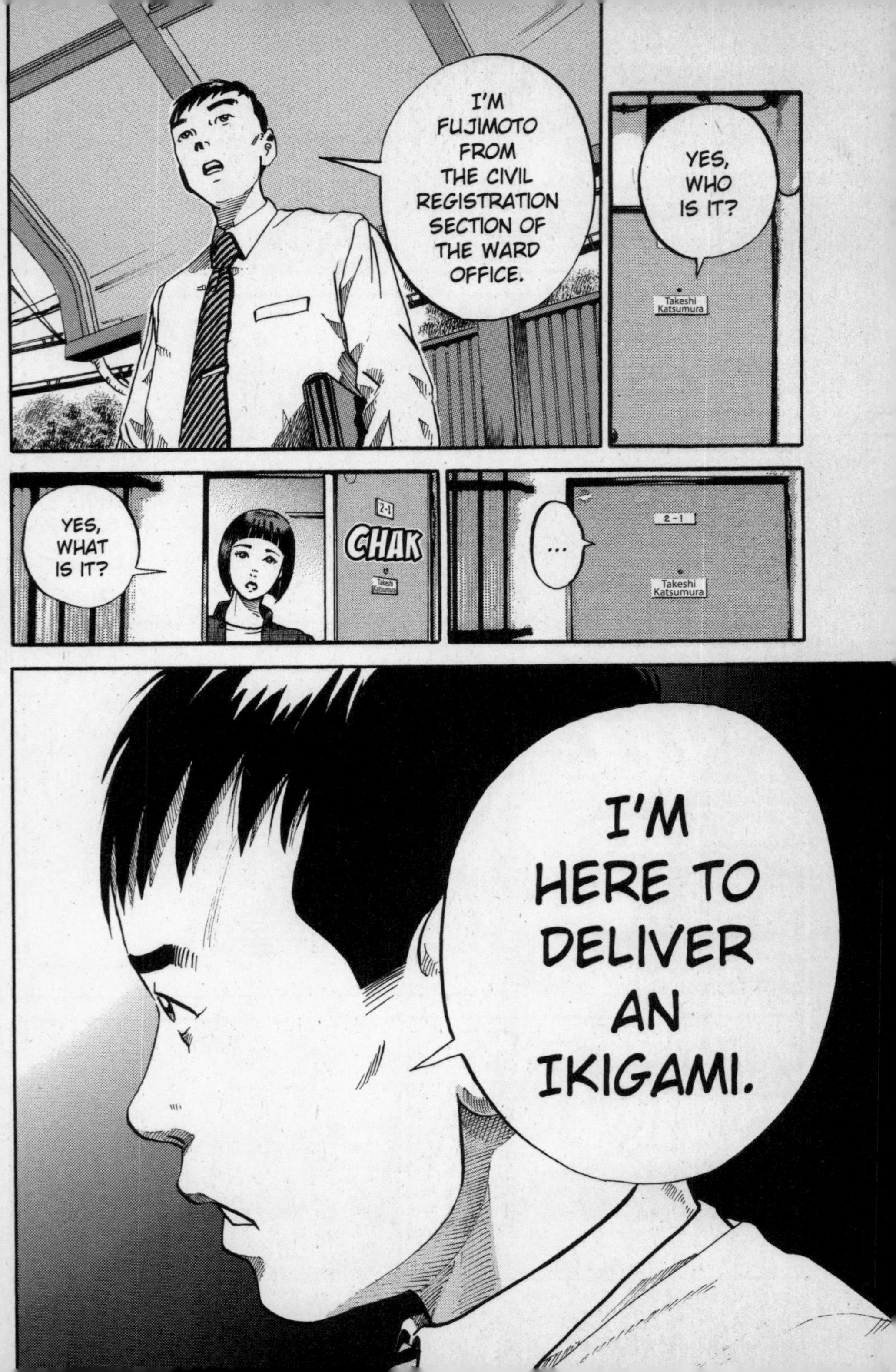
YES, WHO IS IT?
Takeshi Katsumura
I'M FUJIMOTO FROM THE CIVIL REGISTRATION SECTION OF THE WARD OFFICE.
...
2-1
Takeshi Katsumura
2-1
CHAK
Takeshi Katsumura
YES, WHAT IS IT?
I'M HERE TO DELIVER AN IKIGAMI.

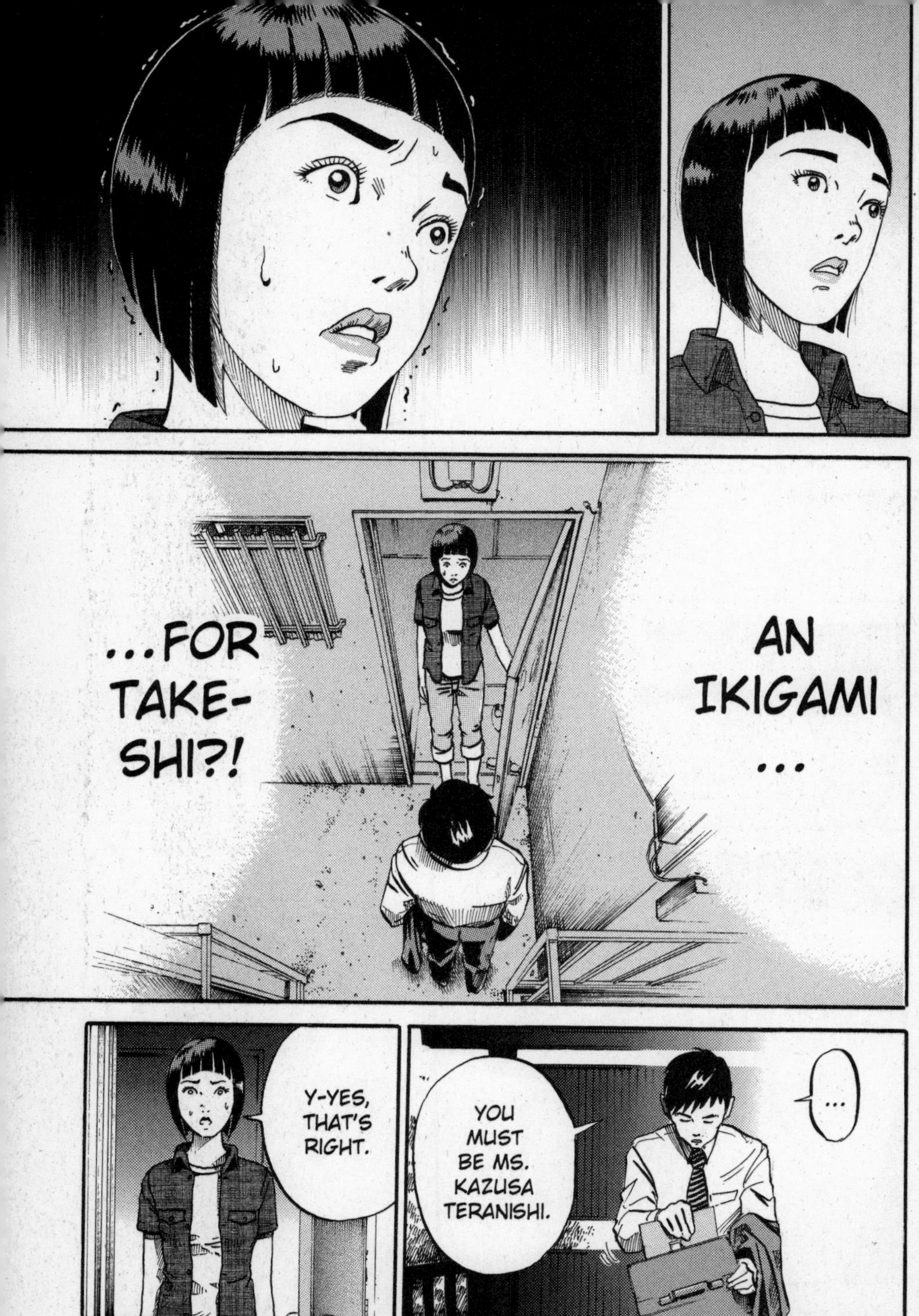
AN IKIGAMI ...
...FOR TAKE-SHI?!
...
YOU MUST BE MS. KAZUSA TERANISHI.
Y-YES, THAT'S RIGHT.

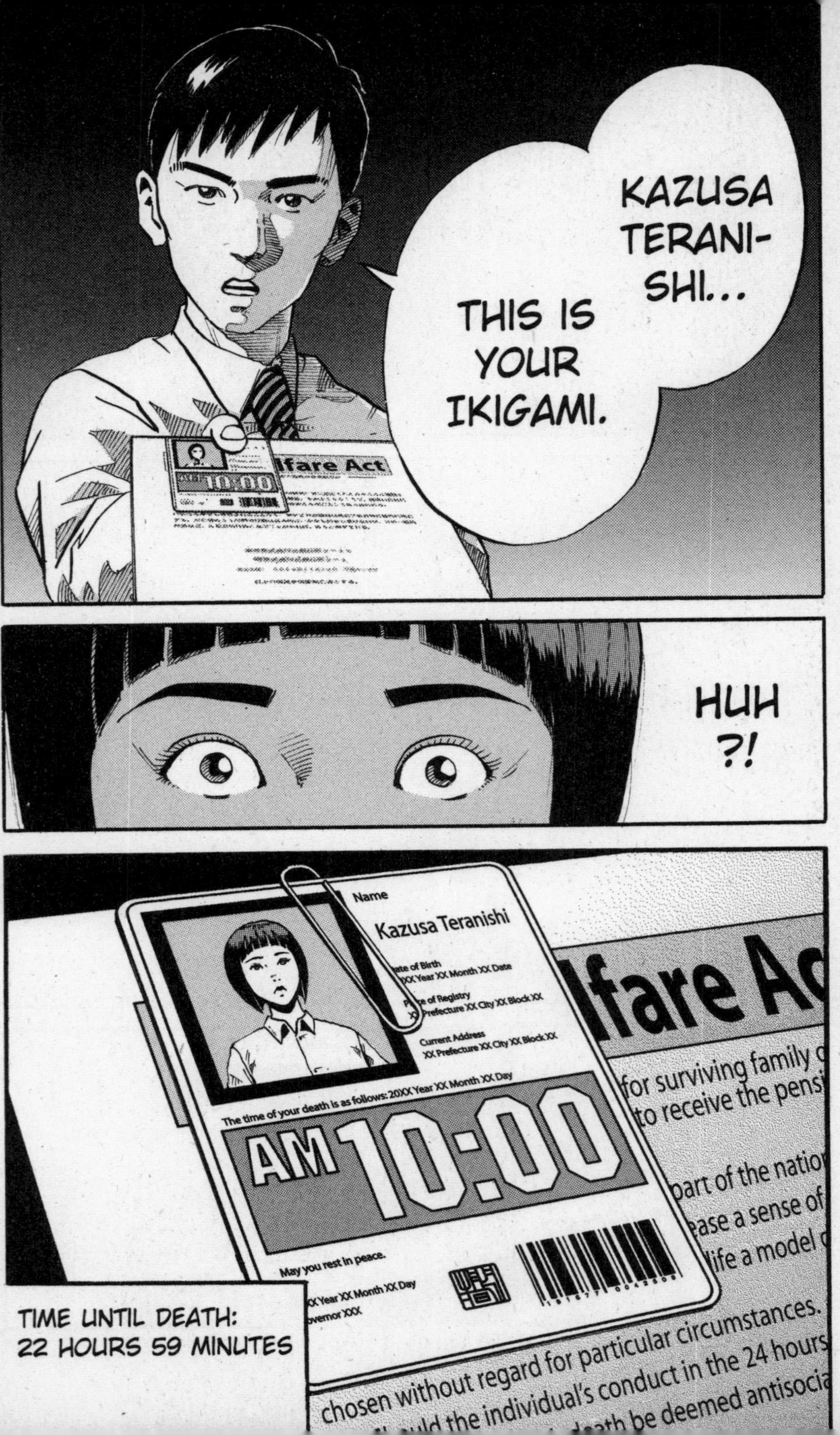
KAZUSA TERANI-SHI...
THIS IS YOUR IKIGAMI.
lfare Act
AM 10:00
HUH ?!
Name
Kazusa Teranishi
Current Address
XX Prefecture XX City XX Block XX
lfare Ac
for surviving family
to receive the pensi
The time of your death is as follows: 20XX Year XX Month XX Day
AM 10:00
part of the natio
ease a sense of
life a model
May you rest in peace.
XX Year XX Month XX Day
overnor XXX
chosen without regard for particular circumstances.
uld the individual's conduct in the 24 hours
death be deemed antisocia
TIME UNTIL DEATH: 22 HOURS 59 MINUTES

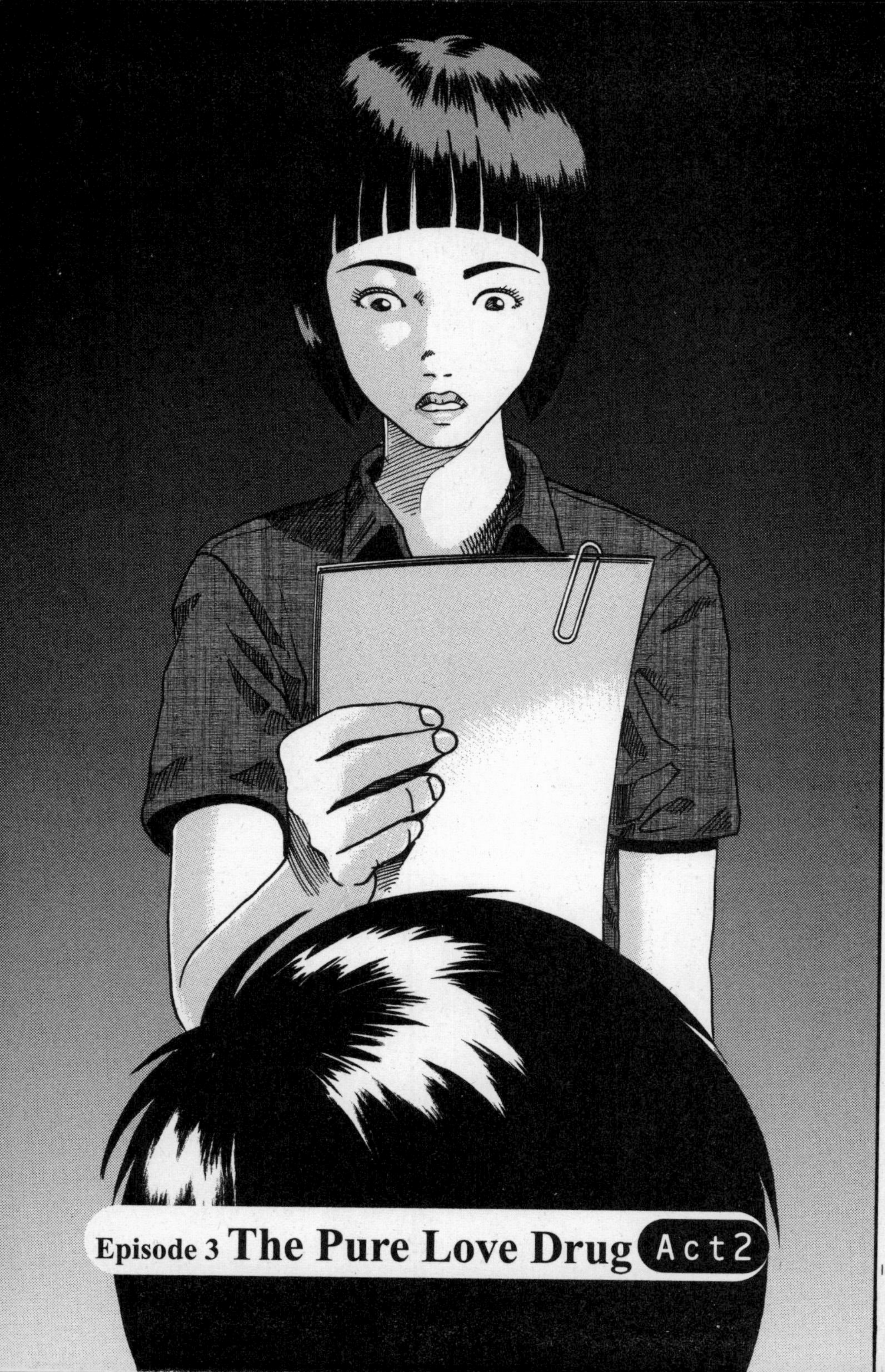

Episode 3 The Pure Love Drug Act 2

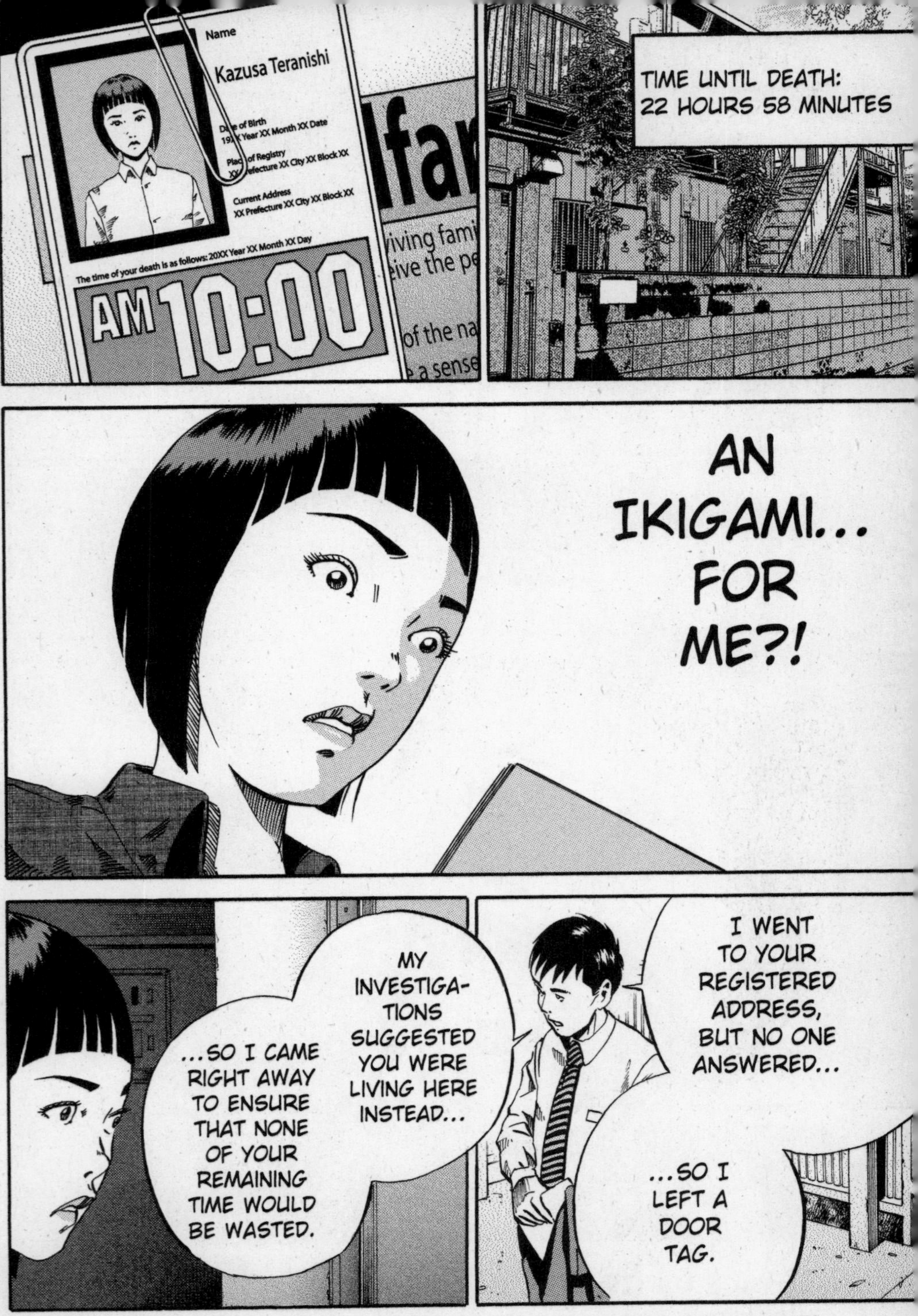
TIME UNTIL DEATH: 22 HOURS 58 MINUTES
Name
Kazusa Teranishi
Date of Birth
19XX Year XX Month XX Date
Place of Registry
XX Prefecture XX City XX Block XX
Current Address
XX Prefecture XX City XX Block XX
The time of your death is as follows: 20XX Year XX Month XX Day
AM 10:00
AN IKIGAMI... FOR ME?!
I WENT TO YOUR REGISTERED ADDRESS, BUT NO ONE ANSWERED...
...SO I LEFT A DOOR TAG.
MY INVESTIGATIONS SUGGESTED YOU WERE LIVING HERE INSTEAD...
...SO I CAME RIGHT AWAY TO ENSURE THAT NONE OF YOUR REMAINING TIME WOULD BE WASTED.

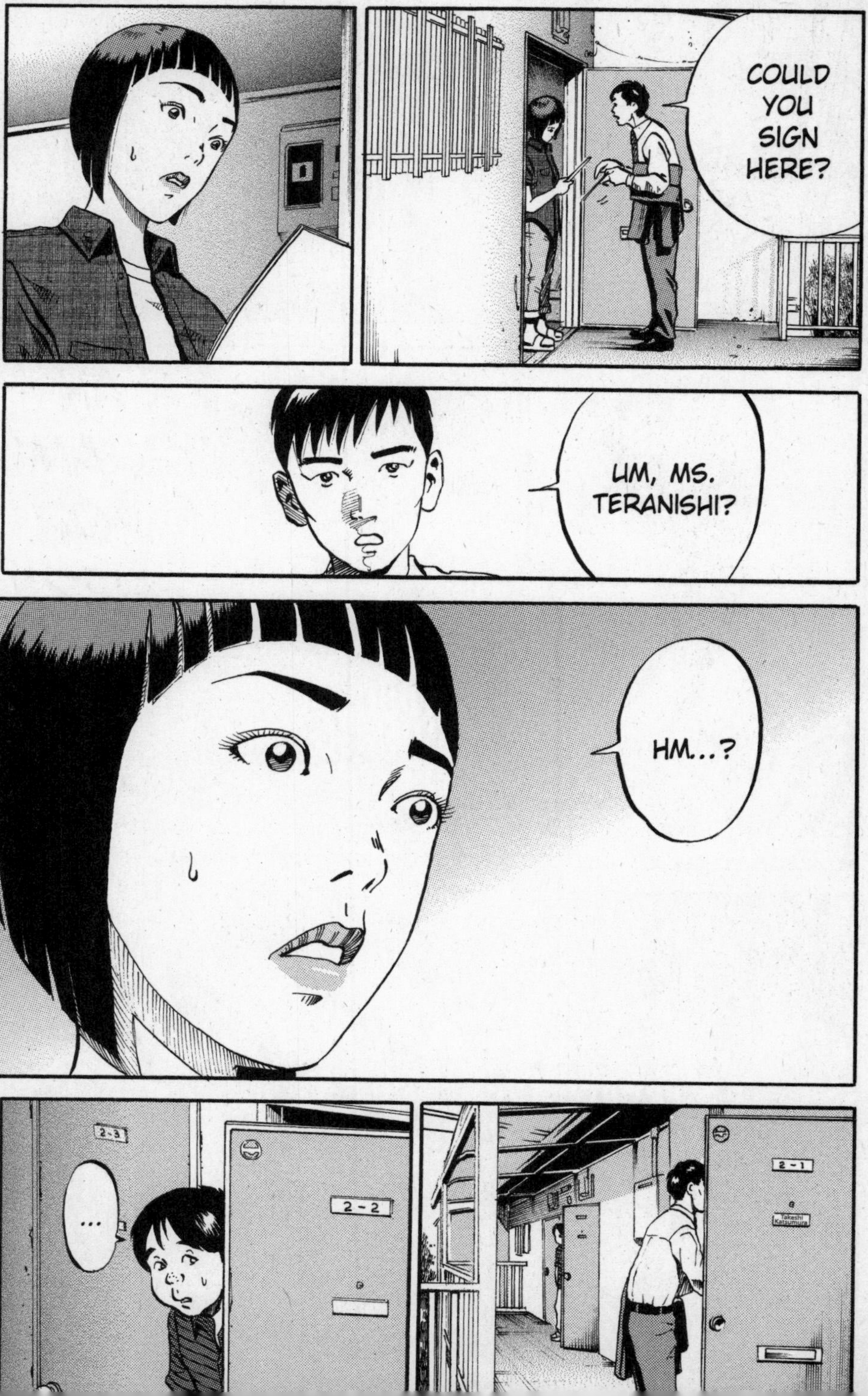
COULD YOU SIGN HERE?
UM, MS. TERANISHI?
HM...?
2-1
2-3
2-2
...

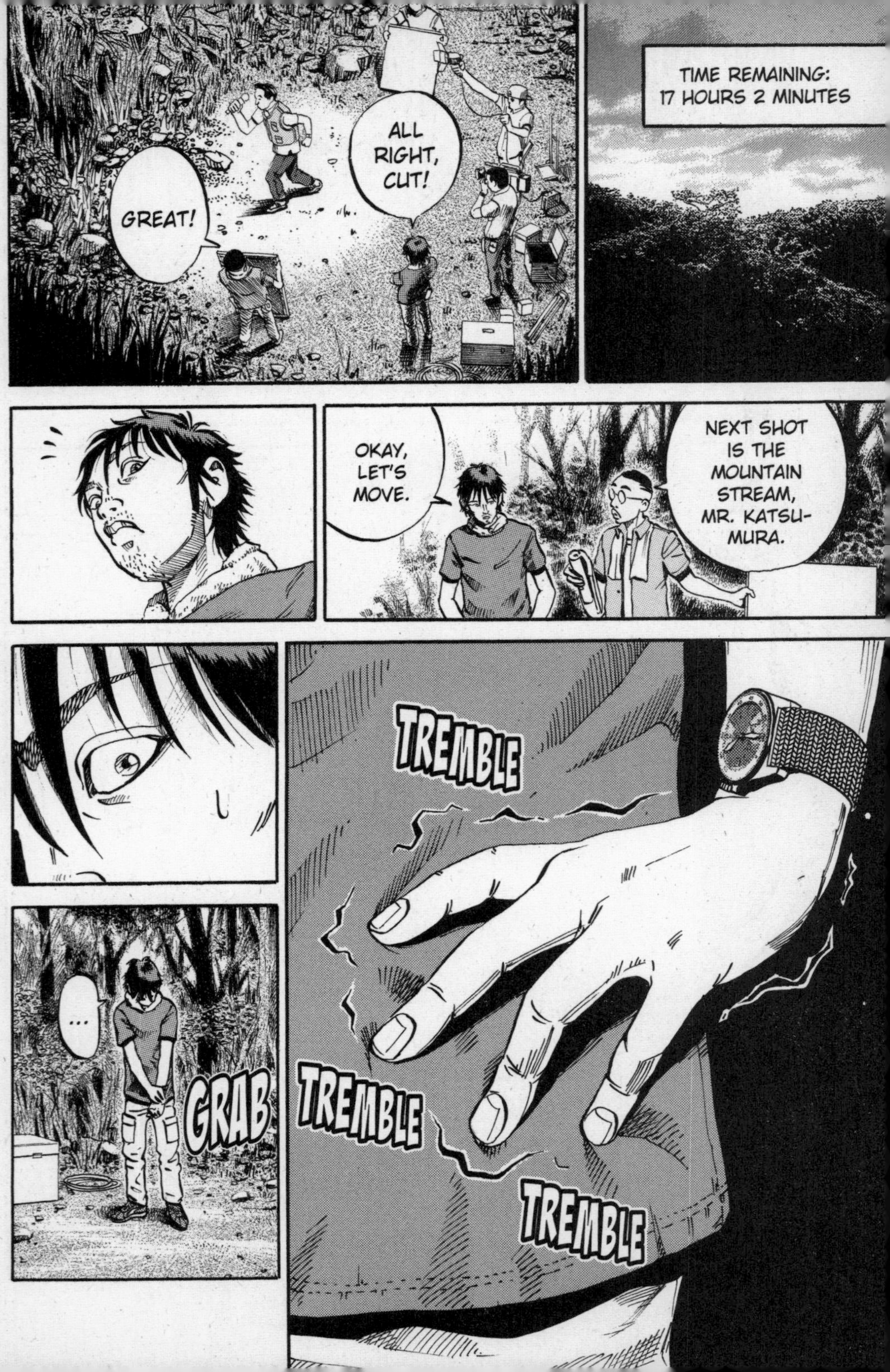
TIME REMAINING: 17 HOURS 2 MINUTES
ALL RIGHT, CUT!
GREAT!
NEXT SHOT IS THE MOUNTAIN STREAM, MR. KATSU-MURA.
OKAY, LET'S MOVE.
TREMBLE
TREMBLE
TREMBLE
...
GRAB

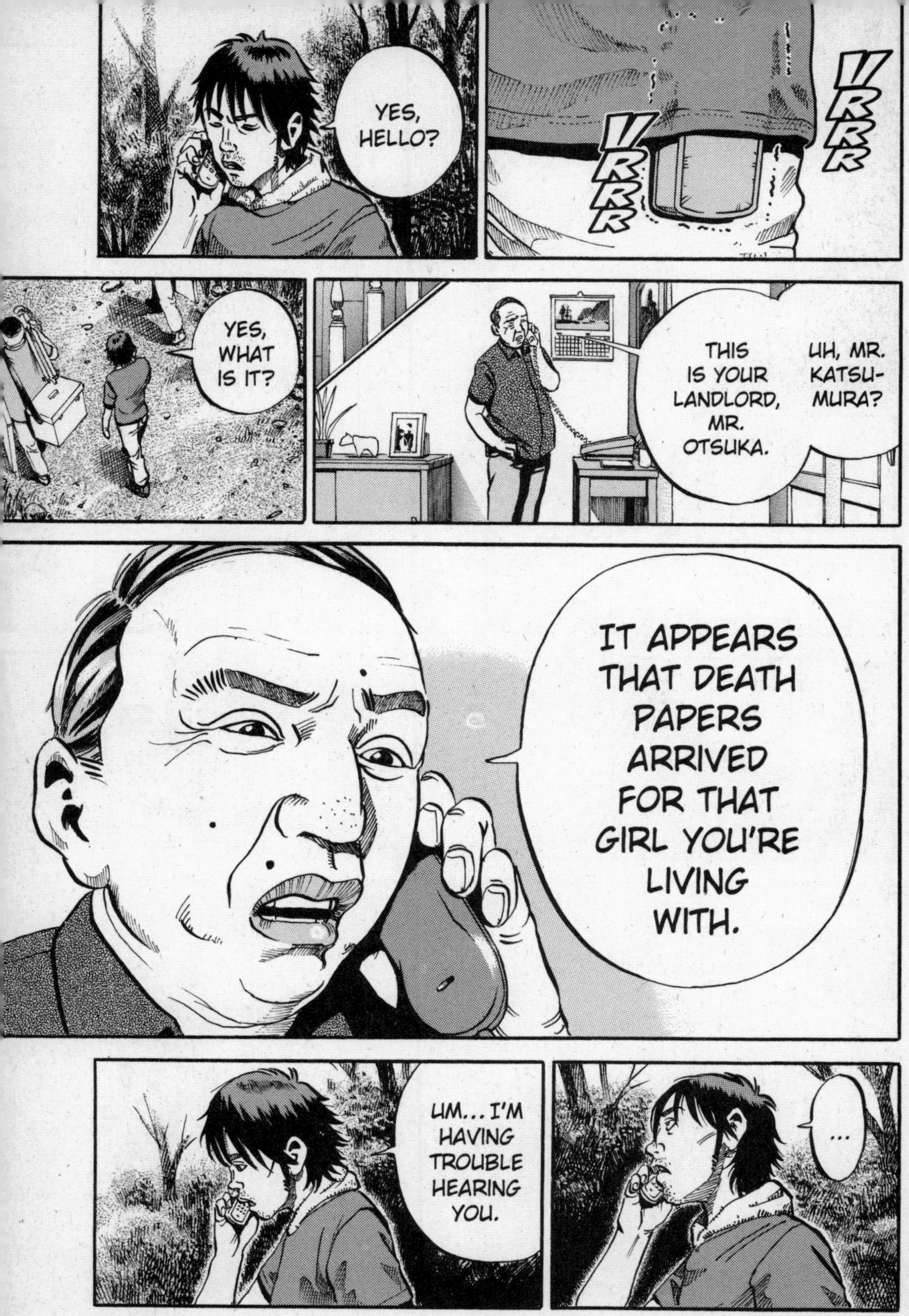
VRRR
VRRR
YES, HELLO?
UH, MR. KATSUMURA?
THIS IS YOUR LANDLORD, MR. OTSUKA.
YES, WHAT IS IT?
IT APPEARS THAT DEATH PAPERS ARRIVED FOR THAT GIRL YOU'RE LIVING WITH.
...
UM... I'M HAVING TROUBLE HEARING YOU.

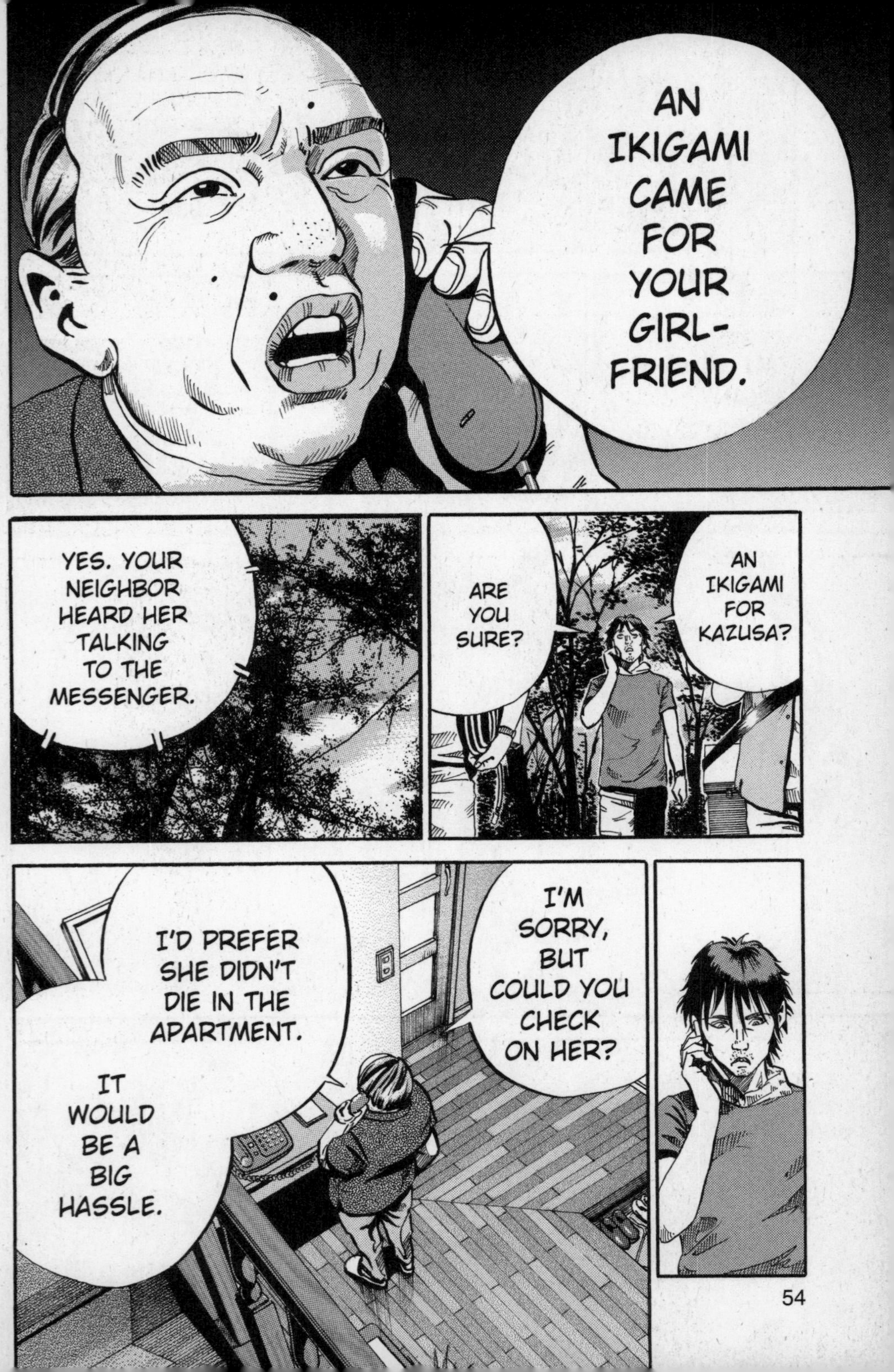
AN IKIGAMI CAME FOR YOUR GIRL-FRIEND.
AN IKIGAMI FOR KAZUSA?
ARE YOU SURE?
YES. YOUR NEIGHBOR HEARD HER TALKING TO THE MESSENGER.
I'M SORRY, BUT COULD YOU CHECK ON HER?
I'D PREFER SHE DIDN'T DIE IN THE APARTMENT.
IT WOULD BE A BIG HASSLE.

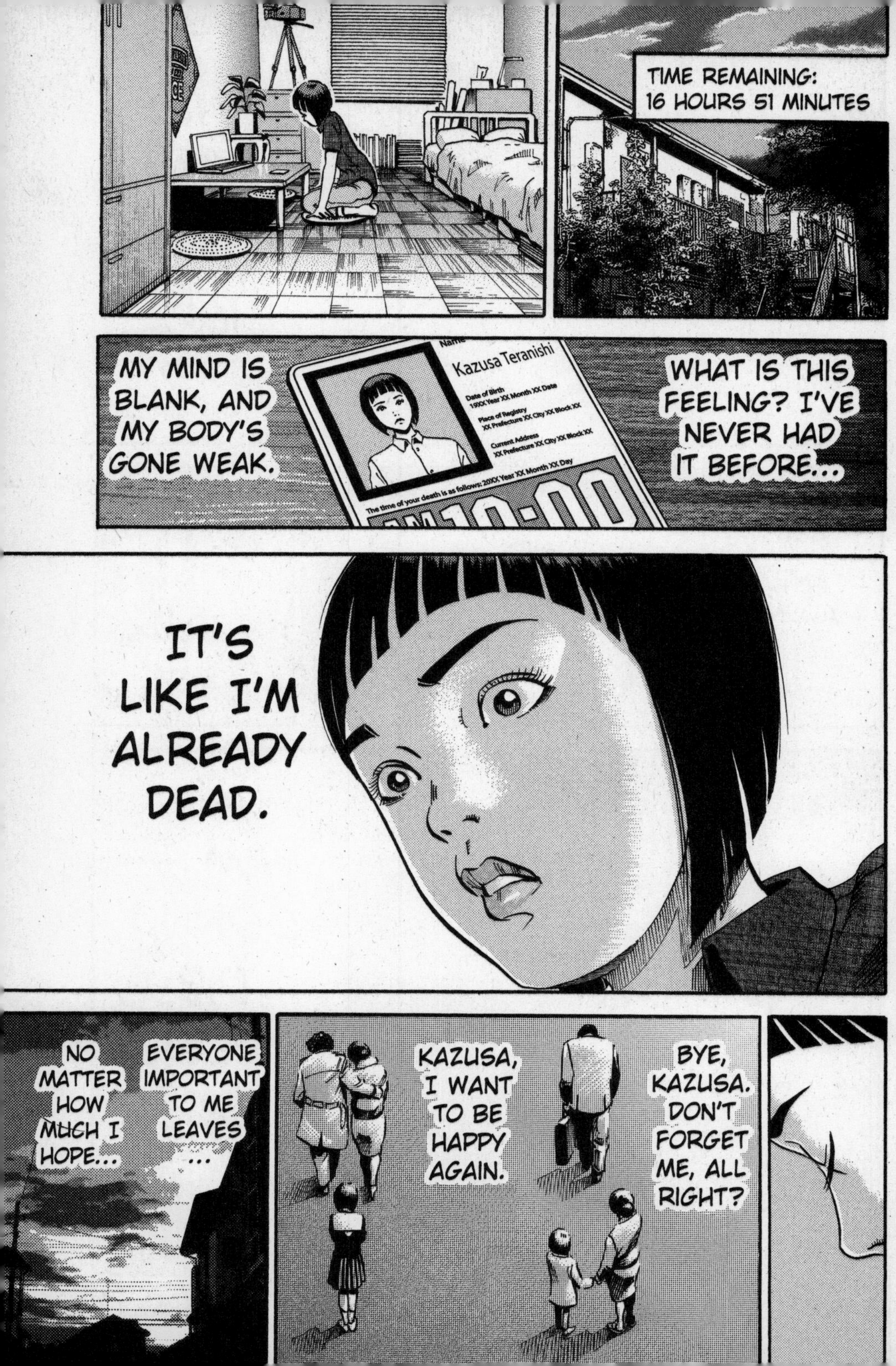
TIME REMAINING: 16 HOURS 51 MINUTES
WHAT IS THIS FEELING? I'VE NEVER HAD IT BEFORE...
Name
Kazusa Teranishi
Date of Birth 19XX Year XX Month XX Date
Place of Registry XX Prefecture XX City XX Block XX
Current Address XX Prefecture XX City XX Block XX
The time of your death is as follows: 20XX Year XX Month XX Day
MY MIND IS BLANK, AND MY BODY'S GONE WEAK.
IT'S LIKE I'M ALREADY DEAD.
BYE, KAZUSA. DON'T FORGET ME, ALL RIGHT?
KAZUSA, I WANT TO BE HAPPY AGAIN.
EVERYONE IMPORTANT TO ME LEAVES...
NO MATTER HOW MUCH I HOPE...

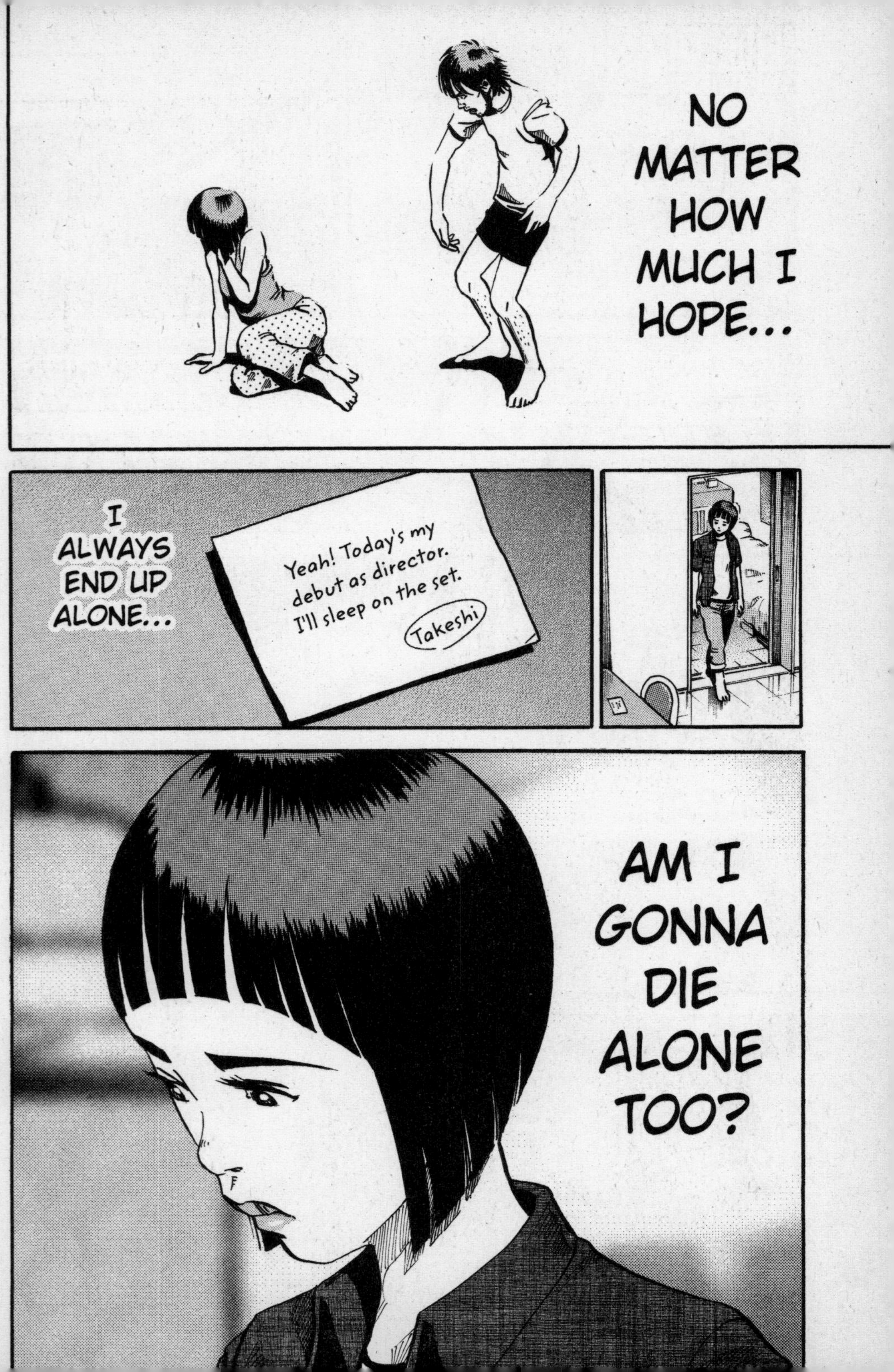
NO MATTER HOW MUCH I HOPE...
Yeah! Today's my debut as director. I'll sleep on the set.
Takeshi
I ALWAYS END UP ALONE...
AM I GONNA DIE ALONE TOO?

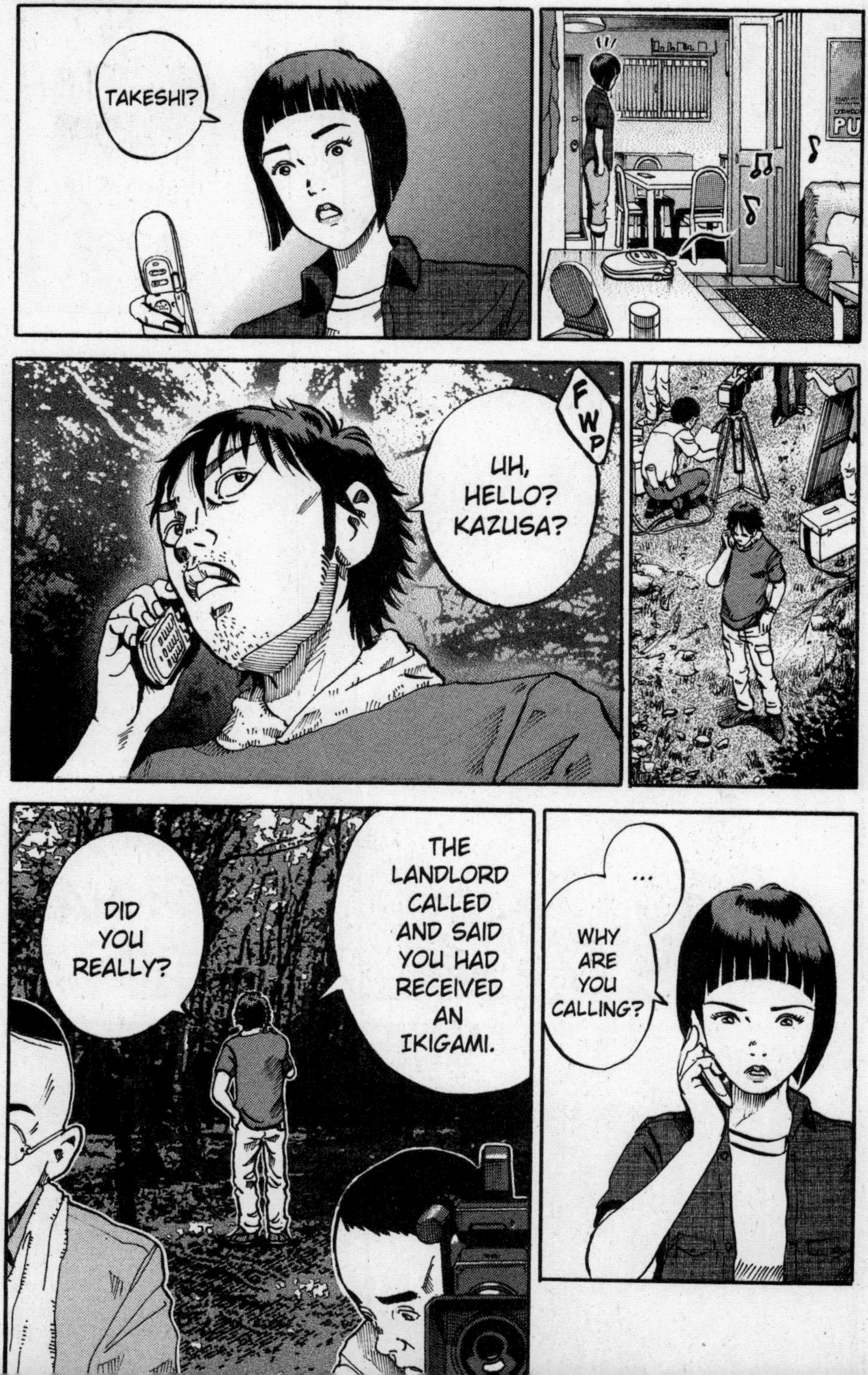
TAKESHI?
FWP
UH, HELLO? KAZUSA?
...
WHY ARE YOU CALLING?
THE LANDLORD CALLED AND SAID YOU HAD RECEIVED AN IKIGAMI.
DID YOU REALLY?

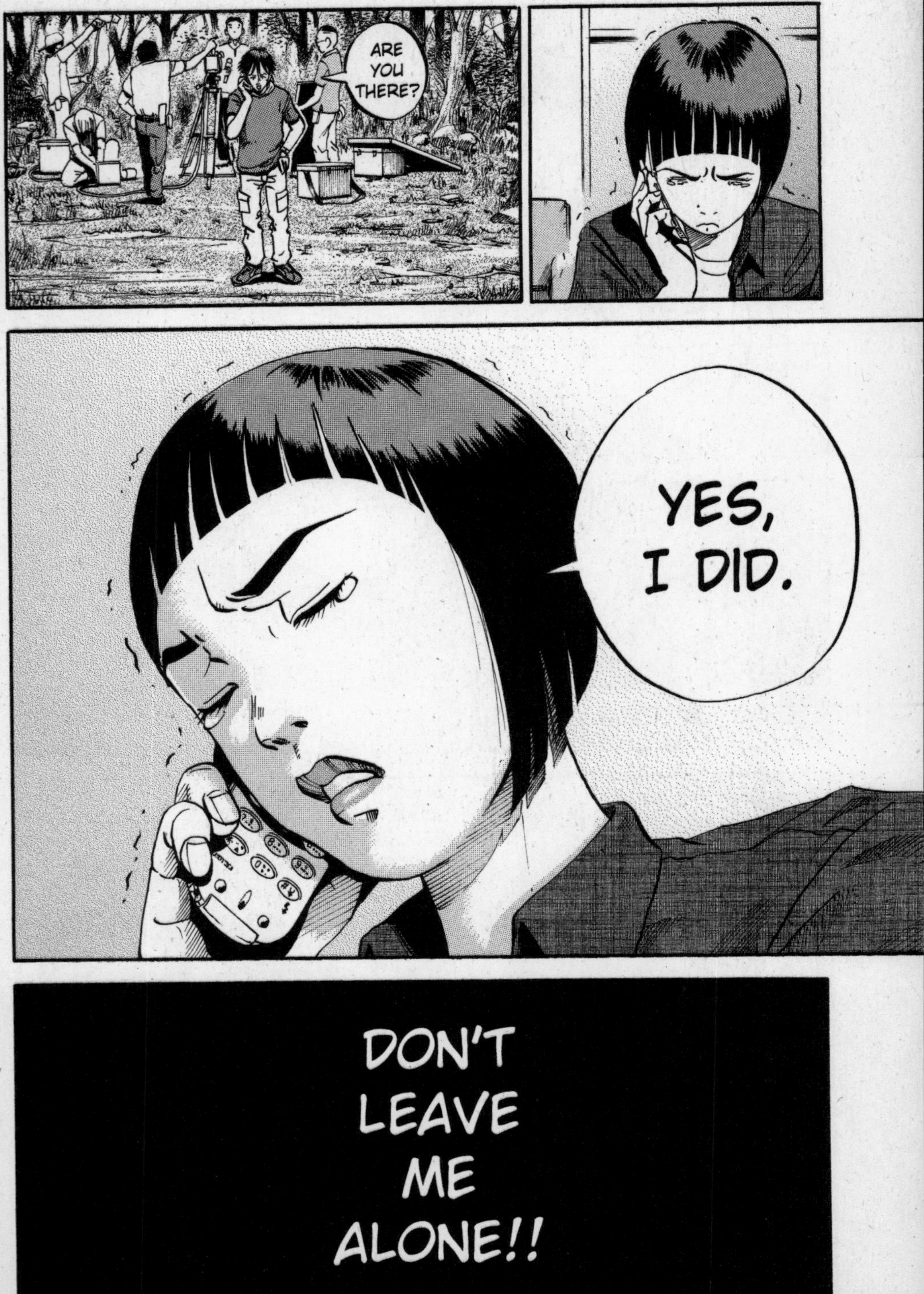
ARE YOU THERE?
YES, I DID.
DON'T LEAVE ME ALONE!!

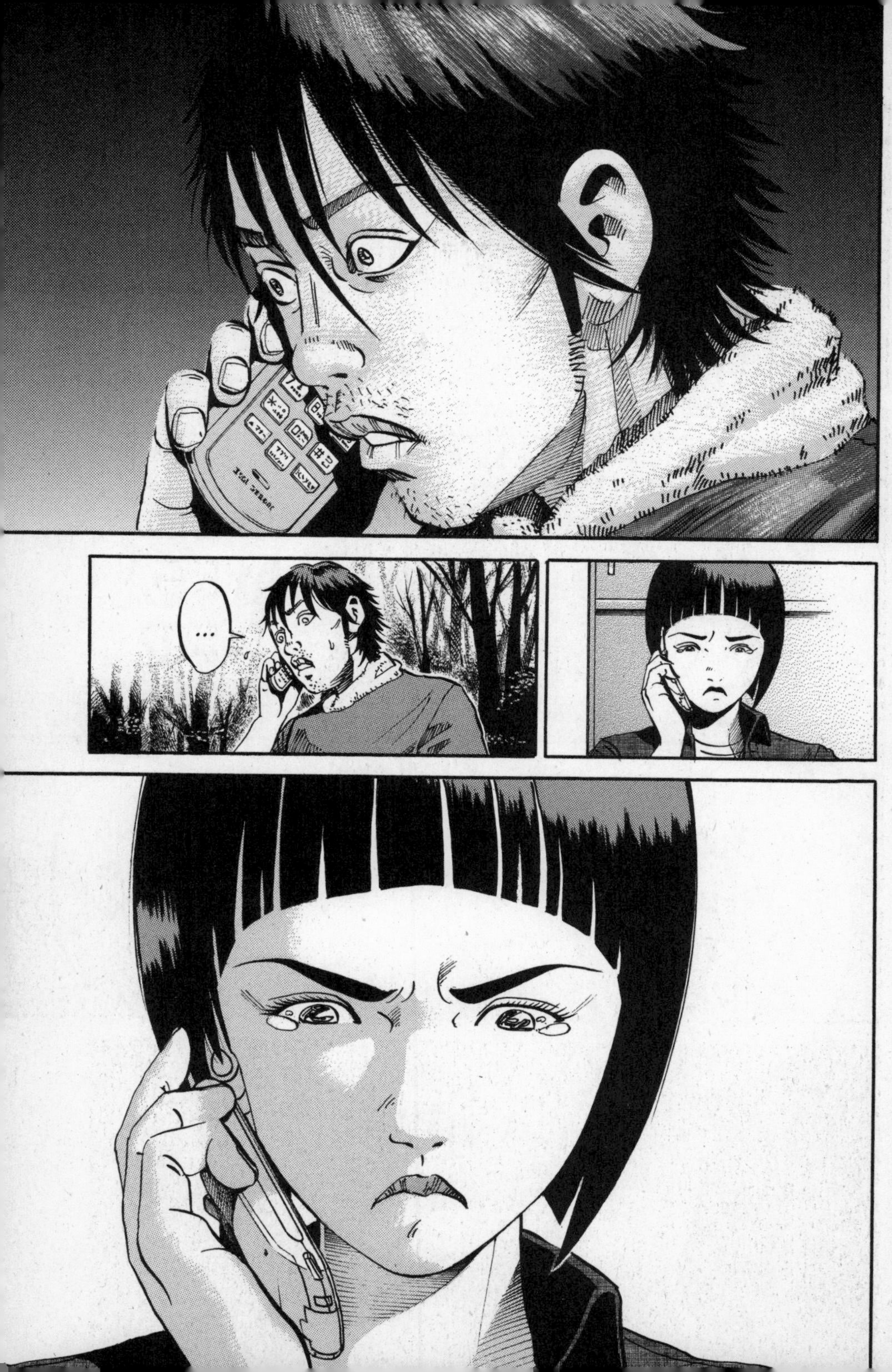
...

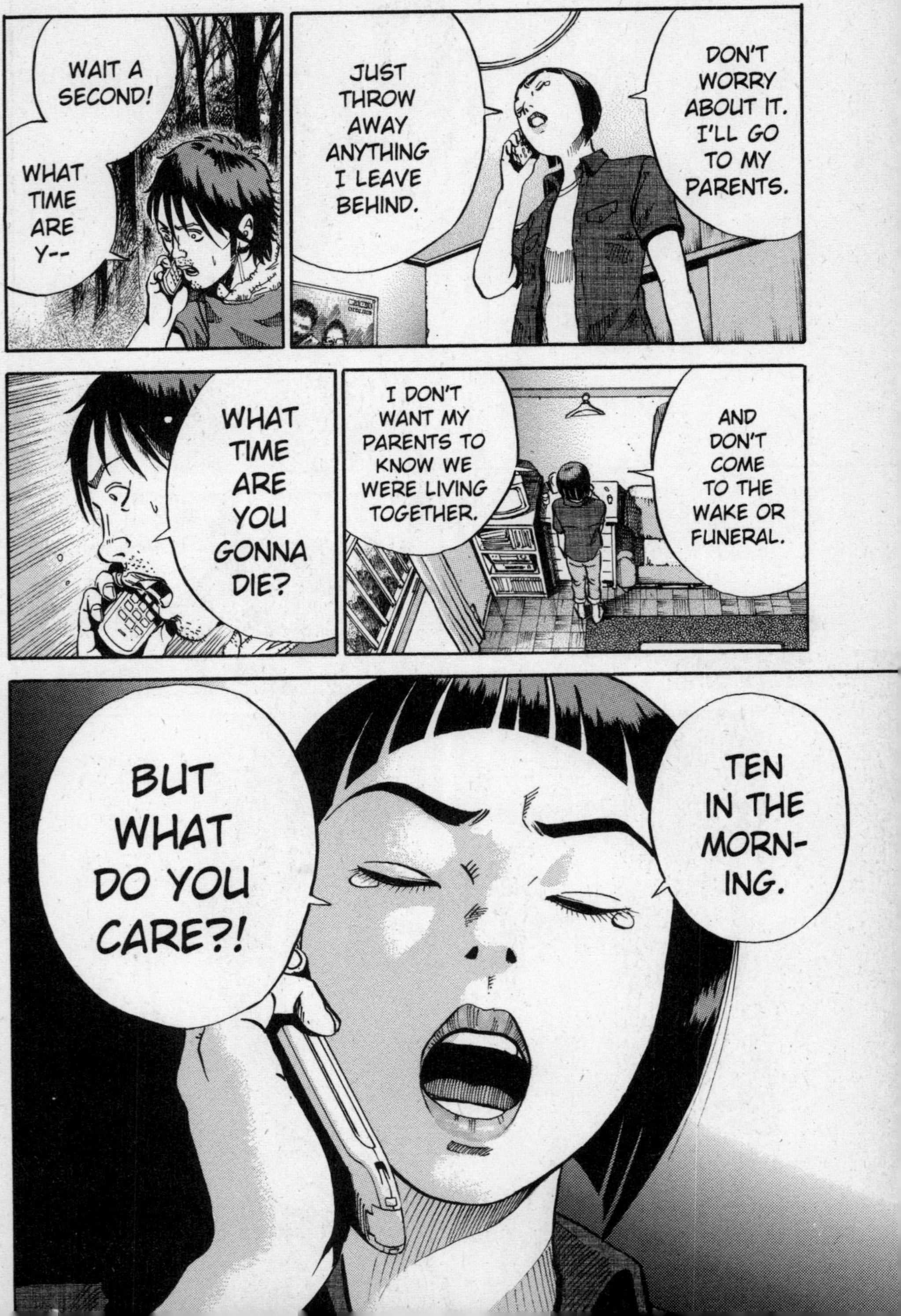
DON'T WORRY ABOUT IT. I'LL GO TO MY PARENTS.
JUST THROW AWAY ANYTHING I LEAVE BEHIND.
WAIT A SECOND!
WHAT TIME ARE Y--
AND DON'T COME TO THE WAKE OR FUNERAL.
I DON'T WANT MY PARENTS TO KNOW WE WERE LIVING TOGETHER.
WHAT TIME ARE YOU GONNA DIE?
TEN IN THE MORN-ING.
BUT WHAT DO YOU CARE?!

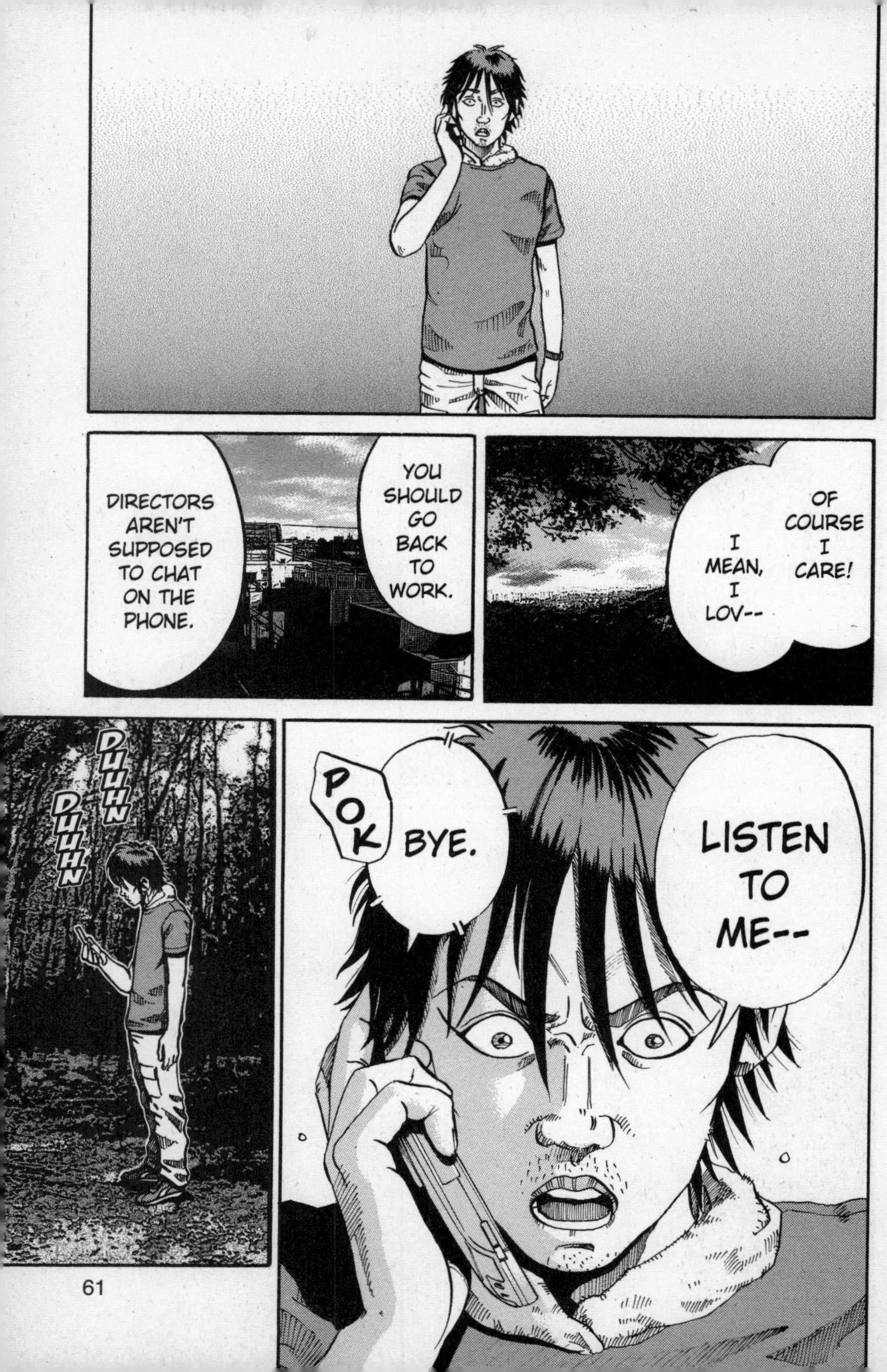
OF COURSE I CARE!
I MEAN, I LOV--
YOU SHOULD GO BACK TO WORK.
DIRECTORS AREN'T SUPPOSED TO CHAT ON THE PHONE.
LISTEN TO ME--
BYE.
POK
DUUHN
DUUHN

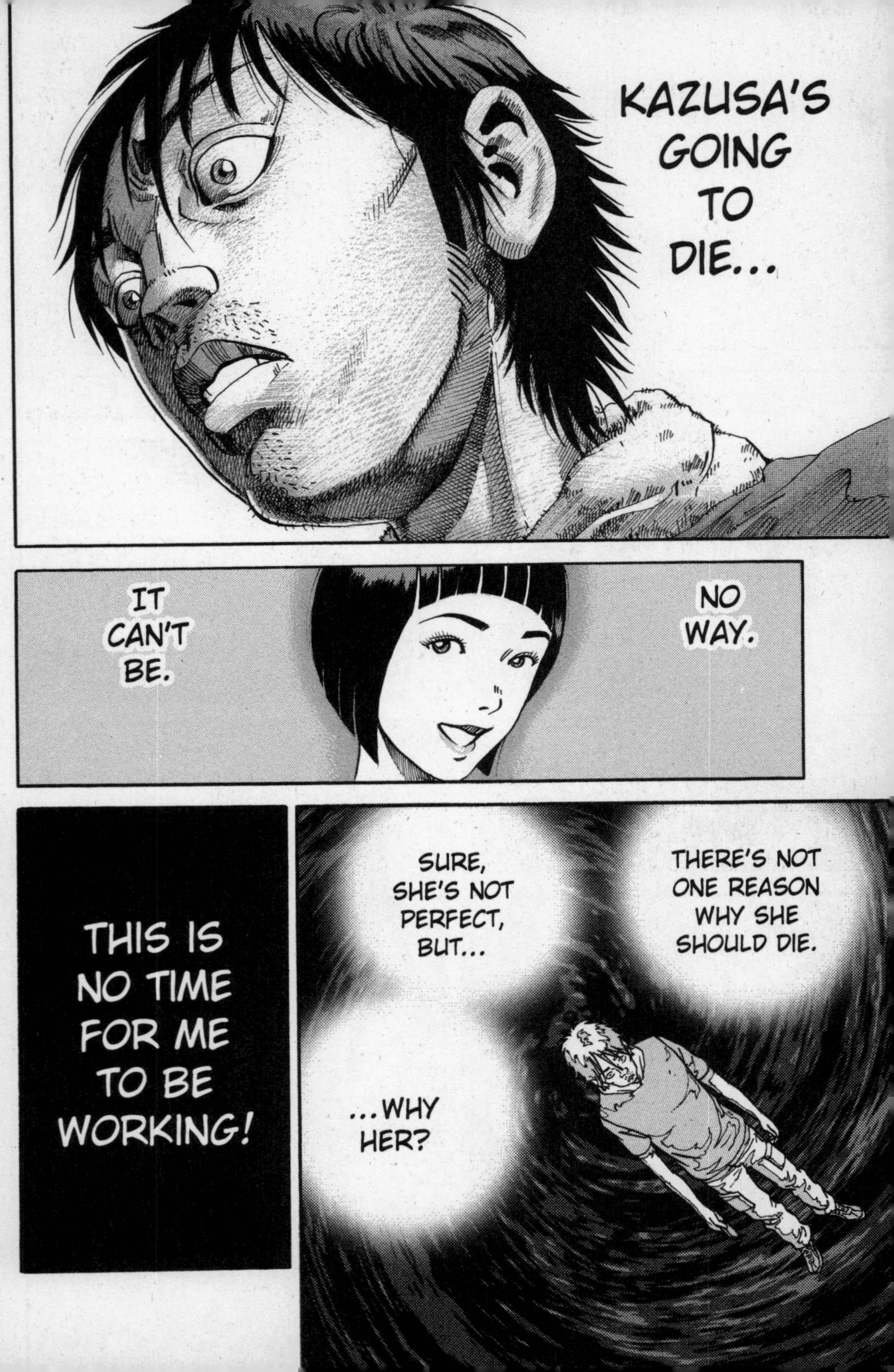
KAZUSA'S GOING TO DIE...
NO WAY.
IT CAN'T BE.
THERE'S NOT ONE REASON WHY SHE SHOULD DIE.
SURE, SHE'S NOT PERFECT, BUT...
...WHY HER?
THIS IS NO TIME FOR ME TO BE WORKING!

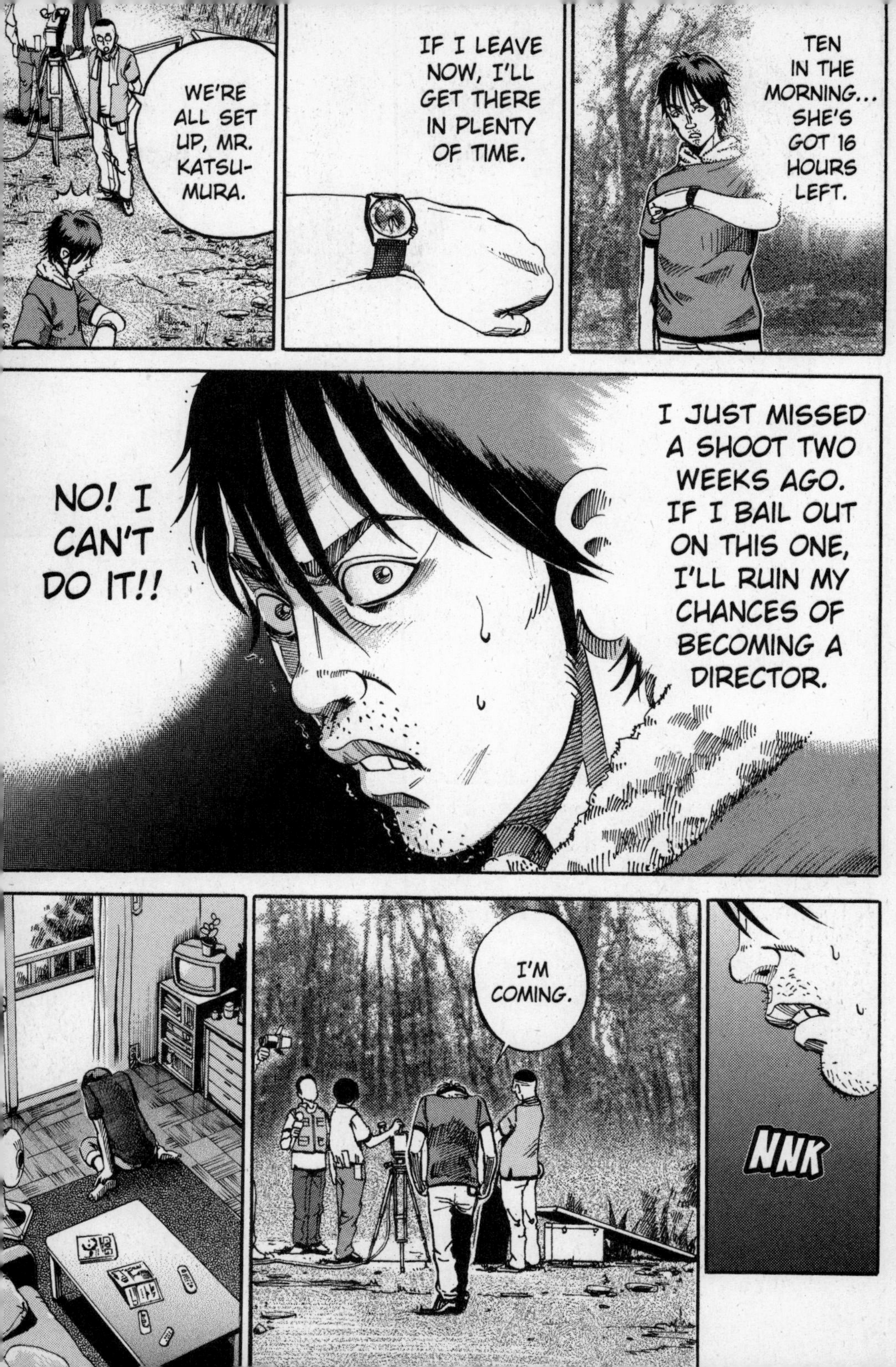
TEN IN THE MORNING... SHE'S GOT 16 HOURS LEFT.
IF I LEAVE NOW, I'LL GET THERE IN PLENTY OF TIME.
WE'RE ALL SET UP, MR. KATSU-MURA.
I JUST MISSED A SHOOT TWO WEEKS AGO. IF I BAIL OUT ON THIS ONE, I'LL RUIN MY CHANCES OF BECOMING A DIRECTOR.
NO! I CAN'T DO IT!!
NNK
I'M COMING.

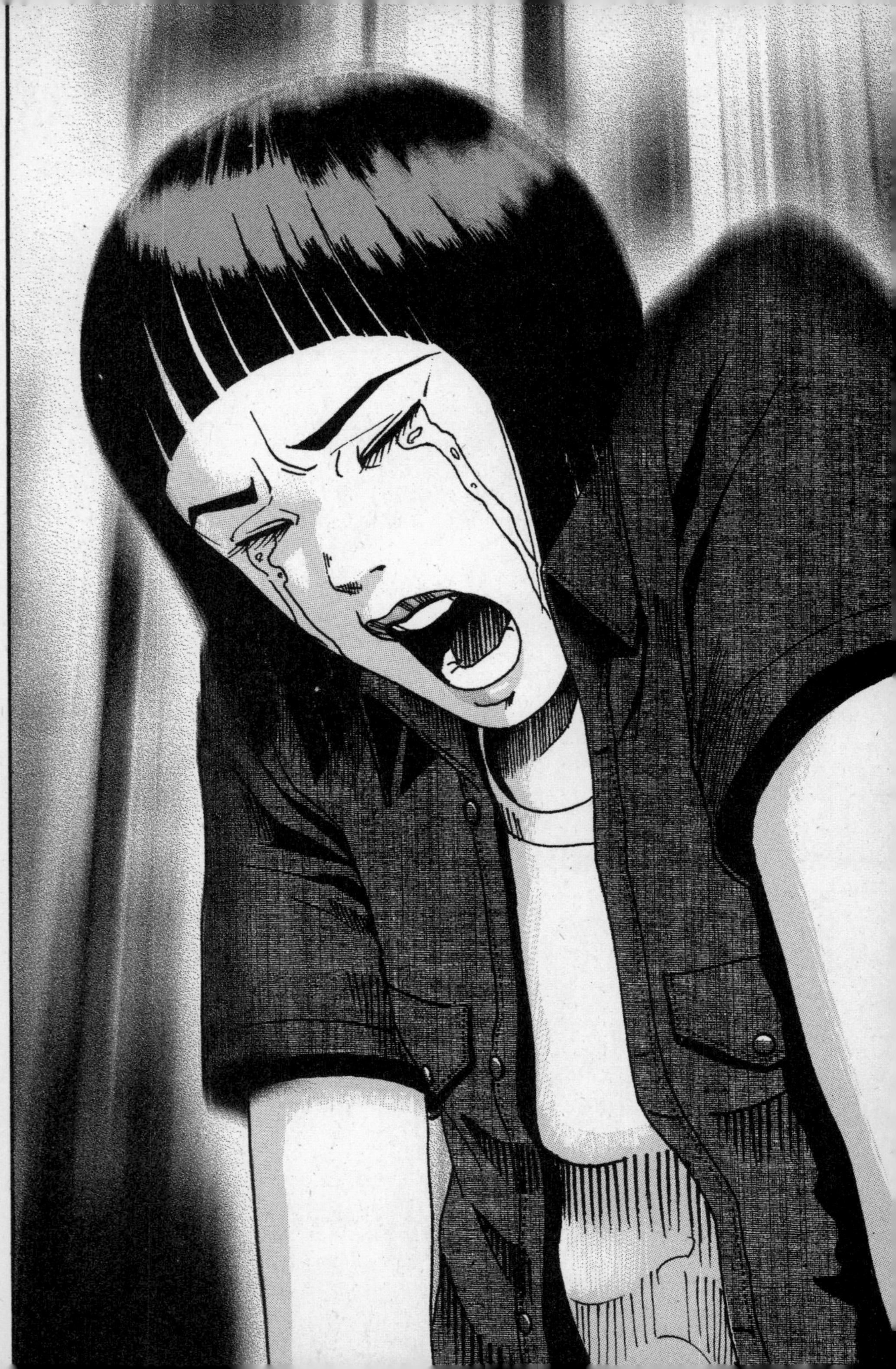

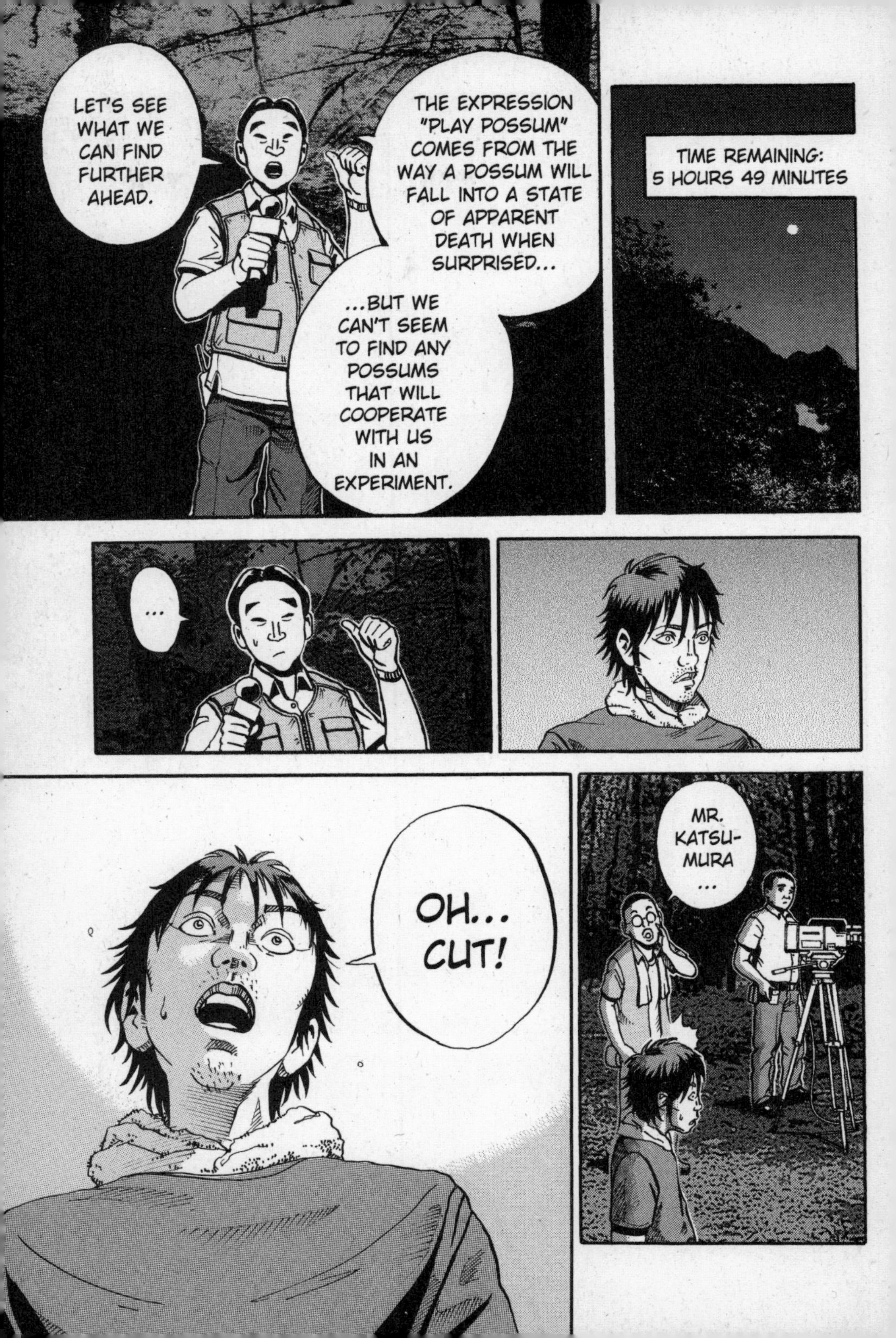
TIME REMAINING: 5 HOURS 49 MINUTES
THE EXPRESSION "PLAY POSSUM" COMES FROM THE WAY A POSSUM WILL FALL INTO A STATE OF APPARENT DEATH WHEN SURPRISED...
...BUT WE CAN'T SEEM TO FIND ANY POSSUMS THAT WILL COOPERATE WITH US IN AN EXPERIMENT.
LET'S SEE WHAT WE CAN FIND FURTHER AHEAD.
...
MR. KATSU-MURA ...
OH... CUT!

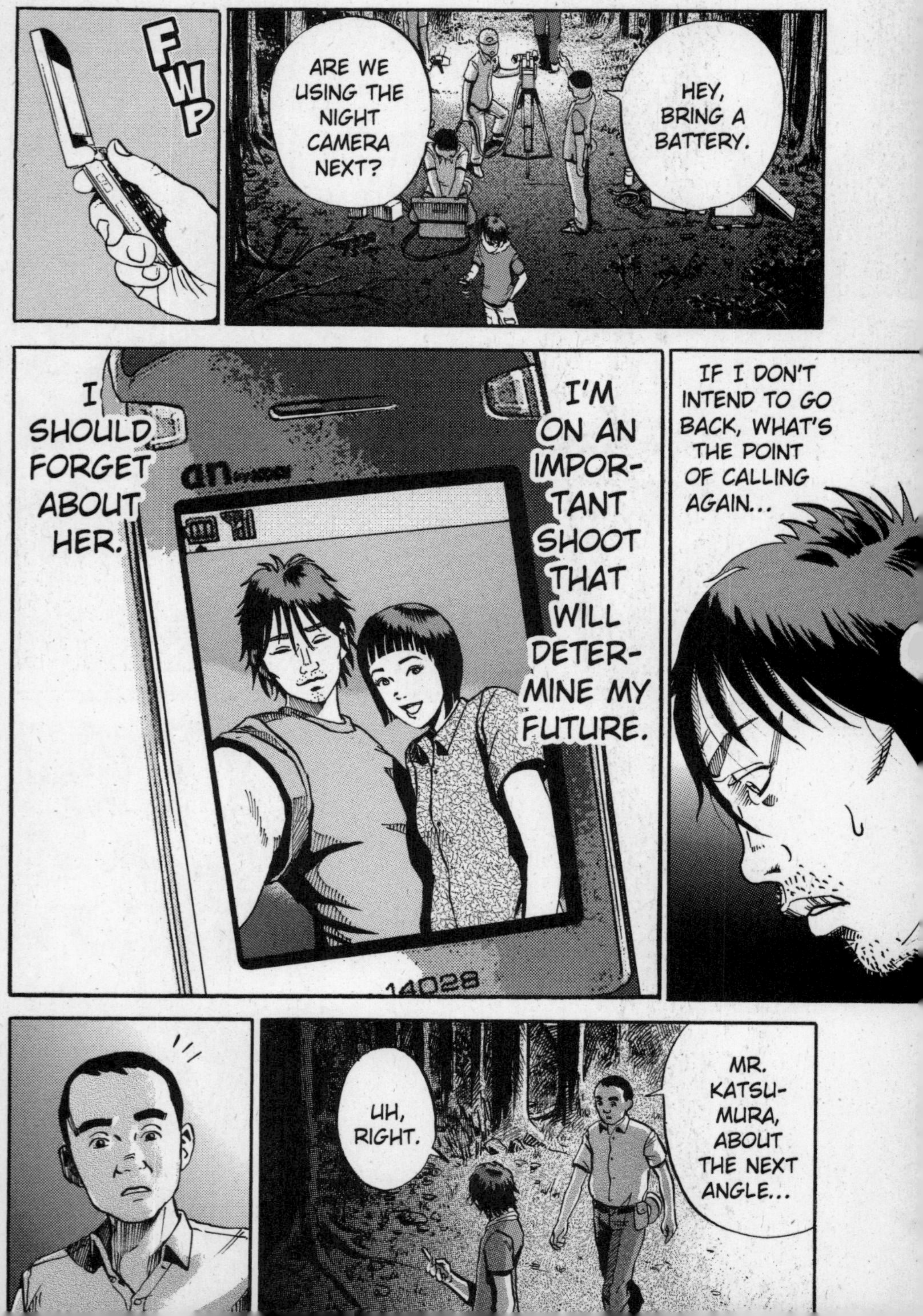
HEY, BRING A BATTERY.
ARE WE USING THE NIGHT CAMERA NEXT?
FWP
IF I DON'T INTEND TO GO BACK, WHAT'S THE POINT OF CALLING AGAIN...
I'M ON AN IMPORTANT SHOOT THAT WILL DETERMINE MY FUTURE.
I SHOULD FORGET ABOUT HER.
14028
MR. KATSUMURA, ABOUT THE NEXT ANGLE...
UH, RIGHT.

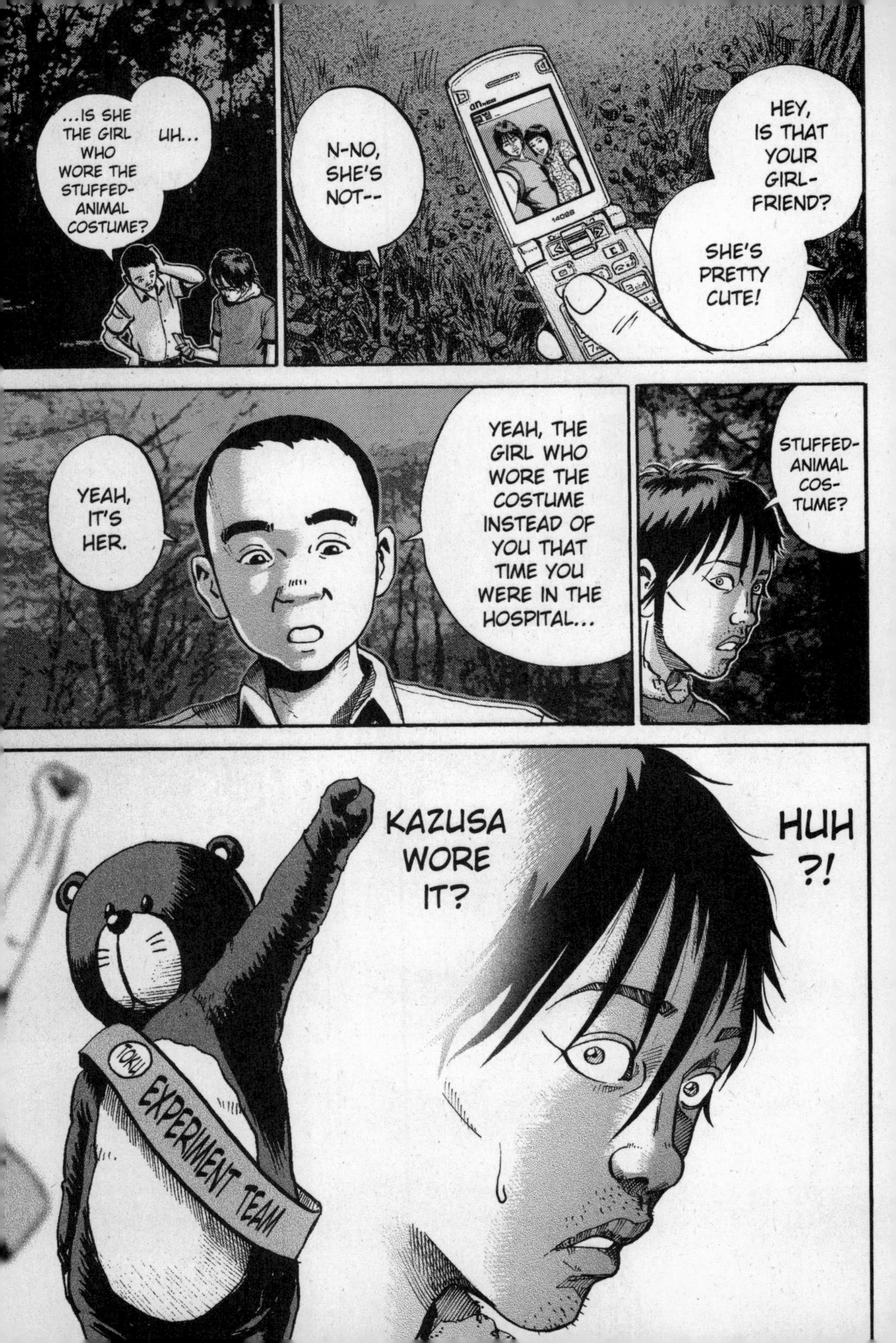
HEY, IS THAT YOUR GIRL-FRIEND?
SHE'S PRETTY CUTE!
N-NO, SHE'S NOT--
UH...
...IS SHE THE GIRL WHO WORE THE STUFFED-ANIMAL COSTUME?
STUFFED-ANIMAL COS-TUME?
YEAH, THE GIRL WHO WORE THE COSTUME INSTEAD OF YOU THAT TIME YOU WERE IN THE HOSPITAL...
YEAH, IT'S HER.
HUH ?!
KAZUSA WORE IT?
TOKU
EXPERIMENT TEAM

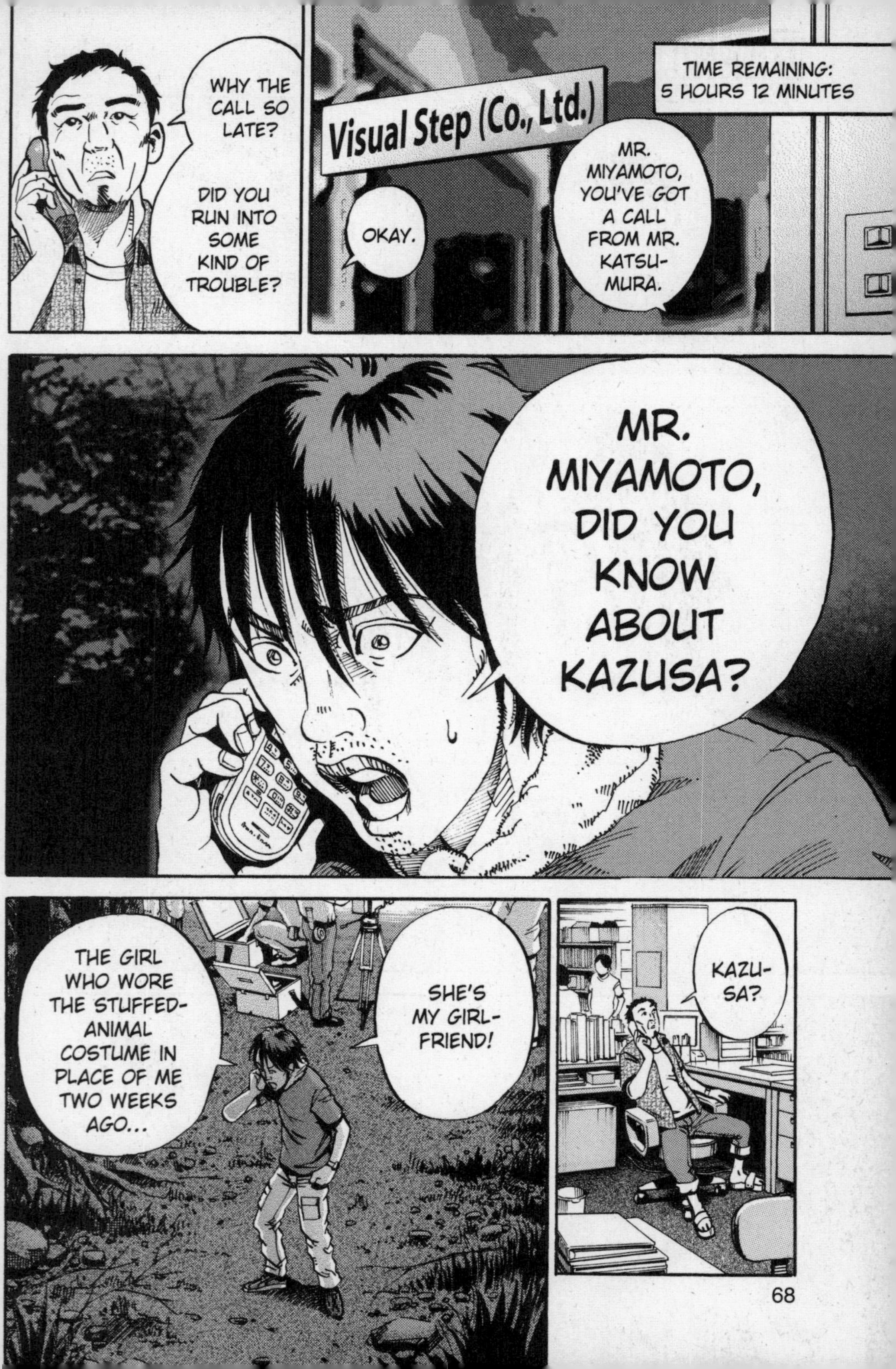
TIME REMAINING: 5 HOURS 12 MINUTES
Visual Step (Co., Ltd.)
MR. MIYAMOTO, YOU'VE GOT A CALL FROM MR. KATSU-MURA.
OKAY.
WHY THE CALL SO LATE?
DID YOU RUN INTO SOME KIND OF TROUBLE?
MR. MIYAMOTO, DID YOU KNOW ABOUT KAZUSA?
KAZU-SA?
SHE'S MY GIRL-FRIEND!
THE GIRL WHO WORE THE STUFFED-ANIMAL COSTUME IN PLACE OF ME TWO WEEKS AGO...

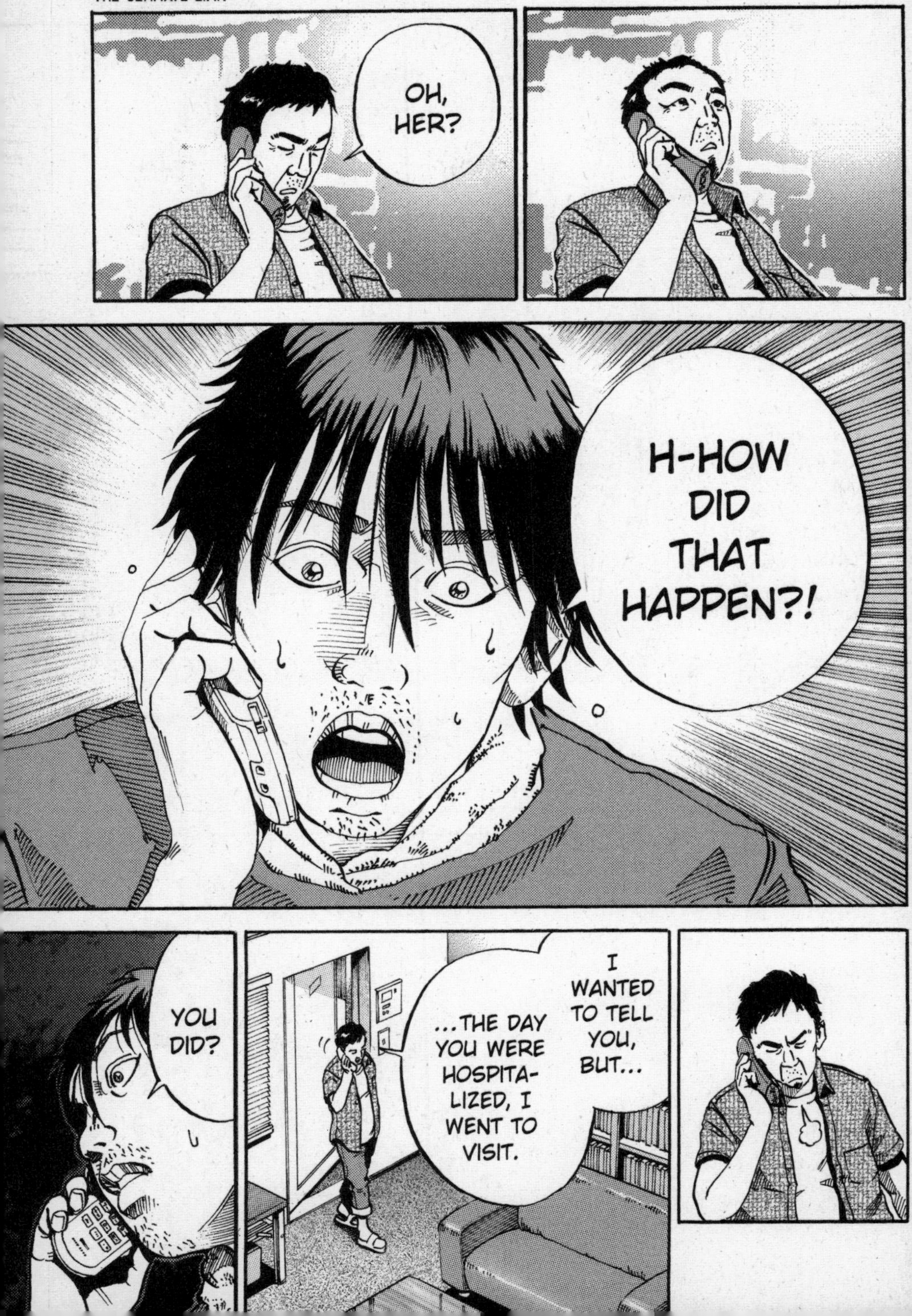
OH, HER?
H-HOW DID THAT HAPPEN?!
I WANTED TO TELL YOU, BUT...
...THE DAY YOU WERE HOSPITA-LIZED, I WENT TO VISIT.
YOU DID?

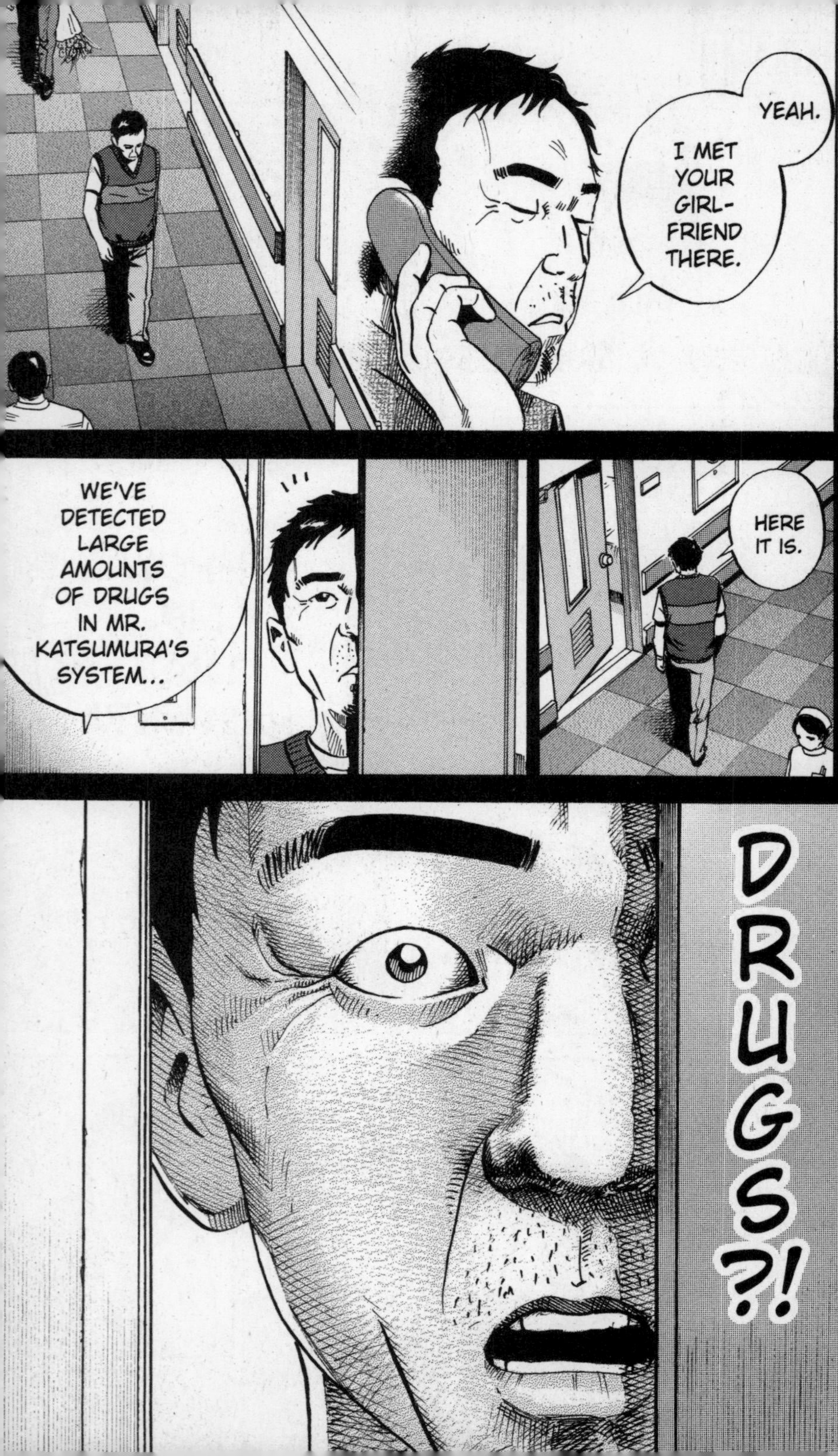
YEAH. I MET YOUR GIRL-FRIEND THERE.
HERE IT IS.
WE'VE DETECTED LARGE AMOUNTS OF DRUGS IN MR. KATSUMURA'S SYSTEM...
DRUGS?!

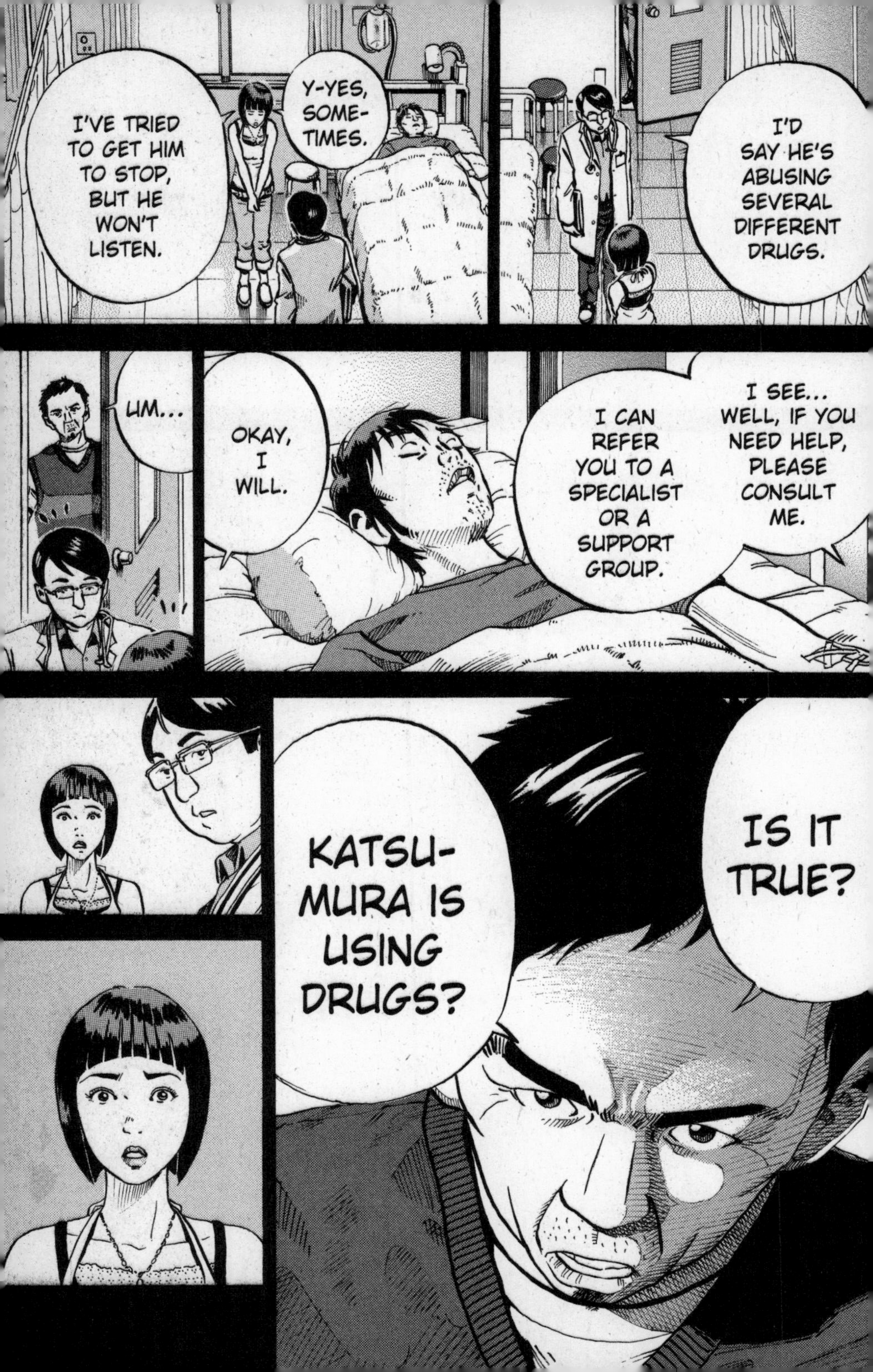
I'D SAY HE'S ABUSING SEVERAL DIFFERENT DRUGS.
Y-YES, SOMETIMES.
I'VE TRIED TO GET HIM TO STOP, BUT HE WON'T LISTEN.
I SEE... WELL, IF YOU NEED HELP, PLEASE CONSULT ME.
I CAN REFER YOU TO A SPECIALIST OR A SUPPORT GROUP.
OKAY, I WILL.
UM...
IS IT TRUE?
KATSUMURA IS USING DRUGS?

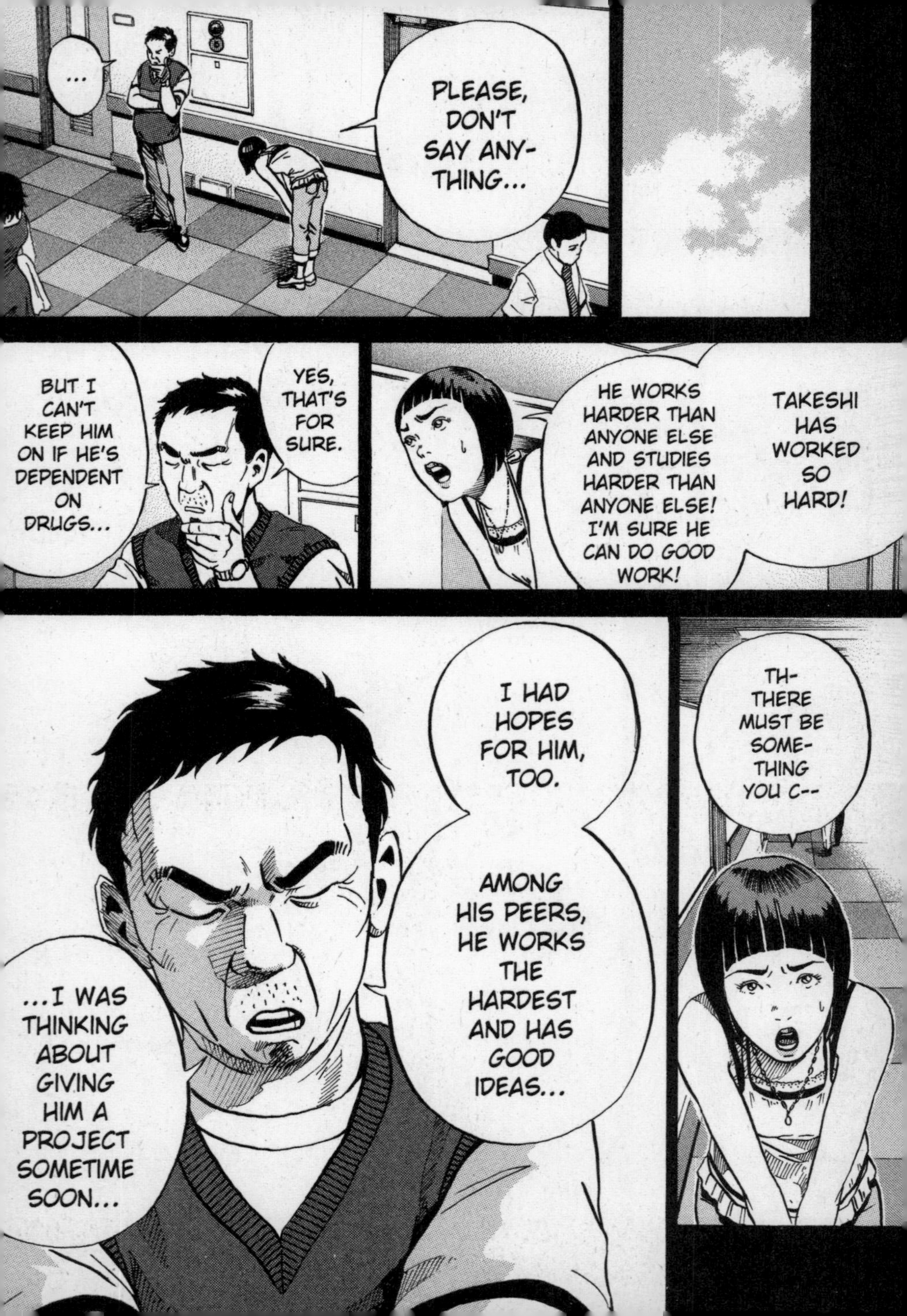
PLEASE, DON'T SAY ANY-THING...
...
TAKESHI HAS WORKED SO HARD!
HE WORKS HARDER THAN ANYONE ELSE AND STUDIES HARDER THAN ANYONE ELSE! I'M SURE HE CAN DO GOOD WORK!
YES, THAT'S FOR SURE.
BUT I CAN'T KEEP HIM ON IF HE'S DEPENDENT ON DRUGS...
TH- THERE MUST BE SOME-THING YOU C--
I HAD HOPES FOR HIM, TOO.
AMONG HIS PEERS, HE WORKS THE HARDEST AND HAS GOOD IDEAS...
...I WAS THINKING ABOUT GIVING HIM A PROJECT SOMETIME SOON...

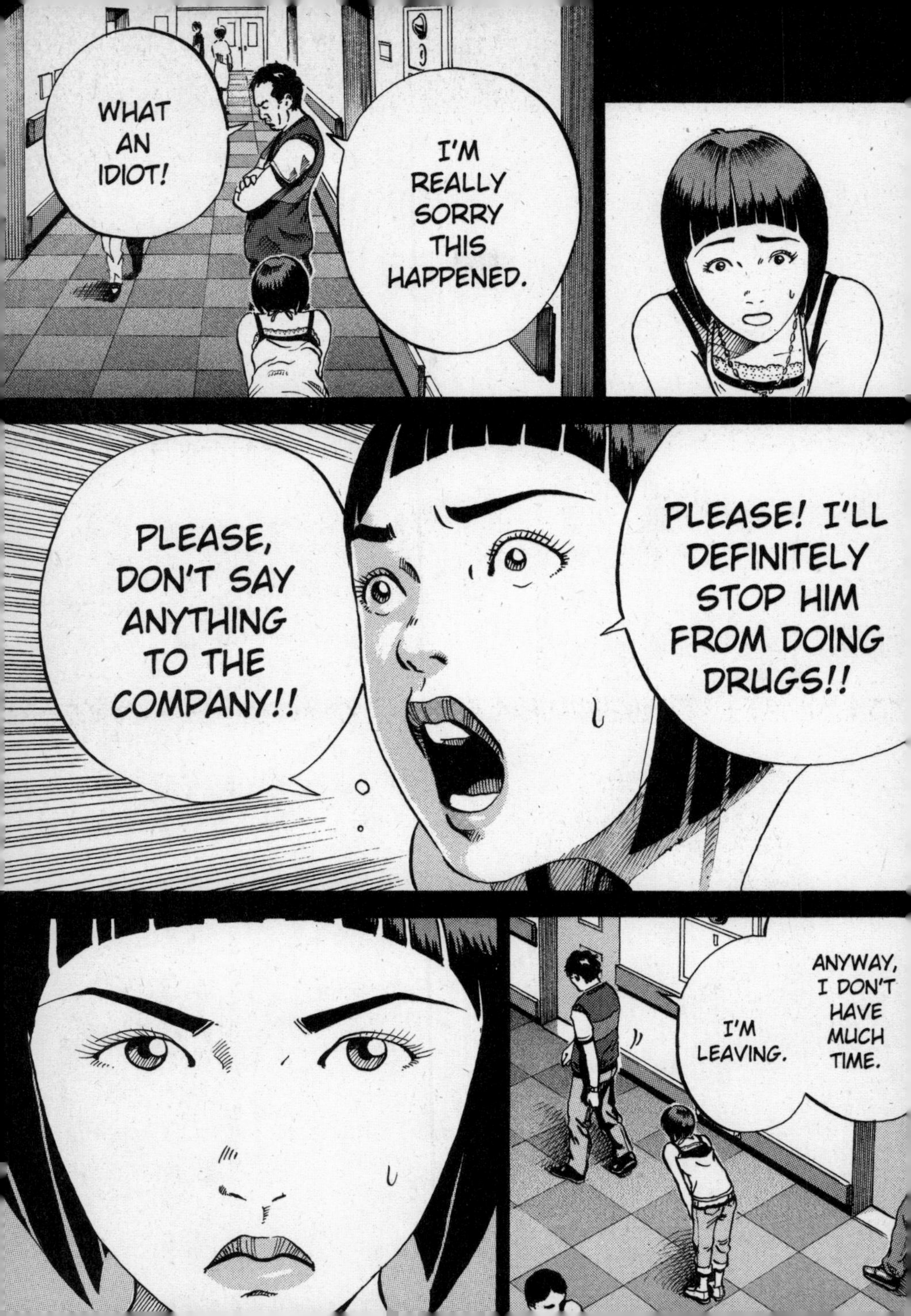
I'M REALLY SORRY THIS HAPPENED.
WHAT AN IDIOT!
PLEASE! I'LL DEFINITELY STOP HIM FROM DOING DRUGS!!
PLEASE, DON'T SAY ANYTHING TO THE COMPANY!!
ANYWAY, I DON'T HAVE MUCH TIME.
I'M LEAVING.

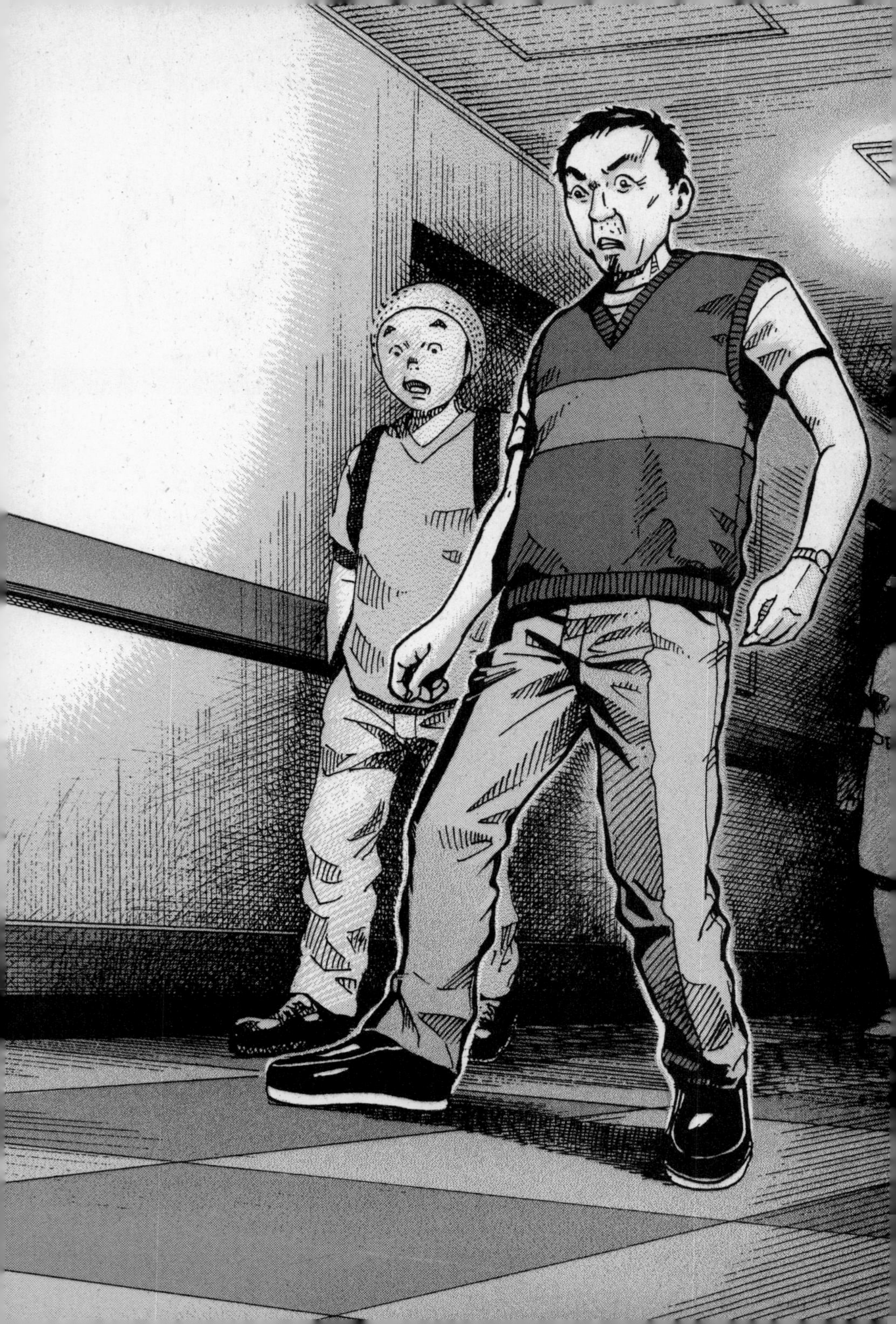

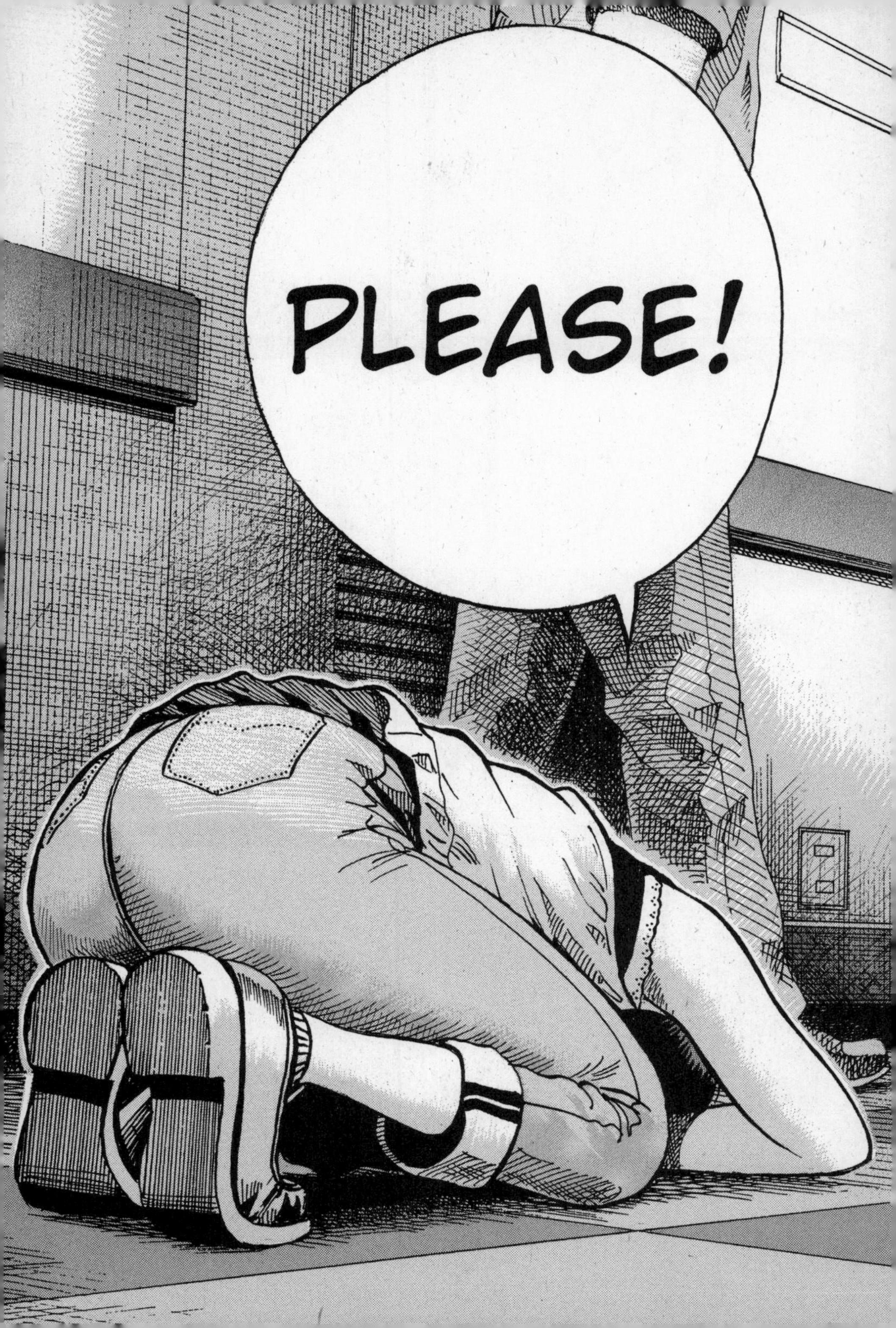
PLEASE!

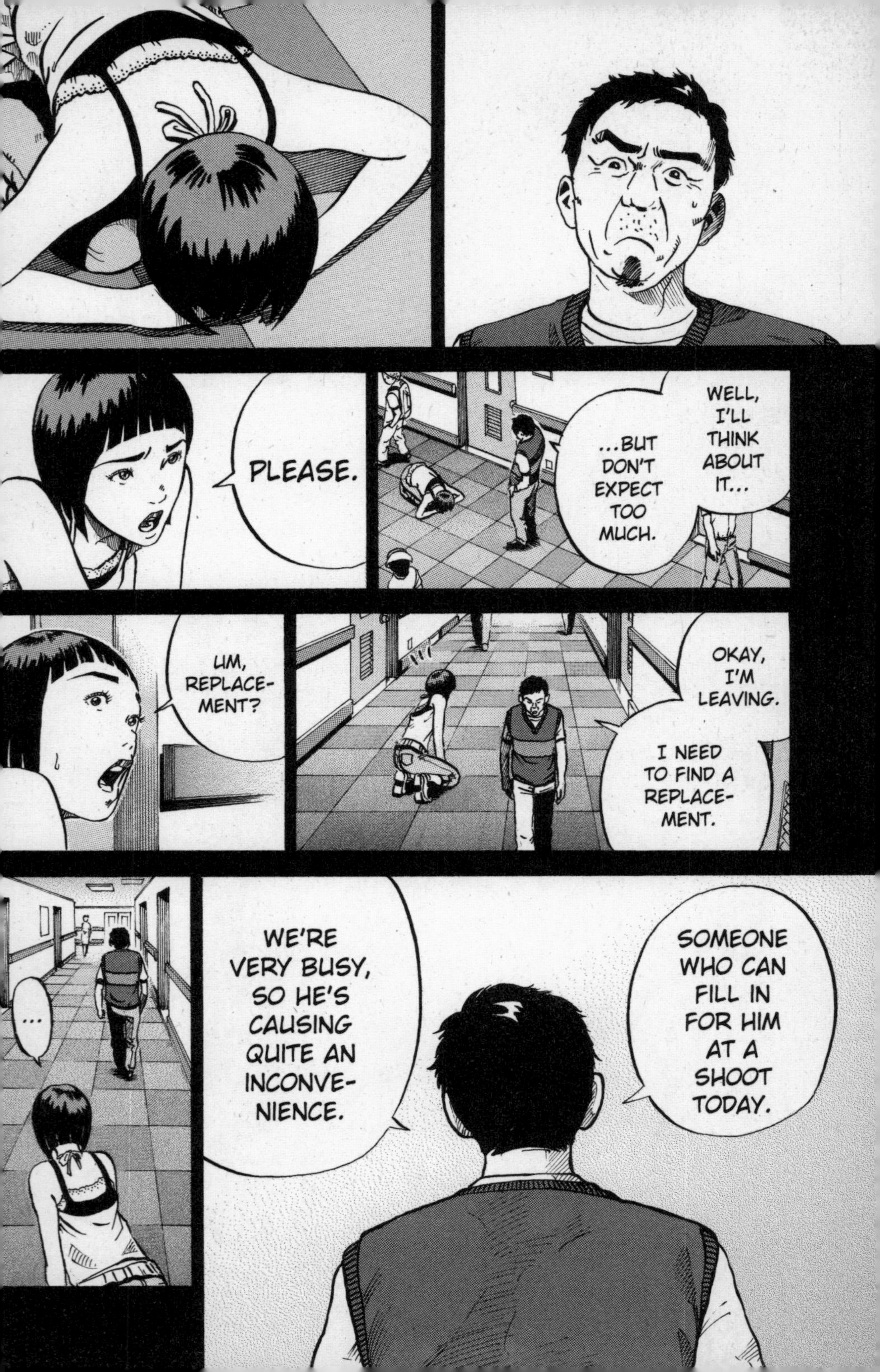
WELL, I'LL THINK ABOUT IT...
...BUT DON'T EXPECT TOO MUCH.
PLEASE.
OKAY, I'M LEAVING.
I NEED TO FIND A REPLACEMENT.
UM, REPLACEMENT?
SOMEONE WHO CAN FILL IN FOR HIM AT A SHOOT TODAY.
WE'RE VERY BUSY, SO HE'S CAUSING QUITE AN INCONVENIENCE.
...

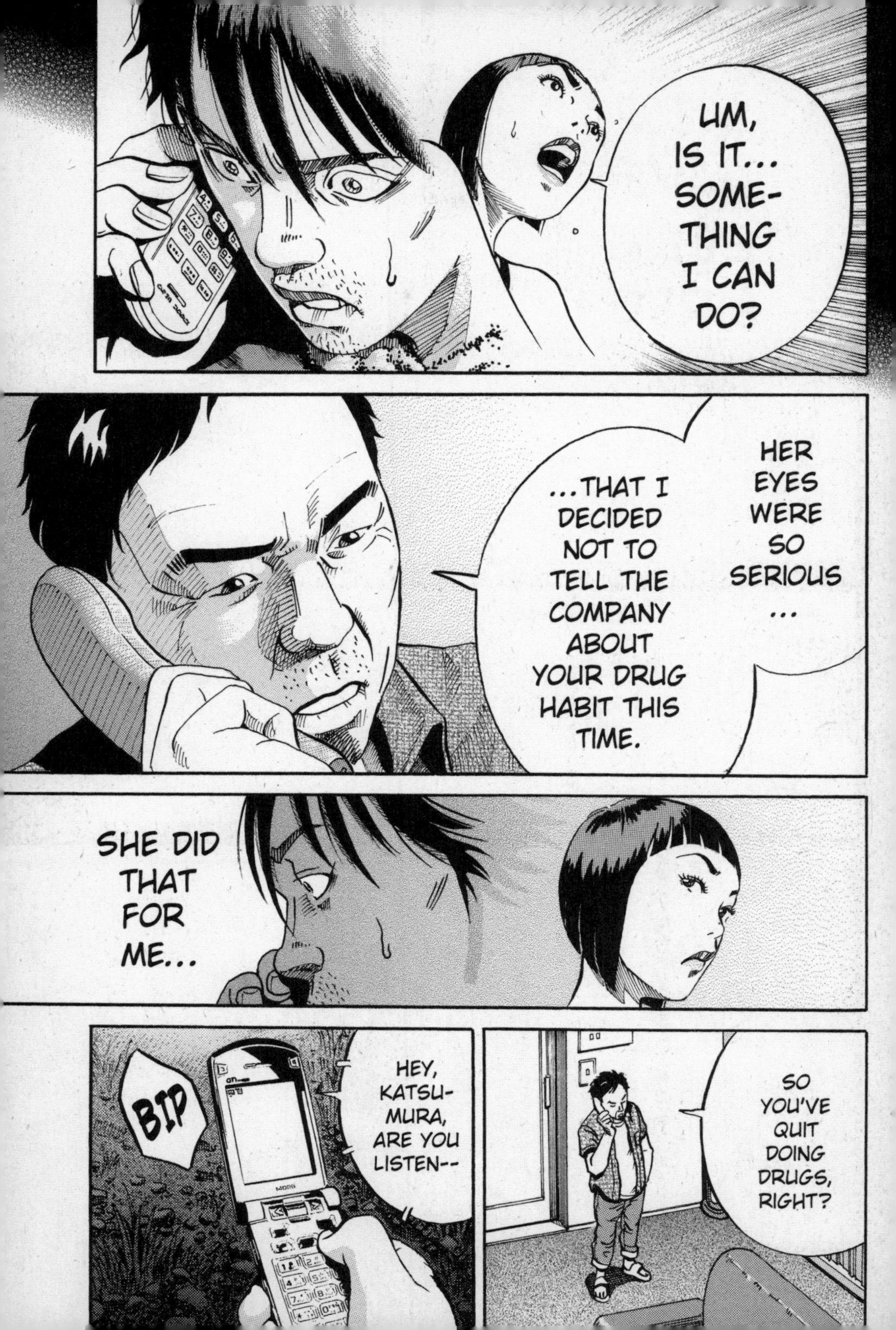
UM, IS IT... SOMETHING I CAN DO?
HER EYES WERE SO SERIOUS...
...THAT I DECIDED NOT TO TELL THE COMPANY ABOUT YOUR DRUG HABIT THIS TIME.
SHE DID THAT FOR ME...
SO YOU'VE QUIT DOING DRUGS, RIGHT?
BIP
HEY, KATSUMURA, ARE YOU LISTEN--

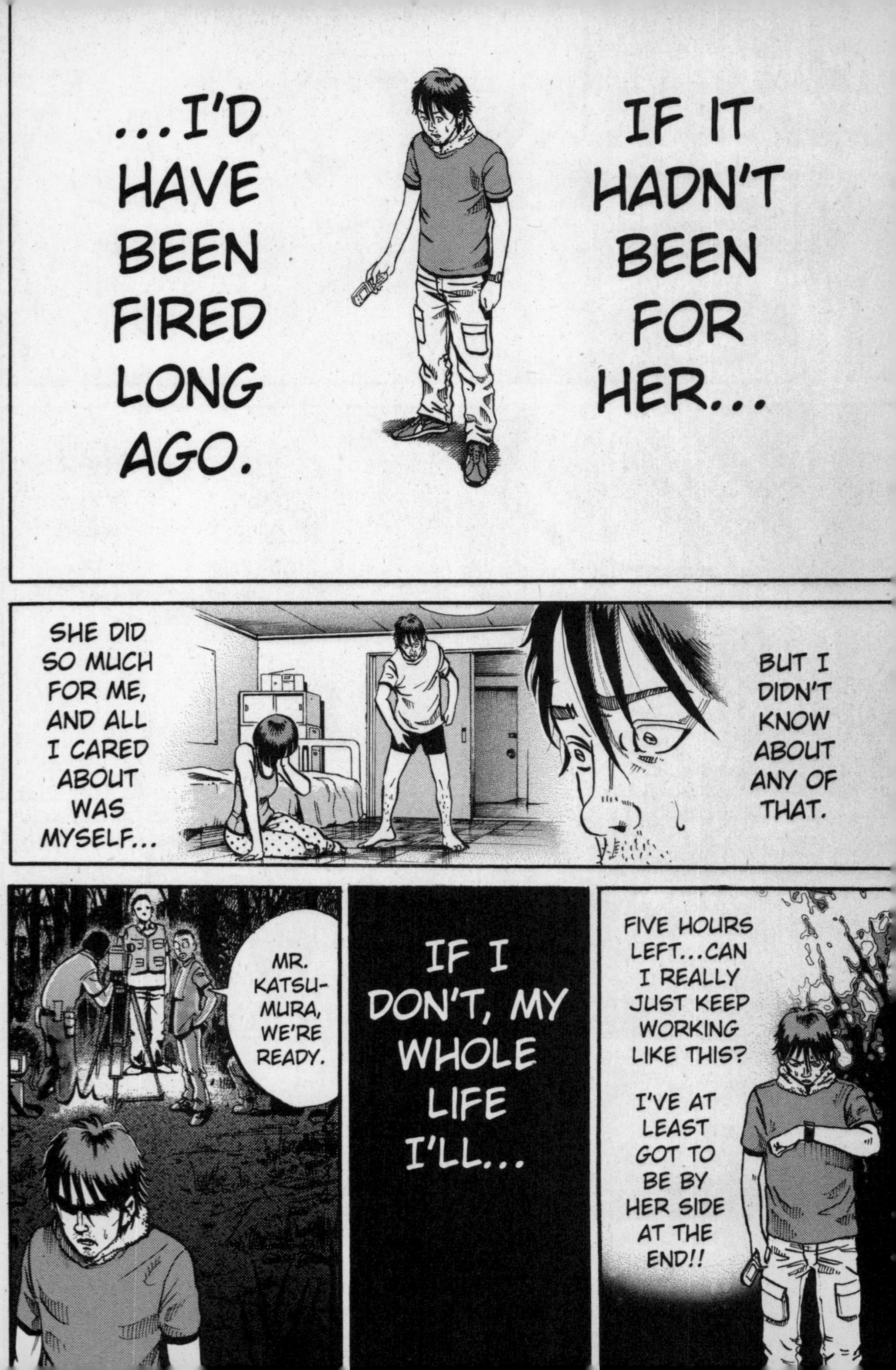
IF IT HADN'T BEEN FOR HER...
...I'D HAVE BEEN FIRED LONG AGO.
BUT I DIDN'T KNOW ABOUT ANY OF THAT.
SHE DID SO MUCH FOR ME, AND ALL I CARED ABOUT WAS MYSELF...
FIVE HOURS LEFT...CAN I REALLY JUST KEEP WORKING LIKE THIS?
I'VE AT LEAST GOT TO BE BY HER SIDE AT THE END!!
IF I DON'T, MY WHOLE LIFE I'LL...
MR. KATSUMURA, WE'RE READY.

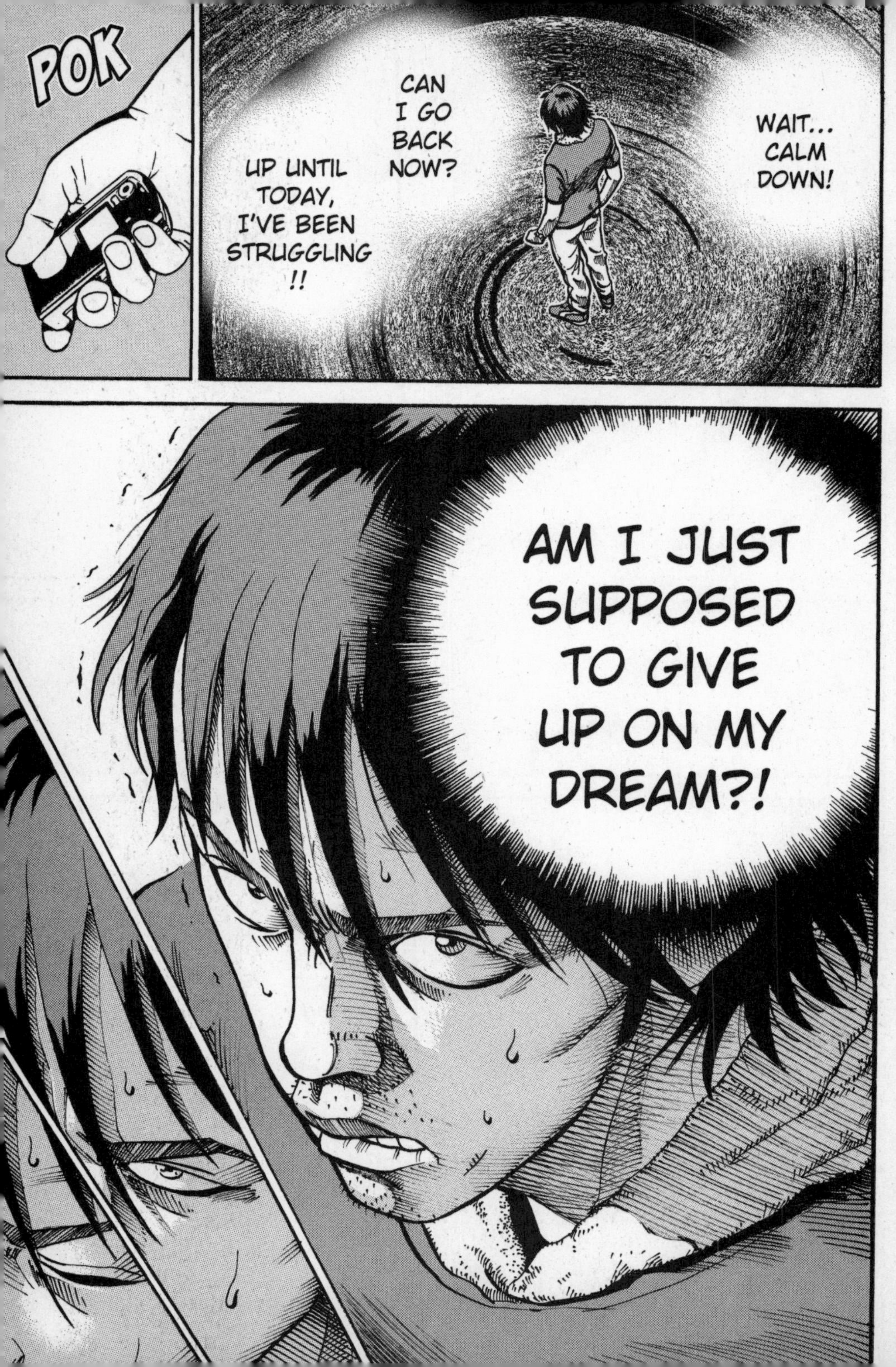
WAIT... CALM DOWN!
CAN I GO BACK NOW?
UP UNTIL TODAY, I'VE BEEN STRUGGLING !!
POK
AM I JUST SUPPOSED TO GIVE UP ON MY DREAM?!

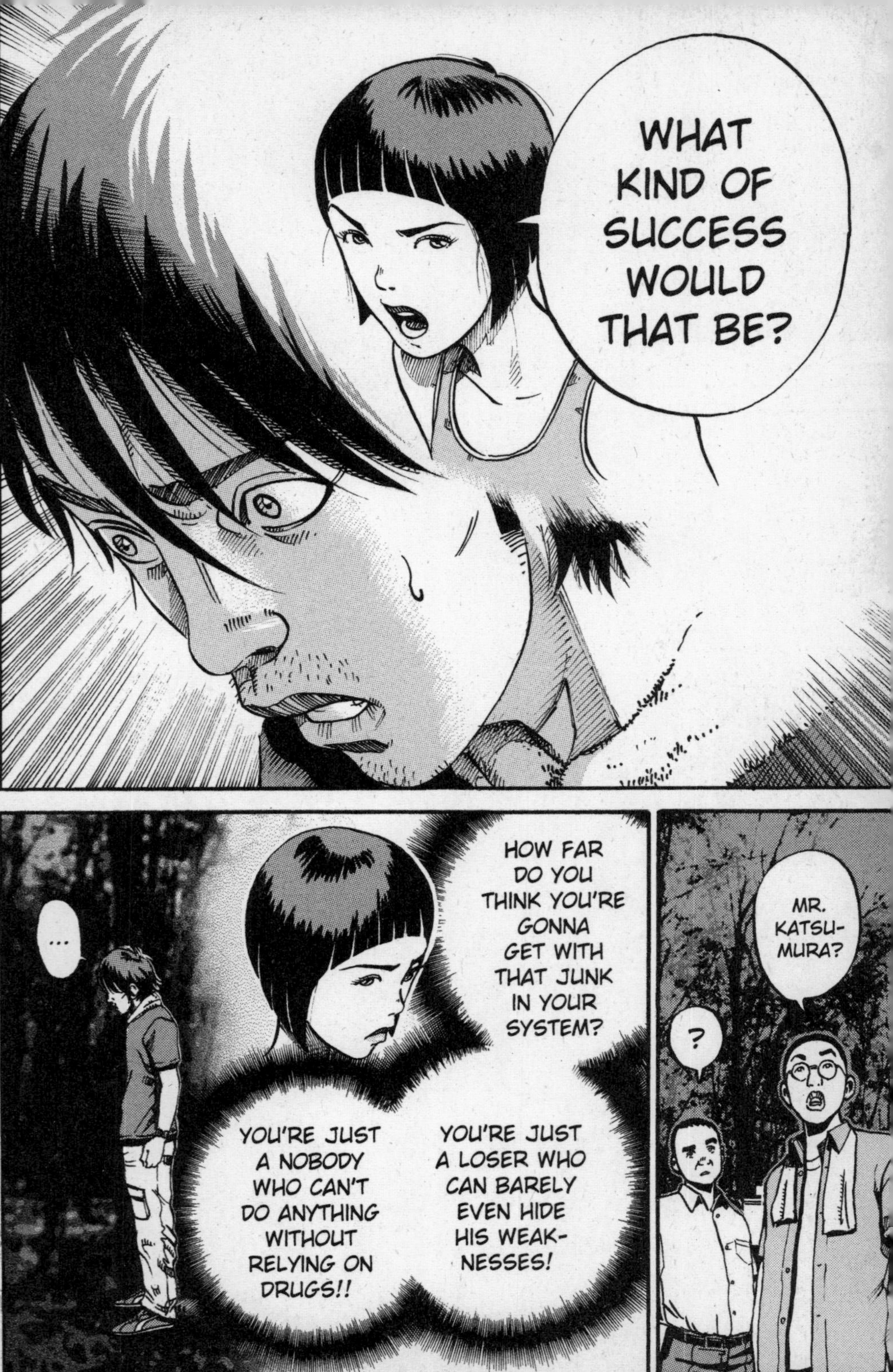
WHAT KIND OF SUCCESS WOULD THAT BE?
MR. KATSUMURA?
?
HOW FAR DO YOU THINK YOU'RE GONNA GET WITH THAT JUNK IN YOUR SYSTEM?
...
YOU'RE JUST A LOSER WHO CAN BARELY EVEN HIDE HIS WEAKNESSES!
YOU'RE JUST A NOBODY WHO CAN'T DO ANYTHING WITHOUT RELYING ON DRUGS!!

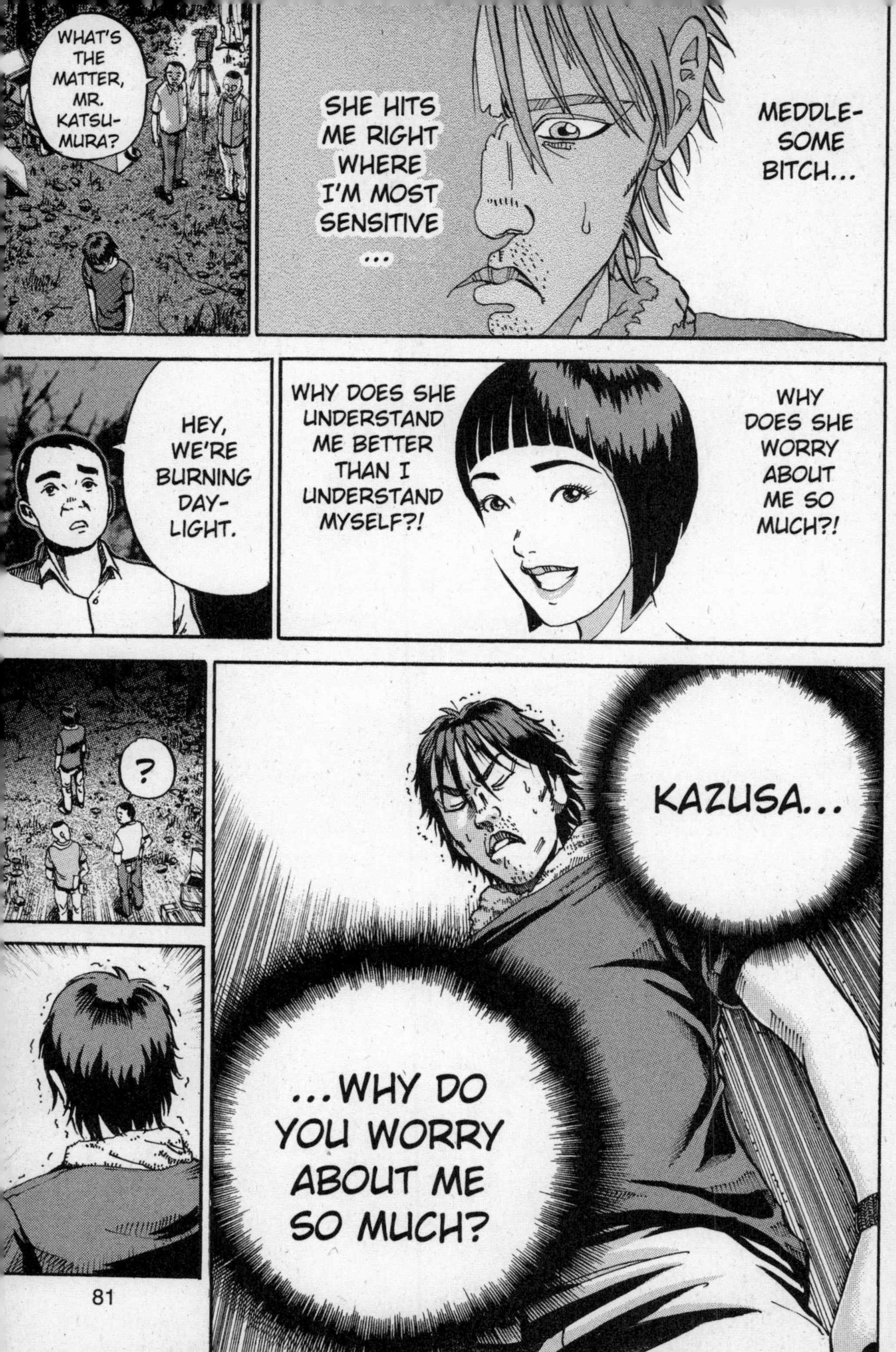
MEDDLE-SOME BITCH...
SHE HITS ME RIGHT WHERE I'M MOST SENSITIVE...
WHAT'S THE MATTER, MR. KATSU-MURA?
WHY DOES SHE WORRY ABOUT ME SO MUCH?!
WHY DOES SHE UNDERSTAND ME BETTER THAN I UNDERSTAND MYSELF?!
HEY, WE'RE BURNING DAY-LIGHT.
KAZUSA...
...WHY DO YOU WORRY ABOUT ME SO MUCH?
?

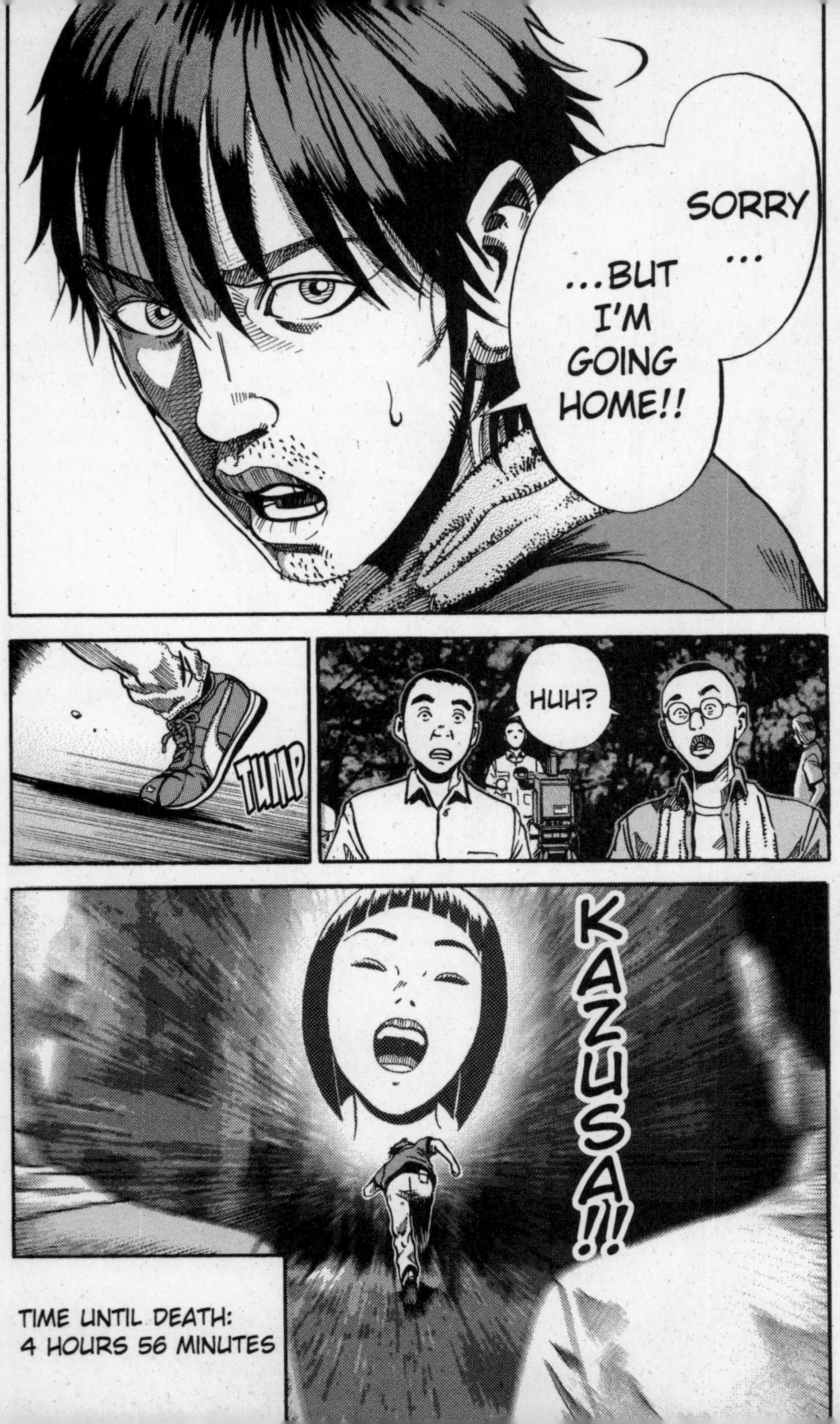
SORRY ...
...BUT I'M GOING HOME!!
HUH?
TUMP
KAZUSA!!
TIME UNTIL DEATH:
4 HOURS 56 MINUTES

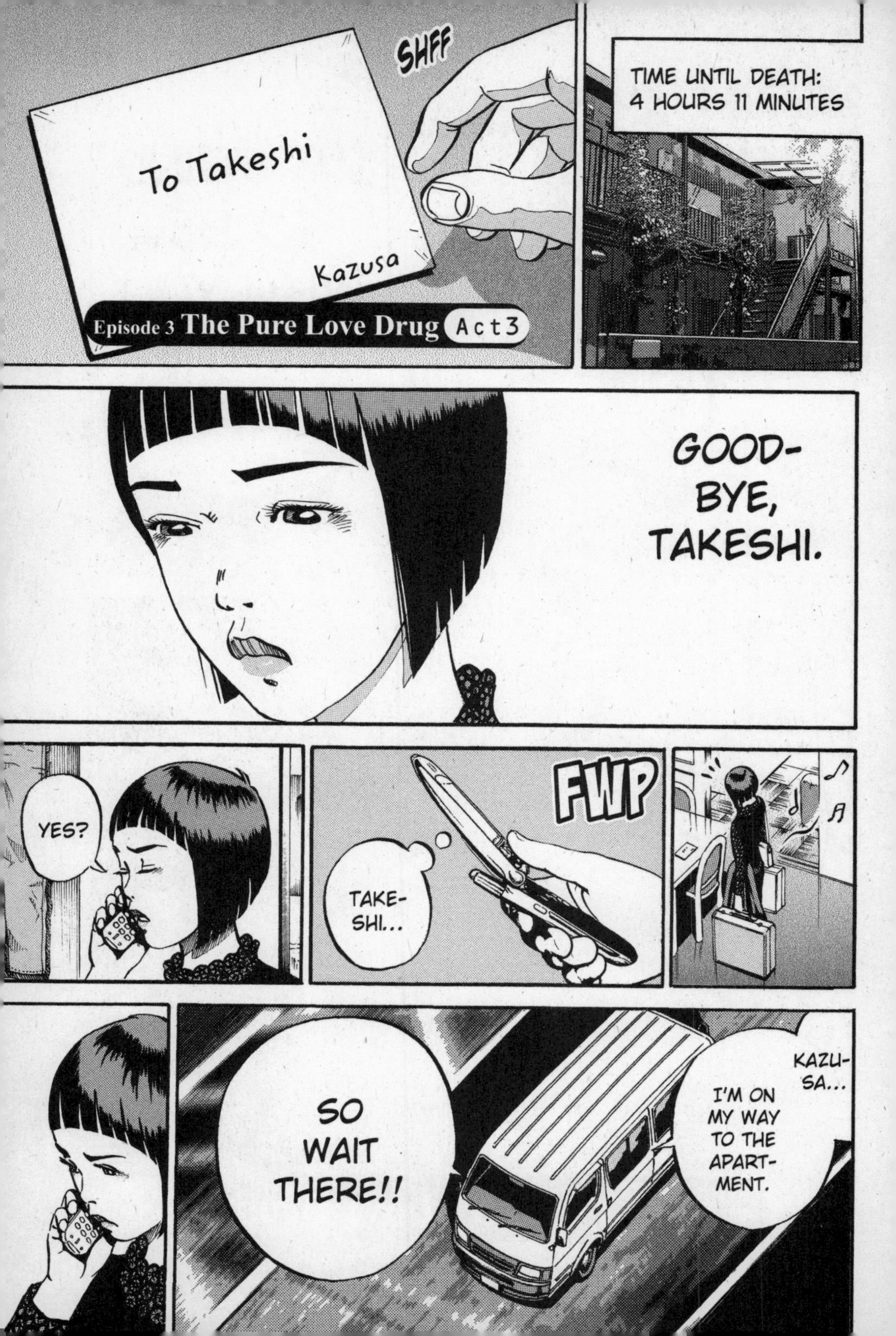
TIME UNTIL DEATH: 4 HOURS 11 MINUTES
SHFF
To Takeshi
Kazusa
Episode 3 The Pure Love Drug Act3
GOOD-BYE, TAKESHI.
FWP
TAKE-SHI...
YES?
KAZU-SA...
I'M ON MY WAY TO THE APART-MENT.
SO WAIT THERE!!

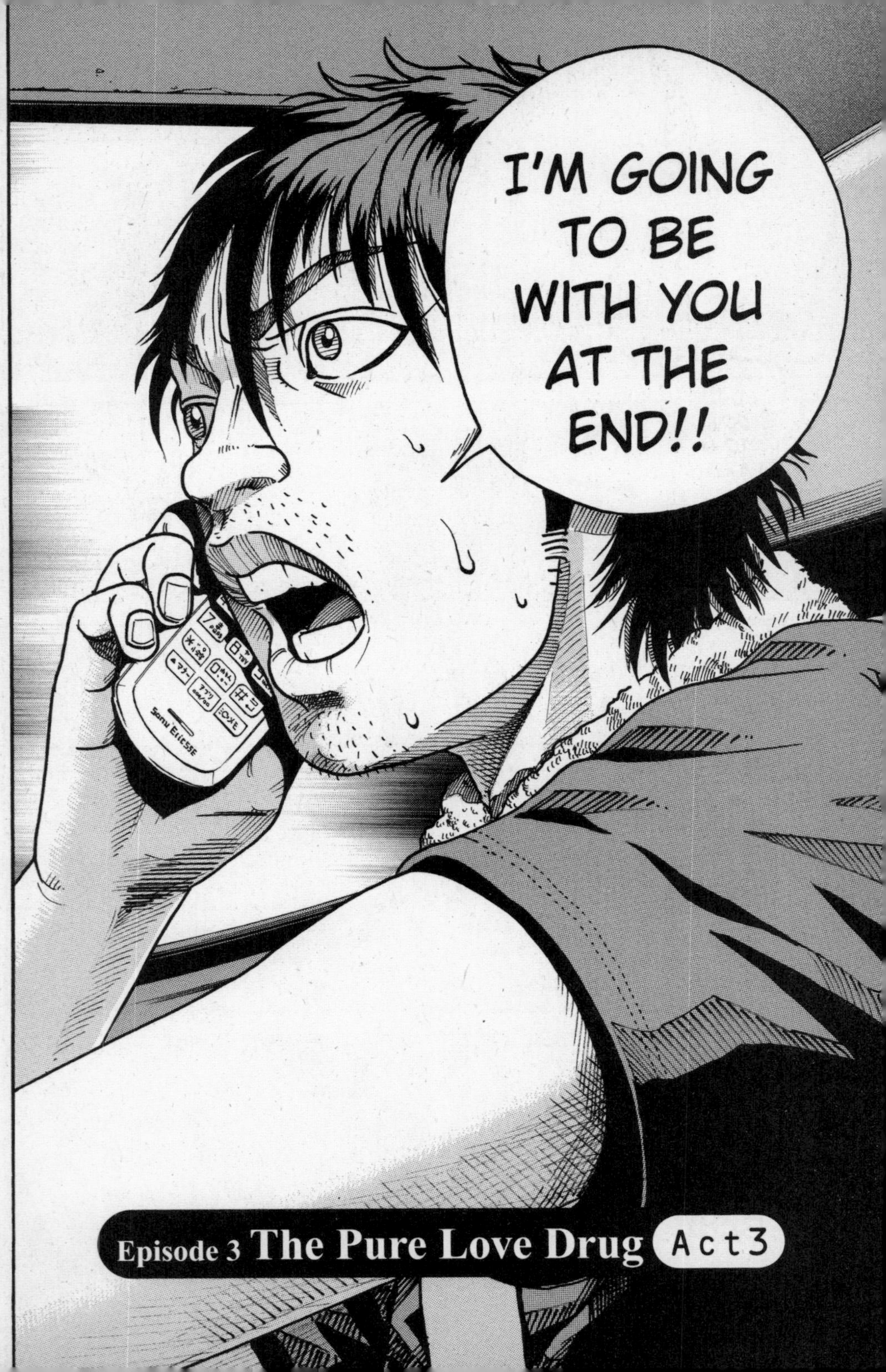
I'M GOING TO BE WITH YOU AT THE END!!

Episode 3 The Pure Love Drug Act 3

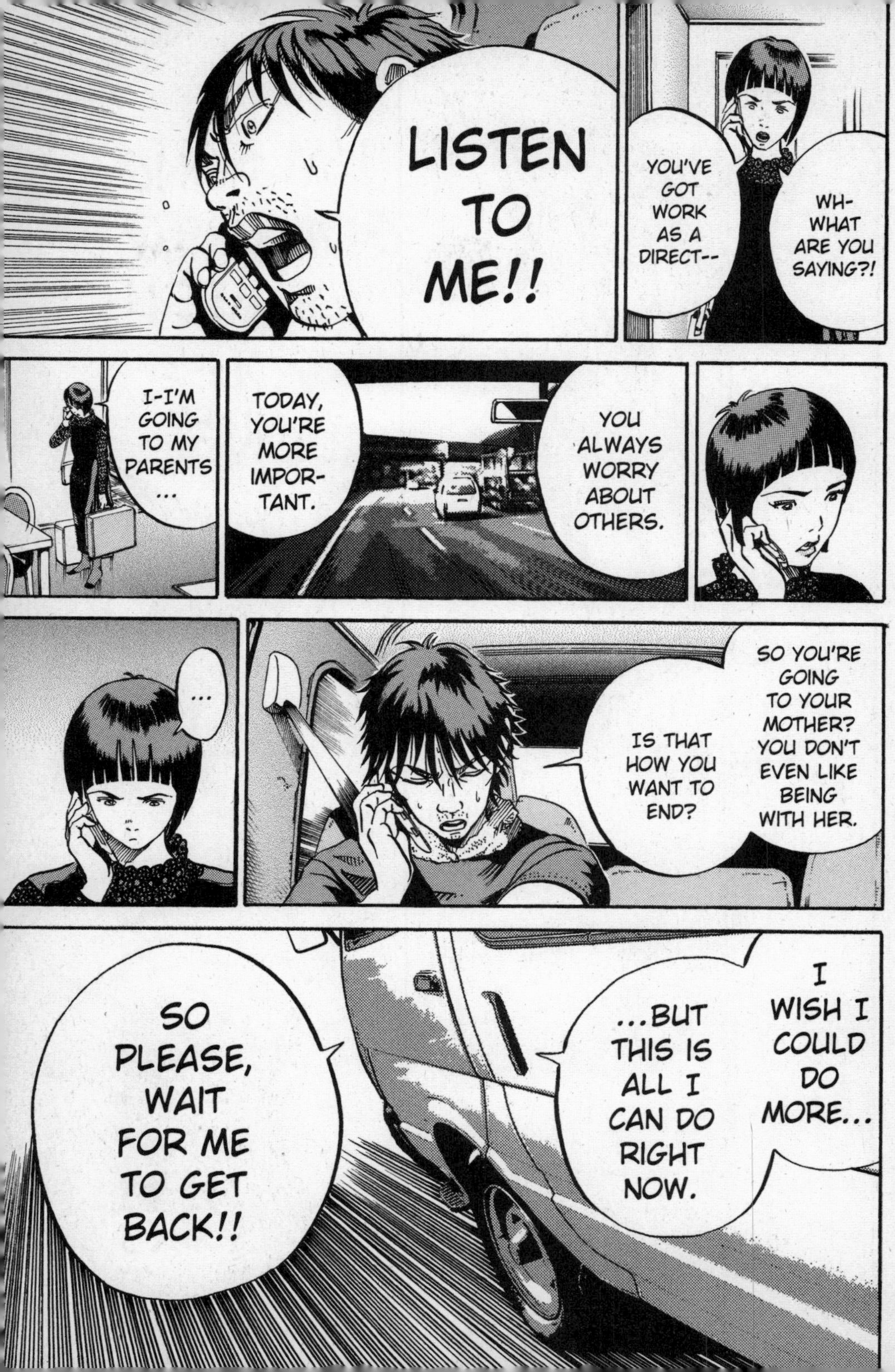
WH- WHAT ARE YOU SAYING?!
YOU'VE GOT WORK AS A DIRECT--
LISTEN TO ME!!
YOU ALWAYS WORRY ABOUT OTHERS.
TODAY, YOU'RE MORE IMPOR-TANT.
I-I'M GOING TO MY PARENTS...
SO YOU'RE GOING TO YOUR MOTHER? YOU DON'T EVEN LIKE BEING WITH HER.
IS THAT HOW YOU WANT TO END?
...
I WISH I COULD DO MORE...
...BUT THIS IS ALL I CAN DO RIGHT NOW.
SO PLEASE, WAIT FOR ME TO GET BACK!!

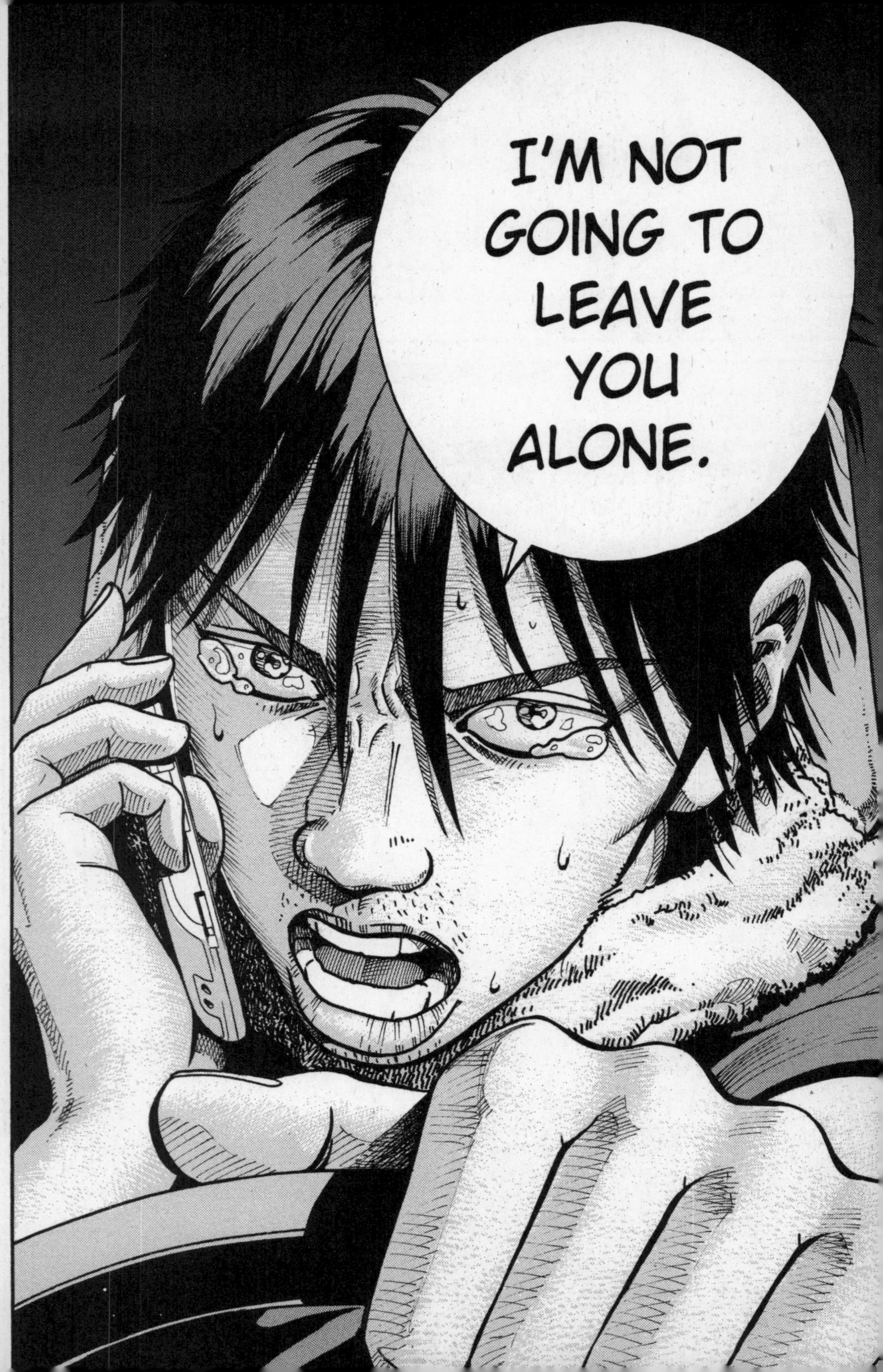
I'M NOT GOING TO LEAVE YOU ALONE.

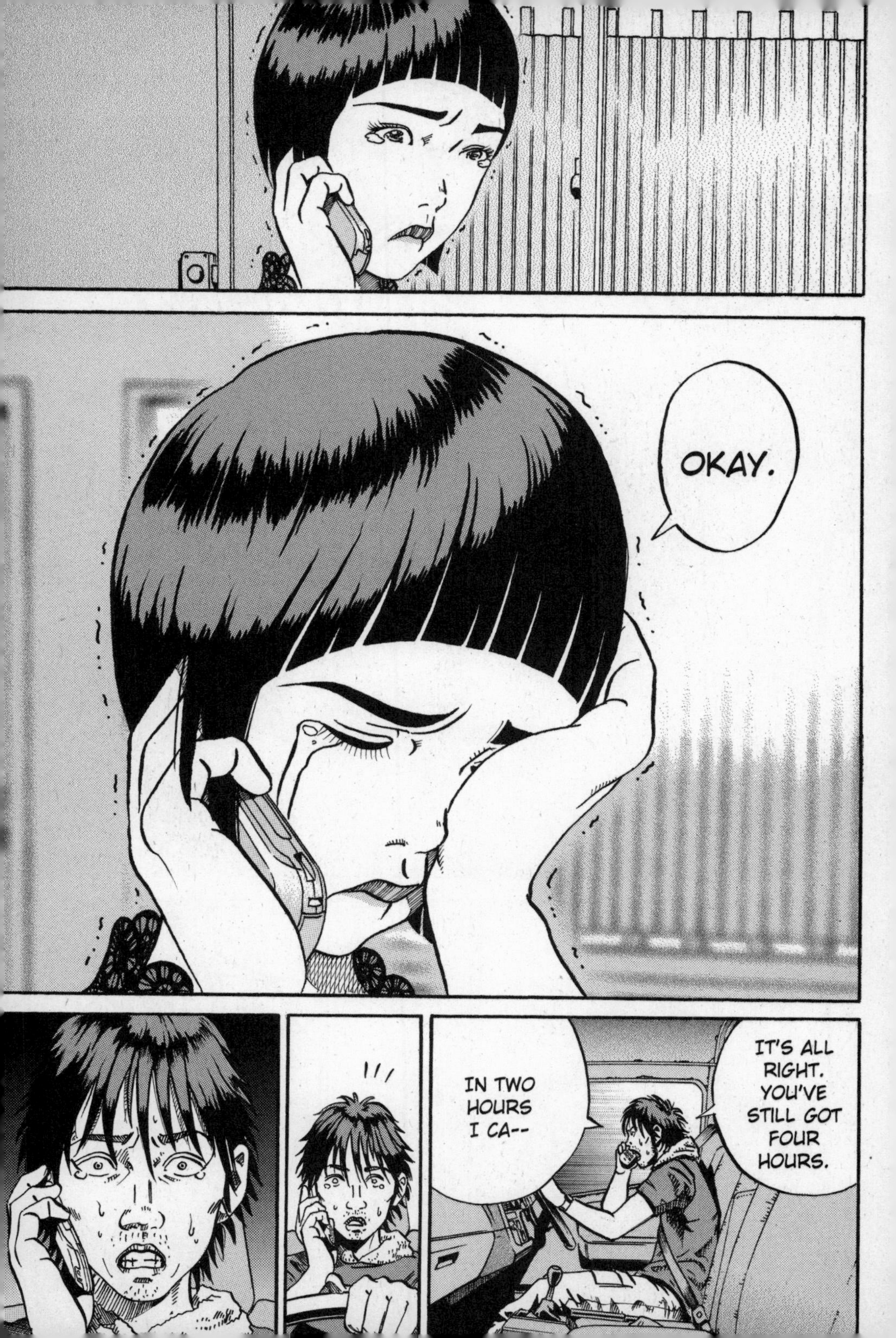
OKAY.
IT'S ALL RIGHT. YOU'VE STILL GOT FOUR HOURS.
IN TWO HOURS I CA--

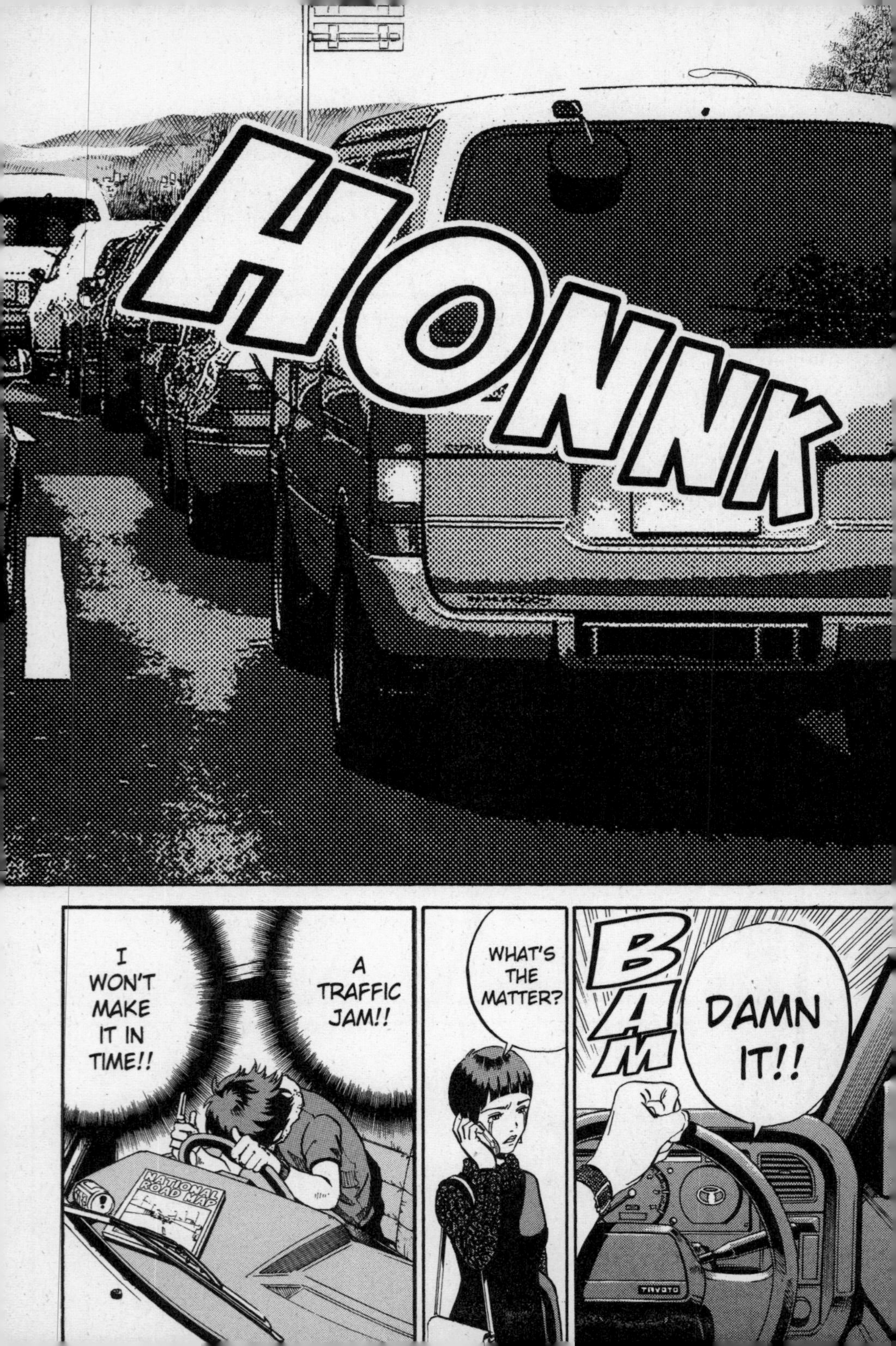
HONNK
BAM
DAMN IT!!
WHAT'S THE MATTER?
A TRAFFIC JAM!!
I WON'T MAKE IT IN TIME!!
NATIONAL ROAD MAP

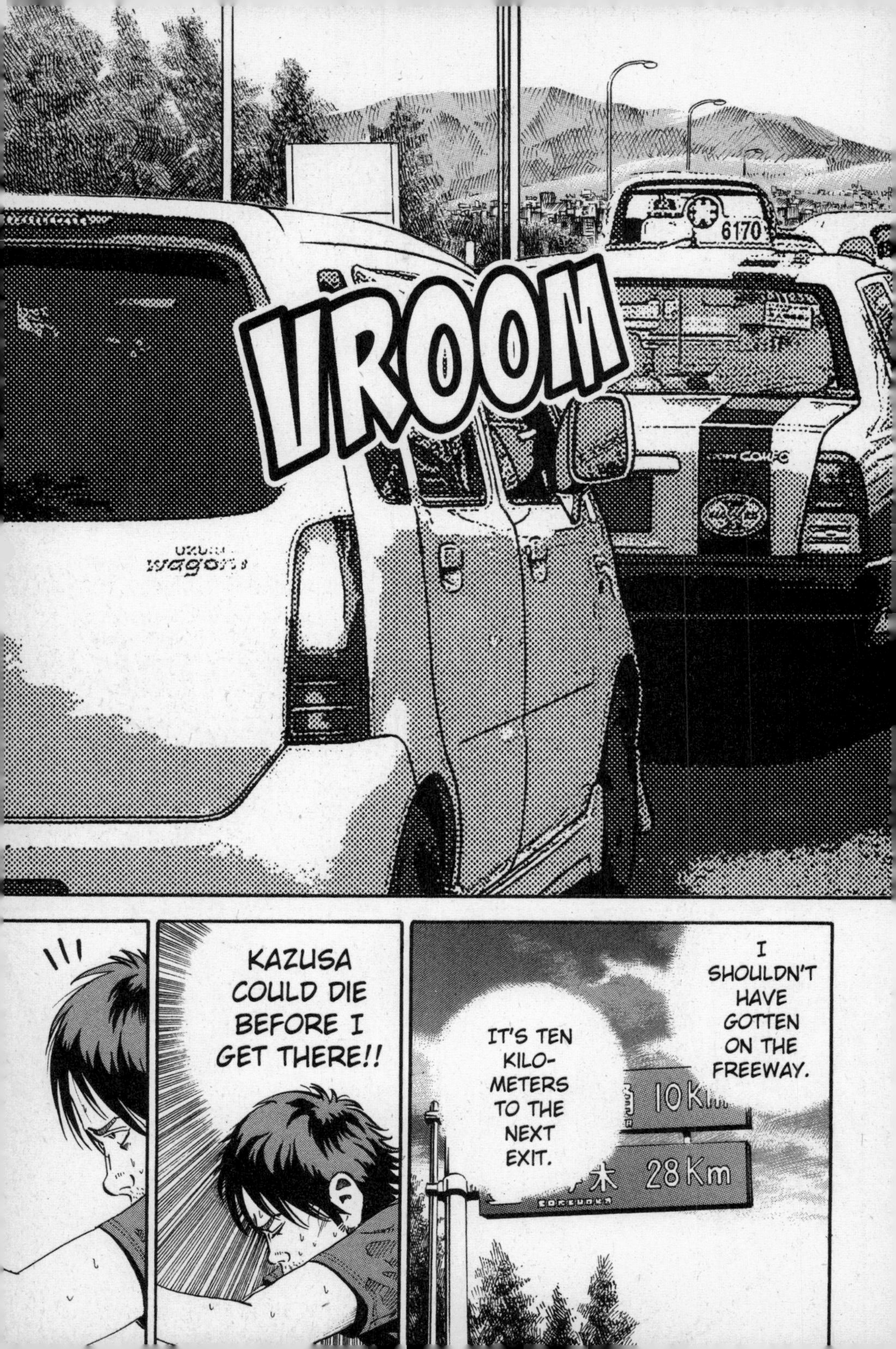
6170
VROOM
I SHOULDN'T HAVE GOTTEN ON THE FREEWAY.
IT'S TEN KILO-METERS TO THE NEXT EXIT.
28Km
KAZUSA COULD DIE BEFORE I GET THERE!!

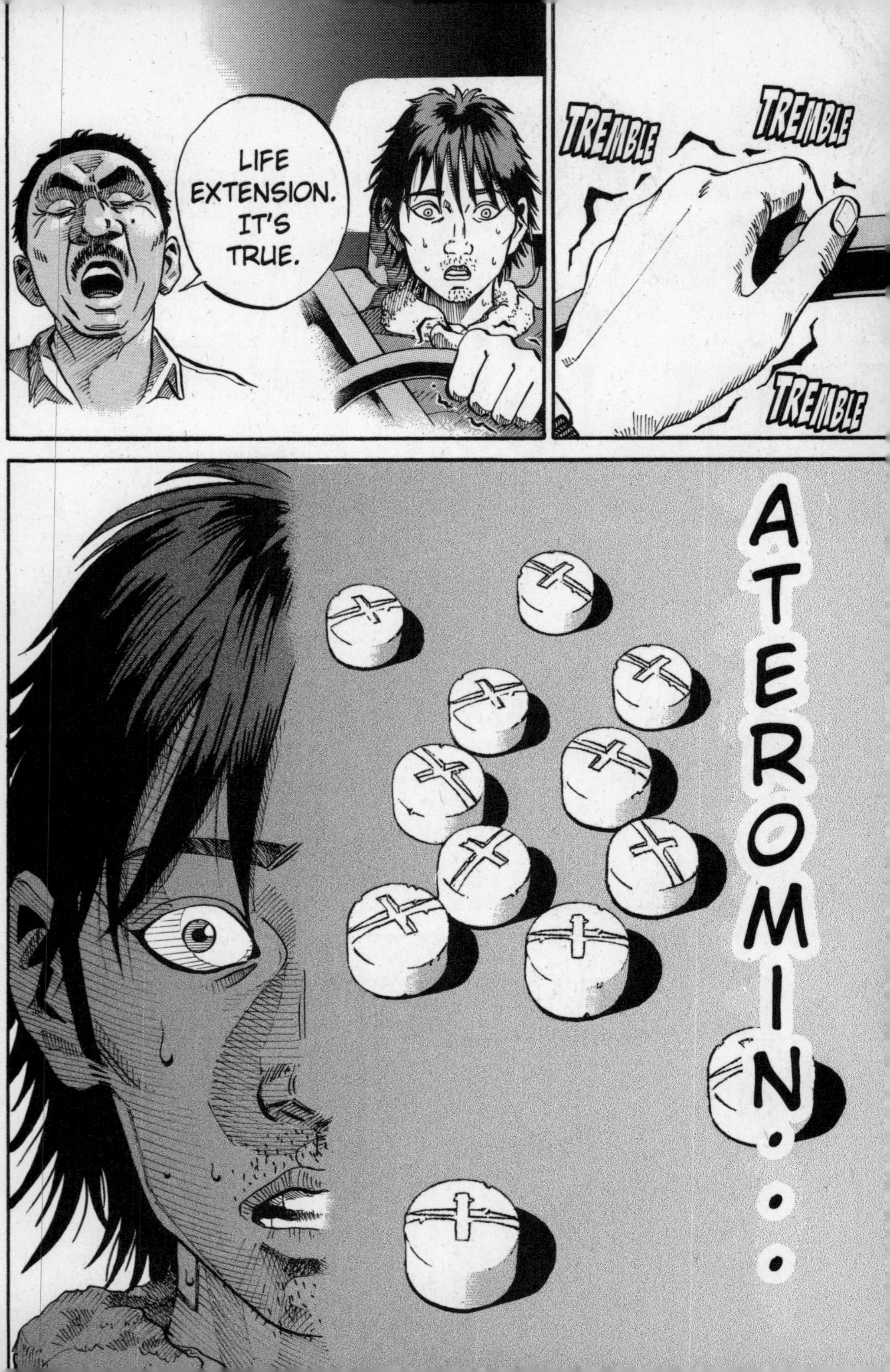
TREMBLE
TREMBLE
TREMBLE
LIFE EXTENSION. IT'S TRUE.
ATEROMIN...

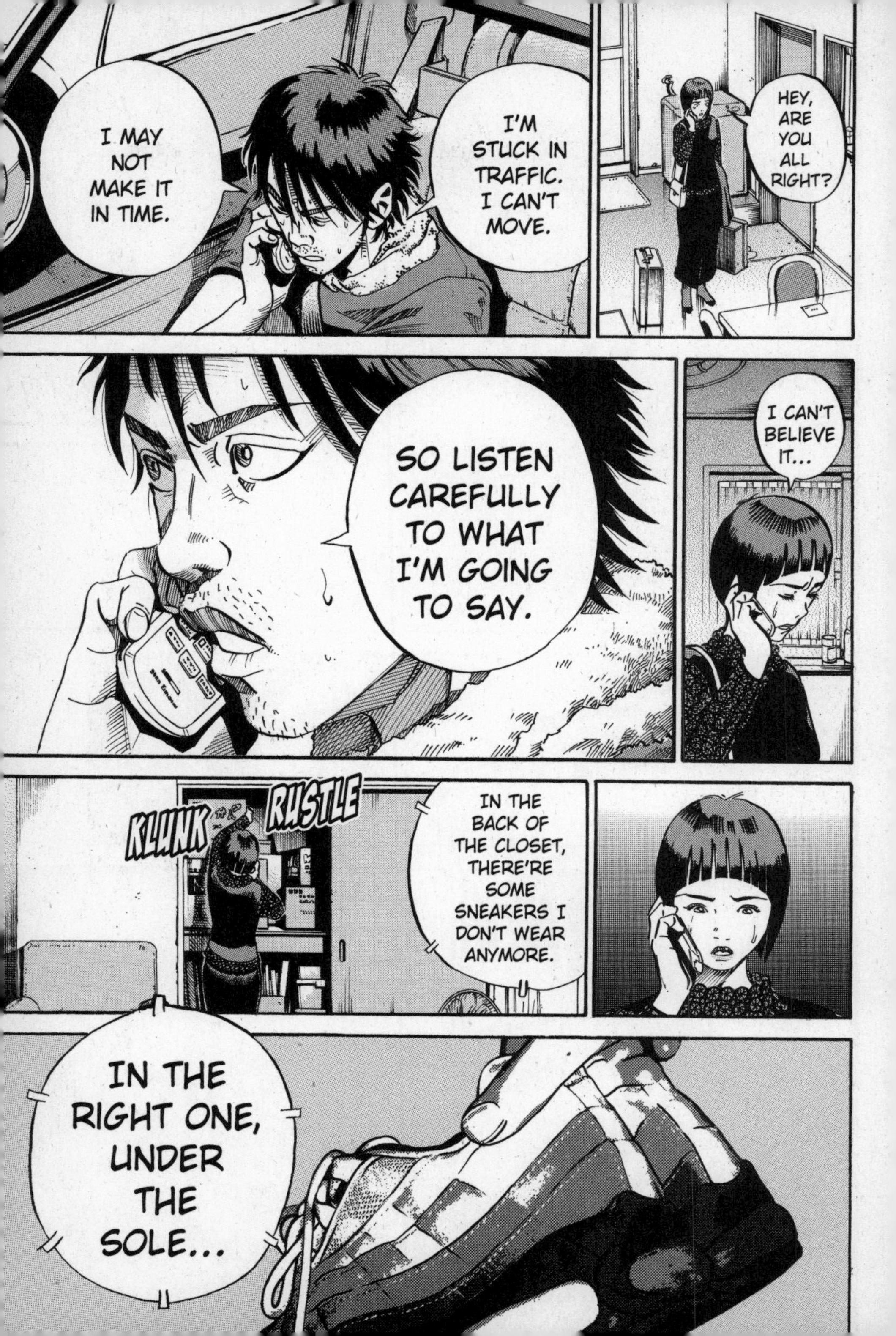
HEY, ARE YOU ALL RIGHT?
I'M STUCK IN TRAFFIC. I CAN'T MOVE.
I MAY NOT MAKE IT IN TIME.
I CAN'T BELIEVE IT...
SO LISTEN CAREFULLY TO WHAT I'M GOING TO SAY.
IN THE BACK OF THE CLOSET, THERE'RE SOME SNEAKERS I DON'T WEAR ANYMORE.
RUSTLE
KLUNK
IN THE RIGHT ONE, UNDER THE SOLE...

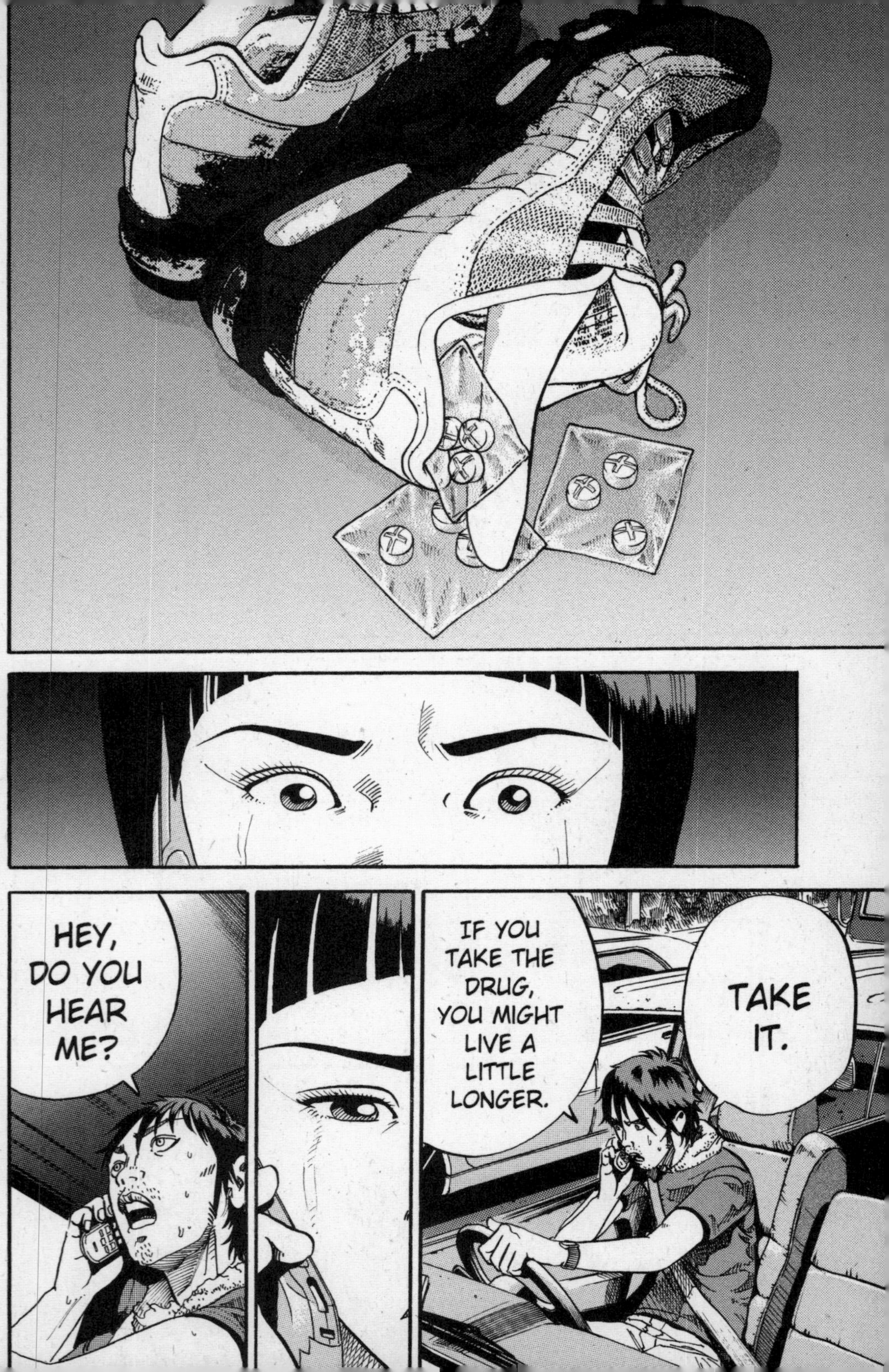
TAKE IT.
IF YOU TAKE THE DRUG, YOU MIGHT LIVE A LITTLE LONGER.
HEY, DO YOU HEAR ME?

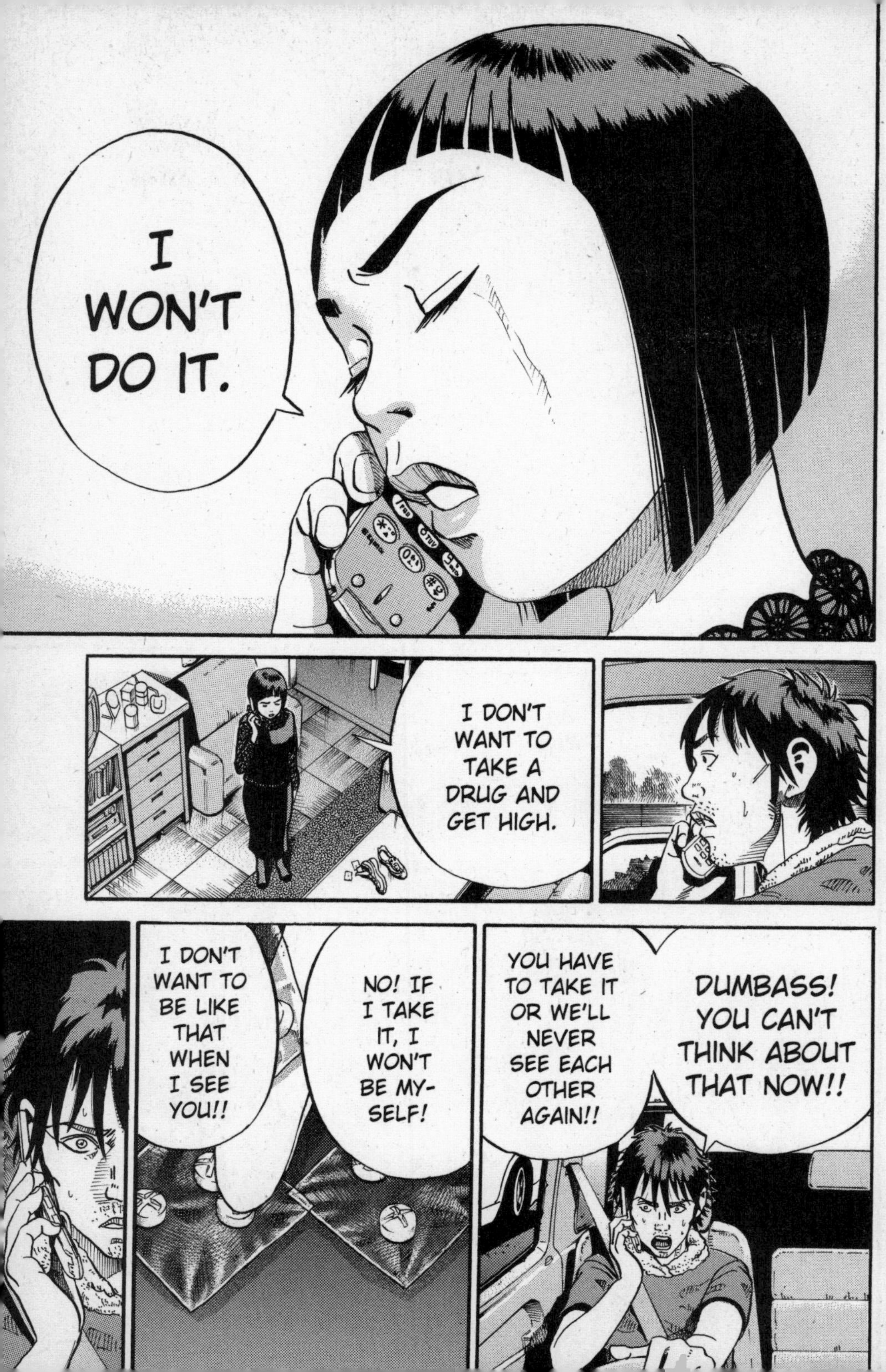
I WON'T DO IT.
I DON'T WANT TO TAKE A DRUG AND GET HIGH.
DUMBASS! YOU CAN'T THINK ABOUT THAT NOW!!
YOU HAVE TO TAKE IT OR WE'LL NEVER SEE EACH OTHER AGAIN!!
NO! IF I TAKE IT, I WON'T BE MY-SELF!
I DON'T WANT TO BE LIKE THAT WHEN I SEE YOU!!

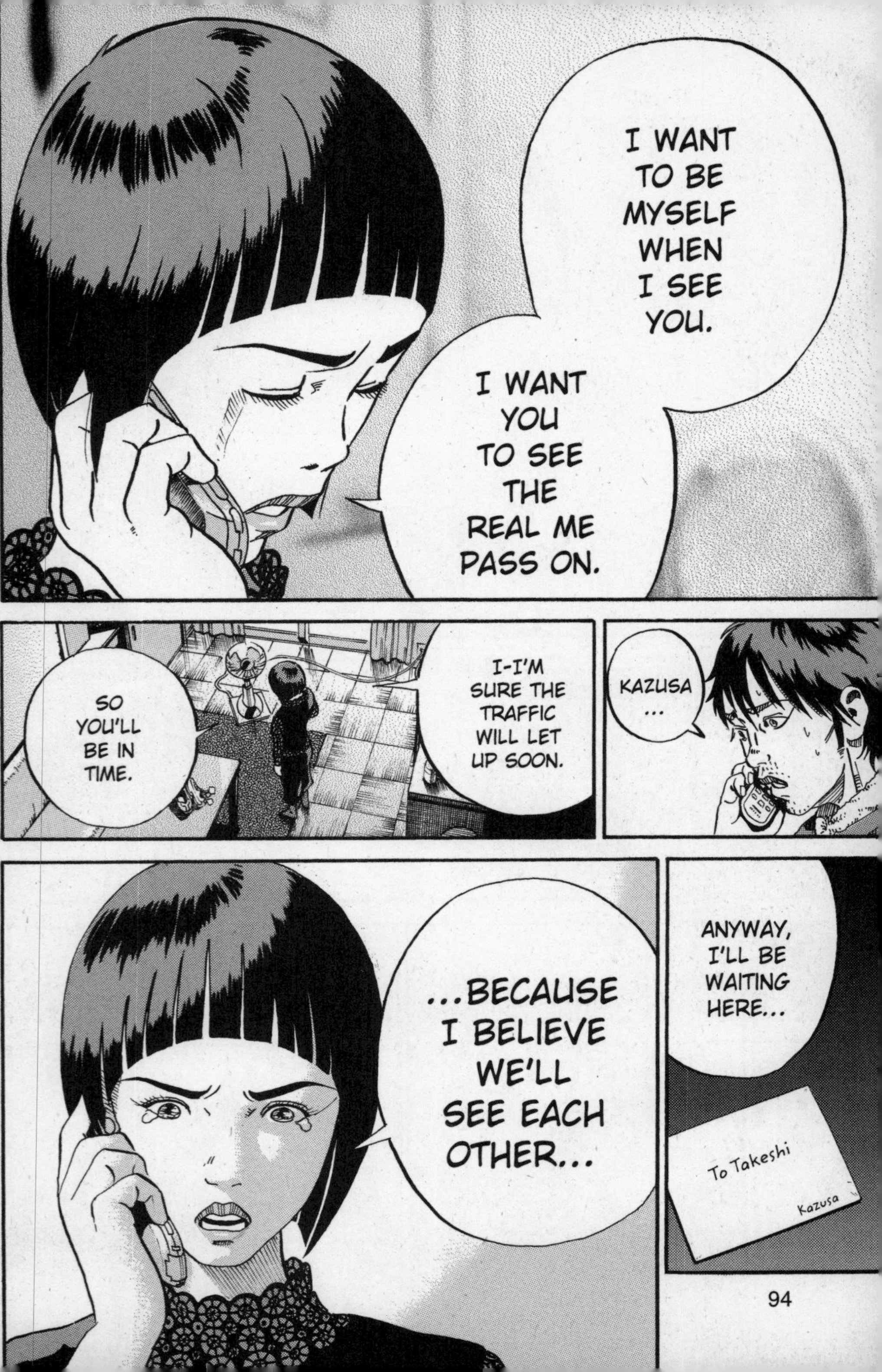
I WANT TO BE MYSELF WHEN I SEE YOU.
I WANT YOU TO SEE THE REAL ME PASS ON.
KAZUSA...
I-I'M SURE THE TRAFFIC WILL LET UP SOON.
SO YOU'LL BE IN TIME.
ANYWAY, I'LL BE WAITING HERE...
To Takeshi
Kazusa
...BECAUSE I BELIEVE WE'LL SEE EACH OTHER...

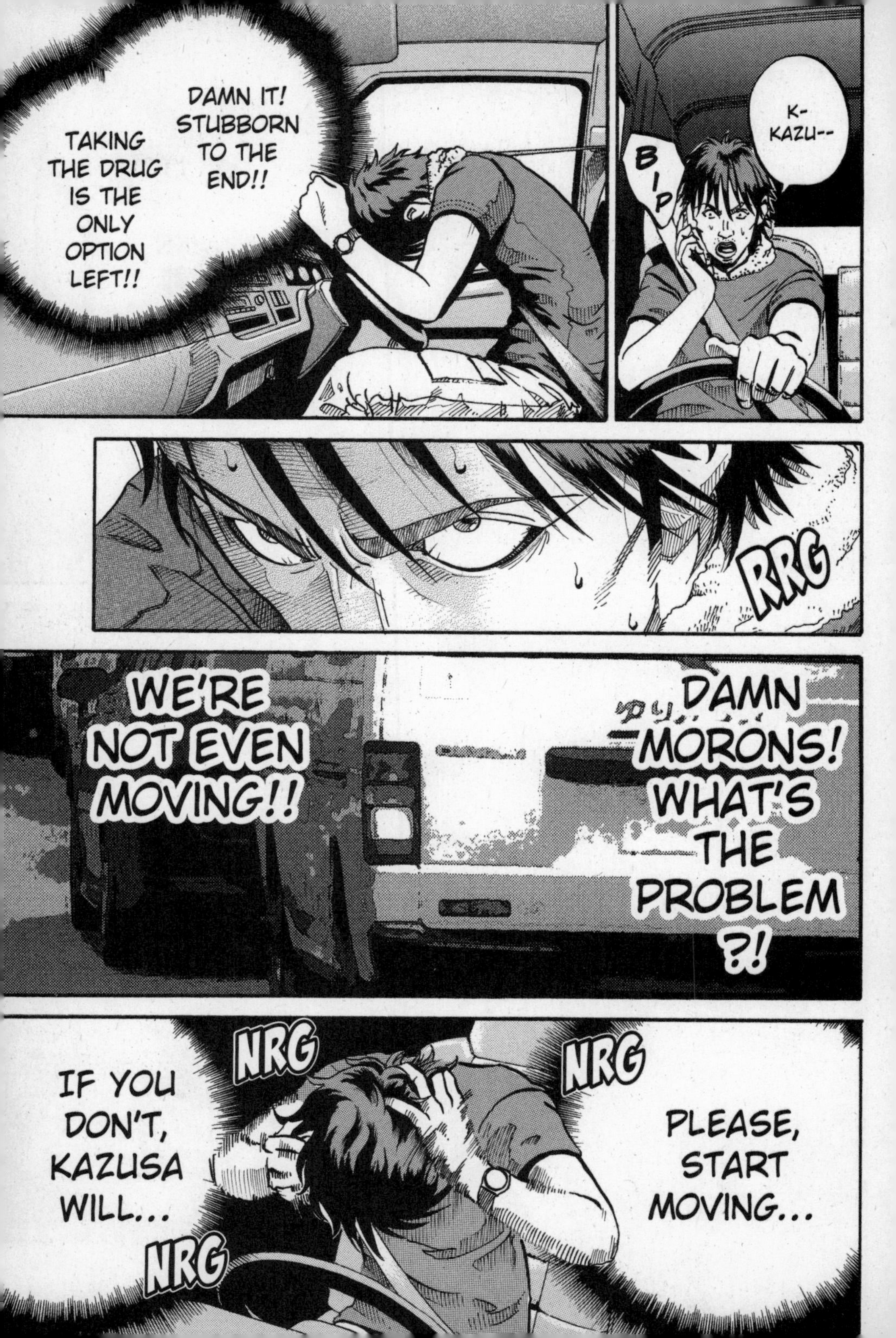
K-KAZU--
BIP
DAMN IT! STUBBORN TO THE END!!
TAKING THE DRUG IS THE ONLY OPTION LEFT!!
RRG
DAMN MORONS! WHAT'S THE PROBLEM?!
WE'RE NOT EVEN MOVING!!
NRG
NRG
PLEASE, START MOVING...
IF YOU DON'T, KAZUSA WILL...
NRG

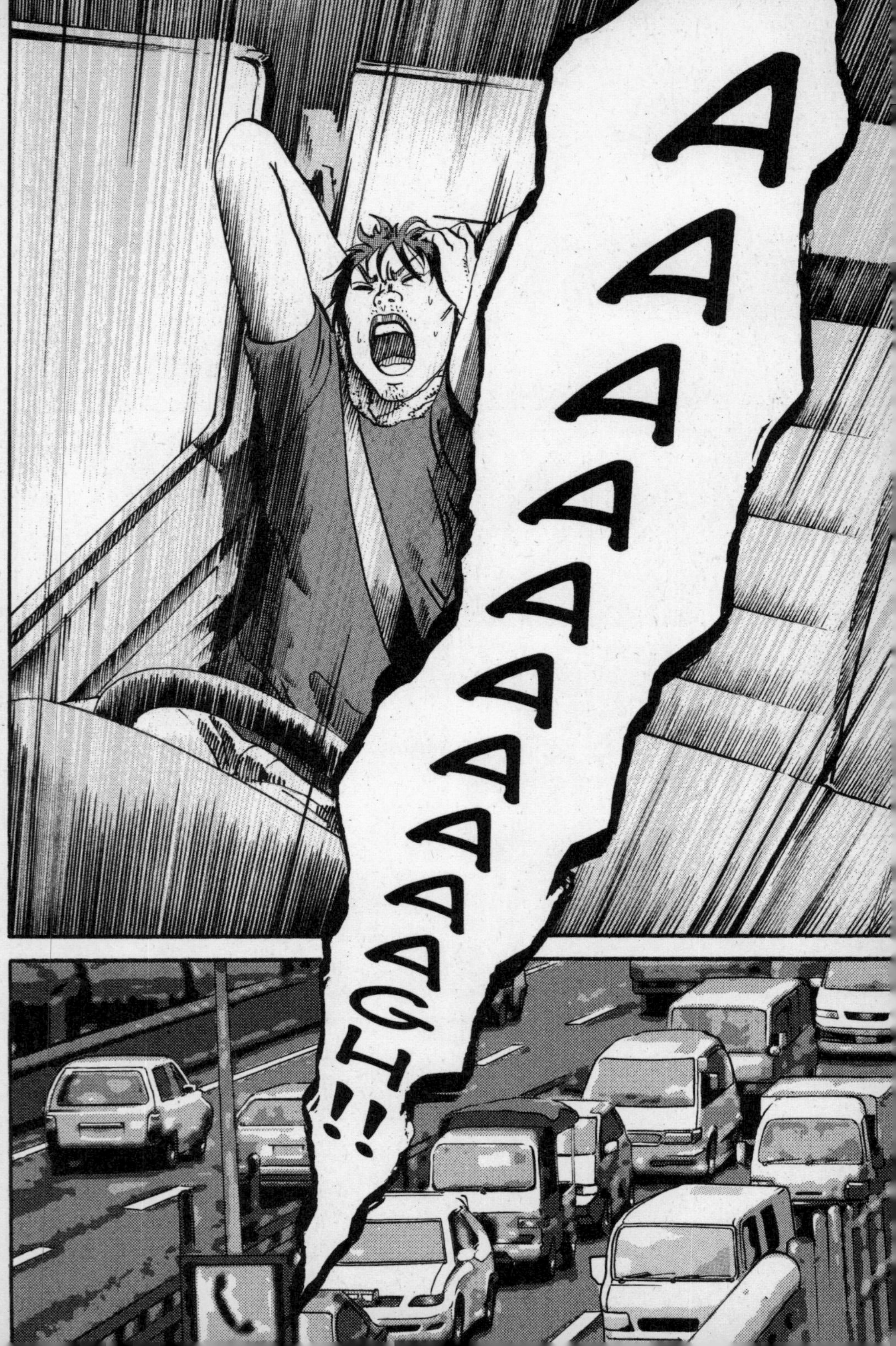
AAAAAAAAAAAGH!!

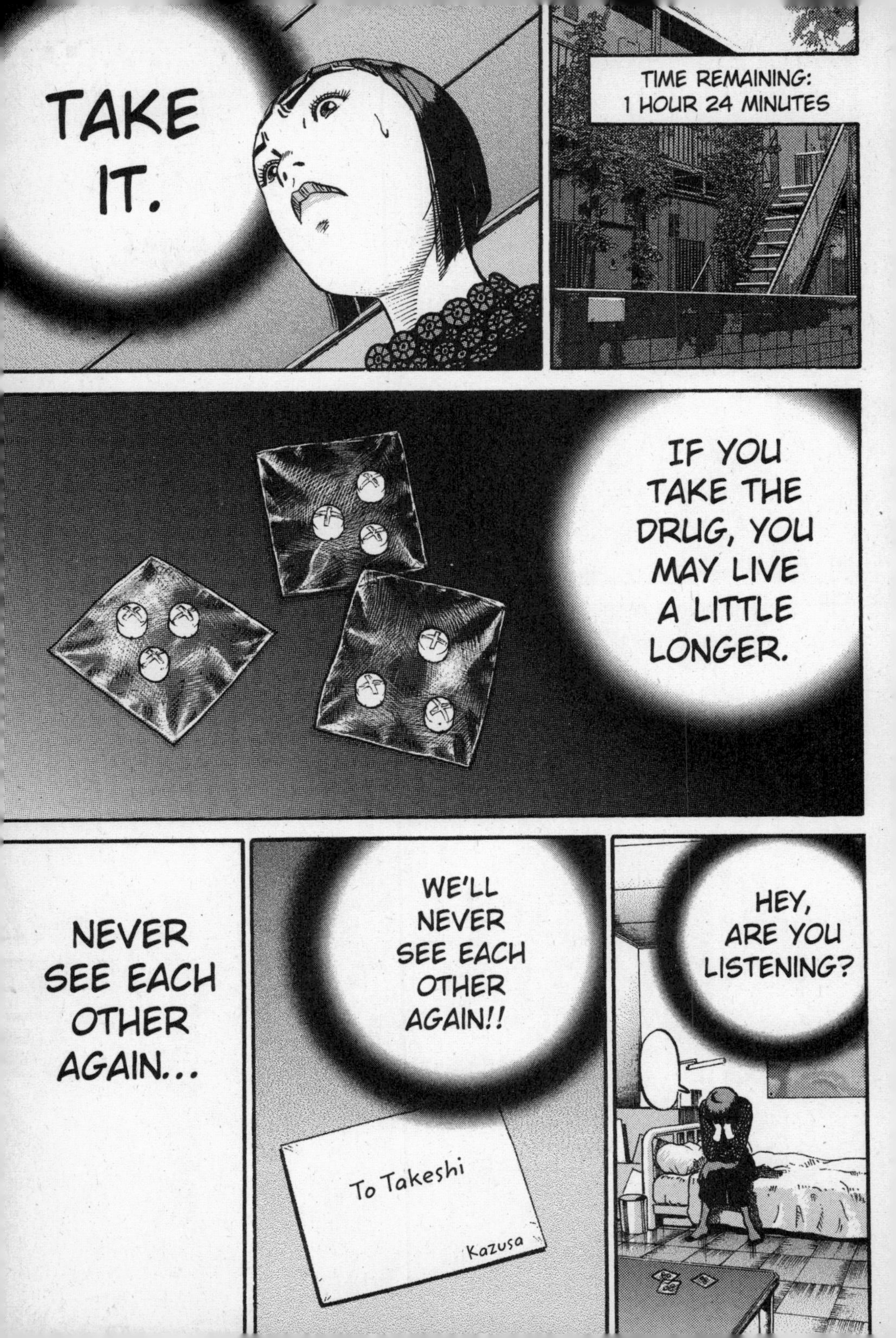
TIME REMAINING: 1 HOUR 24 MINUTES
TAKE IT.
IF YOU TAKE THE DRUG, YOU MAY LIVE A LITTLE LONGER.
HEY, ARE YOU LISTENING?
WE'LL NEVER SEE EACH OTHER AGAIN!!
To Takeshi
Kazusa
NEVER SEE EACH OTHER AGAIN...

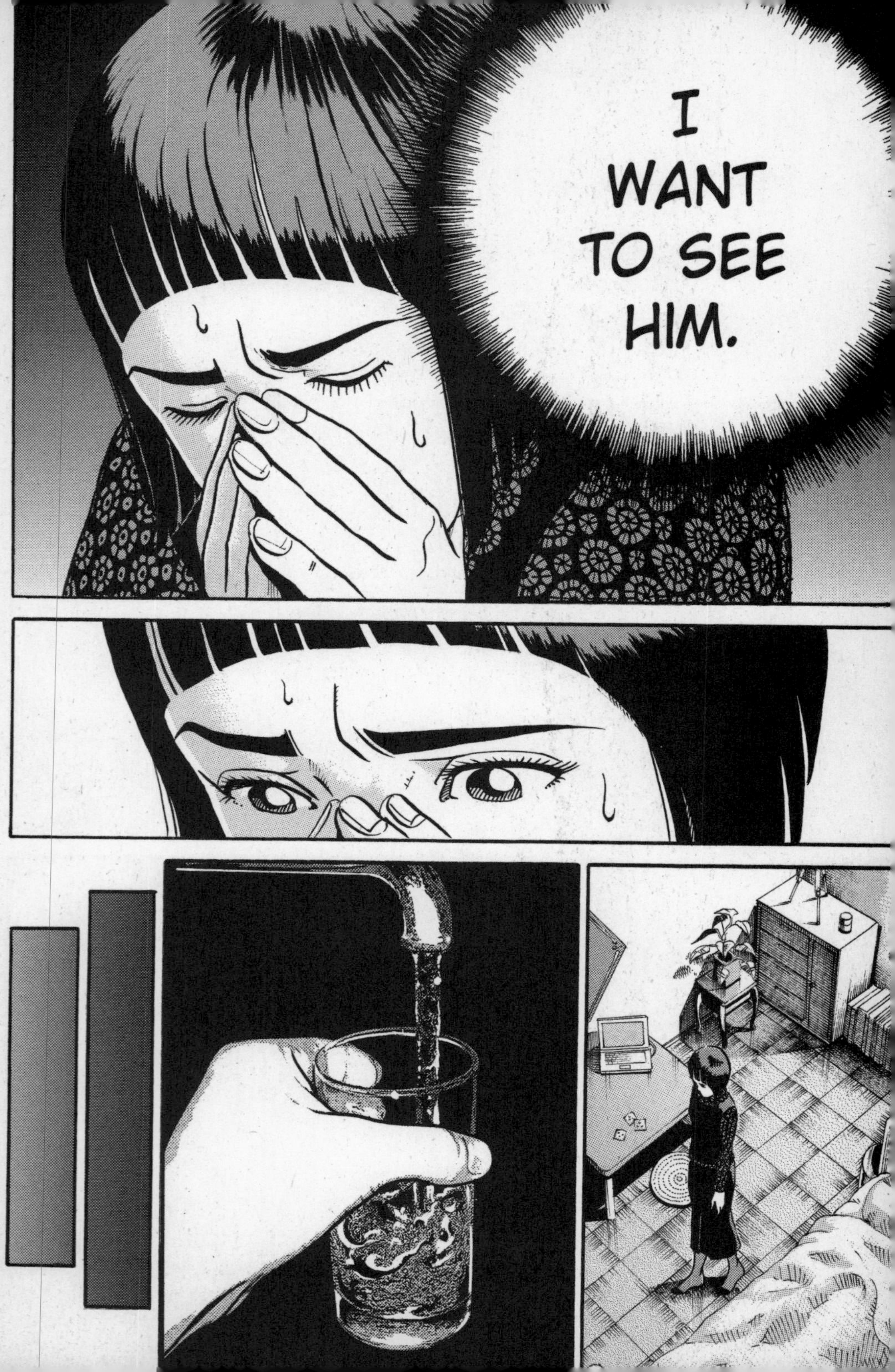
I WANT TO SEE HIM.

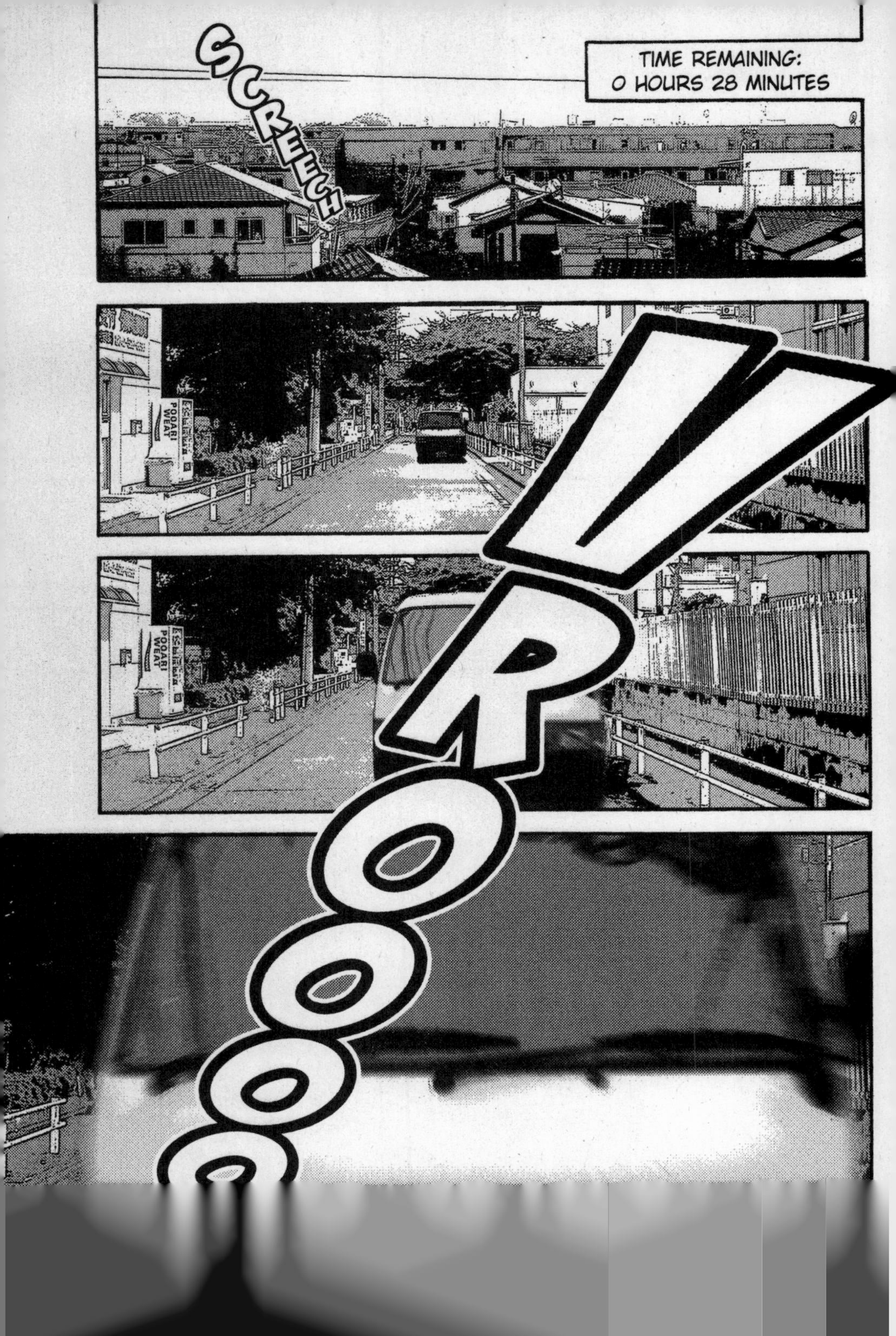
TIME REMAINING:
0 HOURS 28 MINUTES
SCREECH
ROOOO

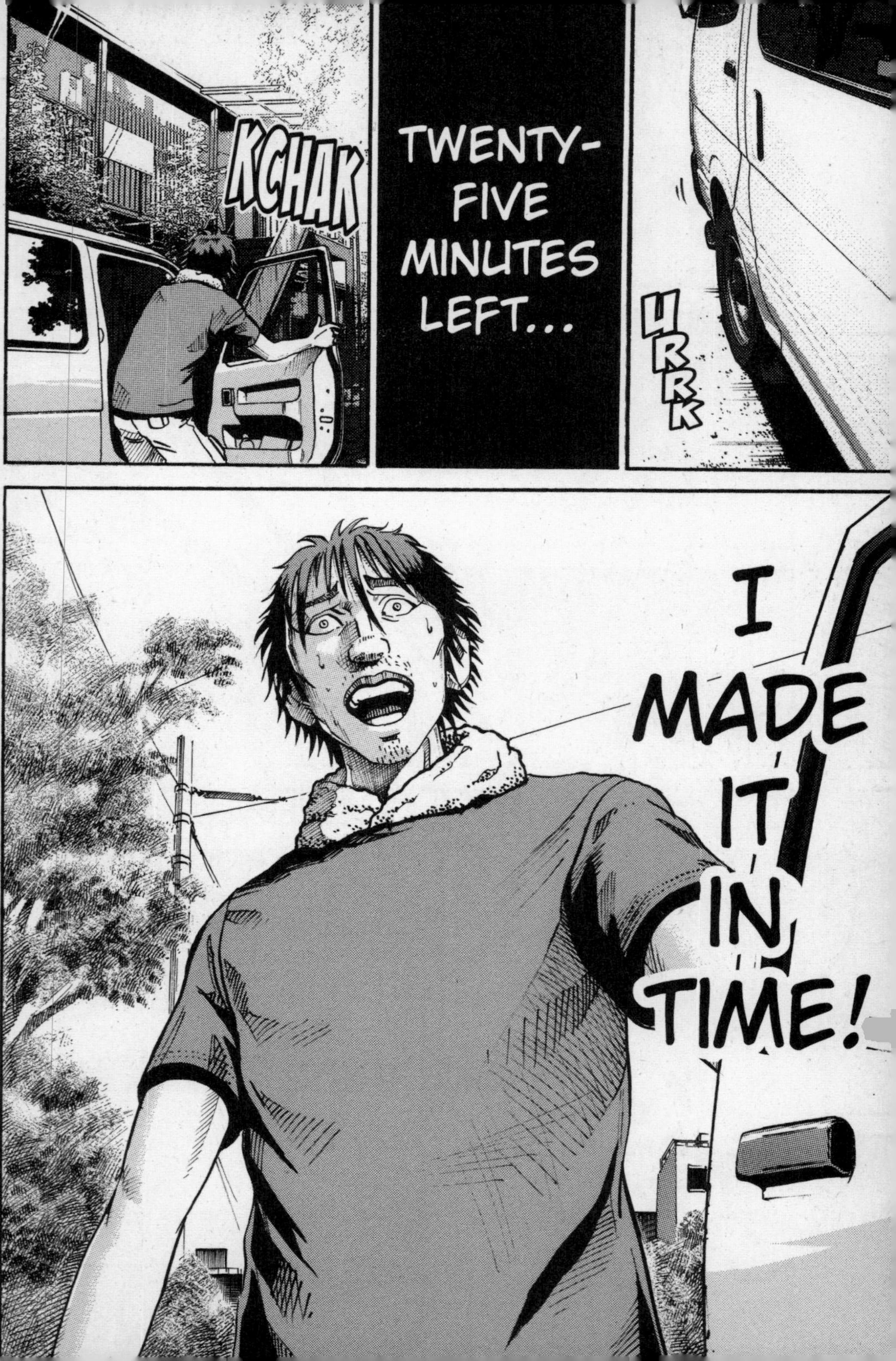
URRK
TWENTY-FIVE MINUTES LEFT...
KCHAK
I MADE IT IN TIME!

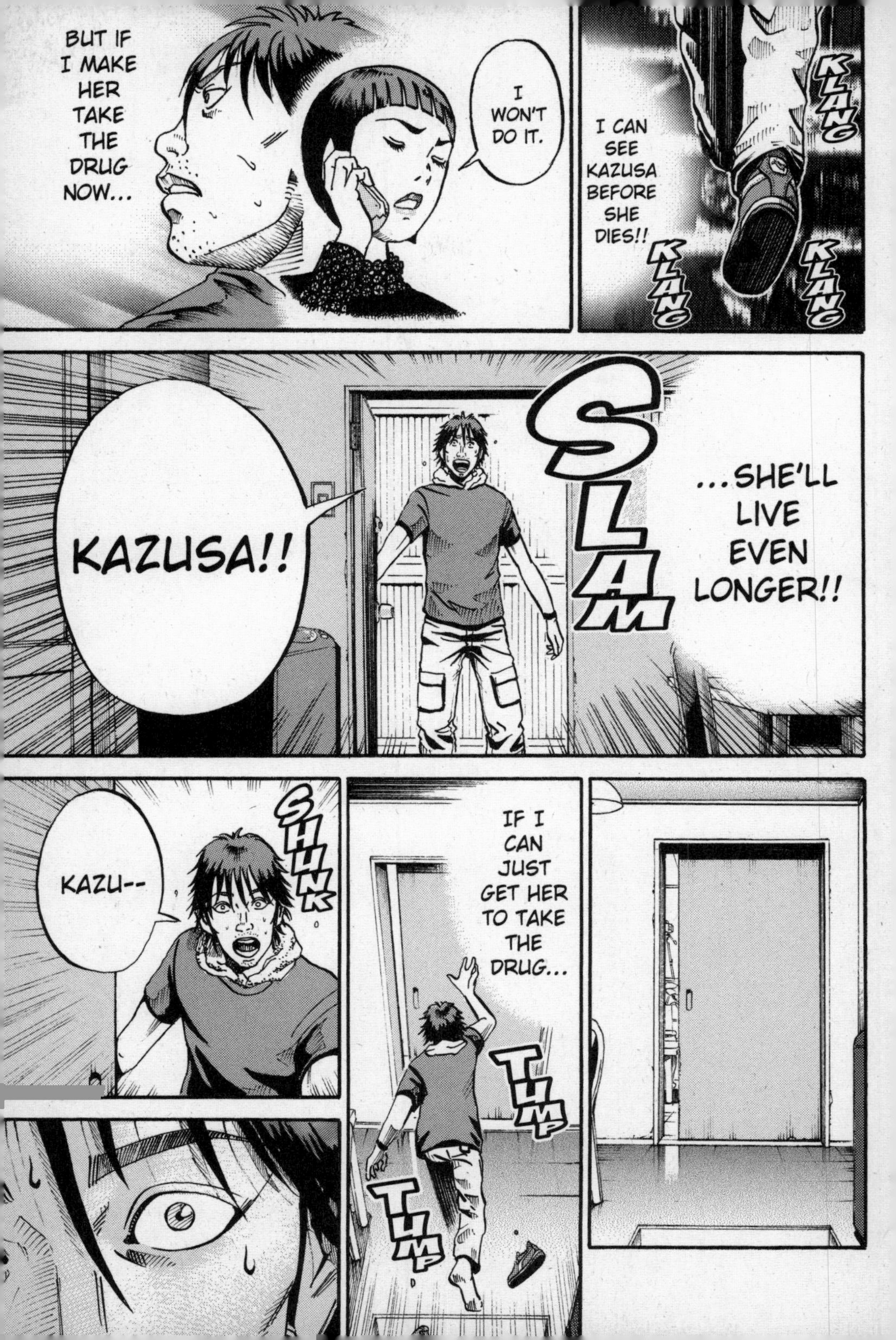
I CAN SEE KAZUSA BEFORE SHE DIES!!
KLANG
KLANG
KLANG
I WON'T DO IT.
BUT IF I MAKE HER TAKE THE DRUG NOW...
...SHE'LL LIVE EVEN LONGER!!
SLAM
KAZUSA!!
IF I CAN JUST GET HER TO TAKE THE DRUG...
TUMP
TUMP
SHUNK
KAZU--

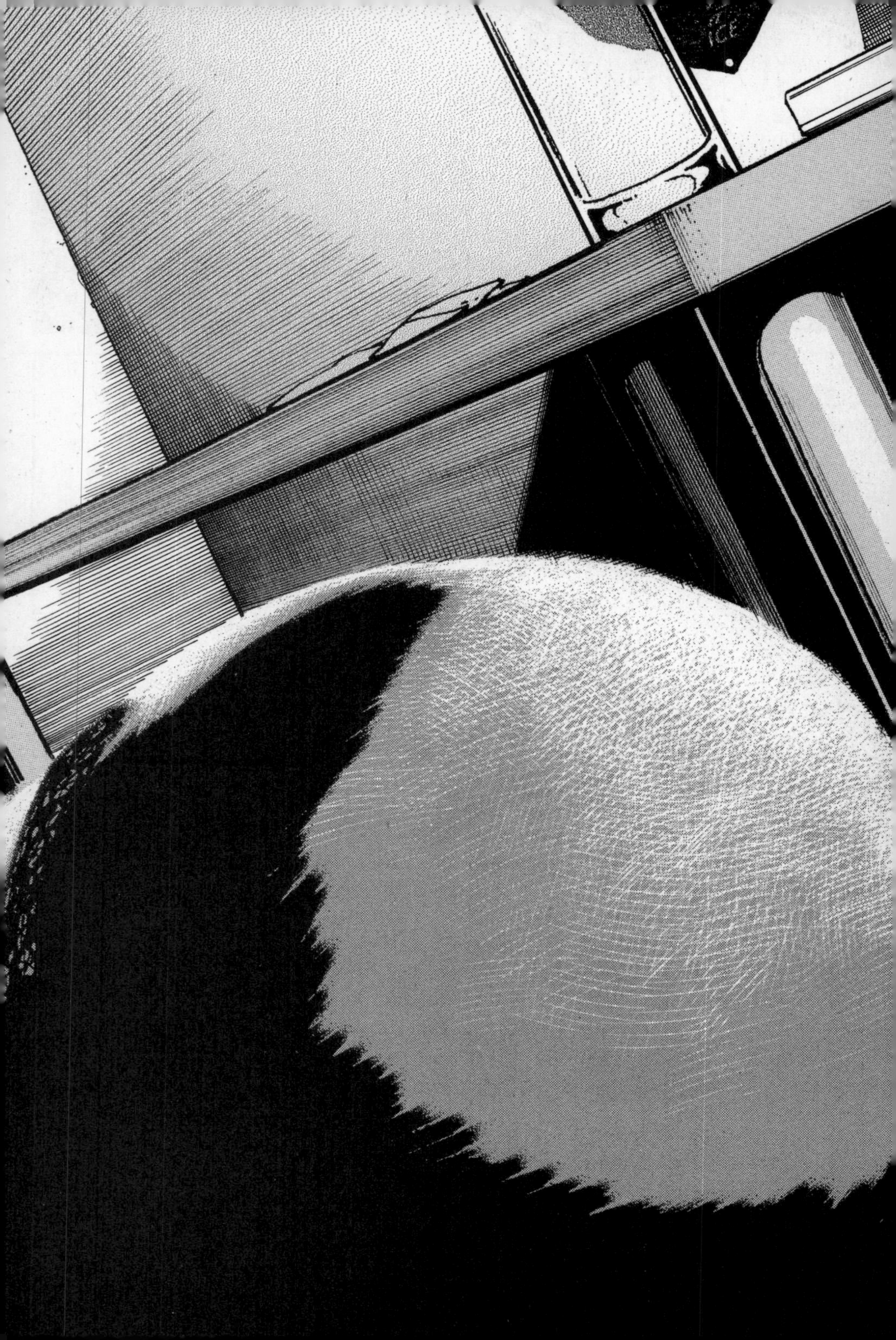

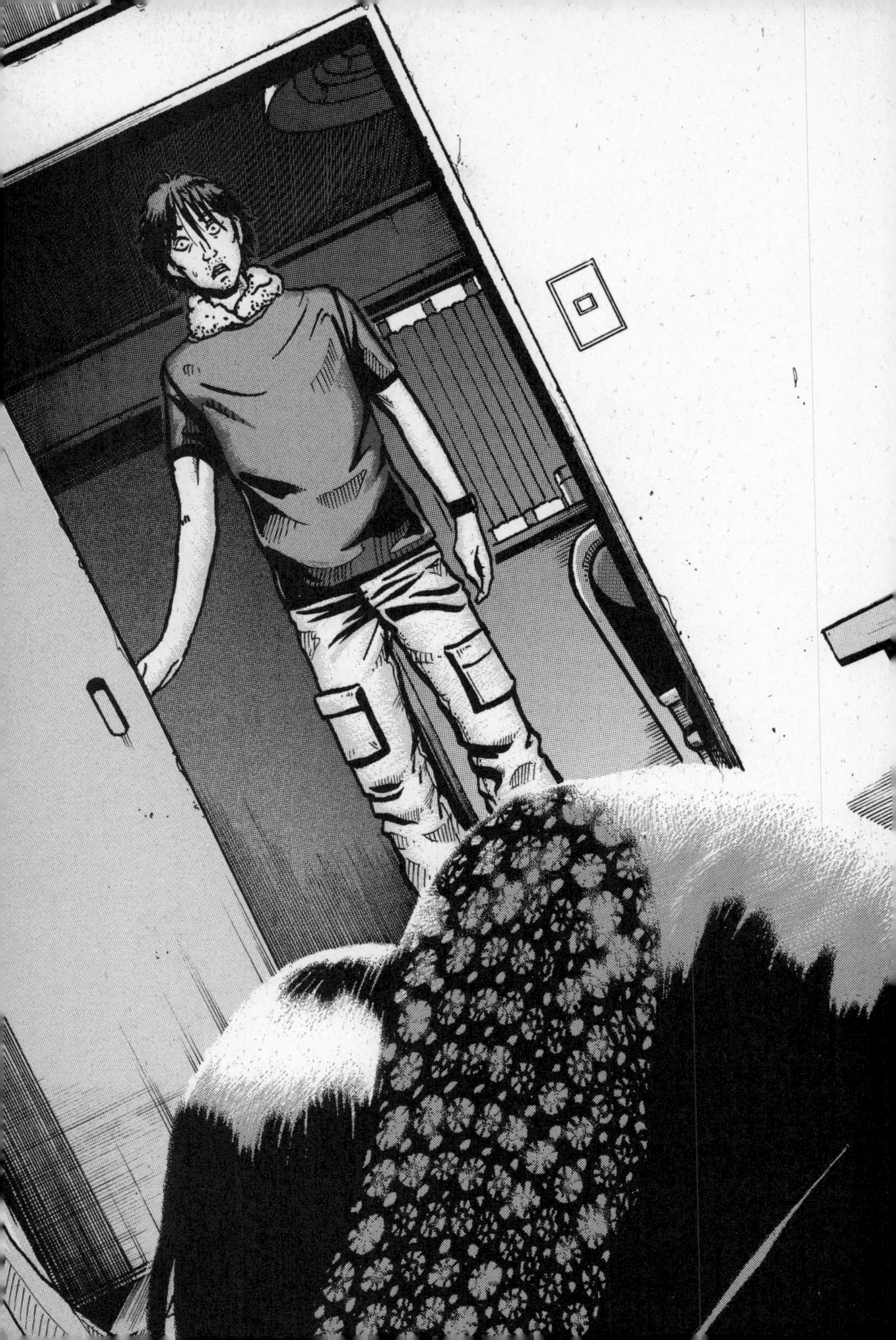

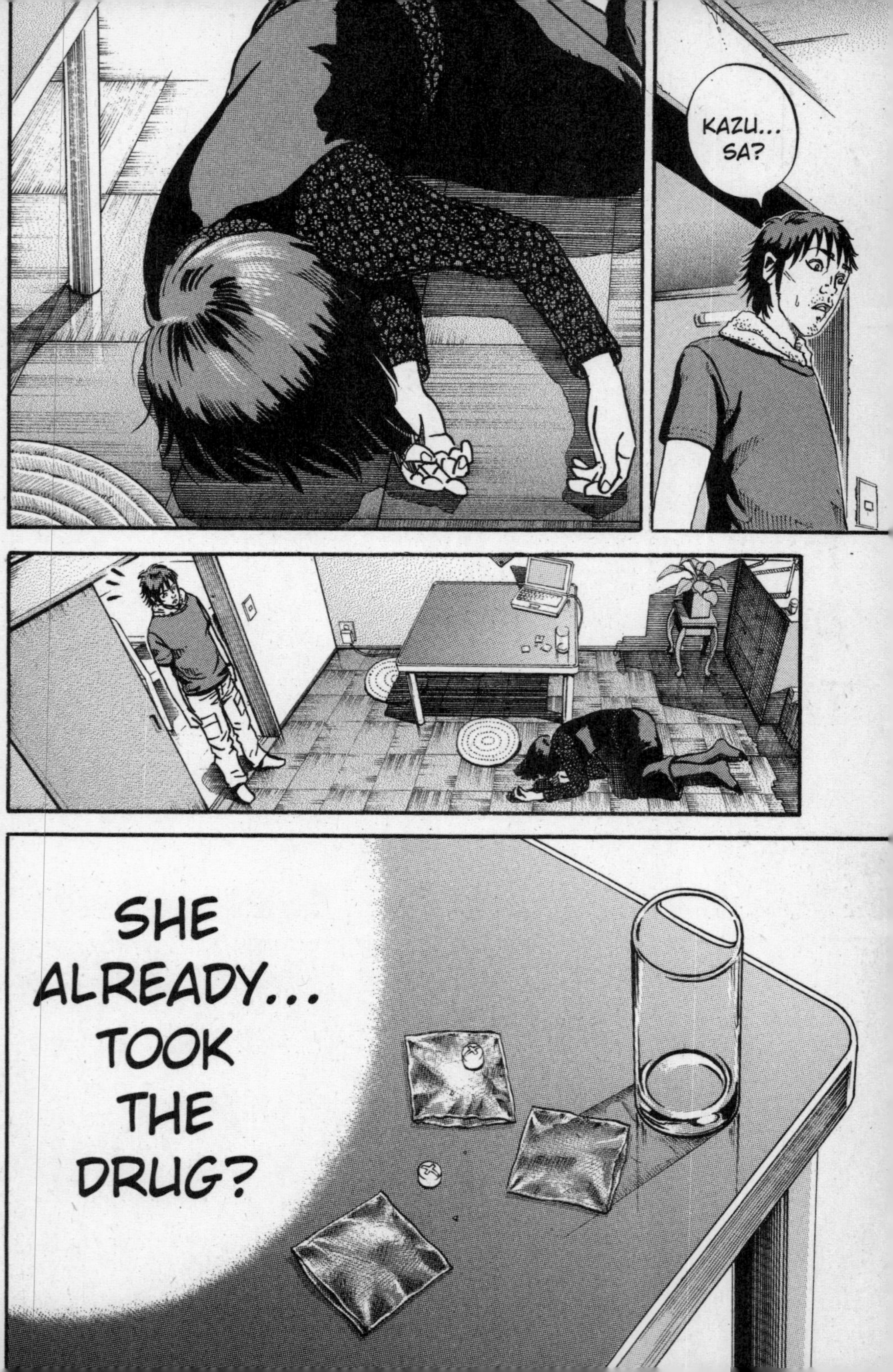
KAZU... SA?
SHE ALREADY... TOOK THE DRUG?

...

ONE
PILL
AT A
TIME.

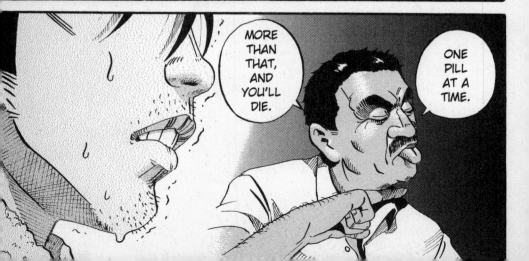

MORE THAN THAT, AND YOU'LL DIE.

ONE PILL AT A TIME.

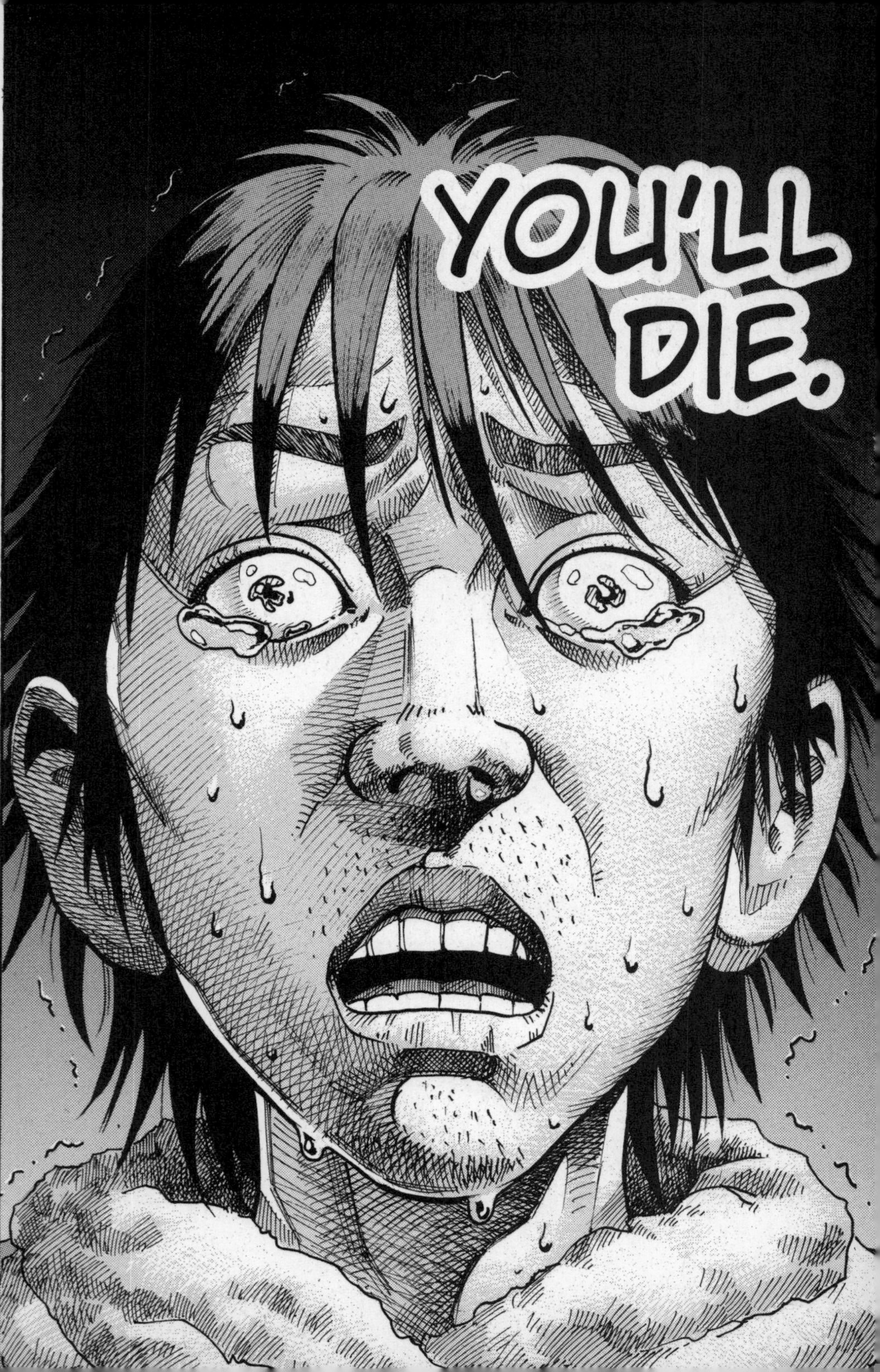
YOU'LL DIE.

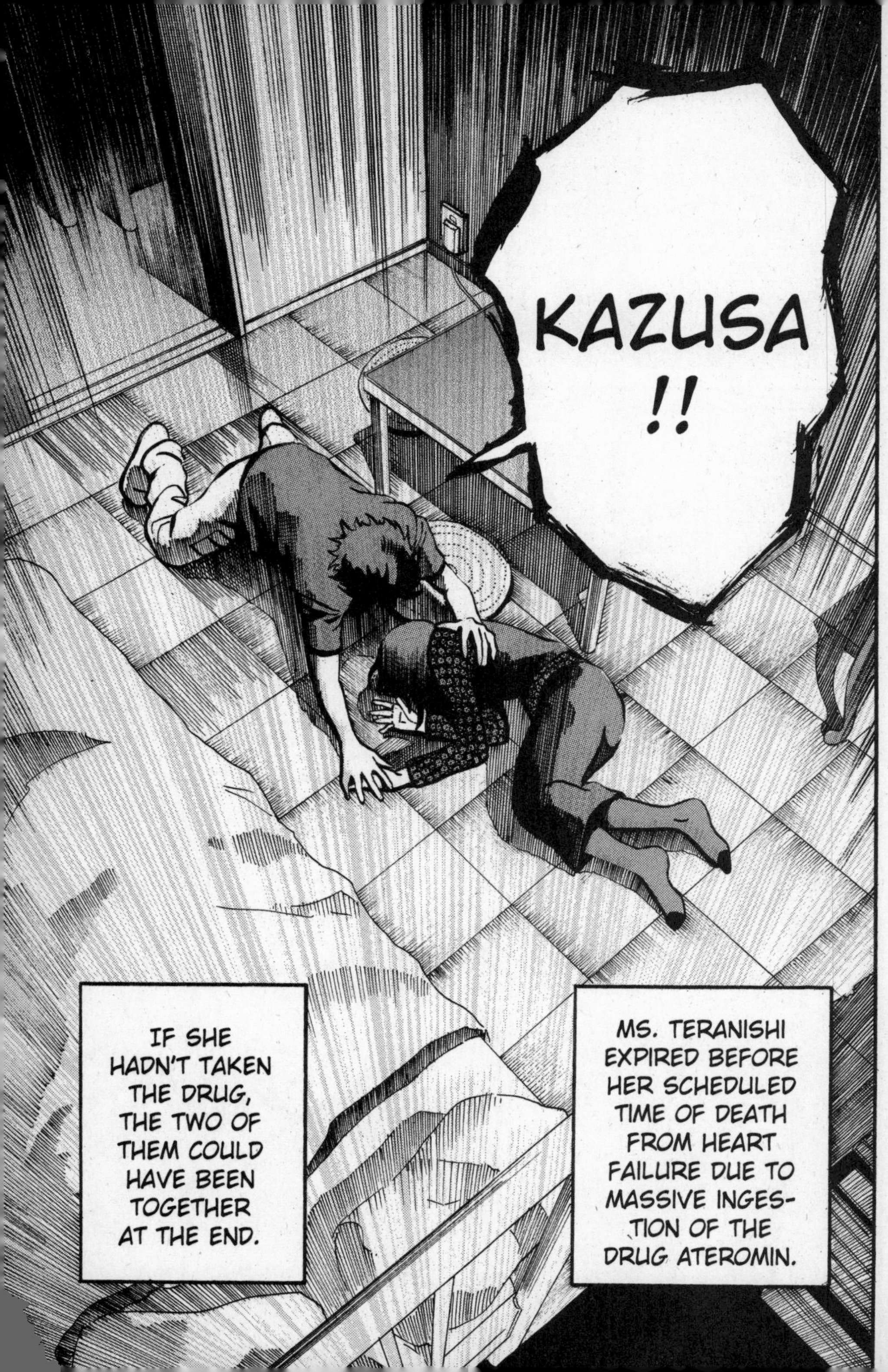
KAZUSA !!
MS. TERANISHI EXPIRED BEFORE HER SCHEDULED TIME OF DEATH FROM HEART FAILURE DUE TO MASSIVE INGES-TION OF THE DRUG ATEROMIN.
IF SHE HADN'T TAKEN THE DRUG, THE TWO OF THEM COULD HAVE BEEN TOGETHER AT THE END.

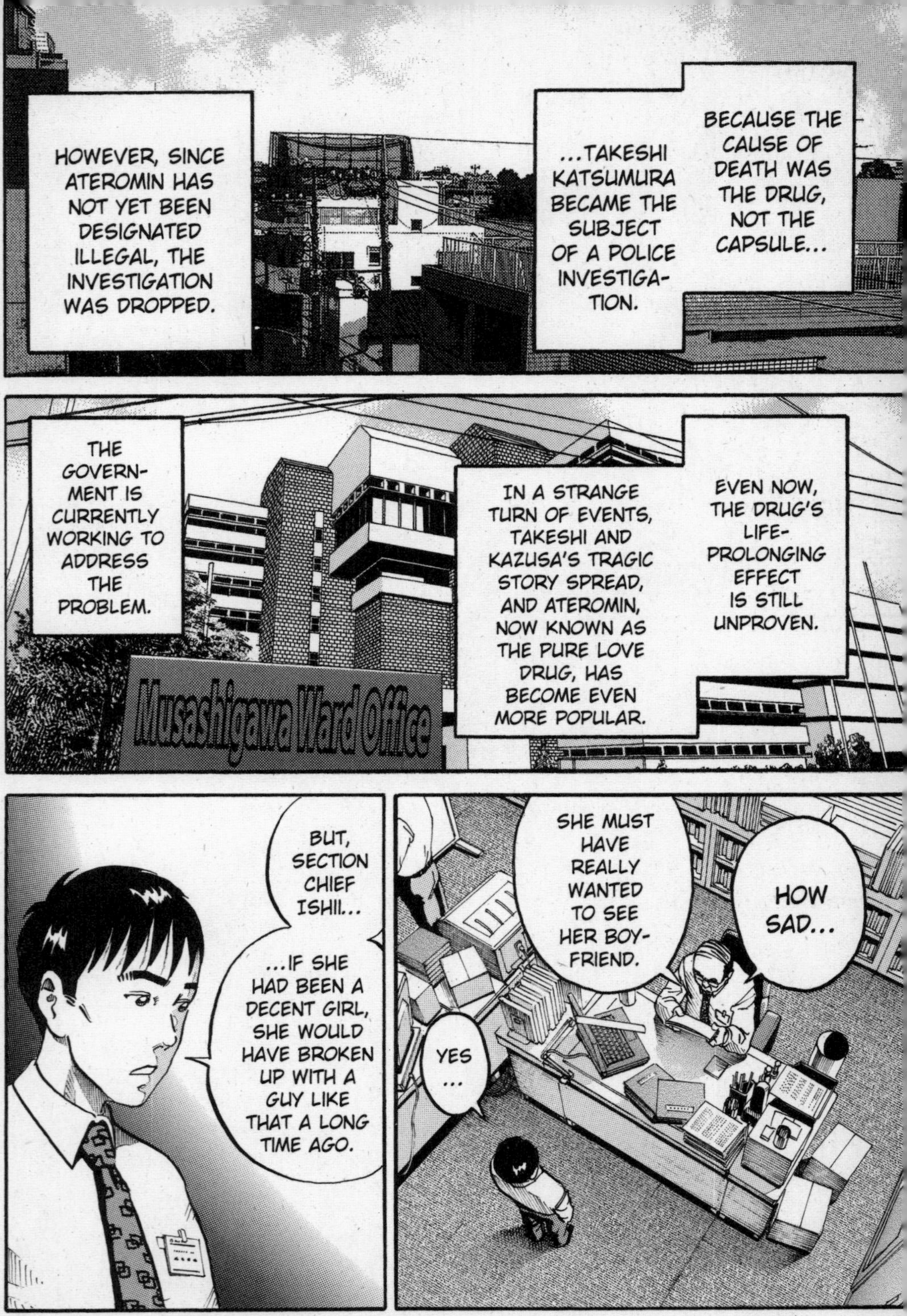
BECAUSE THE CAUSE OF DEATH WAS THE DRUG, NOT THE CAPSULE...
...TAKESHI KATSUMURA BECAME THE SUBJECT OF A POLICE INVESTIGATION.
HOWEVER, SINCE ATEROMIN HAS NOT YET BEEN DESIGNATED ILLEGAL, THE INVESTIGATION WAS DROPPED.
EVEN NOW, THE DRUG'S LIFE-PROLONGING EFFECT IS STILL UNPROVEN.
IN A STRANGE TURN OF EVENTS, TAKESHI AND KAZUSA'S TRAGIC STORY SPREAD, AND ATEROMIN, NOW KNOWN AS THE PURE LOVE DRUG, HAS BECOME EVEN MORE POPULAR.
THE GOVERNMENT IS CURRENTLY WORKING TO ADDRESS THE PROBLEM.
Musashigawa Ward Office
HOW SAD...
SHE MUST HAVE REALLY WANTED TO SEE HER BOYFRIEND.
YES...
BUT, SECTION CHIEF ISHII...
...IF SHE HAD BEEN A DECENT GIRL, SHE WOULD HAVE BROKEN UP WITH A GUY LIKE THAT A LONG TIME AGO.

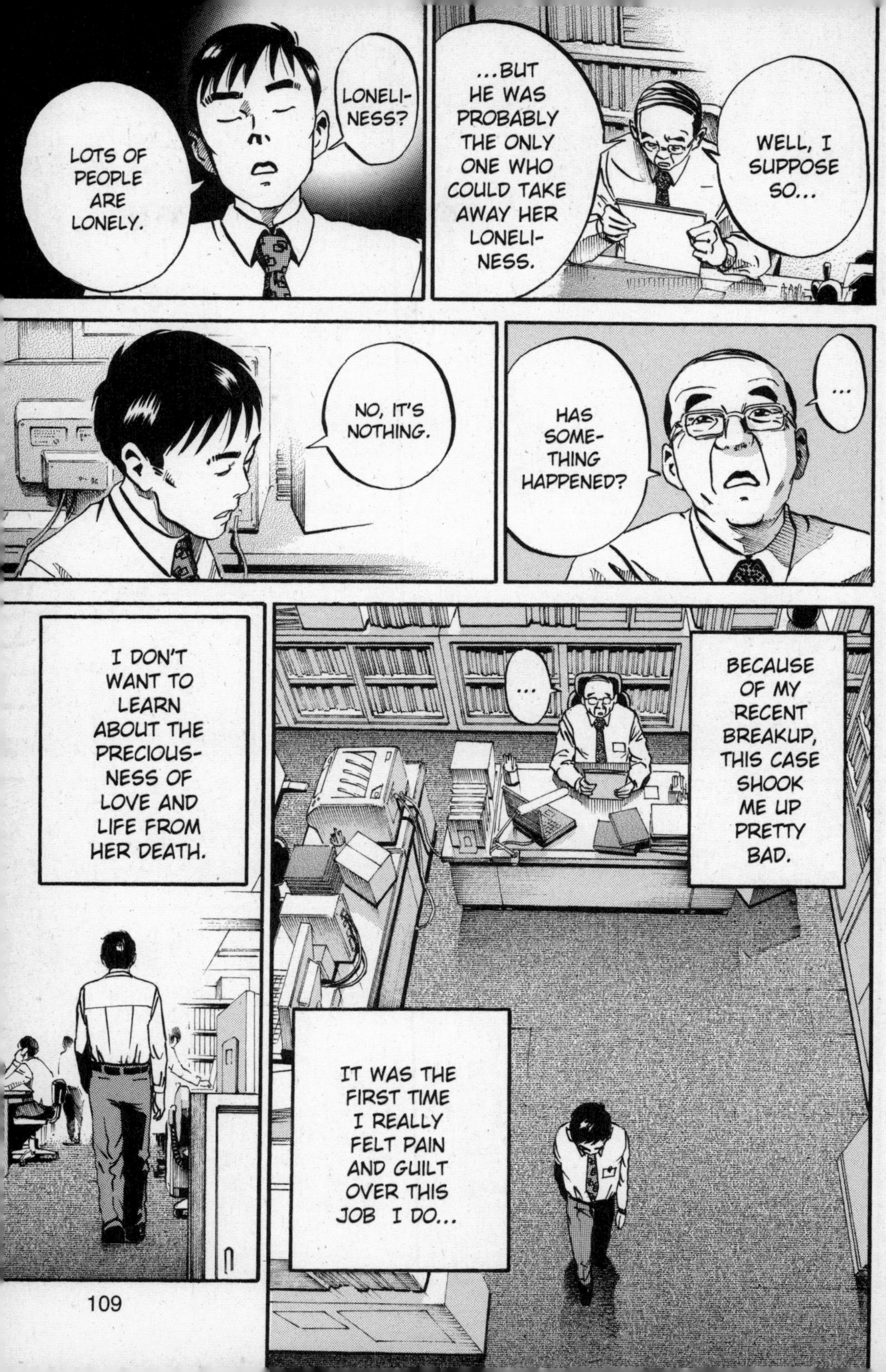
WELL, I SUPPOSE SO...
...BUT HE WAS PROBABLY THE ONLY ONE WHO COULD TAKE AWAY HER LONELINESS.
LONELINESS?
LOTS OF PEOPLE ARE LONELY.
...
HAS SOMETHING HAPPENED?
NO, IT'S NOTHING.
BECAUSE OF MY RECENT BREAKUP, THIS CASE SHOOK ME UP PRETTY BAD.
...
IT WAS THE FIRST TIME I REALLY FELT PAIN AND GUILT OVER THIS JOB I DO...
I DON'T WANT TO LEARN ABOUT THE PRECIOUSNESS OF LOVE AND LIFE FROM HER DEATH.

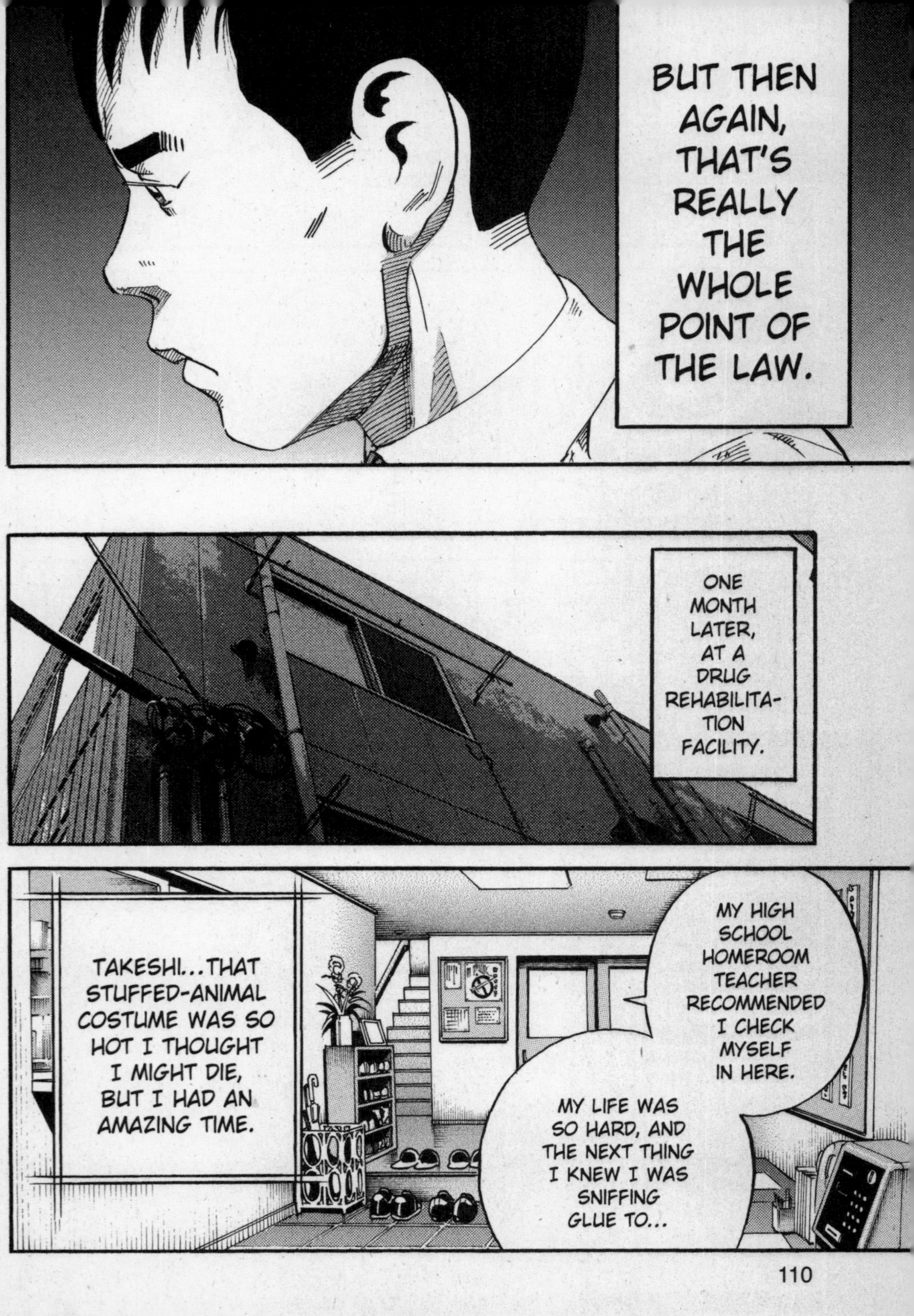
BUT THEN AGAIN, THAT'S REALLY THE WHOLE POINT OF THE LAW.
ONE MONTH LATER, AT A DRUG REHABILITATION FACILITY.
MY HIGH SCHOOL HOMEROOM TEACHER RECOMMENDED I CHECK MYSELF IN HERE.
MY LIFE WAS SO HARD, AND THE NEXT THING I KNEW I WAS SNIFFING GLUE TO...
TAKESHI...THAT STUFFED-ANIMAL COSTUME WAS SO HOT I THOUGHT I MIGHT DIE, BUT I HAD AN AMAZING TIME.

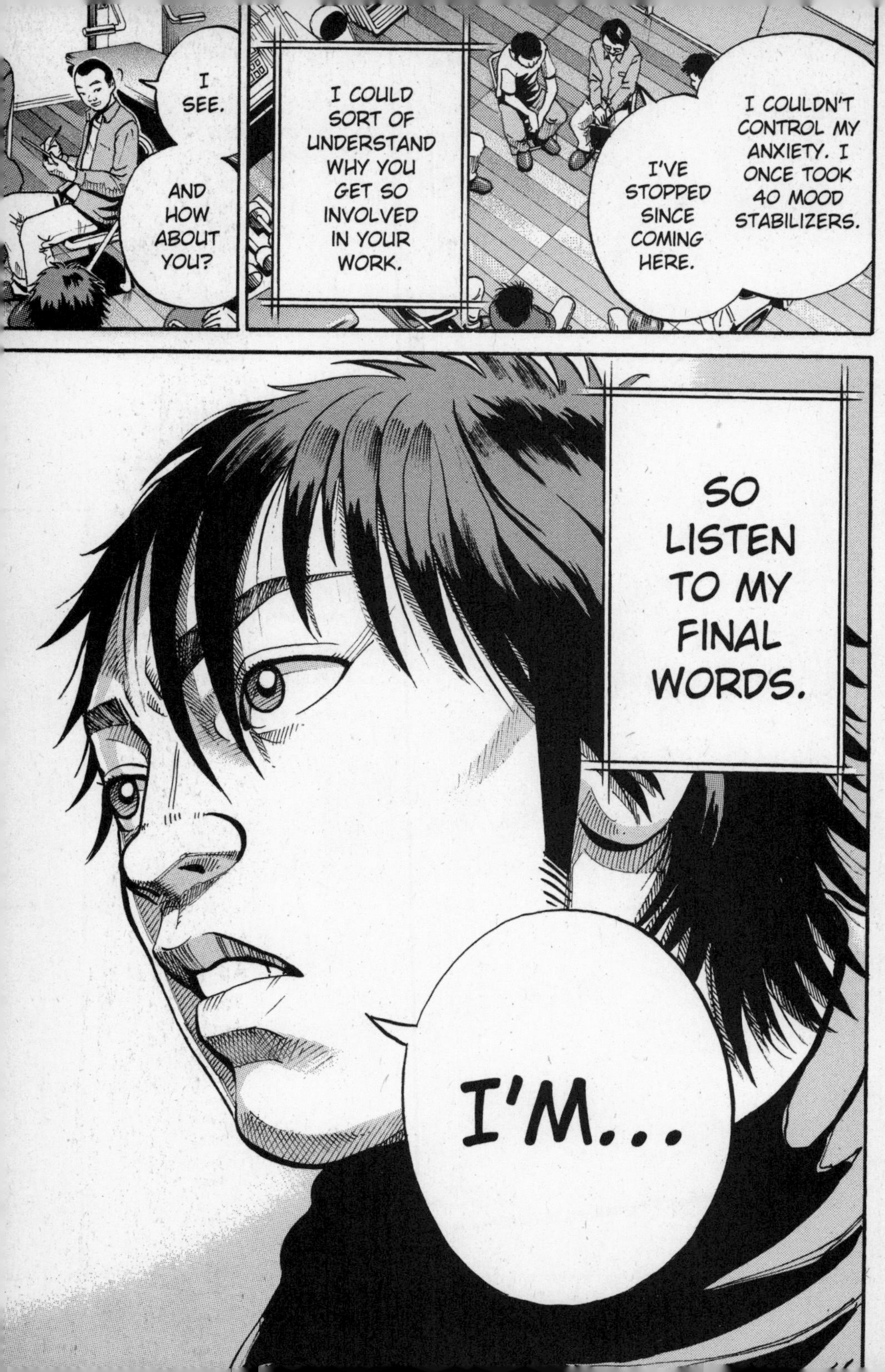
I COULDN'T CONTROL MY ANXIETY. I ONCE TOOK 40 MOOD STABILIZERS.
I'VE STOPPED SINCE COMING HERE.
I COULD SORT OF UNDERSTAND WHY YOU GET SO INVOLVED IN YOUR WORK.
I SEE.
AND HOW ABOUT YOU?
SO LISTEN TO MY FINAL WORDS.
I'M...

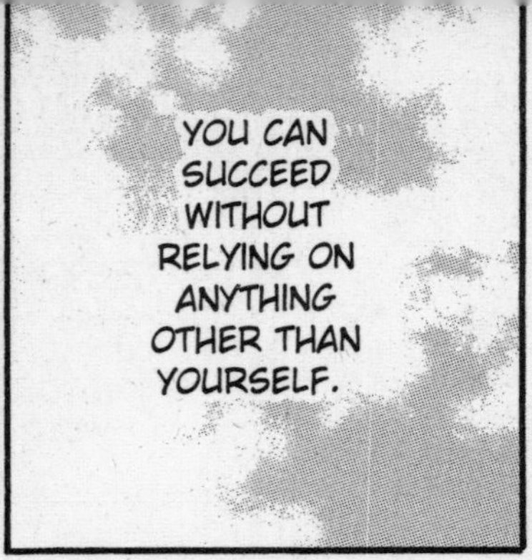
YOU CAN SUCCEED WITHOUT RELYING ON ANYTHING OTHER THAN YOURSELF.

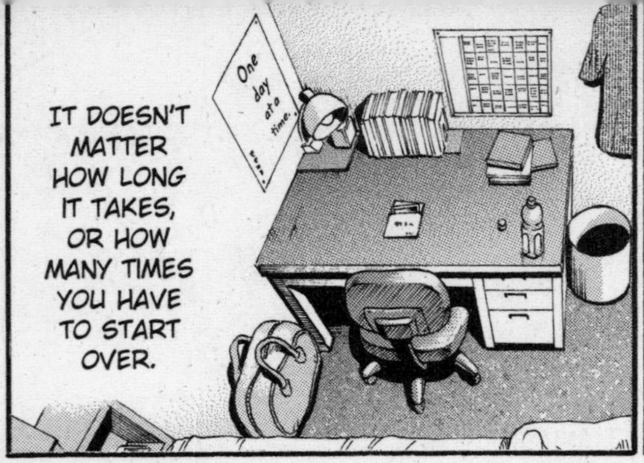
IT DOESN'T MATTER HOW LONG IT TAKES, OR HOW MANY TIMES YOU HAVE TO START OVER.
One day at a time.

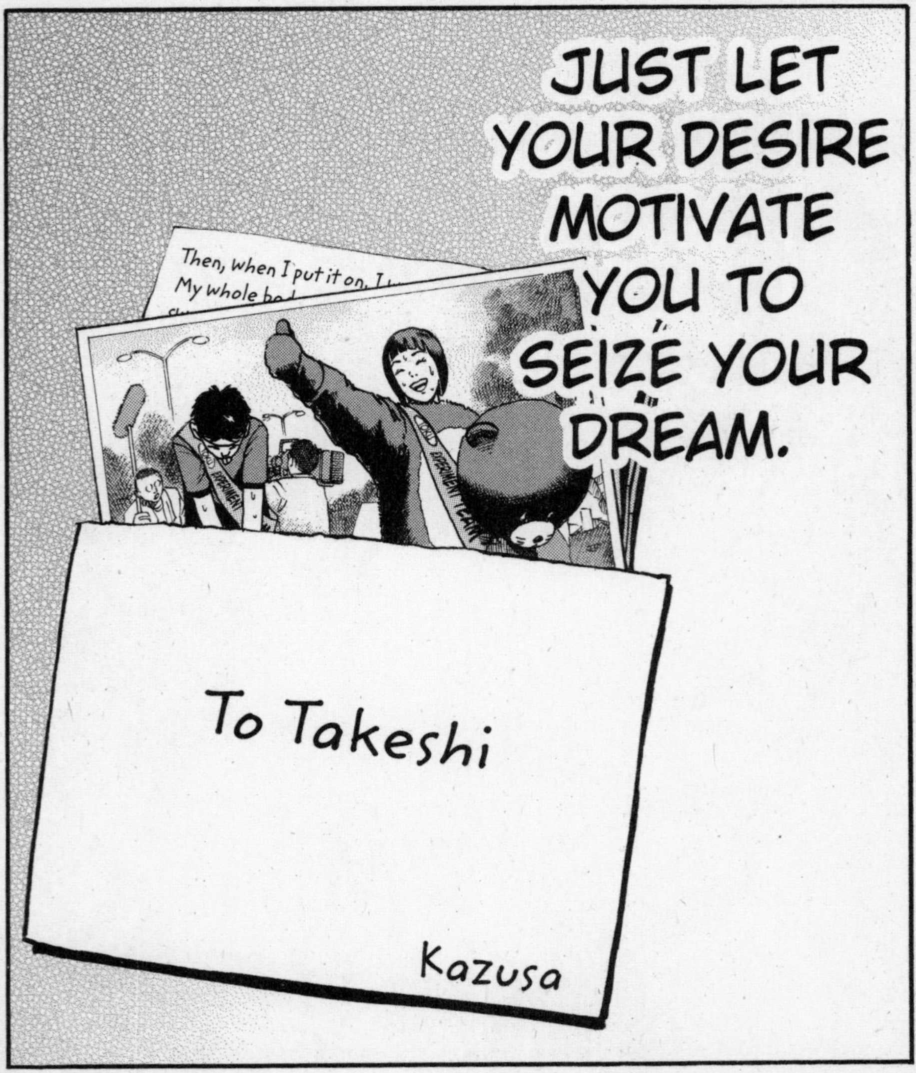
JUST LET YOUR DESIRE MOTIVATE YOU TO SEIZE YOUR DREAM.
Then, when I put it on,
To Takeshi
Kazusa

Episode 4 The Night He Left for War Act 1

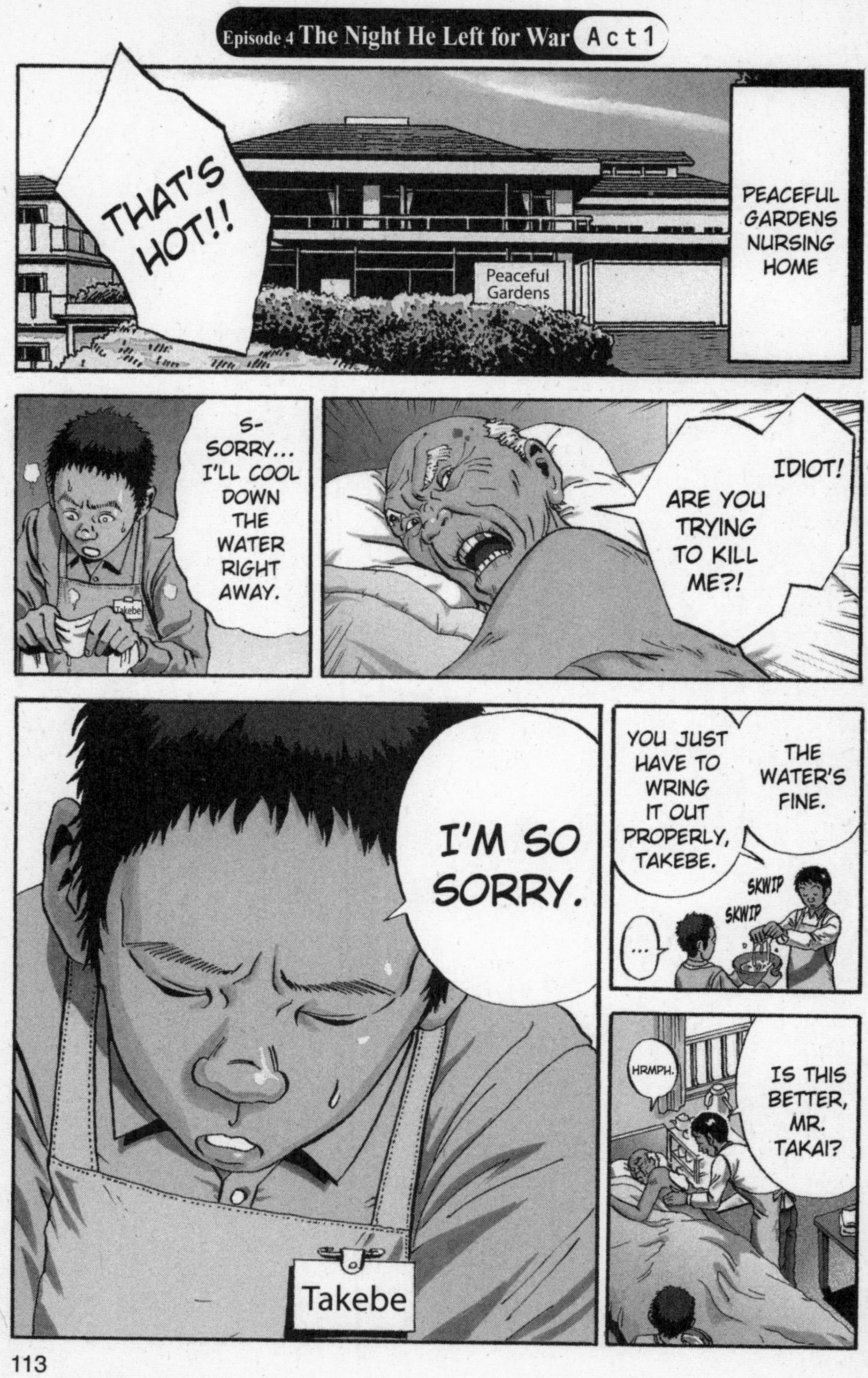
PEACEFUL GARDENS NURSING HOME
THAT'S HOT!!
Peaceful Gardens
IDIOT! ARE YOU TRYING TO KILL ME?!
S-SORRY... I'LL COOL DOWN THE WATER RIGHT AWAY.
Takebe
THE WATER'S FINE.
YOU JUST HAVE TO WRING IT OUT PROPERLY, TAKEBE.
SKWIP
SKWIP
...
IS THIS BETTER, MR. TAKAI?
HRMPH.
I'M SO SORRY.
Takebe

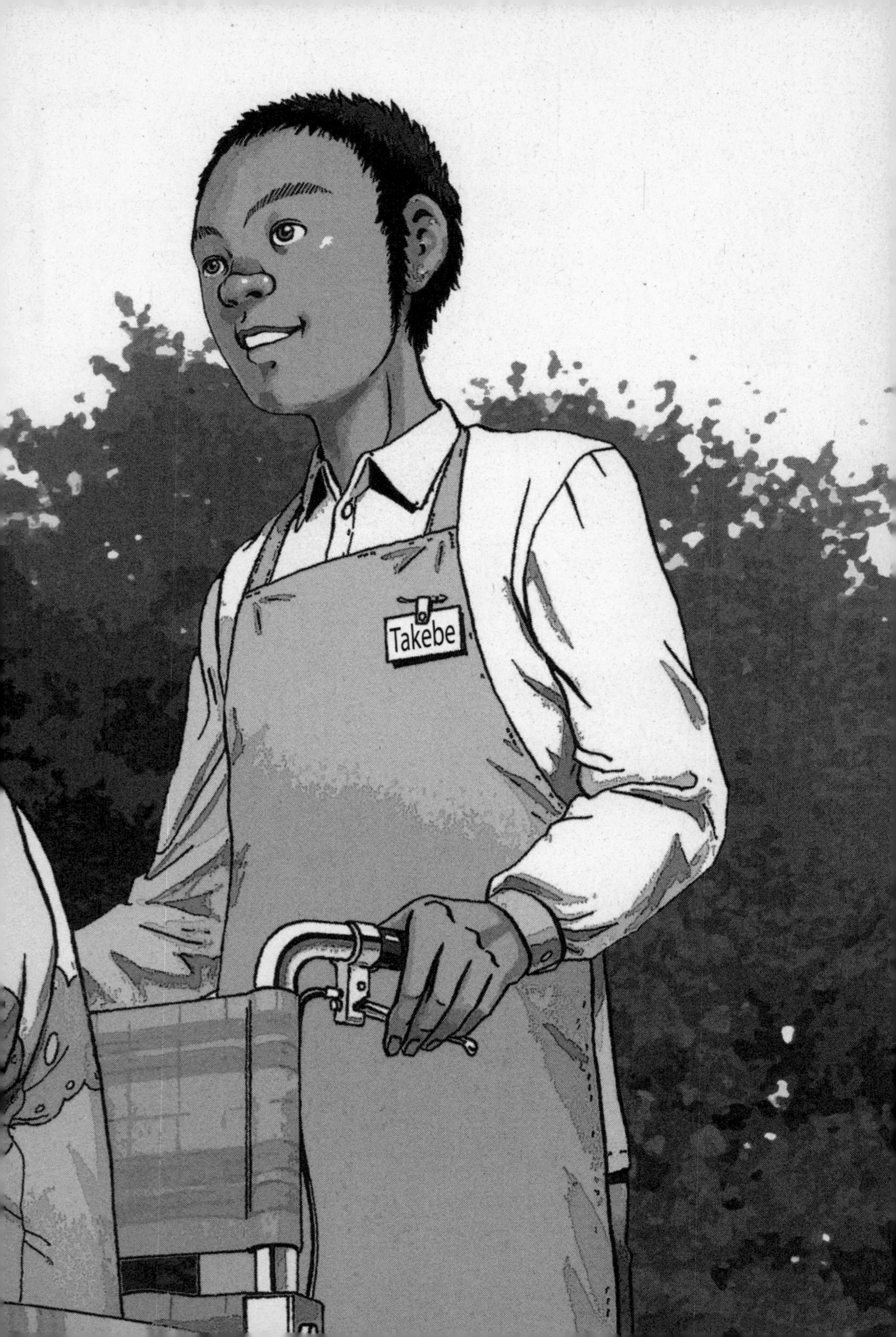
Takebe

Episode 4 The Night He Left for War Act 1

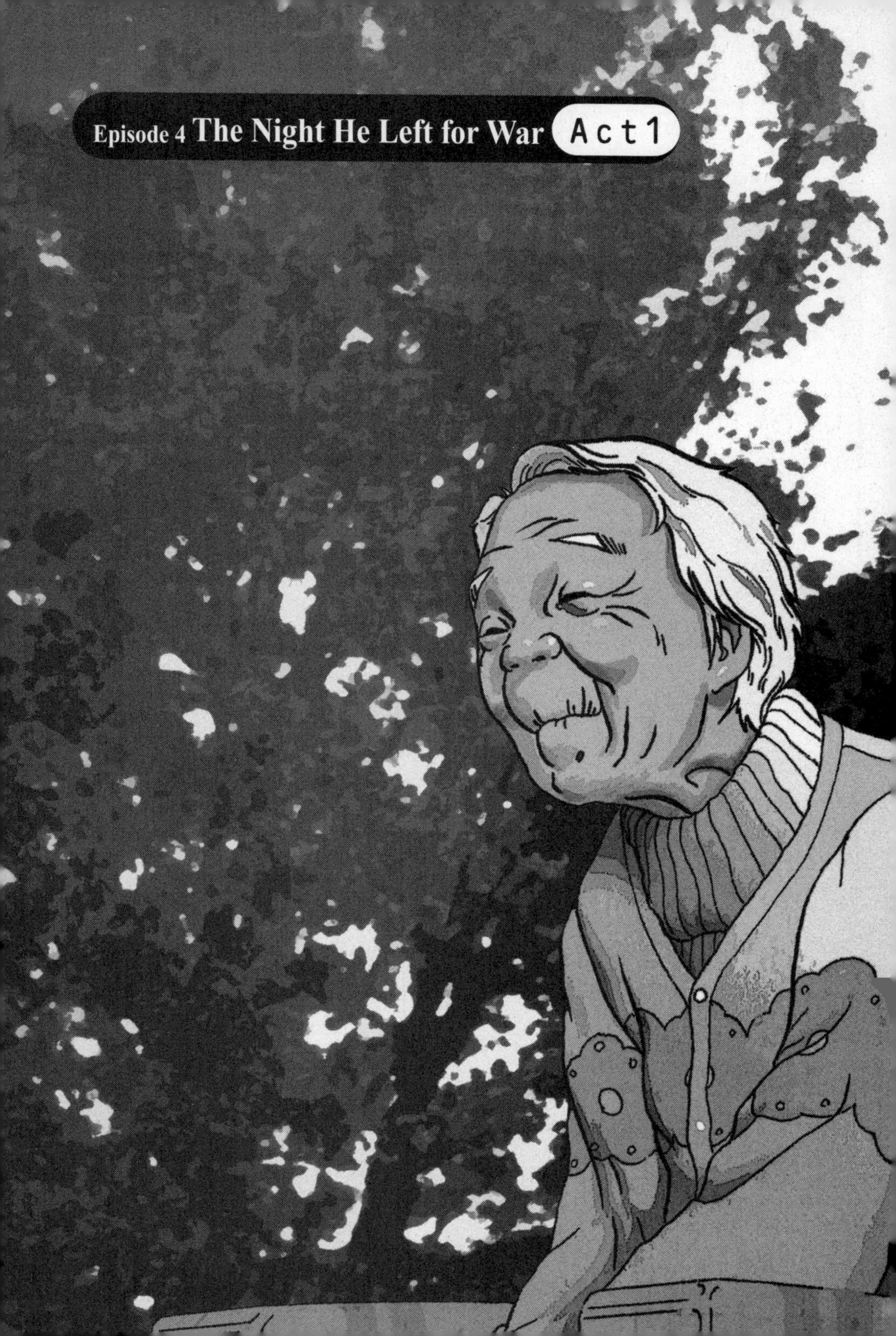

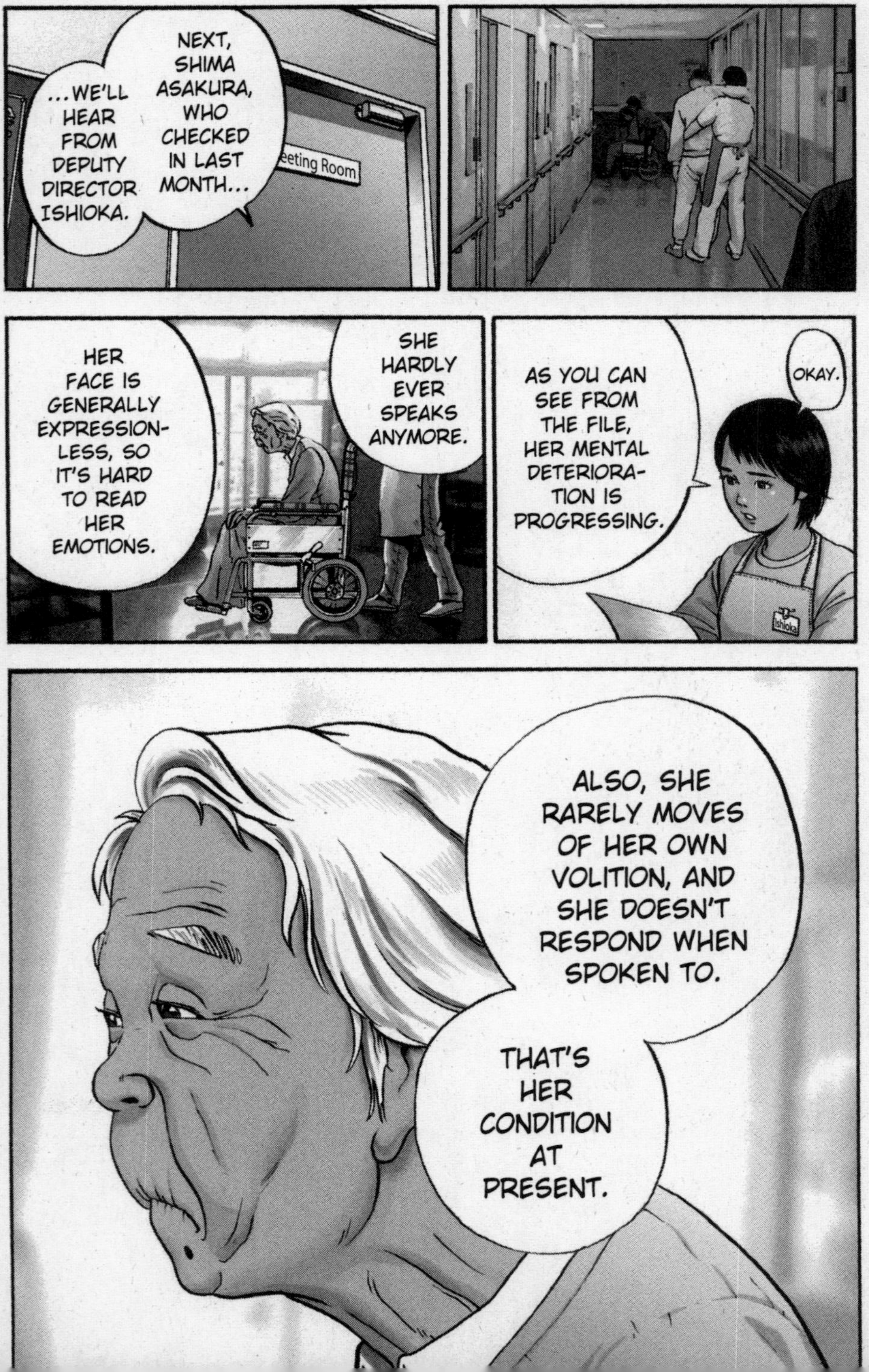
NEXT, SHIMA ASAKURA, WHO CHECKED IN LAST MONTH...
...WE'LL HEAR FROM DEPUTY DIRECTOR ISHIOKA.
eeting Room
OKAY.
AS YOU CAN SEE FROM THE FILE, HER MENTAL DETERIORATION IS PROGRESSING.
Ishioka
SHE HARDLY EVER SPEAKS ANYMORE.
HER FACE IS GENERALLY EXPRESSIONLESS, SO IT'S HARD TO READ HER EMOTIONS.
ALSO, SHE RARELY MOVES OF HER OWN VOLITION, AND SHE DOESN'T RESPOND WHEN SPOKEN TO.
THAT'S HER CONDITION AT PRESENT.

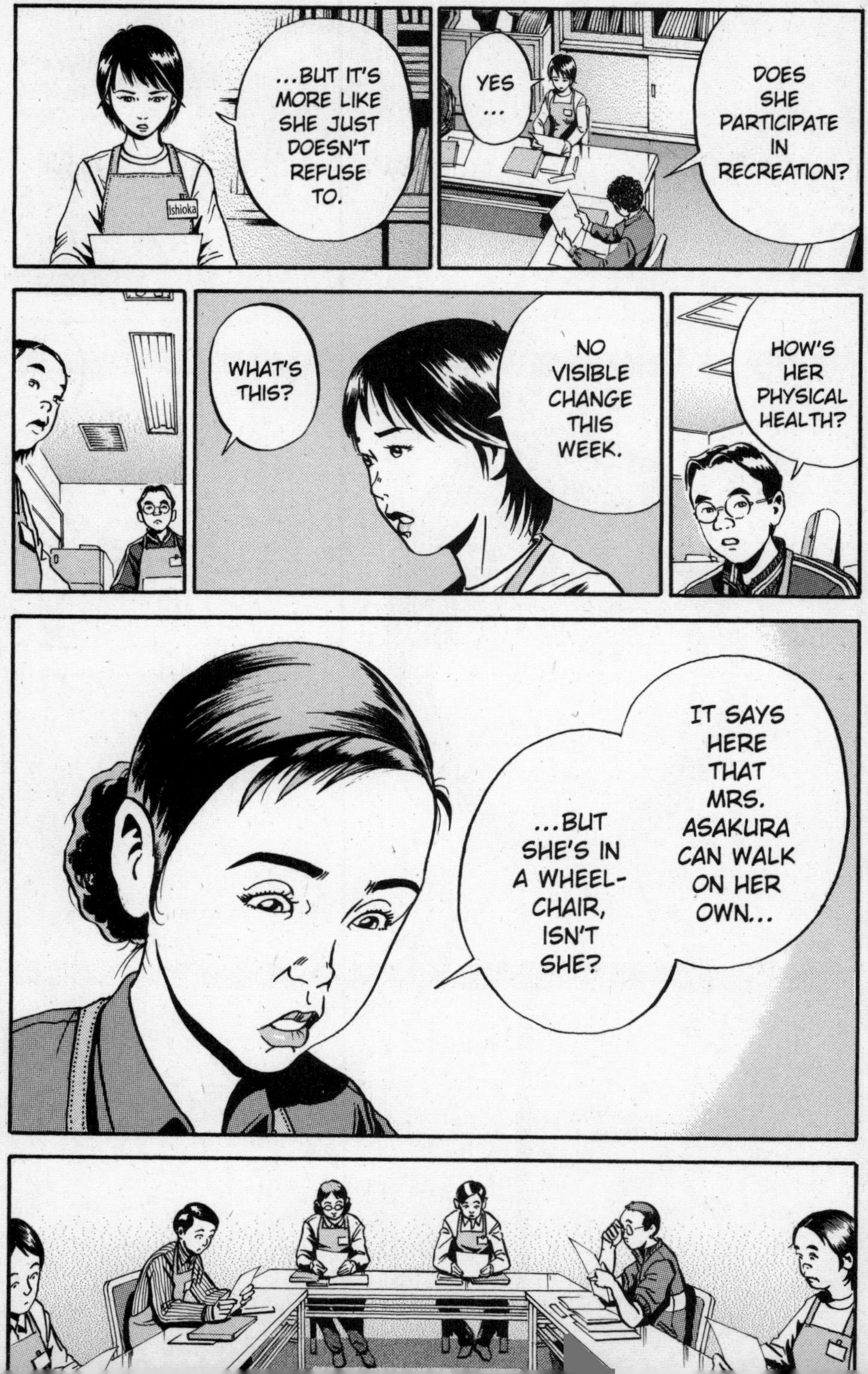
DOES SHE PARTICIPATE IN RECREATION?
YES...
...BUT IT'S MORE LIKE SHE JUST DOESN'T REFUSE TO.
Ishioka
HOW'S HER PHYSICAL HEALTH?
NO VISIBLE CHANGE THIS WEEK.
WHAT'S THIS?
IT SAYS HERE THAT MRS. ASAKURA CAN WALK ON HER OWN...
...BUT SHE'S IN A WHEEL-CHAIR, ISN'T SHE?

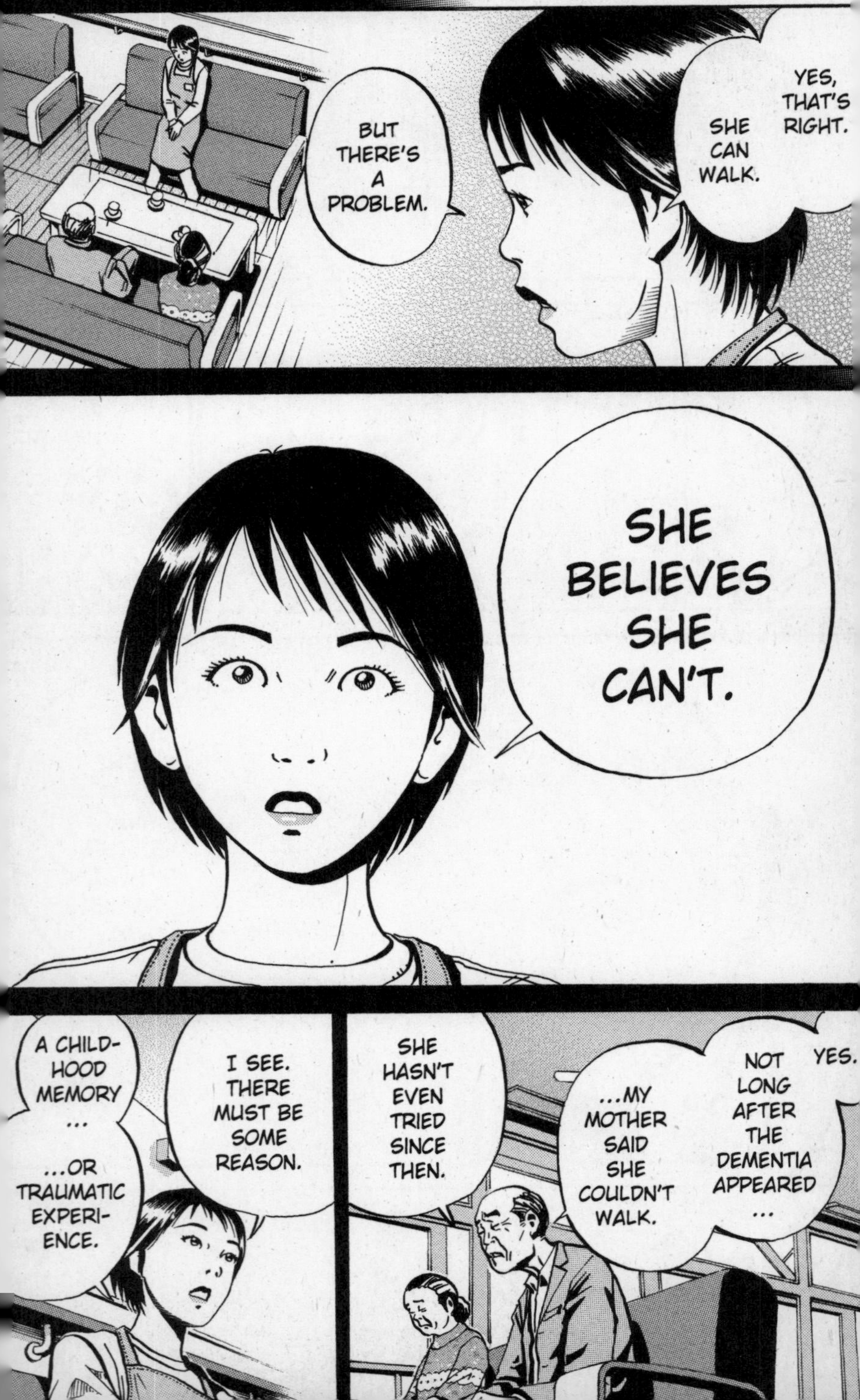
YES, THAT'S RIGHT.
SHE CAN WALK.
BUT THERE'S A PROBLEM.
SHE BELIEVES SHE CAN'T.
YES.
NOT LONG AFTER THE DEMENTIA APPEARED...
...MY MOTHER SAID SHE COULDN'T WALK.
SHE HASN'T EVEN TRIED SINCE THEN.
I SEE. THERE MUST BE SOME REASON.
A CHILDHOOD MEMORY...
...OR TRAUMATIC EXPERIENCE.

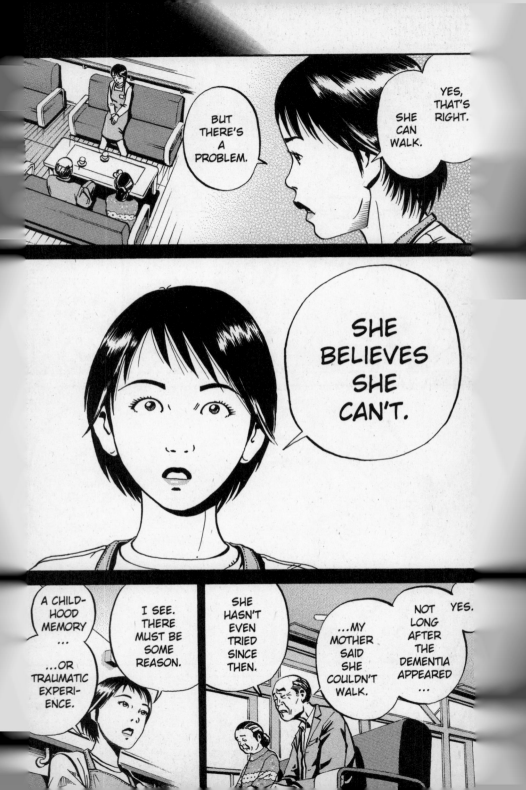

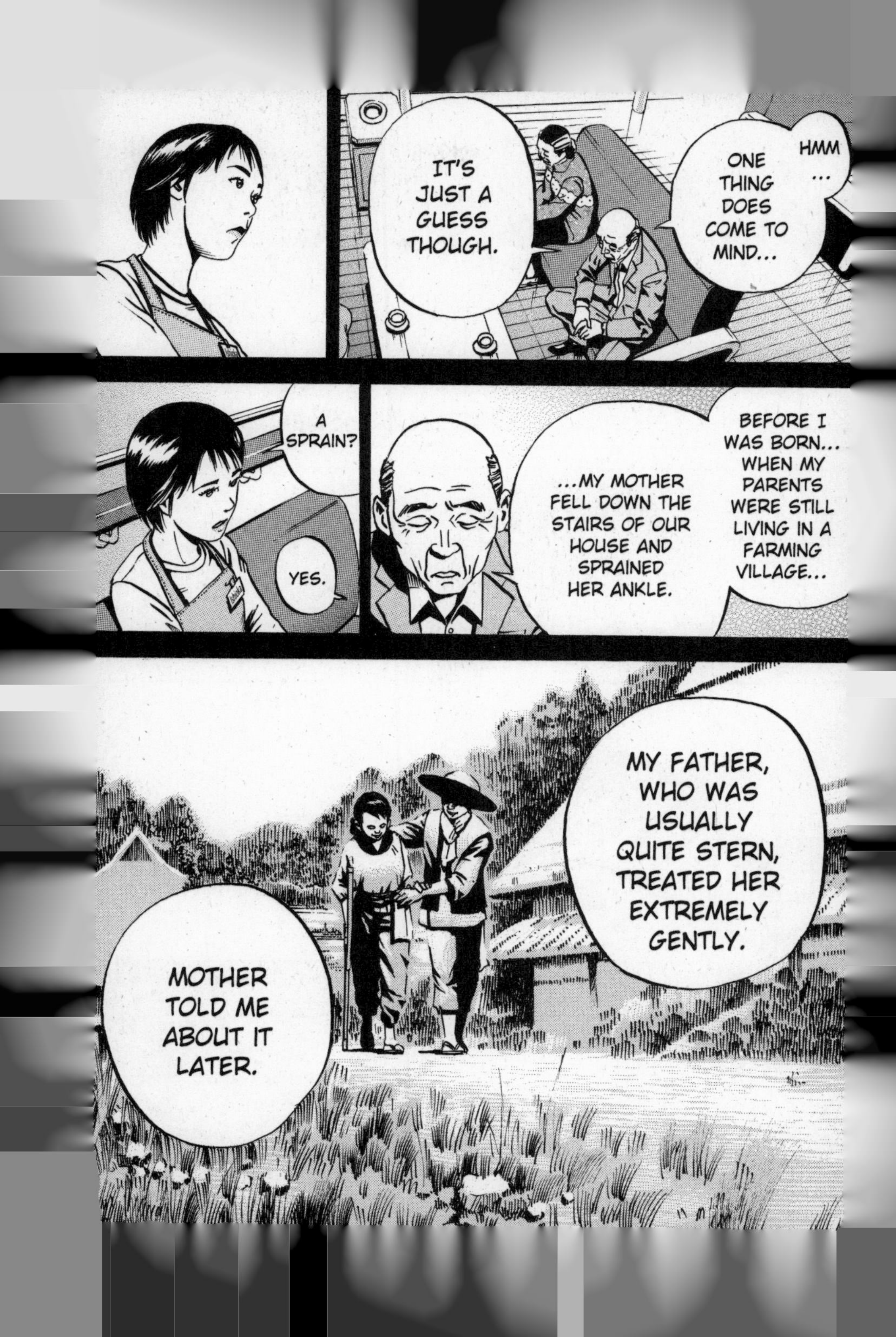
HMM ...
ONE THING DOES COME TO MIND...
IT'S JUST A GUESS THOUGH.
BEFORE I WAS BORN... WHEN MY PARENTS WERE STILL LIVING IN A FARMING VILLAGE...
...MY MOTHER FELL DOWN THE STAIRS OF OUR HOUSE AND SPRAINED HER ANKLE.
A SPRAIN?
YES.
MY FATHER, WHO WAS USUALLY QUITE STERN, TREATED HER EXTREMELY GENTLY.
MOTHER TOLD ME ABOUT IT LATER.

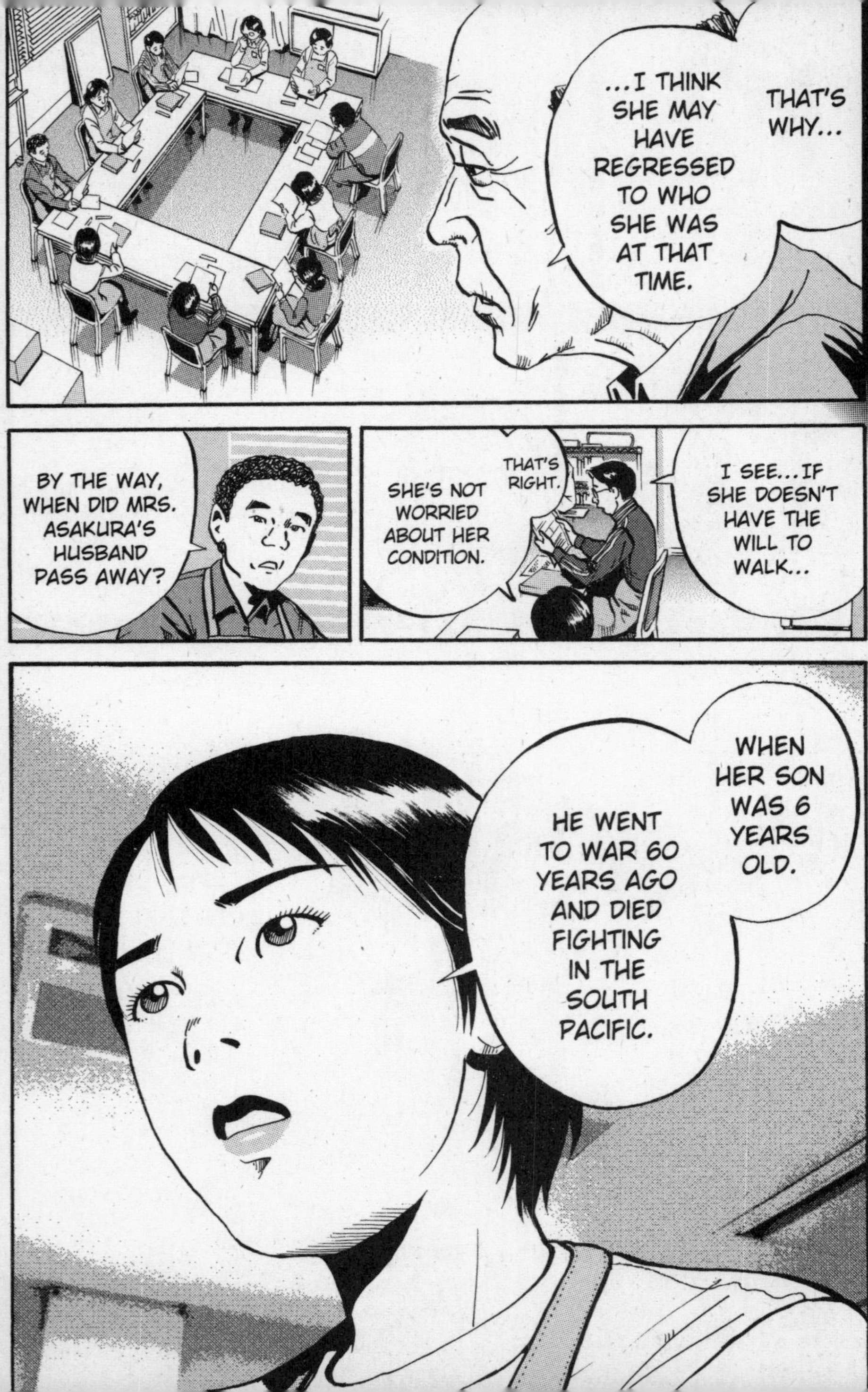
THAT'S WHY...
...I THINK SHE MAY HAVE REGRESSED TO WHO SHE WAS AT THAT TIME.
I SEE...IF SHE DOESN'T HAVE THE WILL TO WALK...
THAT'S RIGHT.
SHE'S NOT WORRIED ABOUT HER CONDITION.
BY THE WAY, WHEN DID MRS. ASAKURA'S HUSBAND PASS AWAY?
WHEN HER SON WAS 6 YEARS OLD.
HE WENT TO WAR 60 YEARS AGO AND DIED FIGHTING IN THE SOUTH PACIFIC.

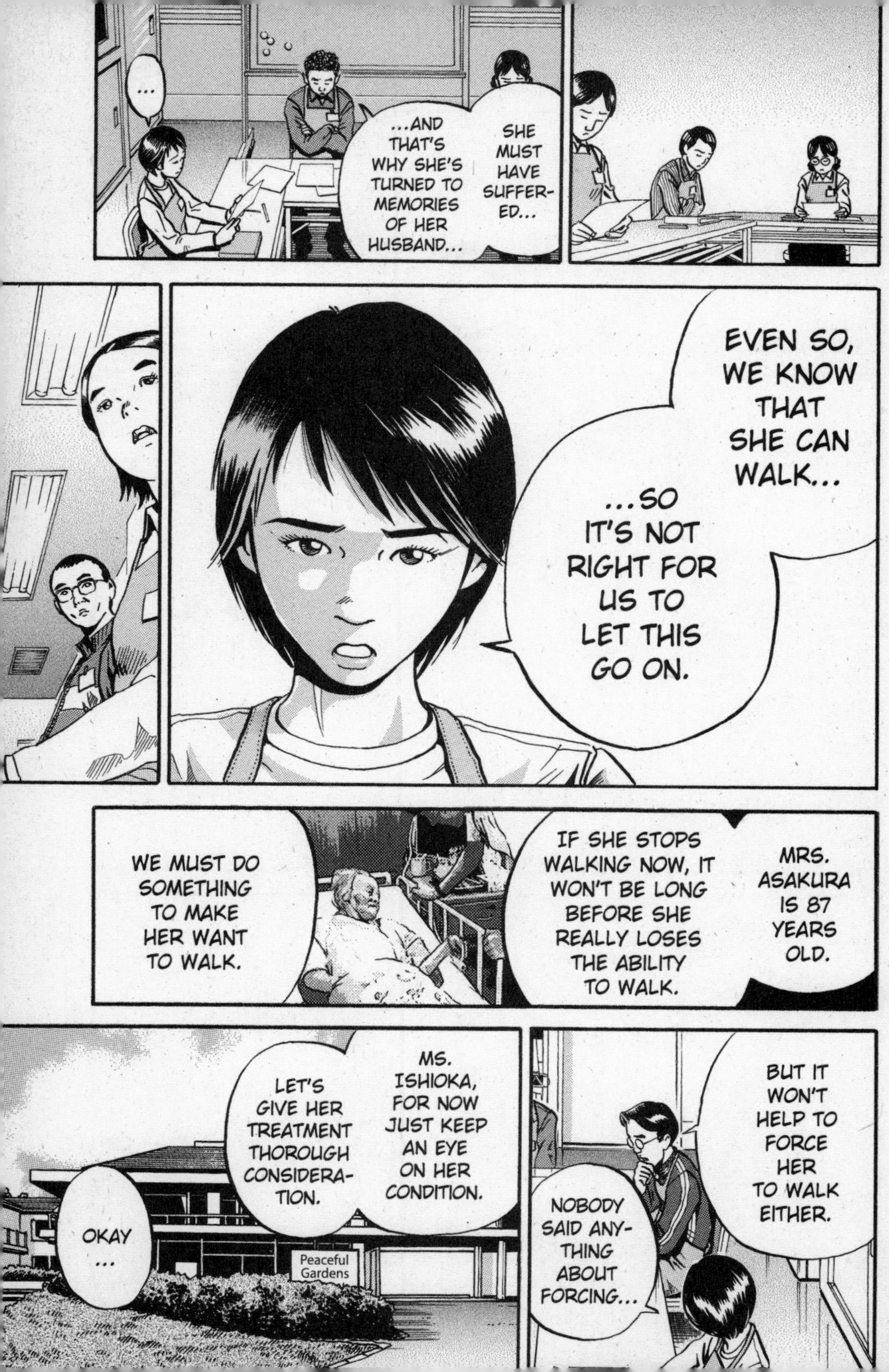
SHE MUST HAVE SUFFERED...
...AND THAT'S WHY SHE'S TURNED TO MEMORIES OF HER HUSBAND...
...
EVEN SO, WE KNOW THAT SHE CAN WALK...
...SO IT'S NOT RIGHT FOR US TO LET THIS GO ON.
MRS. ASAKURA IS 87 YEARS OLD.
IF SHE STOPS WALKING NOW, IT WON'T BE LONG BEFORE SHE REALLY LOSES THE ABILITY TO WALK.
WE MUST DO SOMETHING TO MAKE HER WANT TO WALK.
BUT IT WON'T HELP TO FORCE HER TO WALK EITHER.
NOBODY SAID ANYTHING ABOUT FORCING...
MS. ISHIOKA, FOR NOW JUST KEEP AN EYE ON HER CONDITION.
LET'S GIVE HER TREATMENT THOROUGH CONSIDERATION.
Peaceful Gardens
OKAY ...

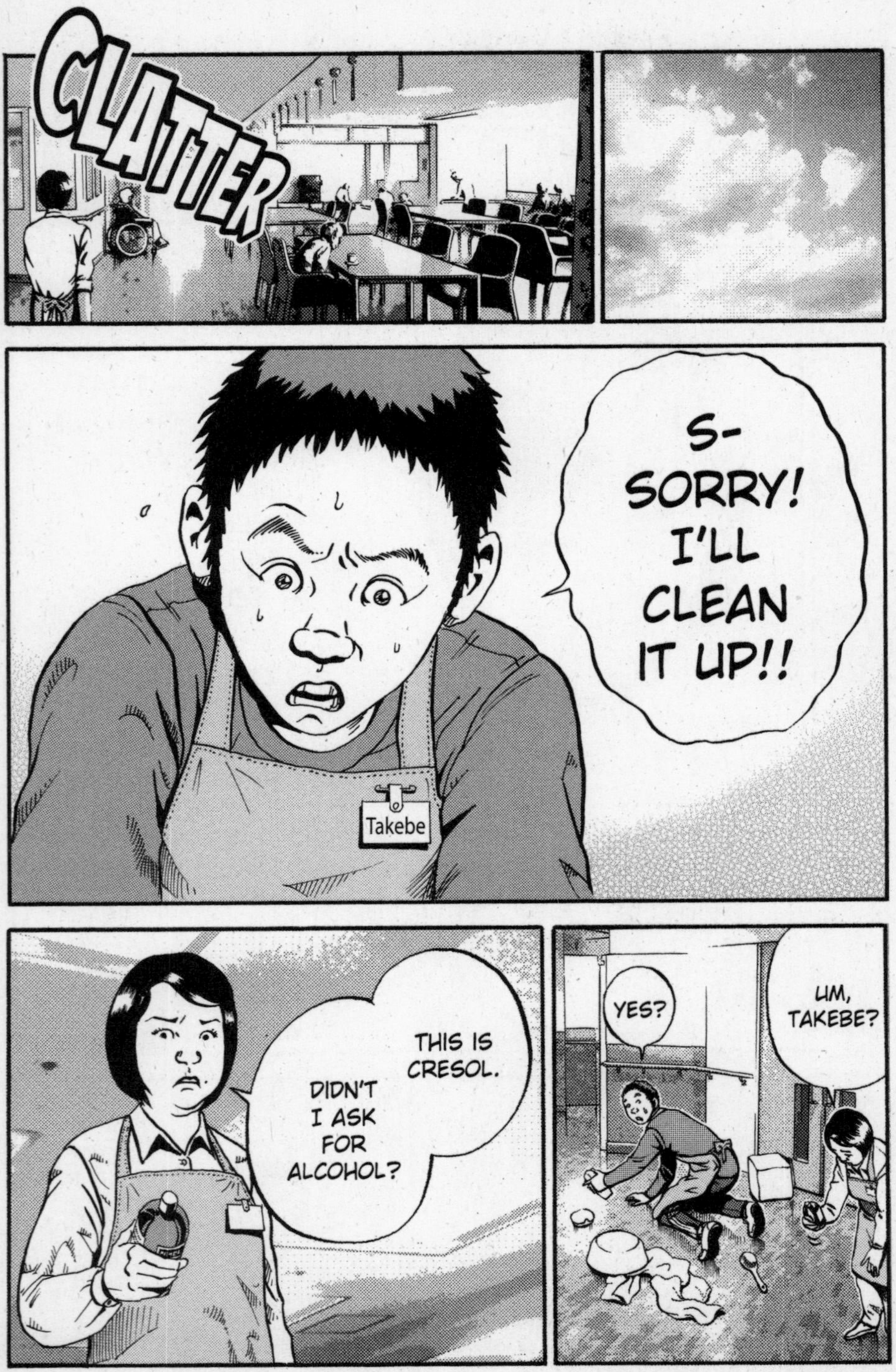
CLATTER
S-SORRY! I'LL CLEAN IT UP!!
Takebe
UM, TAKEBE?
YES?
THIS IS CRESOL.
DIDN'T I ASK FOR ALCOHOL?

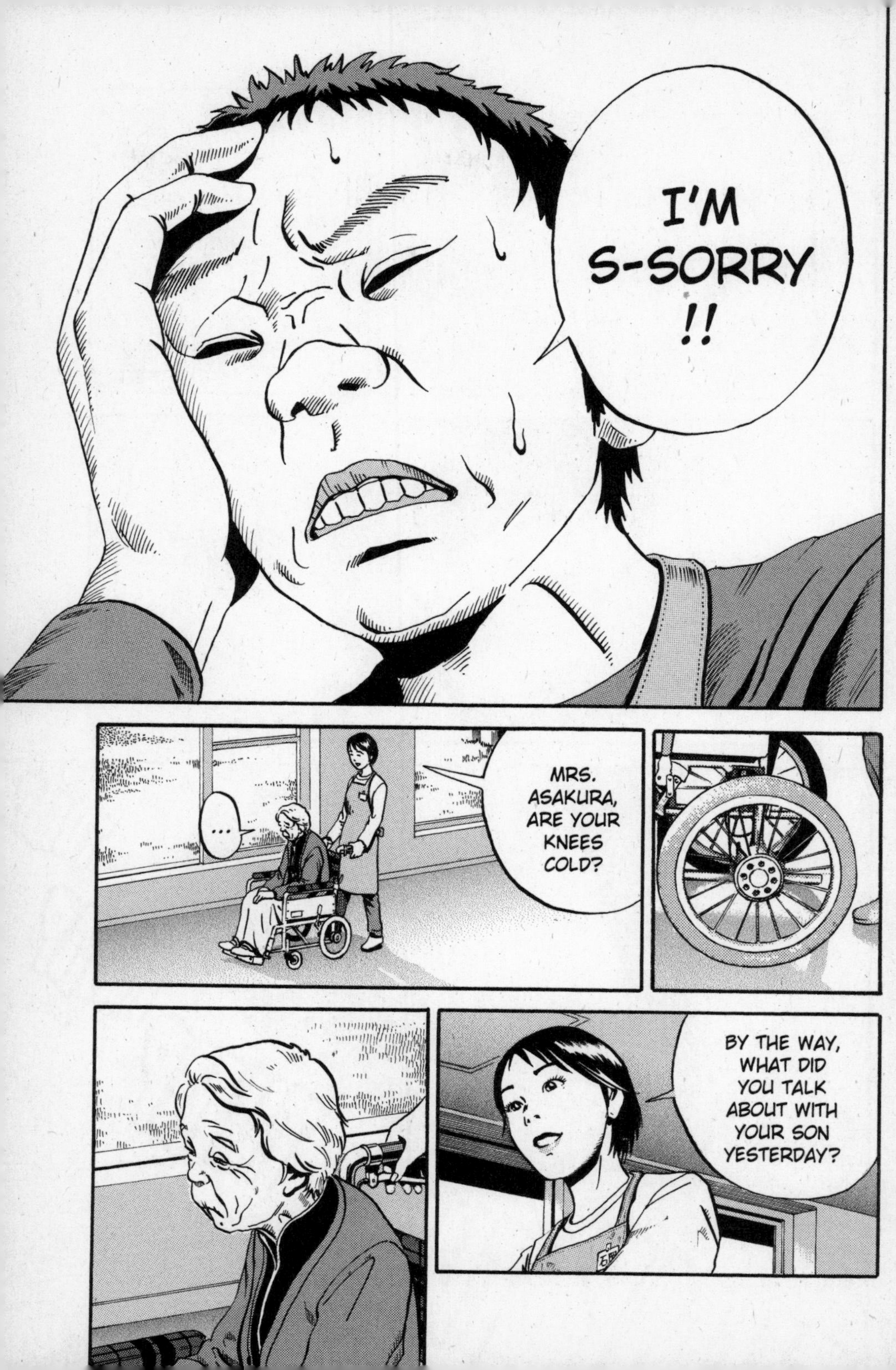
I'M S-SORRY !!
MRS. ASAKURA, ARE YOUR KNEES COLD?
...
BY THE WAY, WHAT DID YOU TALK ABOUT WITH YOUR SON YESTERDAY?

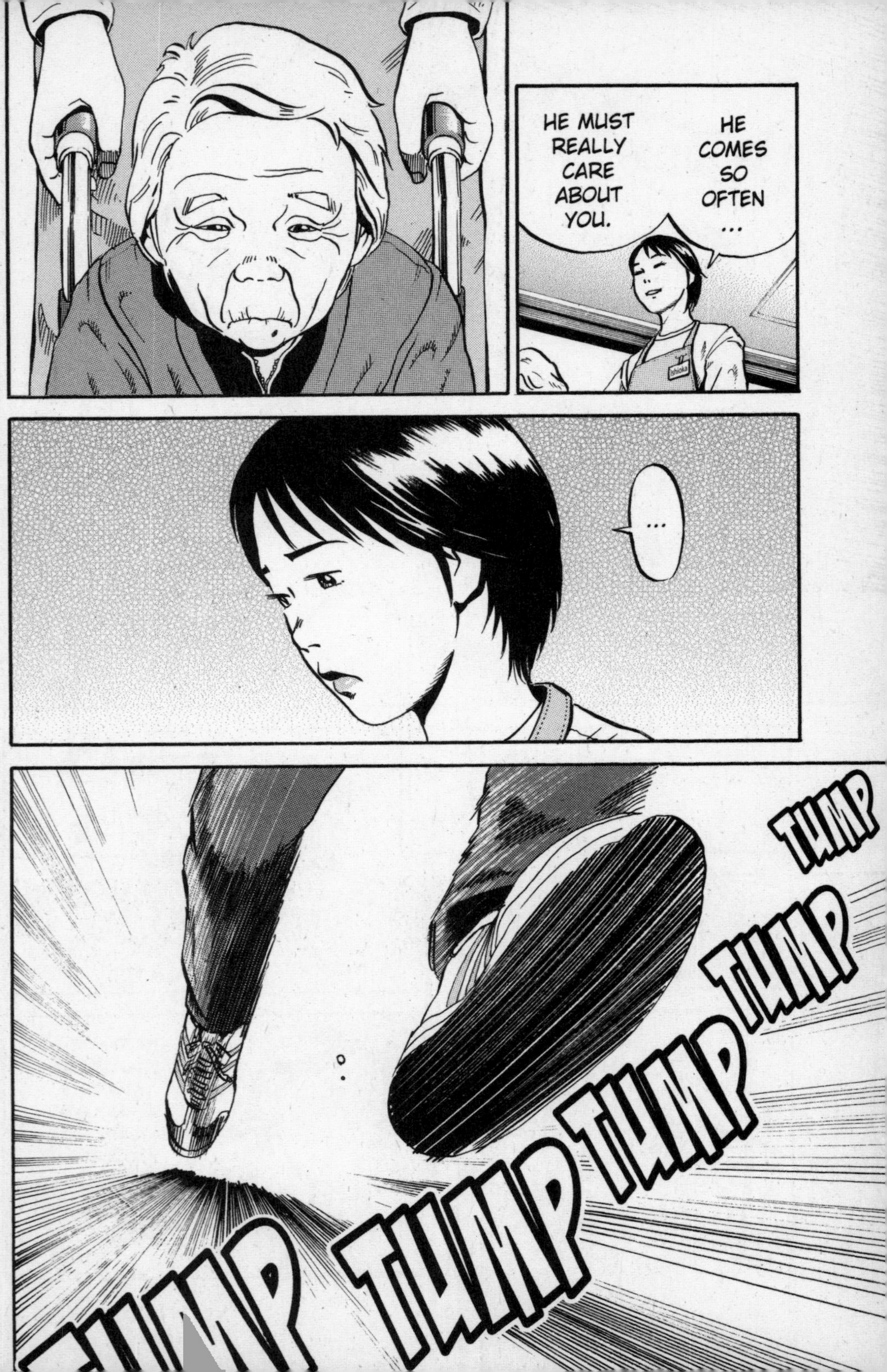
HE COMES SO OFTEN ...
HE MUST REALLY CARE ABOUT YOU.
...
TUMP
TUMP
TUMP
TUMP
TUMP

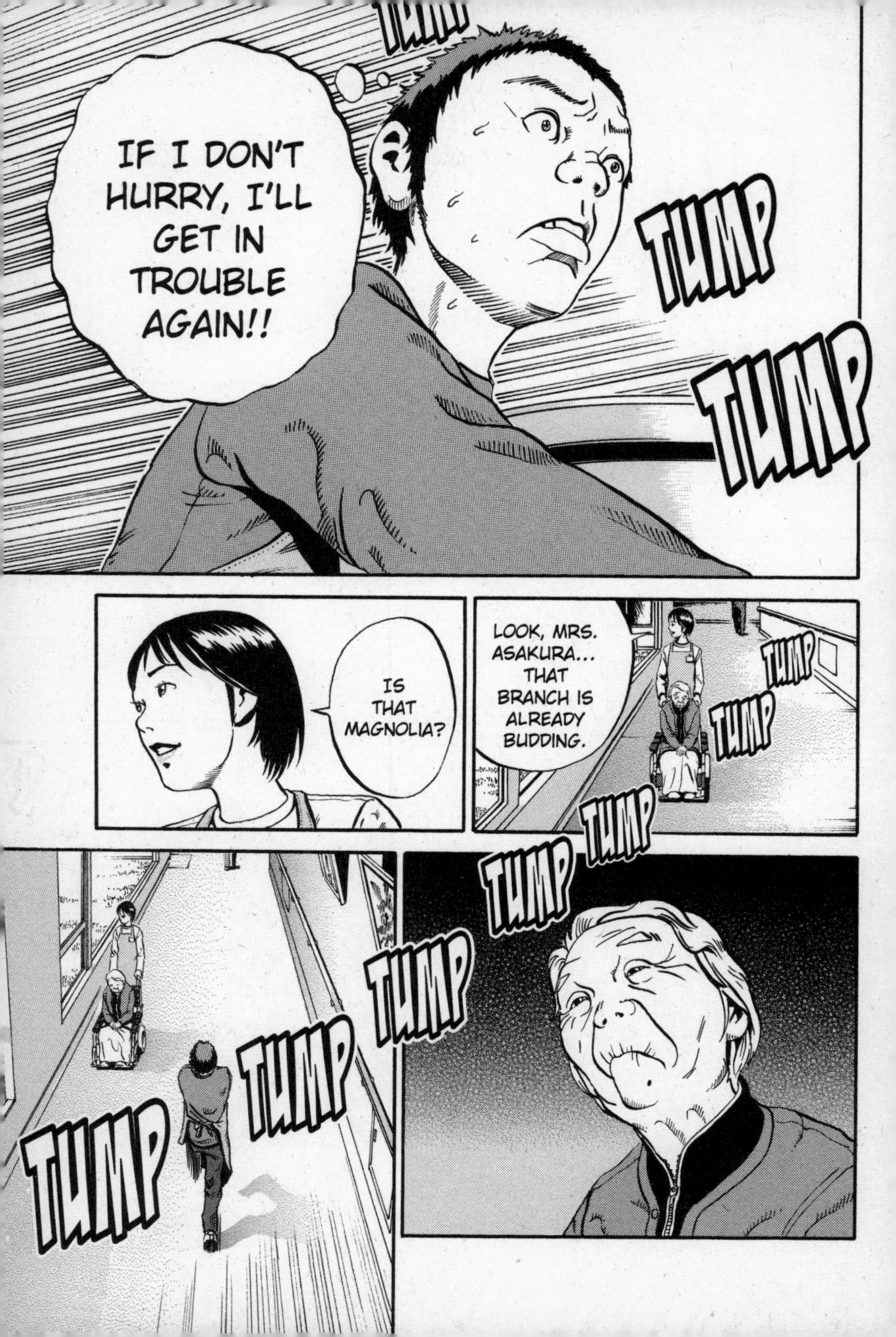
IF I DON'T HURRY, I'LL GET IN TROUBLE AGAIN!!
TUMP
TUMP
LOOK, MRS. ASAKURA... THAT BRANCH IS ALREADY BUDDING.
TUMP
TUMP
TUMP
IS THAT MAGNOLIA?
TUMP
TUMP
TUMP
TUMP

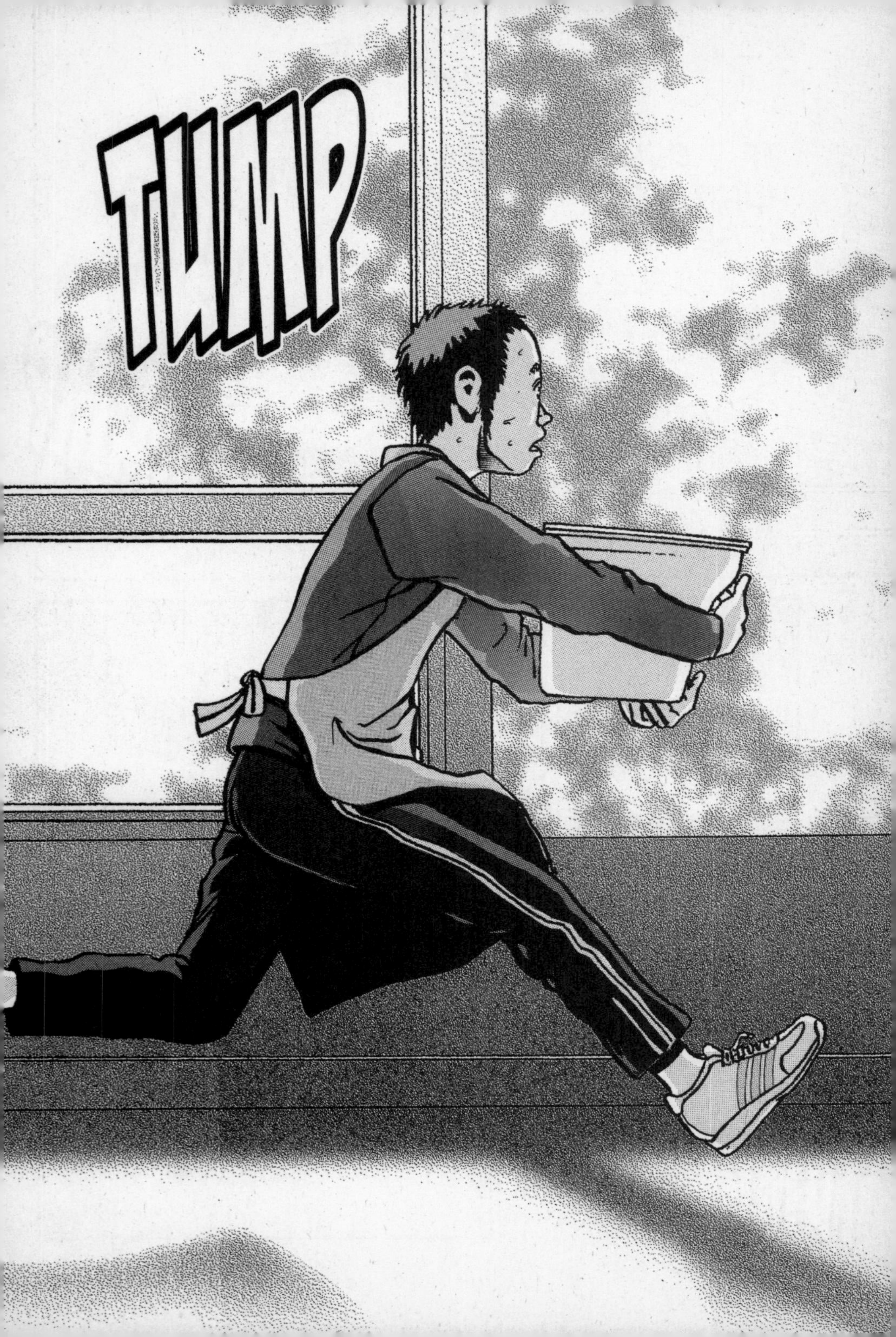
TUMP

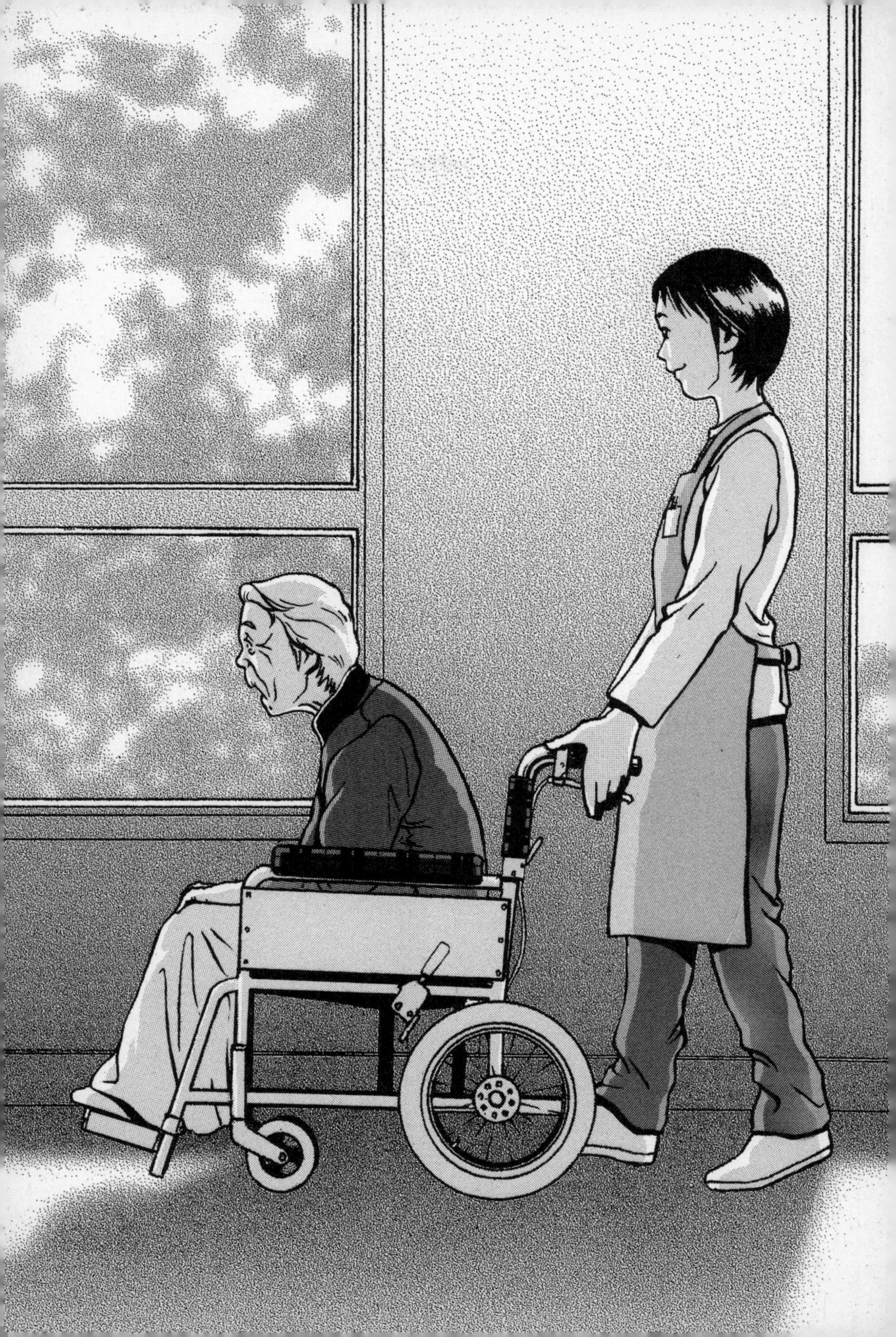

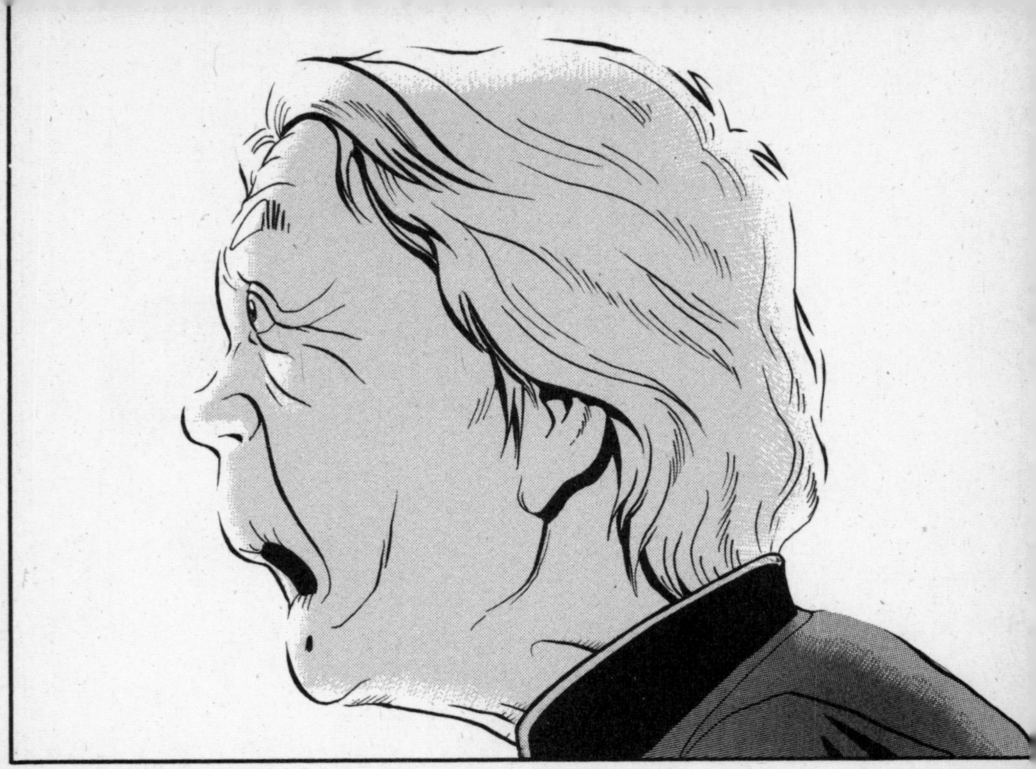
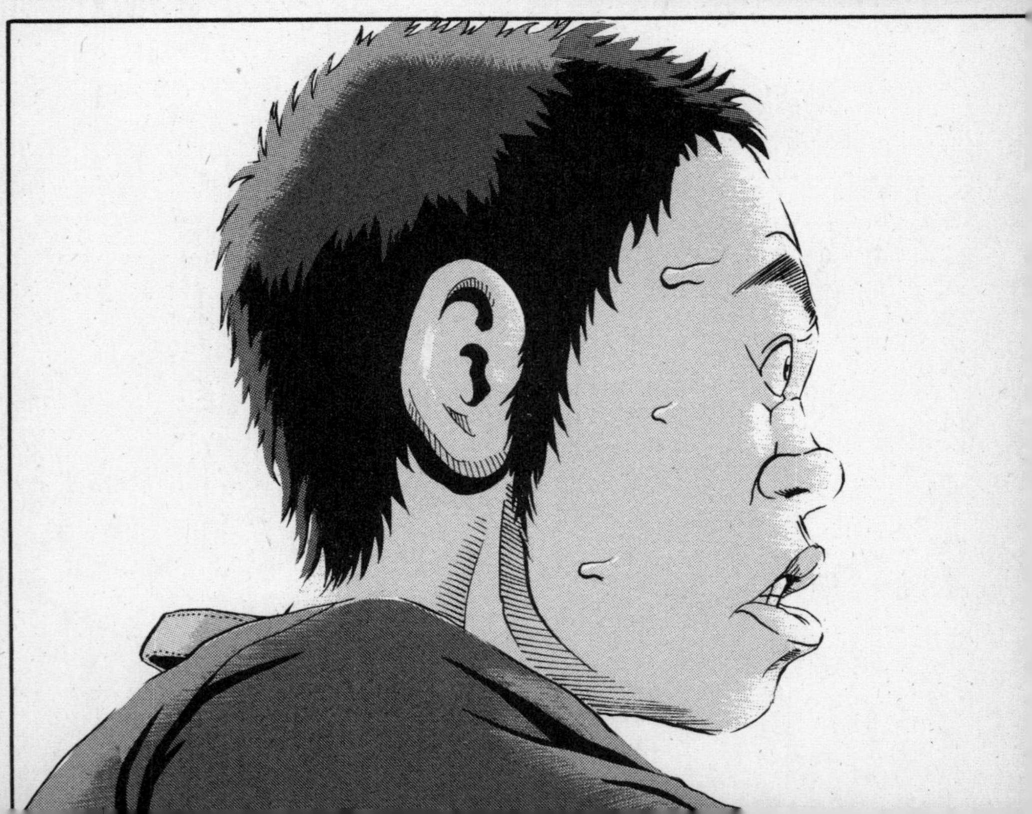

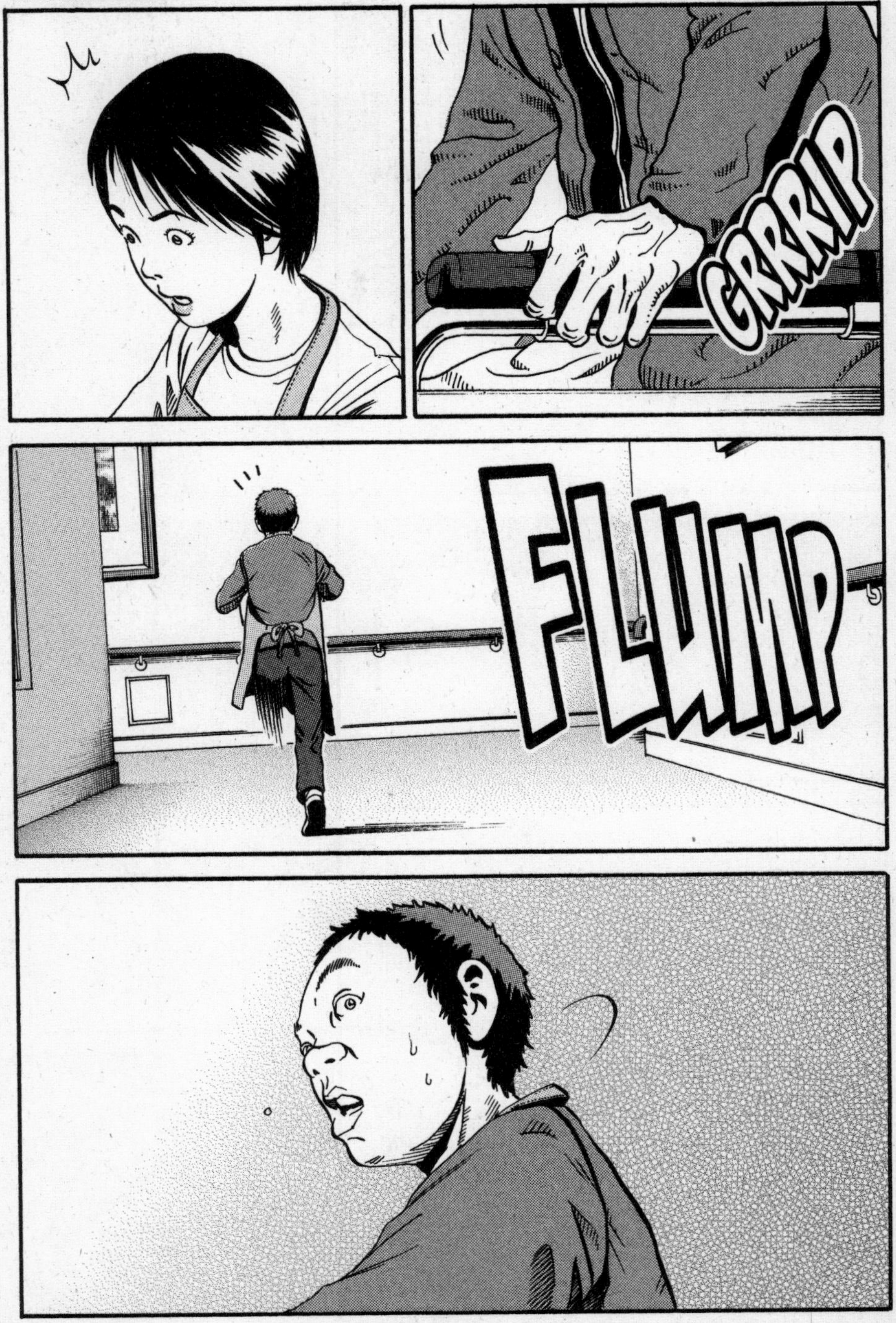
GRRRIP
FLUMP

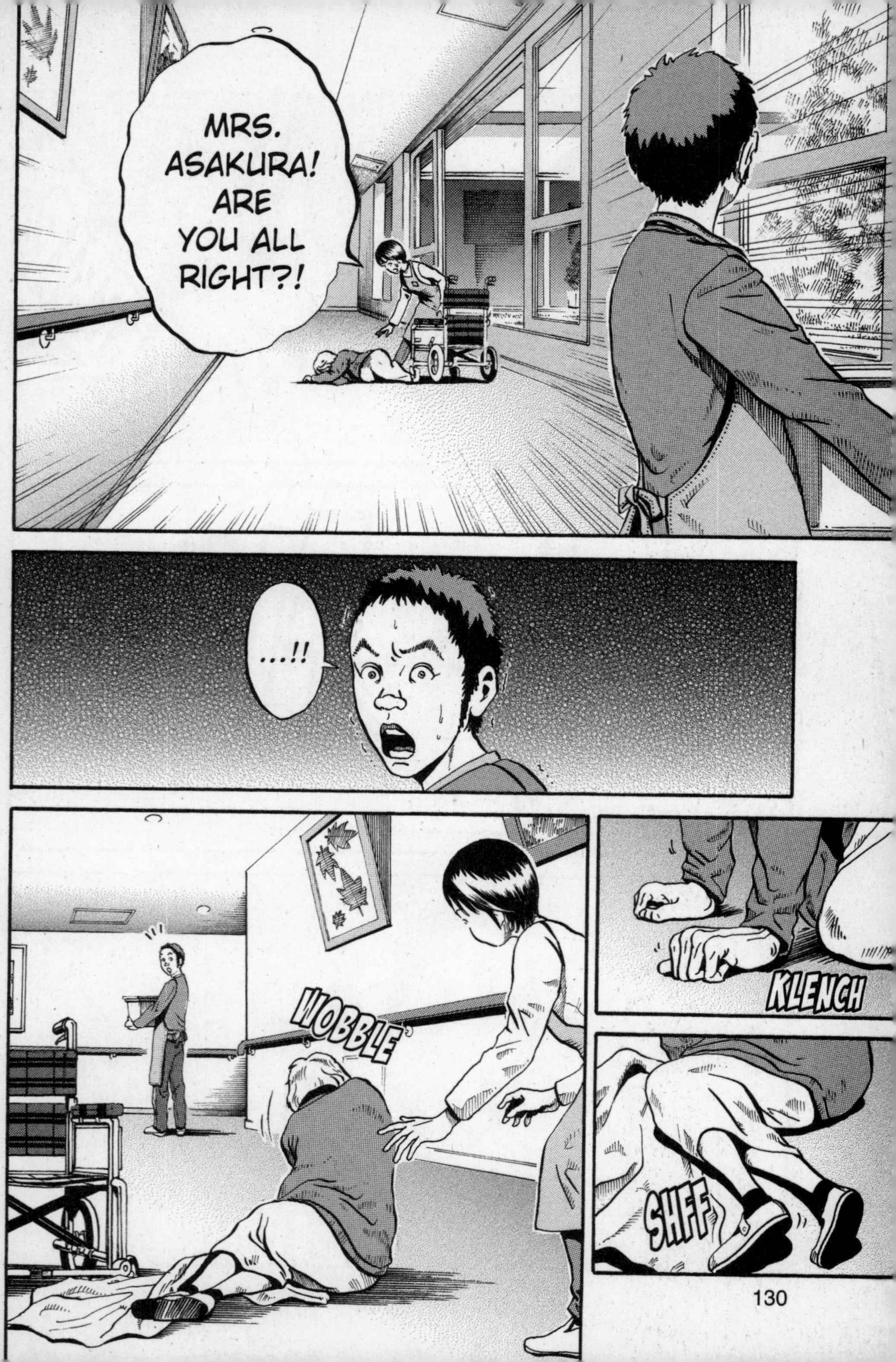
MRS. ASAKURA! ARE YOU ALL RIGHT?!
...!!
KLENCH
SHFF
WOBBLE

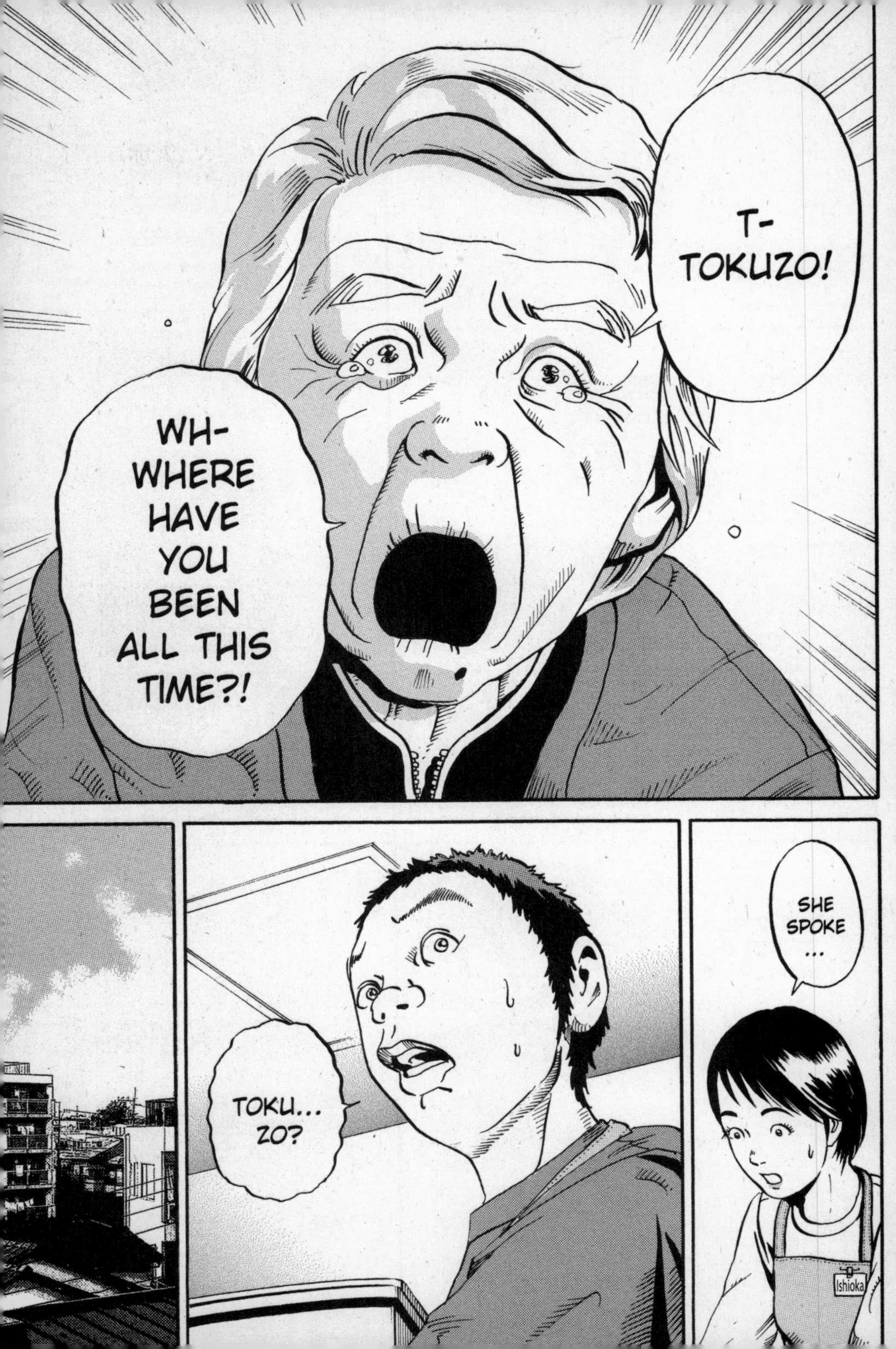
T-TOKUZO!
WH-WHERE HAVE YOU BEEN ALL THIS TIME?!
SHE SPOKE ...
Ishioka
TOKU... ZO?

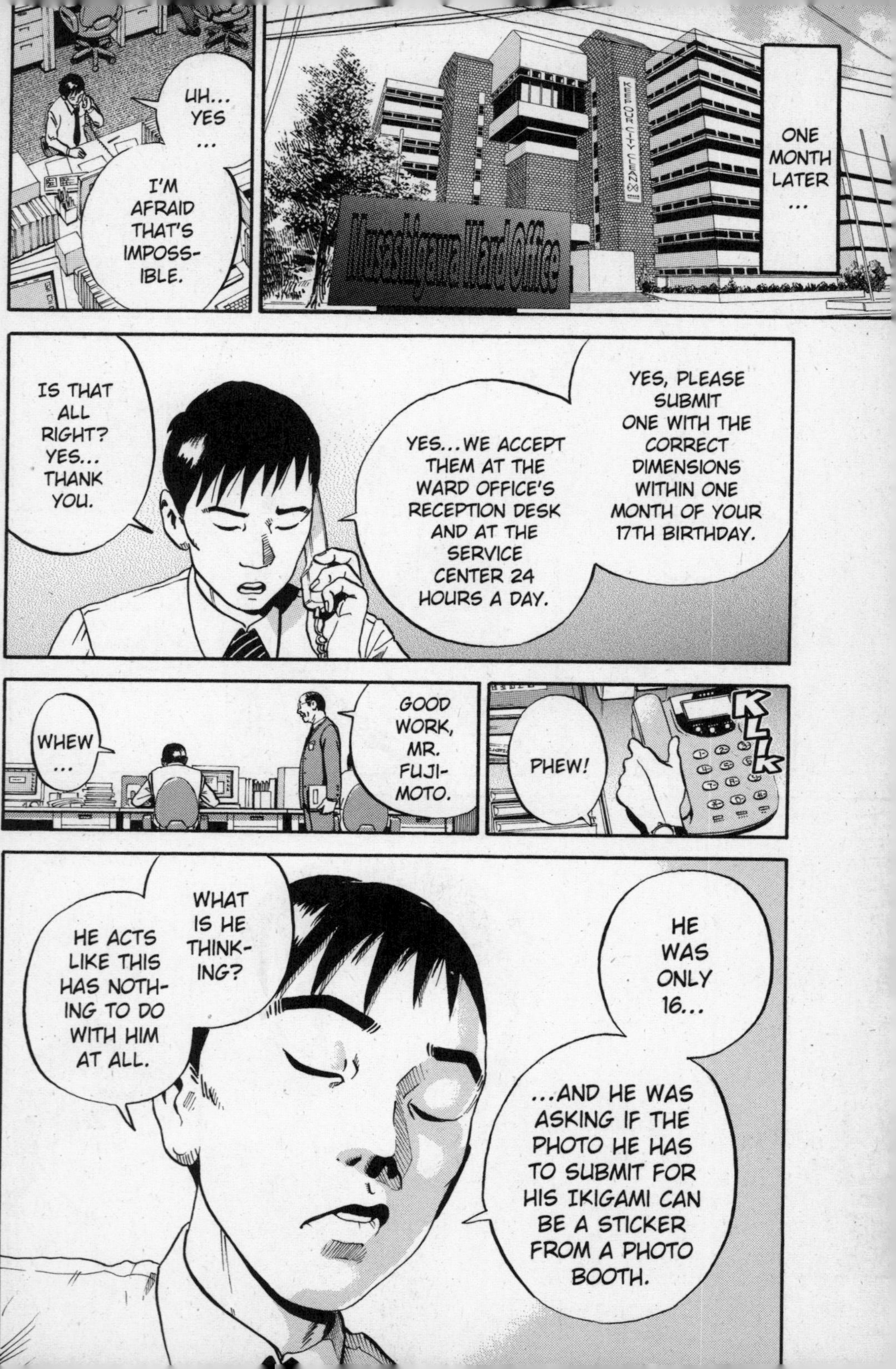
ONE MONTH LATER...
KEEP OUR CITY CLEAN
Musashigawa Ward Office
UH... YES...
I'M AFRAID THAT'S IMPOSS-IBLE.
YES, PLEASE SUBMIT ONE WITH THE CORRECT DIMENSIONS WITHIN ONE MONTH OF YOUR 17TH BIRTHDAY.
YES...WE ACCEPT THEM AT THE WARD OFFICE'S RECEPTION DESK AND AT THE SERVICE CENTER 24 HOURS A DAY.
IS THAT ALL RIGHT? YES... THANK YOU.
KLIK
PHEW!
GOOD WORK, MR. FUJI-MOTO.
WHEW...
HE WAS ONLY 16...
...AND HE WAS ASKING IF THE PHOTO HE HAS TO SUBMIT FOR HIS IKIGAMI CAN BE A STICKER FROM A PHOTO BOOTH.
WHAT IS HE THINK-ING?
HE ACTS LIKE THIS HAS NOTH-ING TO DO WITH HIM AT ALL.

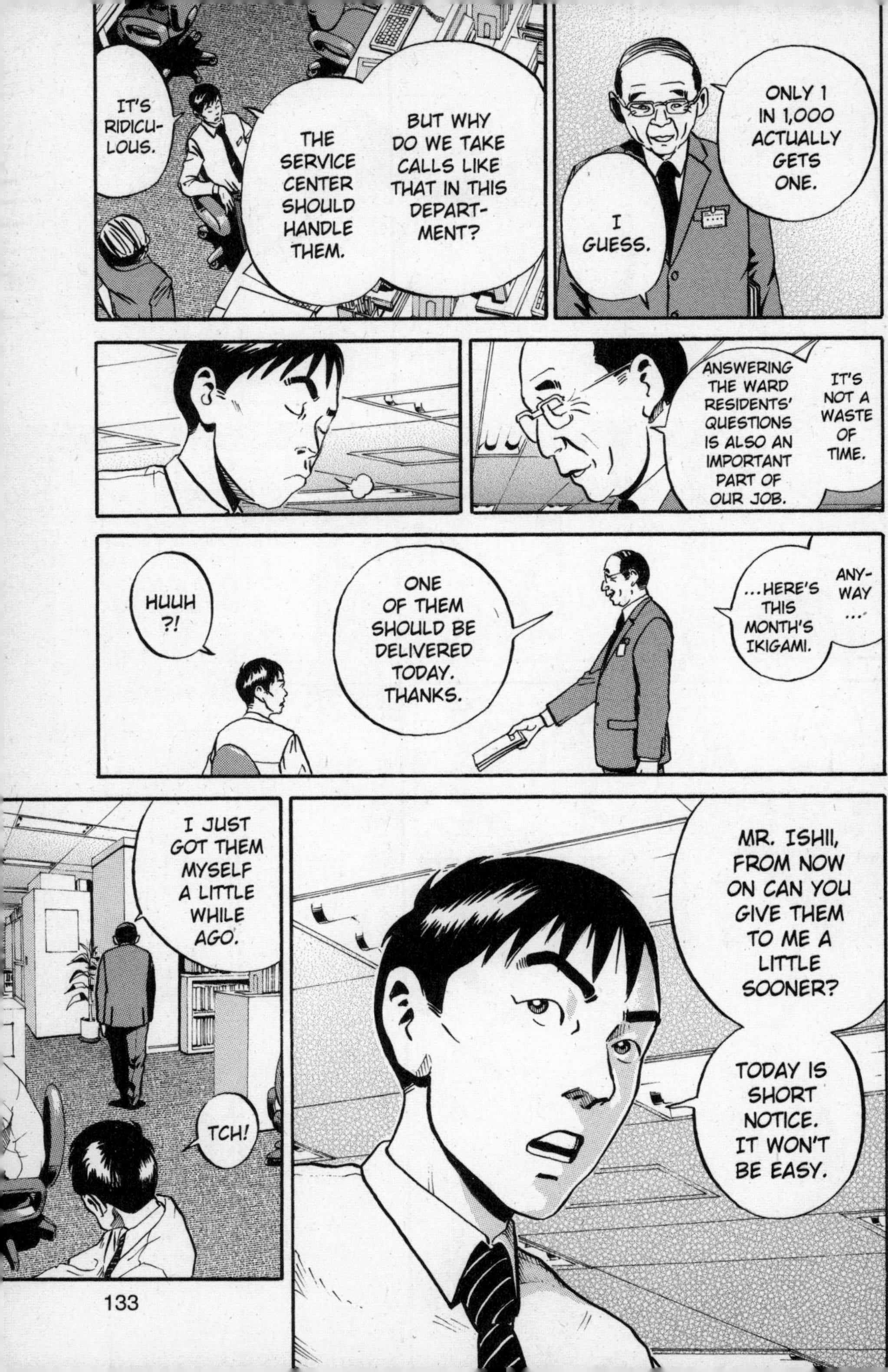
ONLY 1 IN 1,000 ACTUALLY GETS ONE.
I GUESS.
BUT WHY DO WE TAKE CALLS LIKE THAT IN THIS DEPART-MENT?
THE SERVICE CENTER SHOULD HANDLE THEM.
IT'S RIDICU-LOUS.
IT'S NOT A WASTE OF TIME.
ANSWERING THE WARD RESIDENTS' QUESTIONS IS ALSO AN IMPORTANT PART OF OUR JOB.
ANY-WAY...
...HERE'S THIS MONTH'S IKIGAMI.
ONE OF THEM SHOULD BE DELIVERED TODAY. THANKS.
HUUH ?!
MR. ISHII, FROM NOW ON CAN YOU GIVE THEM TO ME A LITTLE SOONER?
TODAY IS SHORT NOTICE. IT WON'T BE EASY.
I JUST GOT THEM MYSELF A LITTLE WHILE AGO.
TCH!

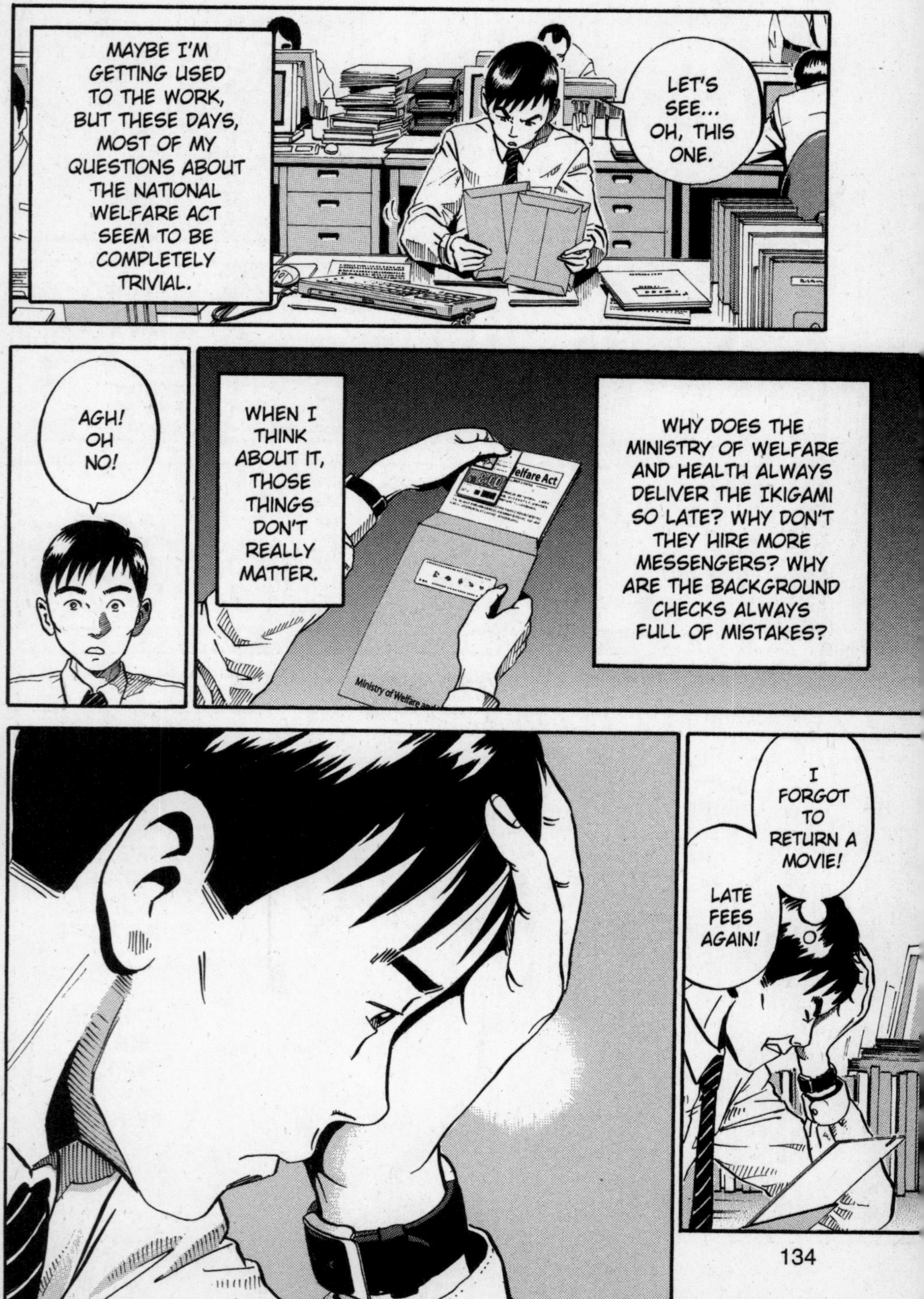
LET'S SEE... OH, THIS ONE.
MAYBE I'M GETTING USED TO THE WORK, BUT THESE DAYS, MOST OF MY QUESTIONS ABOUT THE NATIONAL WELFARE ACT SEEM TO BE COMPLETELY TRIVIAL.
WHY DOES THE MINISTRY OF WELFARE AND HEALTH ALWAYS DELIVER THE IKIGAMI SO LATE? WHY DON'T THEY HIRE MORE MESSENGERS? WHY ARE THE BACKGROUND CHECKS ALWAYS FULL OF MISTAKES?
WHEN I THINK ABOUT IT, THOSE THINGS DON'T REALLY MATTER.
AGH! OH NO!
I FORGOT TO RETURN A MOVIE!
LATE FEES AGAIN!

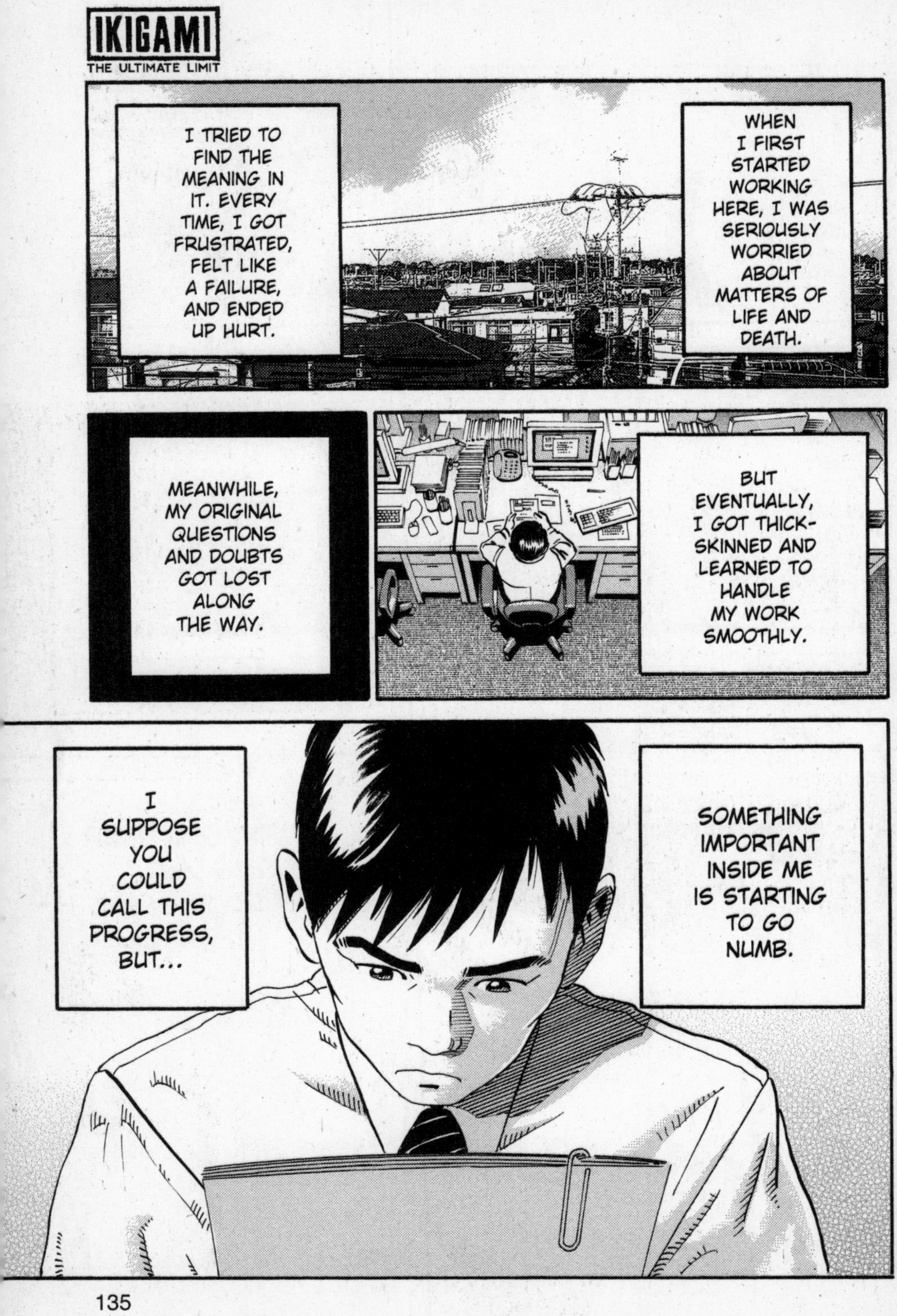
WHEN I FIRST STARTED WORKING HERE, I WAS SERIOUSLY WORRIED ABOUT MATTERS OF LIFE AND DEATH.
I TRIED TO FIND THE MEANING IN IT. EVERY TIME, I GOT FRUSTRATED, FELT LIKE A FAILURE, AND ENDED UP HURT.
BUT EVENTUALLY, I GOT THICK-SKINNED AND LEARNED TO HANDLE MY WORK SMOOTHLY.
MEANWHILE, MY ORIGINAL QUESTIONS AND DOUBTS GOT LOST ALONG THE WAY.
I SUPPOSE YOU COULD CALL THIS PROGRESS, BUT...
SOMETHING IMPORTANT INSIDE ME IS STARTING TO GO NUMB.

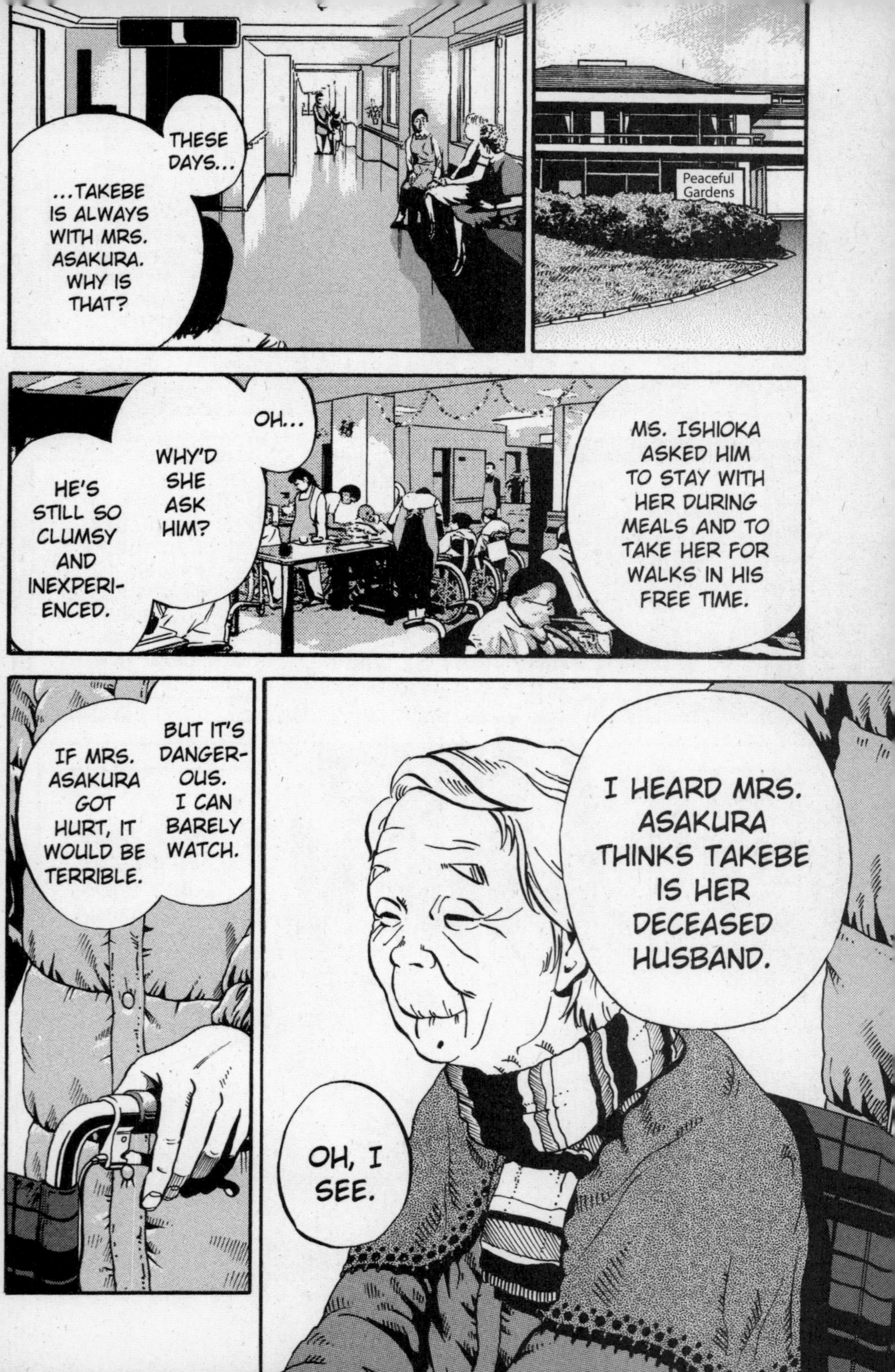
Peaceful Gardens
THESE DAYS...
...TAKEBE IS ALWAYS WITH MRS. ASAKURA. WHY IS THAT?
MS. ISHIOKA ASKED HIM TO STAY WITH HER DURING MEALS AND TO TAKE HER FOR WALKS IN HIS FREE TIME.
OH...
WHY'D SHE ASK HIM?
HE'S STILL SO CLUMSY AND INEXPERI-ENCED.
I HEARD MRS. ASAKURA THINKS TAKEBE IS HER DECEASED HUSBAND.
OH, I SEE.
BUT IT'S DANGER-OUS. I CAN BARELY WATCH.
IF MRS. ASAKURA GOT HURT, IT WOULD BE TERRIBLE.

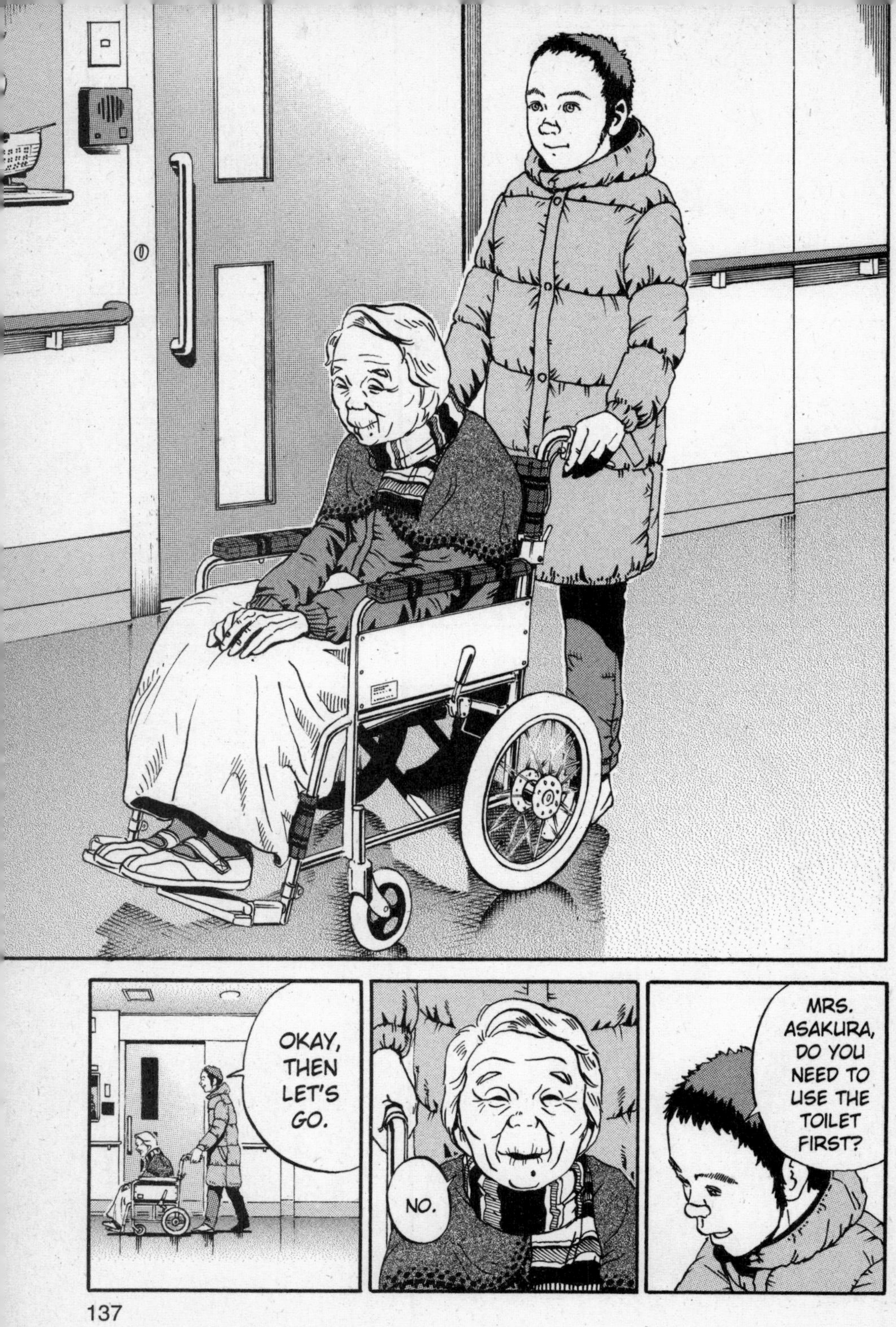
MRS. ASAKURA, DO YOU NEED TO USE THE TOILET FIRST?
NO.
OKAY, THEN LET'S GO.

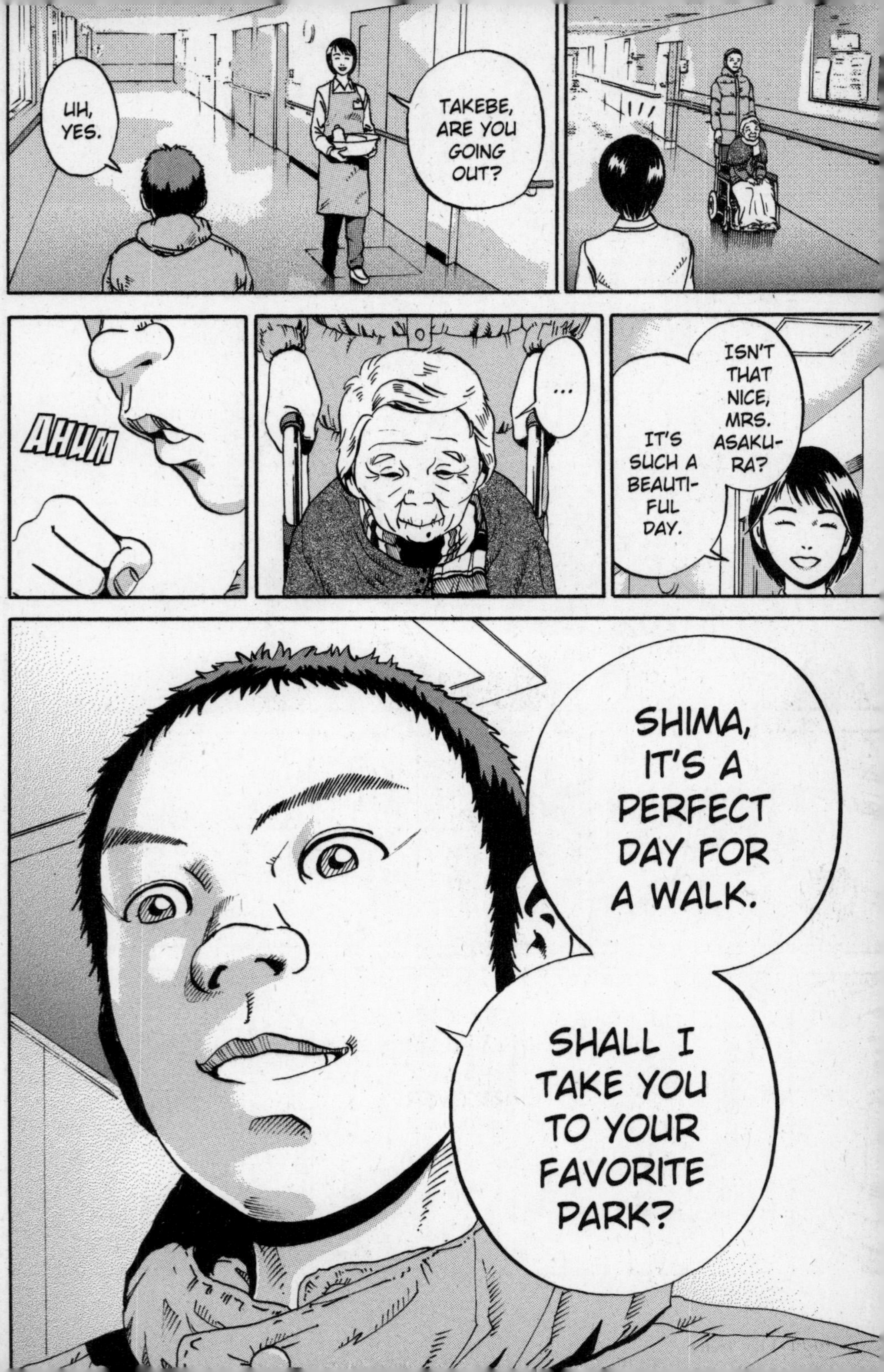
TAKEBE, ARE YOU GOING OUT?
UH, YES.
ISN'T THAT NICE, MRS. ASAKURA?
IT'S SUCH A BEAUTIFUL DAY.
...
AHUM
SHIMA, IT'S A PERFECT DAY FOR A WALK.
SHALL I TAKE YOU TO YOUR FAVORITE PARK?

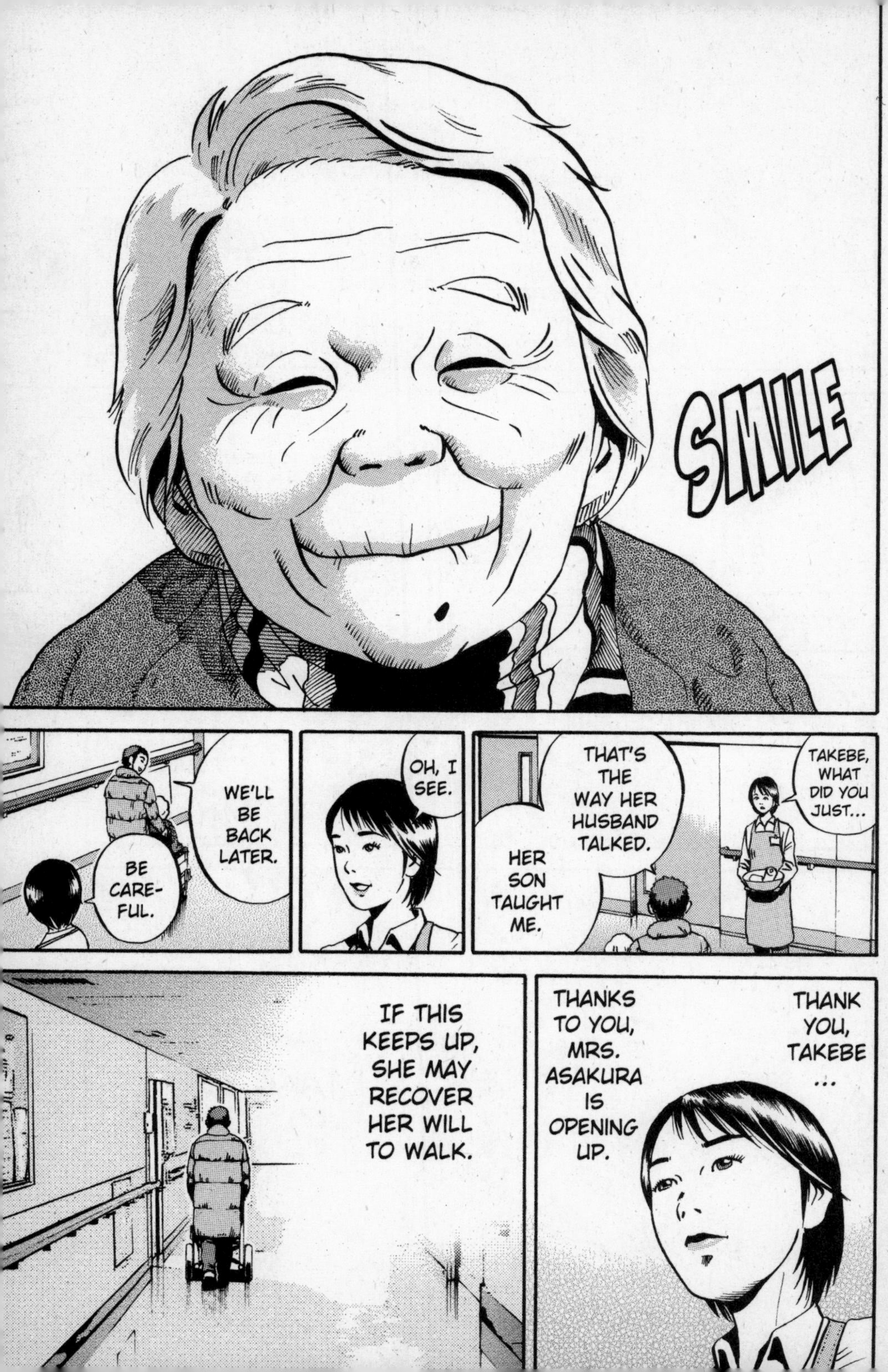

SMILE
TAKEBE, WHAT DID YOU JUST...
THAT'S THE WAY HER HUSBAND TALKED.
HER SON TAUGHT ME.
OH, I SEE.
WE'LL BE BACK LATER.
BE CARE-FUL.
THANK YOU, TAKEBE...
THANKS TO YOU, MRS. ASAKURA IS OPENING UP.
IF THIS KEEPS UP, SHE MAY RECOVER HER WILL TO WALK.

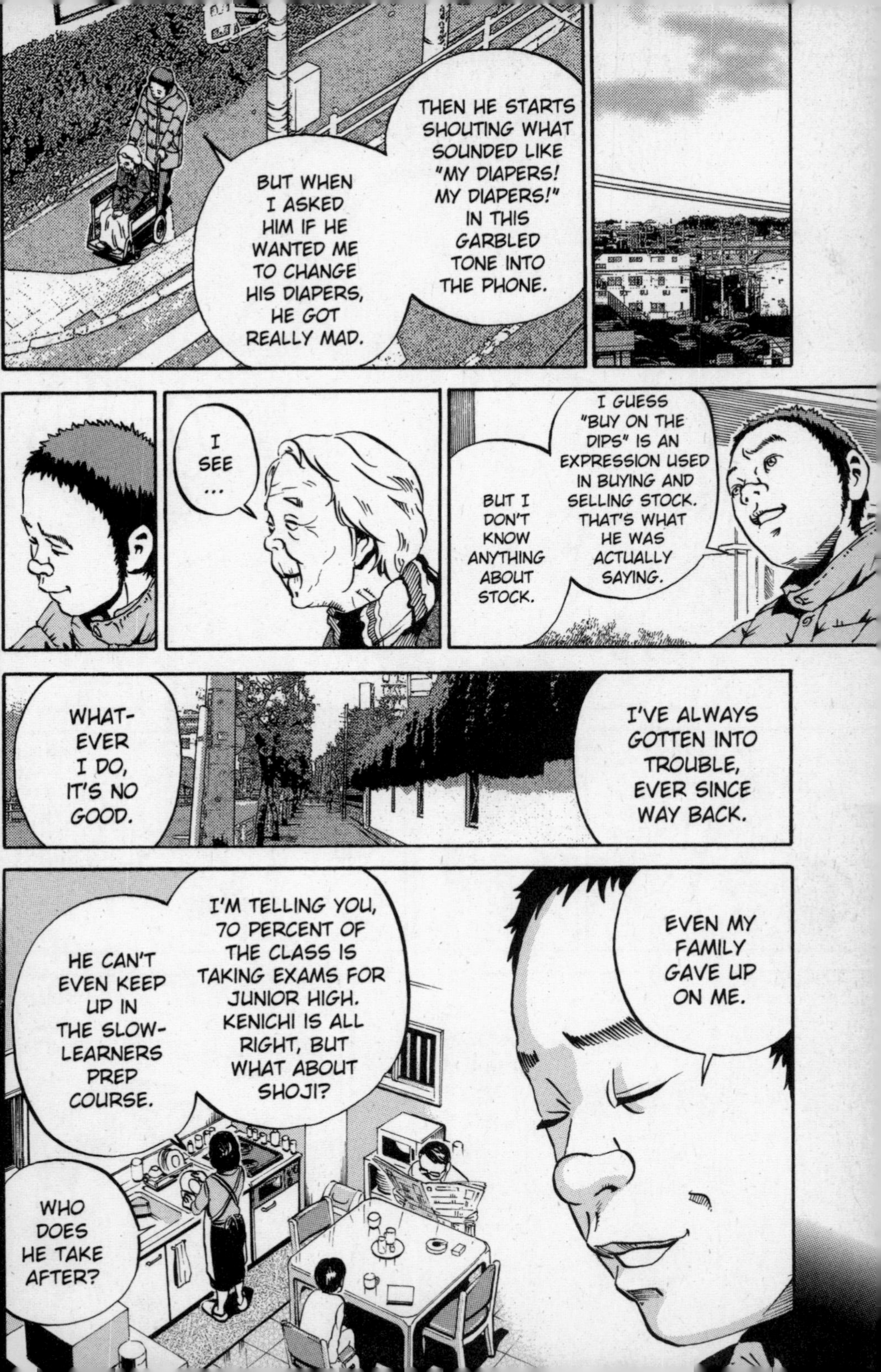
THEN HE STARTS SHOUTING WHAT SOUNDED LIKE "MY DIAPERS! MY DIAPERS!" IN THIS GARBLED TONE INTO THE PHONE.
BUT WHEN I ASKED HIM IF HE WANTED ME TO CHANGE HIS DIAPERS, HE GOT REALLY MAD.
I GUESS "BUY ON THE DIPS" IS AN EXPRESSION USED IN BUYING AND SELLING STOCK. THAT'S WHAT HE WAS ACTUALLY SAYING.
BUT I DON'T KNOW ANYTHING ABOUT STOCK.
I SEE ...
I'VE ALWAYS GOTTEN INTO TROUBLE, EVER SINCE WAY BACK.
WHAT-EVER I DO, IT'S NO GOOD.
EVEN MY FAMILY GAVE UP ON ME.
I'M TELLING YOU, 70 PERCENT OF THE CLASS IS TAKING EXAMS FOR JUNIOR HIGH. KENICHI IS ALL RIGHT, BUT WHAT ABOUT SHOJI?
HE CAN'T EVEN KEEP UP IN THE SLOW-LEARNERS PREP COURSE.
WHO DOES HE TAKE AFTER?

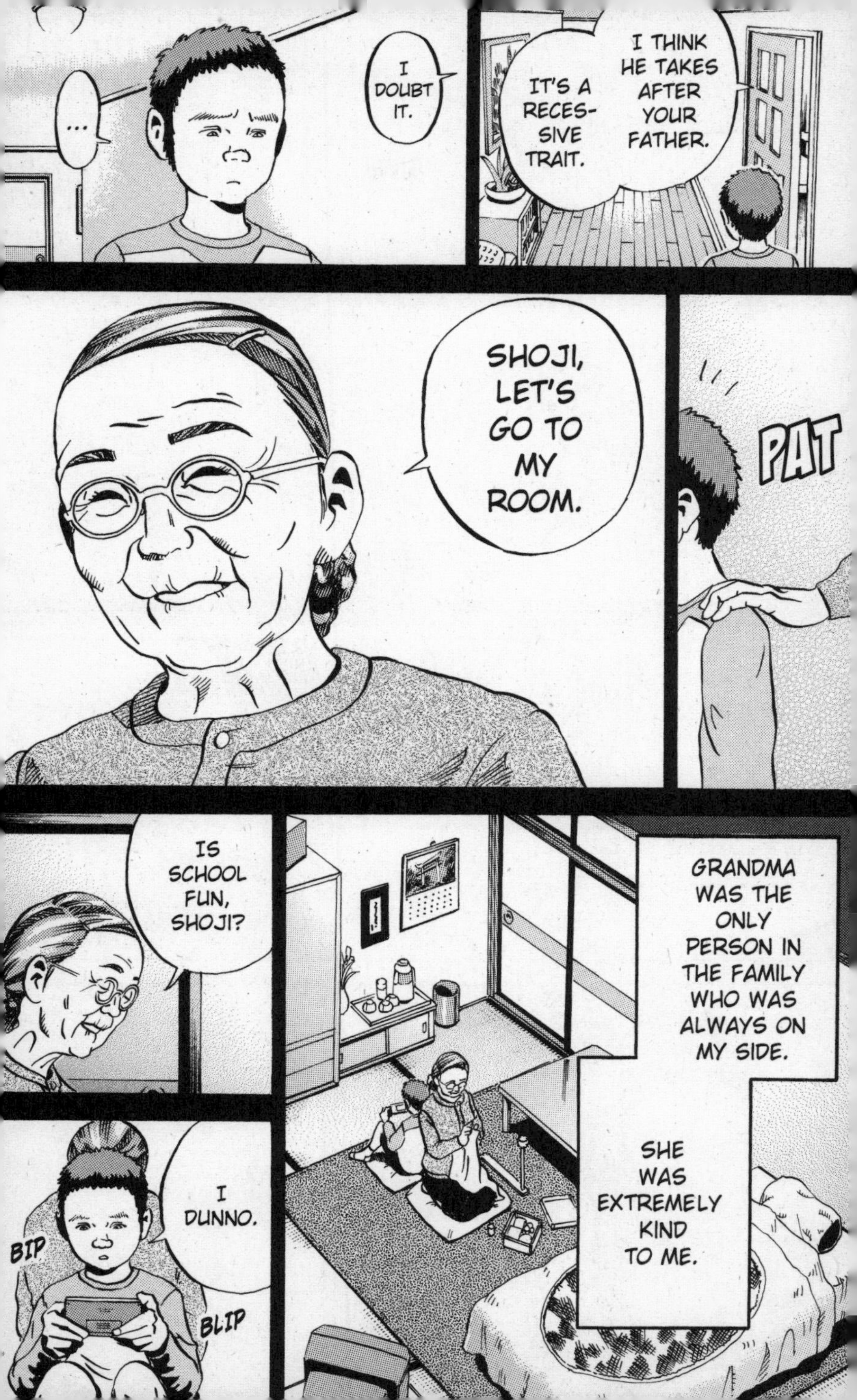
I THINK HE TAKES AFTER YOUR FATHER.
IT'S A RECESSIVE TRAIT.
I DOUBT IT.
...
PAT
SHOJI, LET'S GO TO MY ROOM.
GRANDMA WAS THE ONLY PERSON IN THE FAMILY WHO WAS ALWAYS ON MY SIDE.
SHE WAS EXTREMELY KIND TO ME.
IS SCHOOL FUN, SHOJI?
I DUNNO.
BIP
BLIP

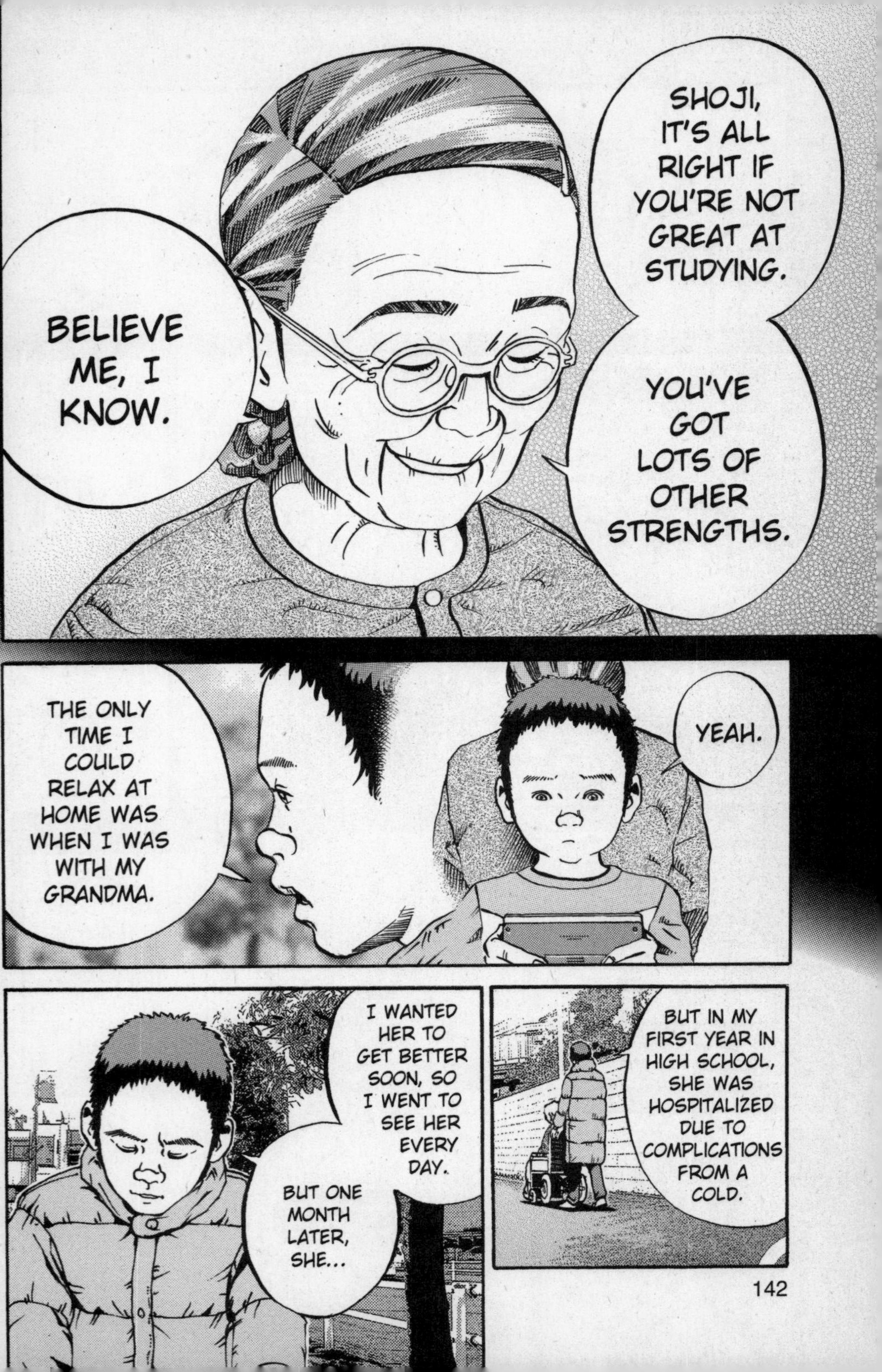
SHOJI, IT'S ALL RIGHT IF YOU'RE NOT GREAT AT STUDYING.
YOU'VE GOT LOTS OF OTHER STRENGTHS.
BELIEVE ME, I KNOW.
YEAH.
THE ONLY TIME I COULD RELAX AT HOME WAS WHEN I WAS WITH MY GRANDMA.
BUT IN MY FIRST YEAR IN HIGH SCHOOL, SHE WAS HOSPITALIZED DUE TO COMPLICATIONS FROM A COLD.
I WANTED HER TO GET BETTER SOON, SO I WENT TO SEE HER EVERY DAY.
BUT ONE MONTH LATER, SHE...

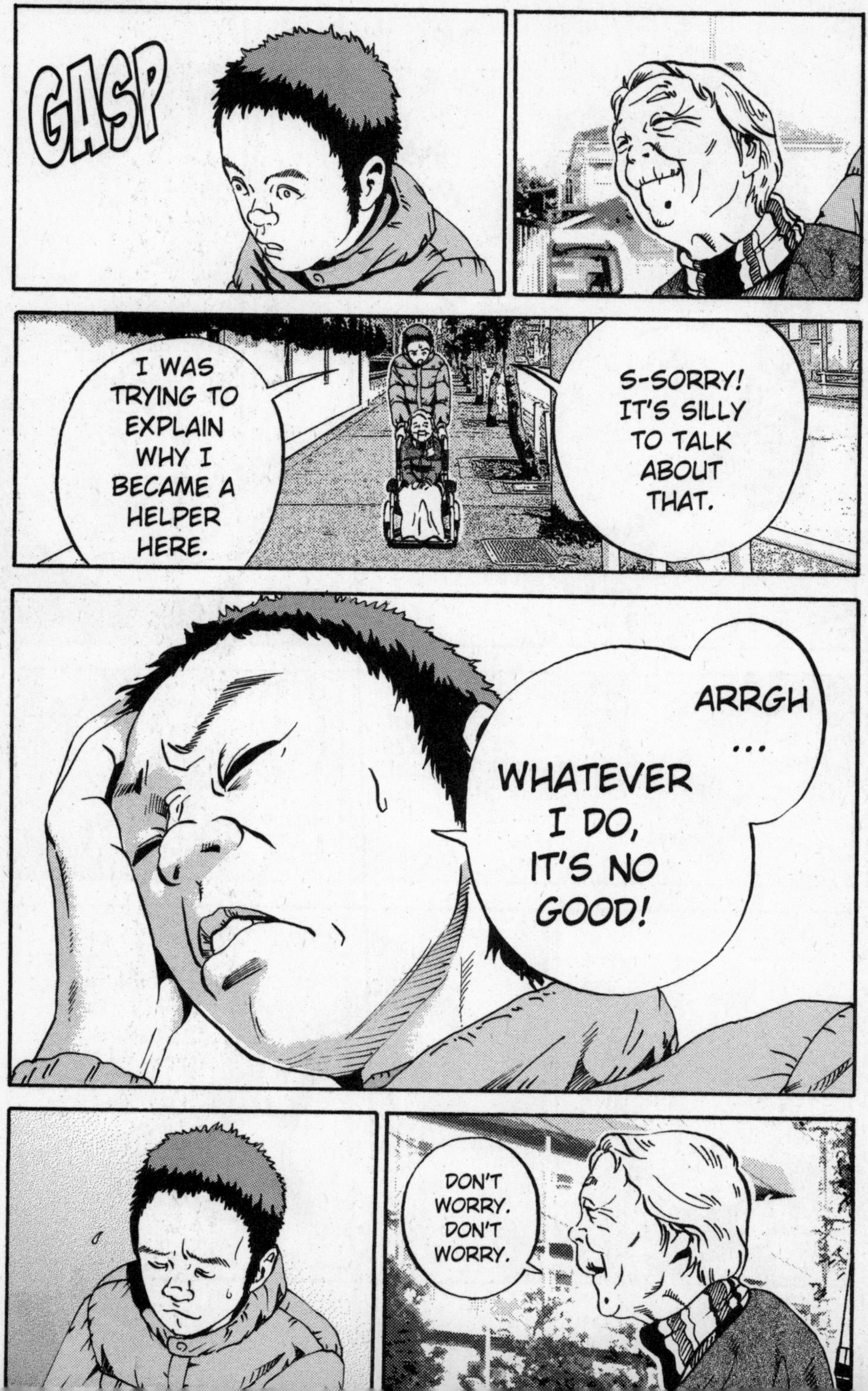
GASP
S-SORRY! IT'S SILLY TO TALK ABOUT THAT.
I WAS TRYING TO EXPLAIN WHY I BECAME A HELPER HERE.
ARRGH ... WHATEVER I DO, IT'S NO GOOD!
DON'T WORRY. DON'T WORRY.

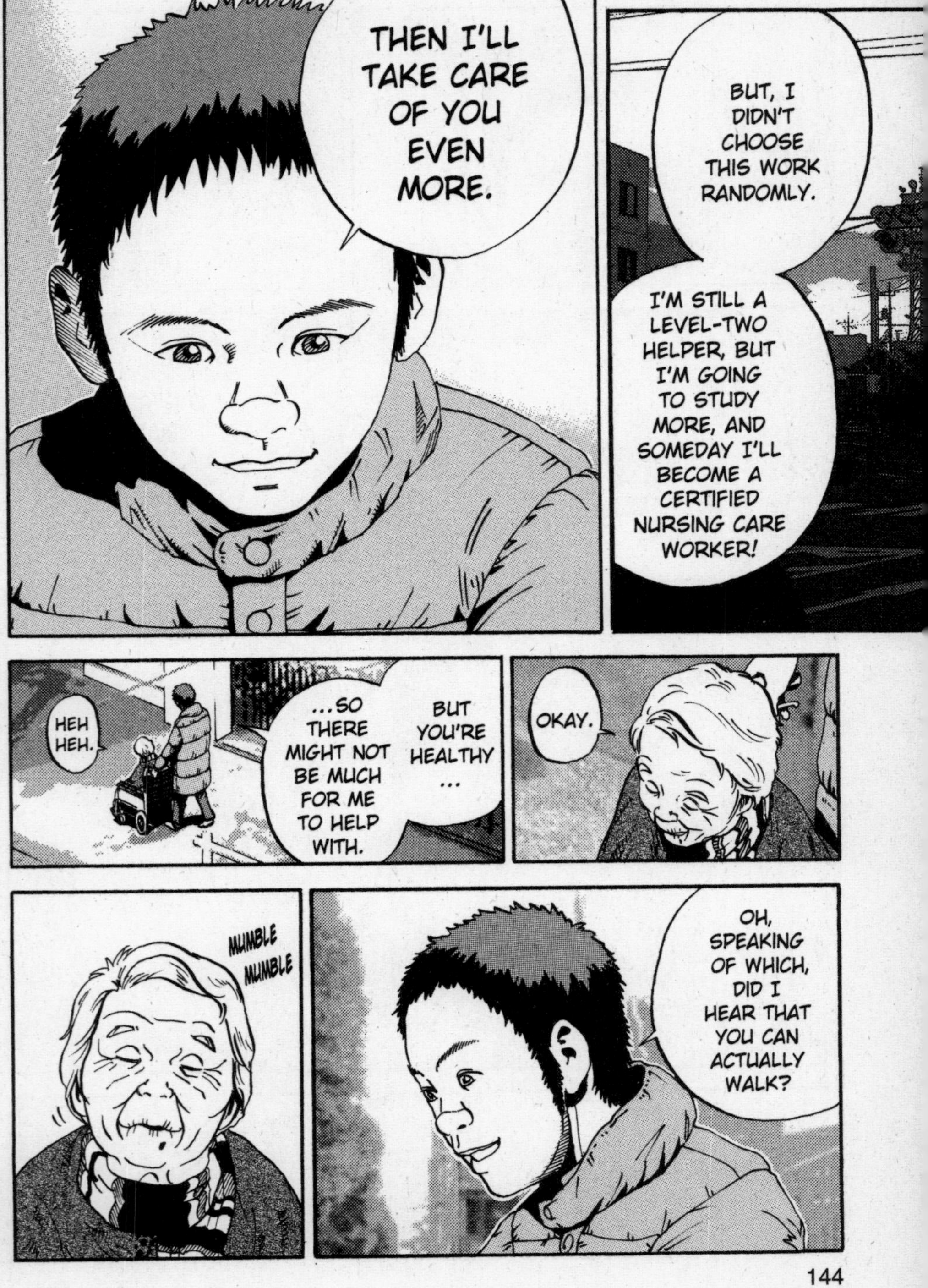
BUT, I DIDN'T CHOOSE THIS WORK RANDOMLY.
I'M STILL A LEVEL-TWO HELPER, BUT I'M GOING TO STUDY MORE, AND SOMEDAY I'LL BECOME A CERTIFIED NURSING CARE WORKER!
THEN I'LL TAKE CARE OF YOU EVEN MORE.
OKAY.
BUT YOU'RE HEALTHY...
...SO THERE MIGHT NOT BE MUCH FOR ME TO HELP WITH.
HEH HEH.
OH, SPEAKING OF WHICH, DID I HEAR THAT YOU CAN ACTUALLY WALK?
MUMBLE MUMBLE

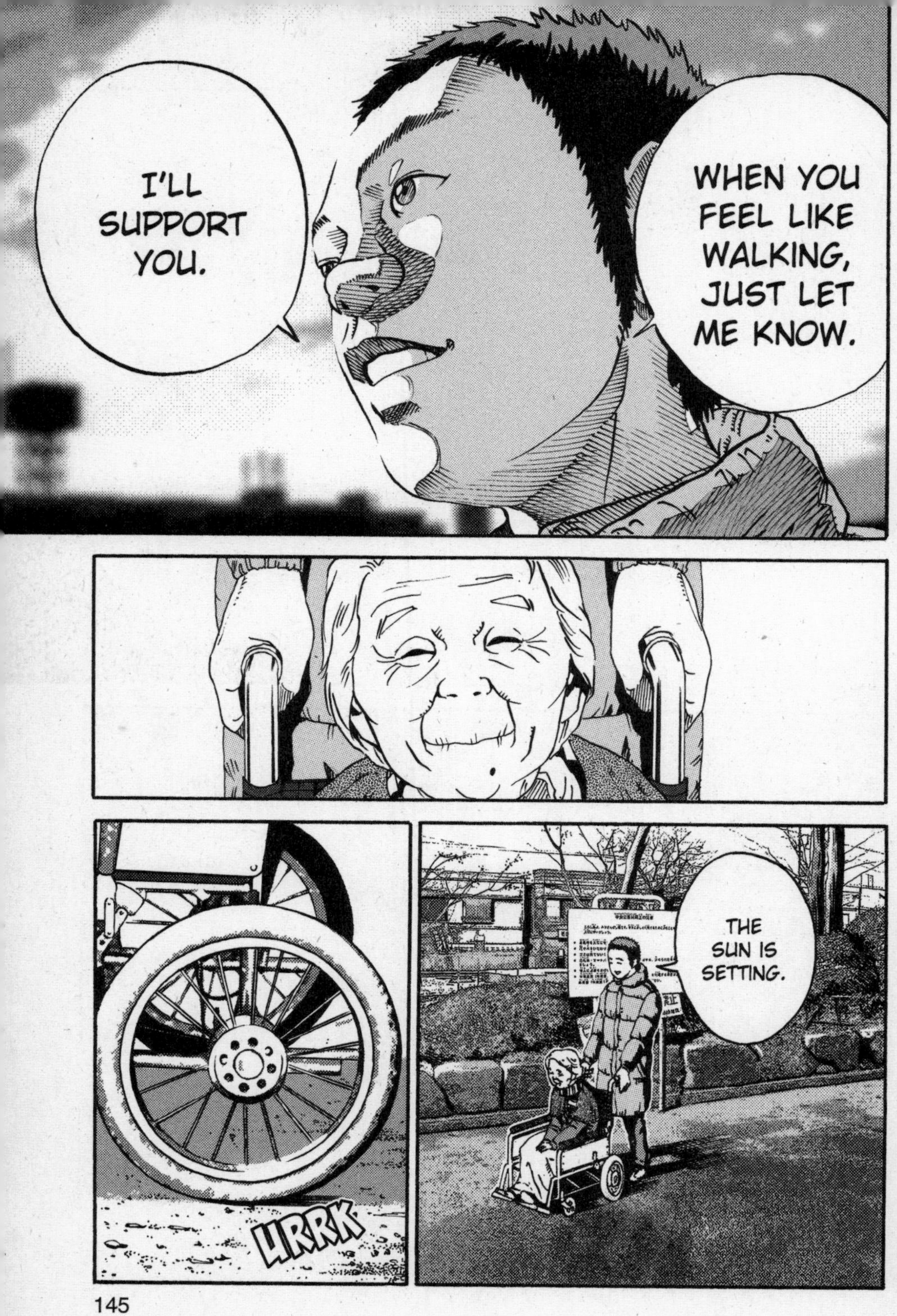
WHEN YOU FEEL LIKE WALKING, JUST LET ME KNOW.
I'LL SUPPORT YOU.
THE SUN IS SETTING.
URRK

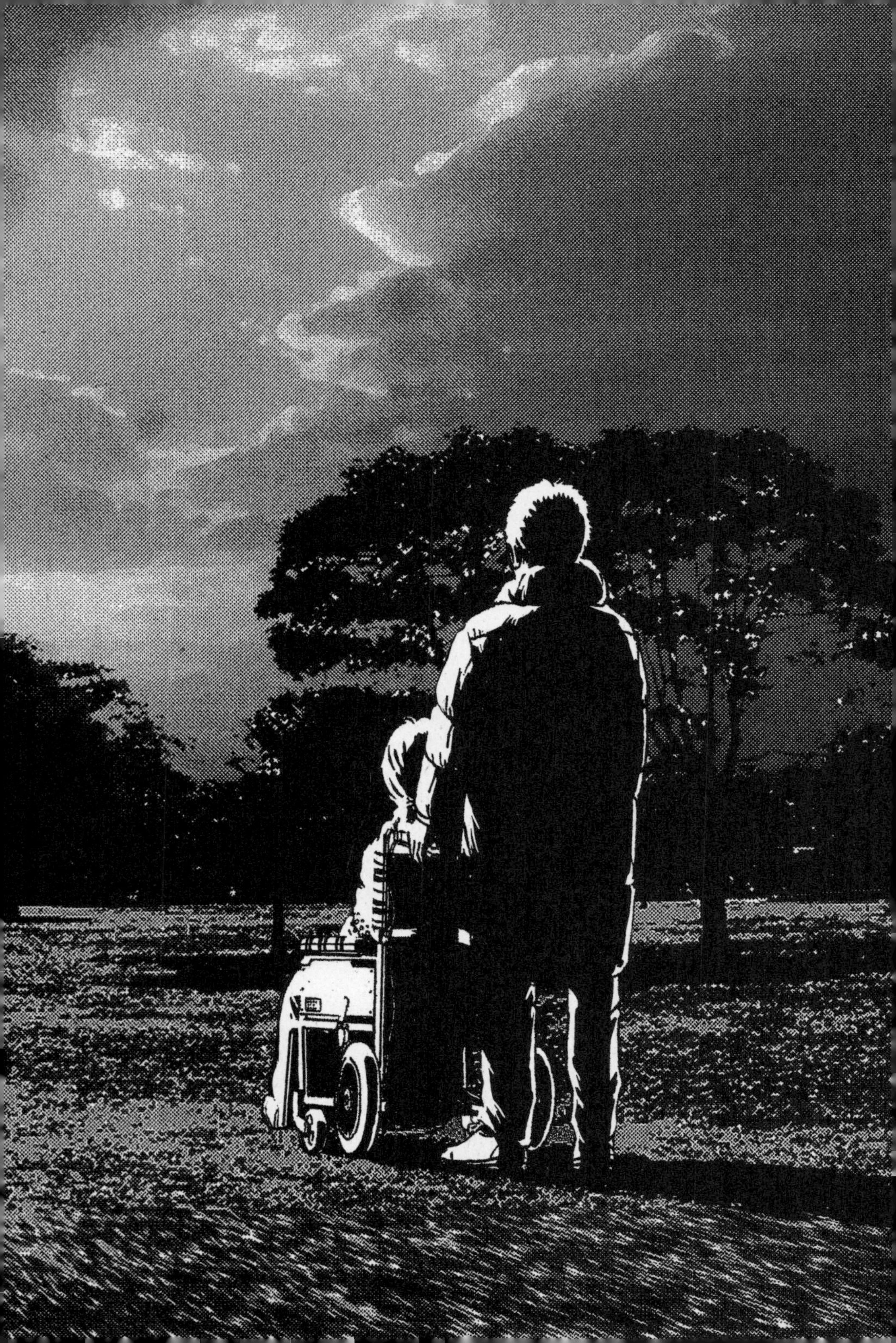

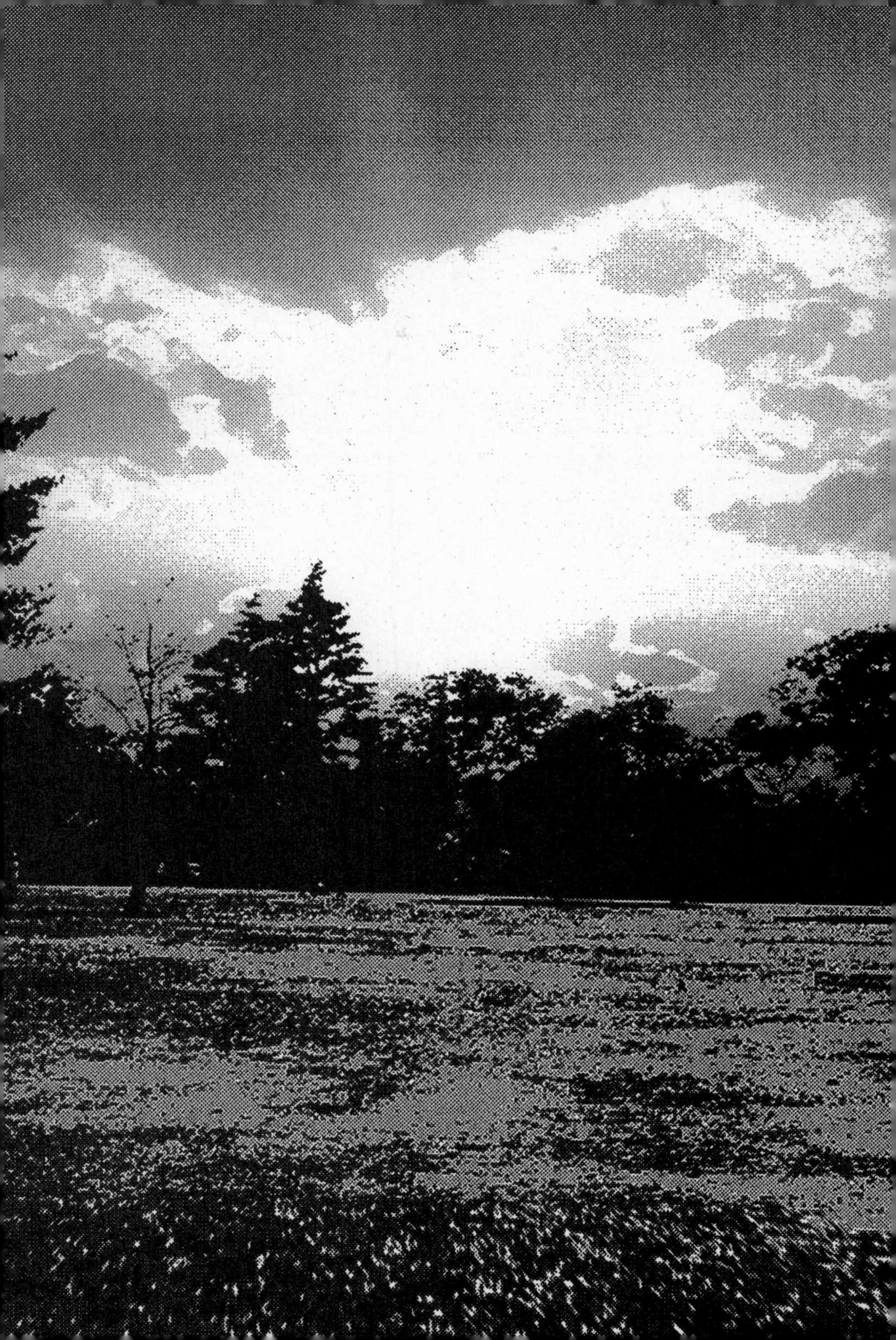

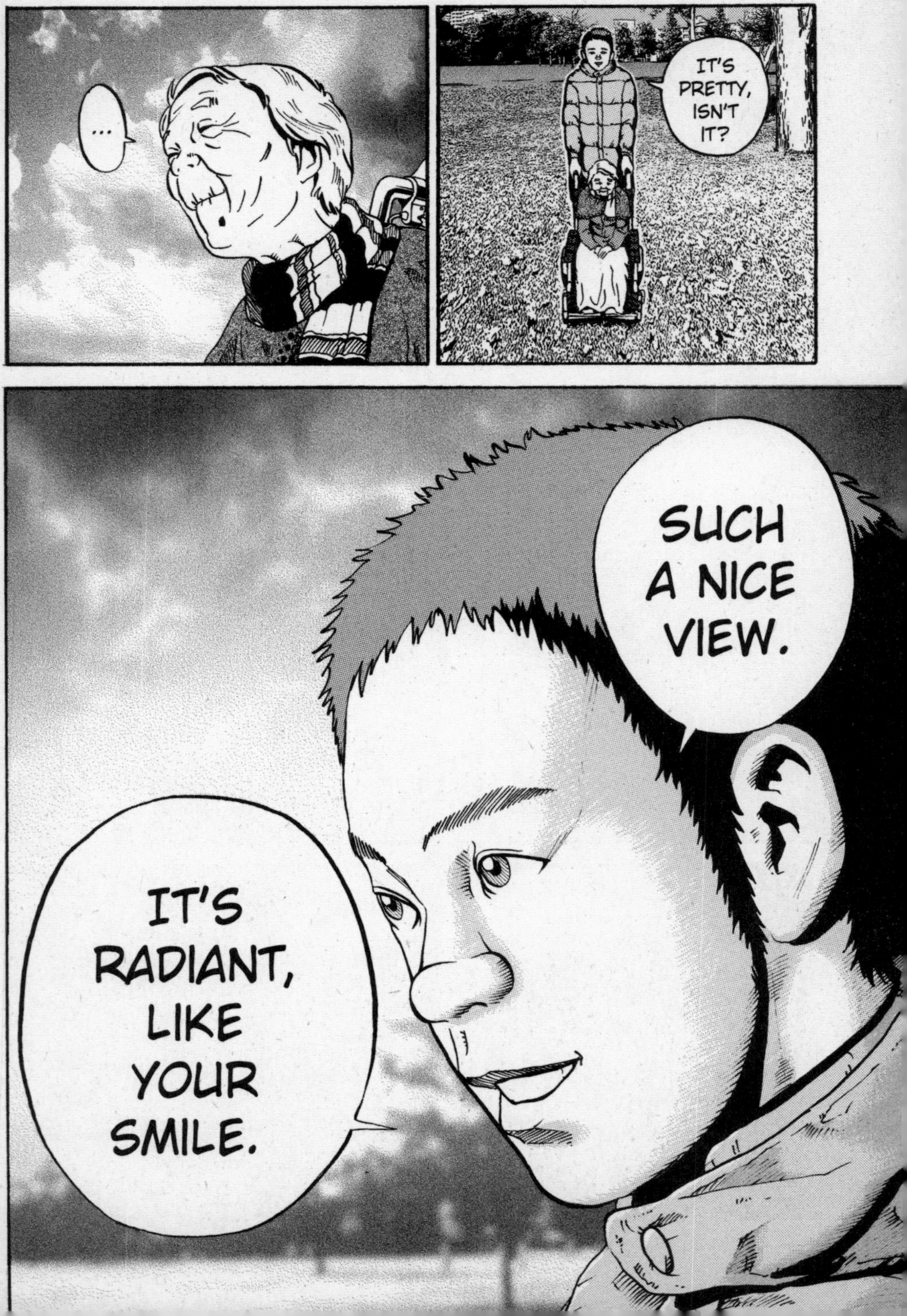
IT'S PRETTY, ISN'T IT?
...
SUCH A NICE VIEW.
IT'S RADIANT, LIKE YOUR SMILE.

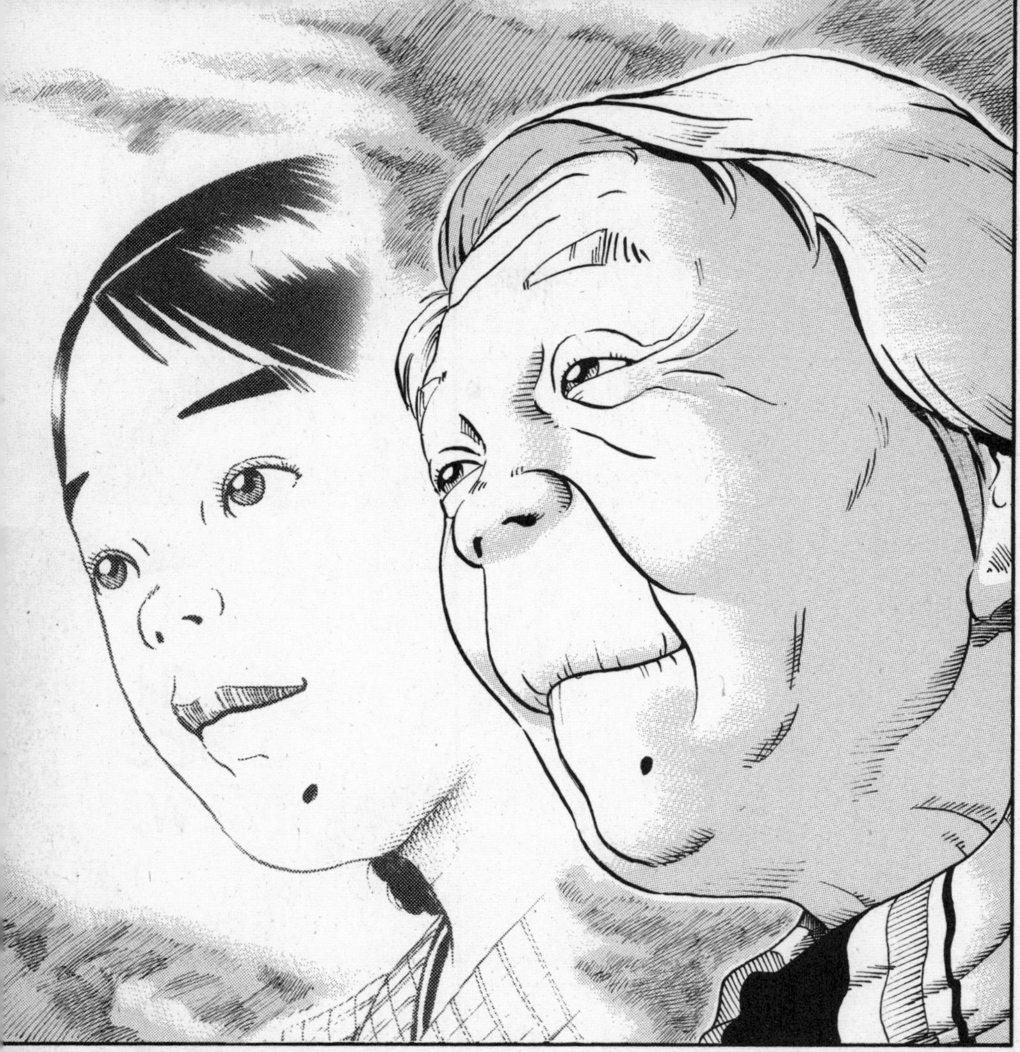
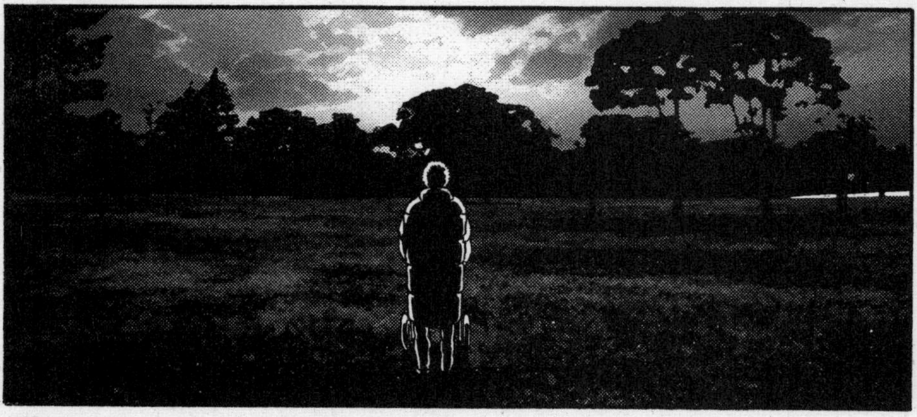

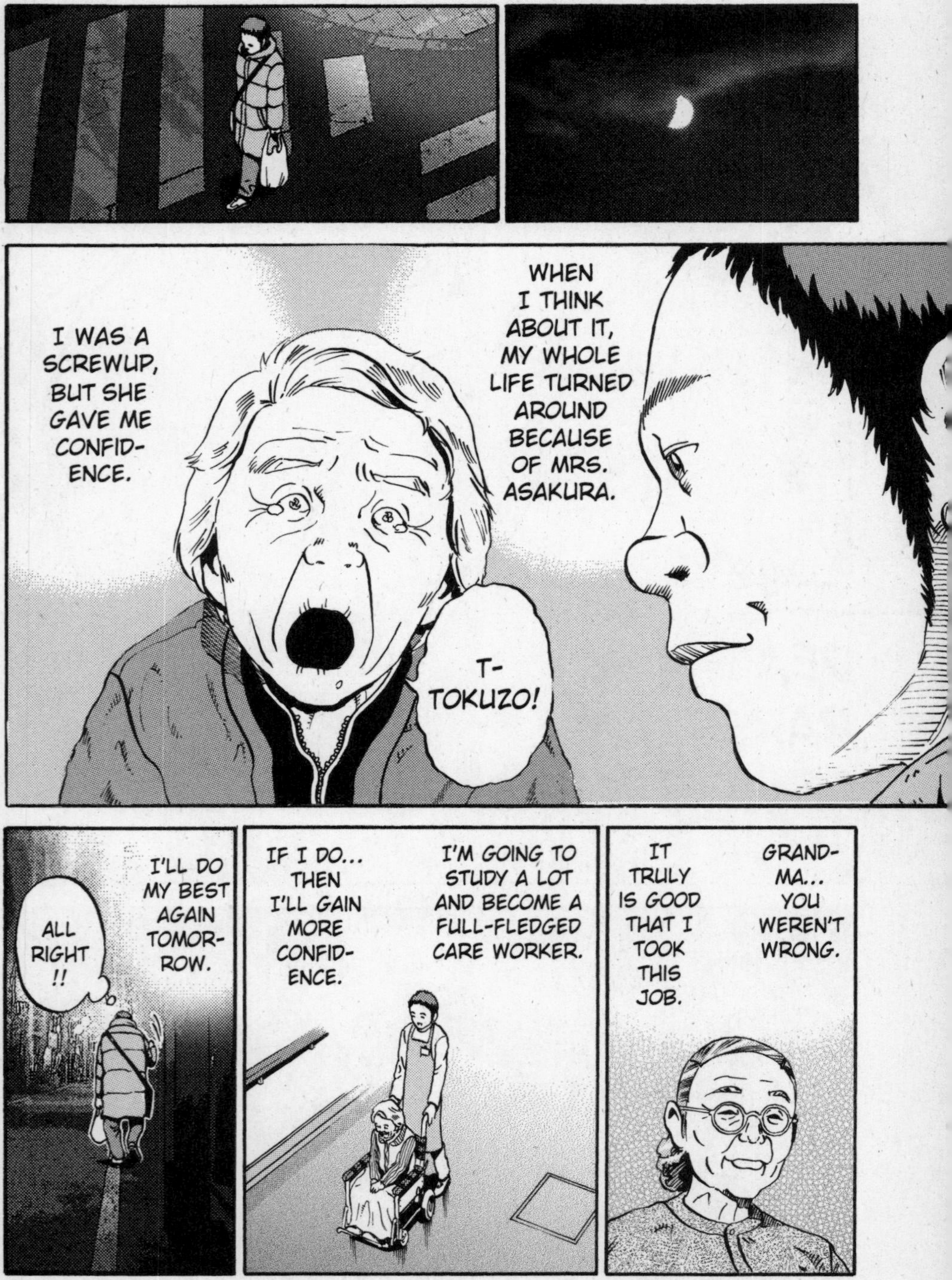
WHEN I THINK ABOUT IT, MY WHOLE LIFE TURNED AROUND BECAUSE OF MRS. ASAKURA.
I WAS A SCREWUP, BUT SHE GAVE ME CONFIDENCE.
T-TOKUZO!
GRANDMA... YOU WEREN'T WRONG.
IT TRULY IS GOOD THAT I TOOK THIS JOB.
I'M GOING TO STUDY A LOT AND BECOME A FULL-FLEDGED CARE WORKER.
IF I DO... THEN I'LL GAIN MORE CONFIDENCE.
I'LL DO MY BEST AGAIN TOMORROW.
ALL RIGHT!!

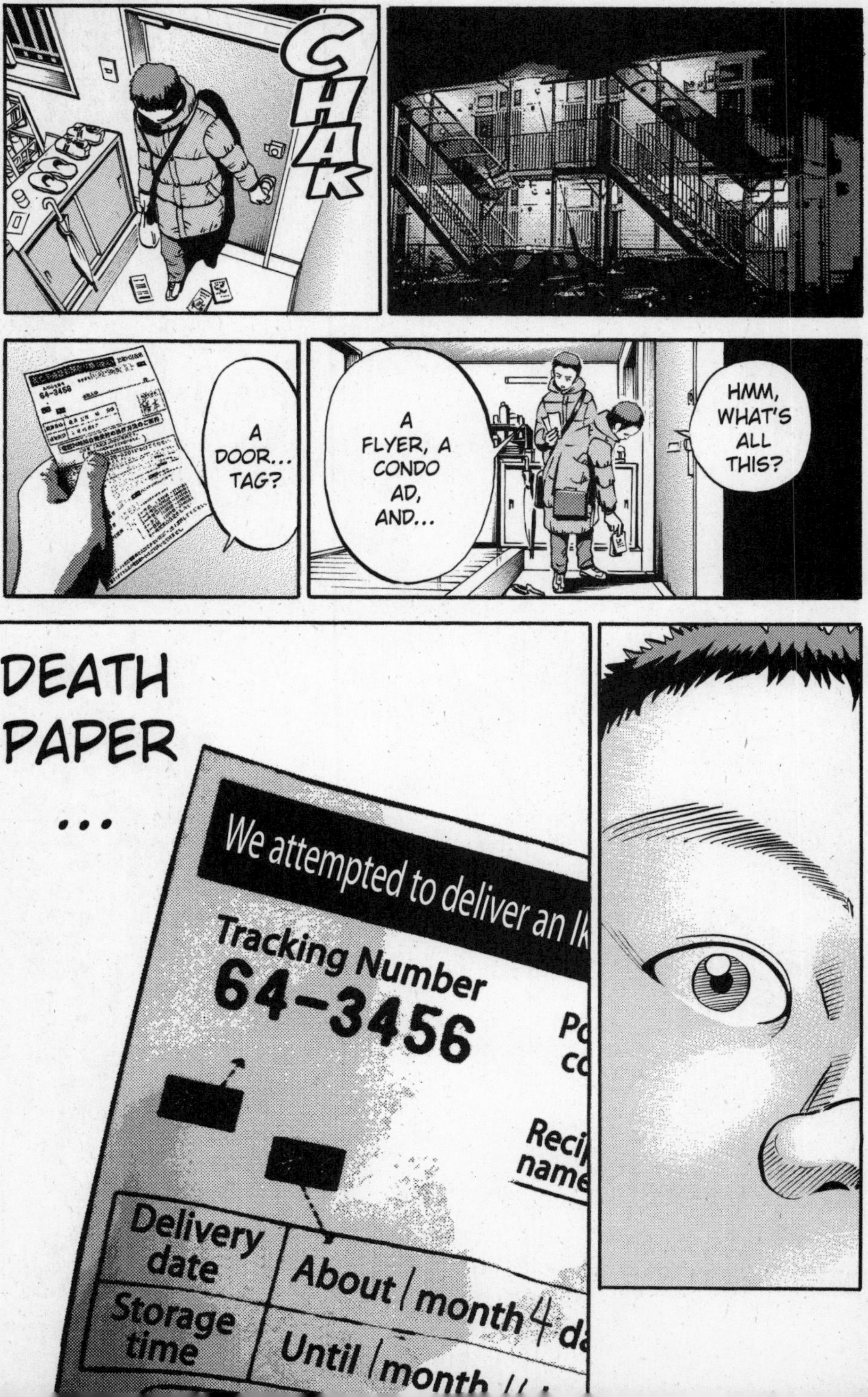
CHAK
HMM, WHAT'S ALL THIS?
A FLYER, A CONDO AD, AND...
A DOOR... TAG?
DEATH PAPER
...
We attempted to deliver an Ik
Tracking Number
64-3456
Delivery date
About / month 4
Storage time
Until / month

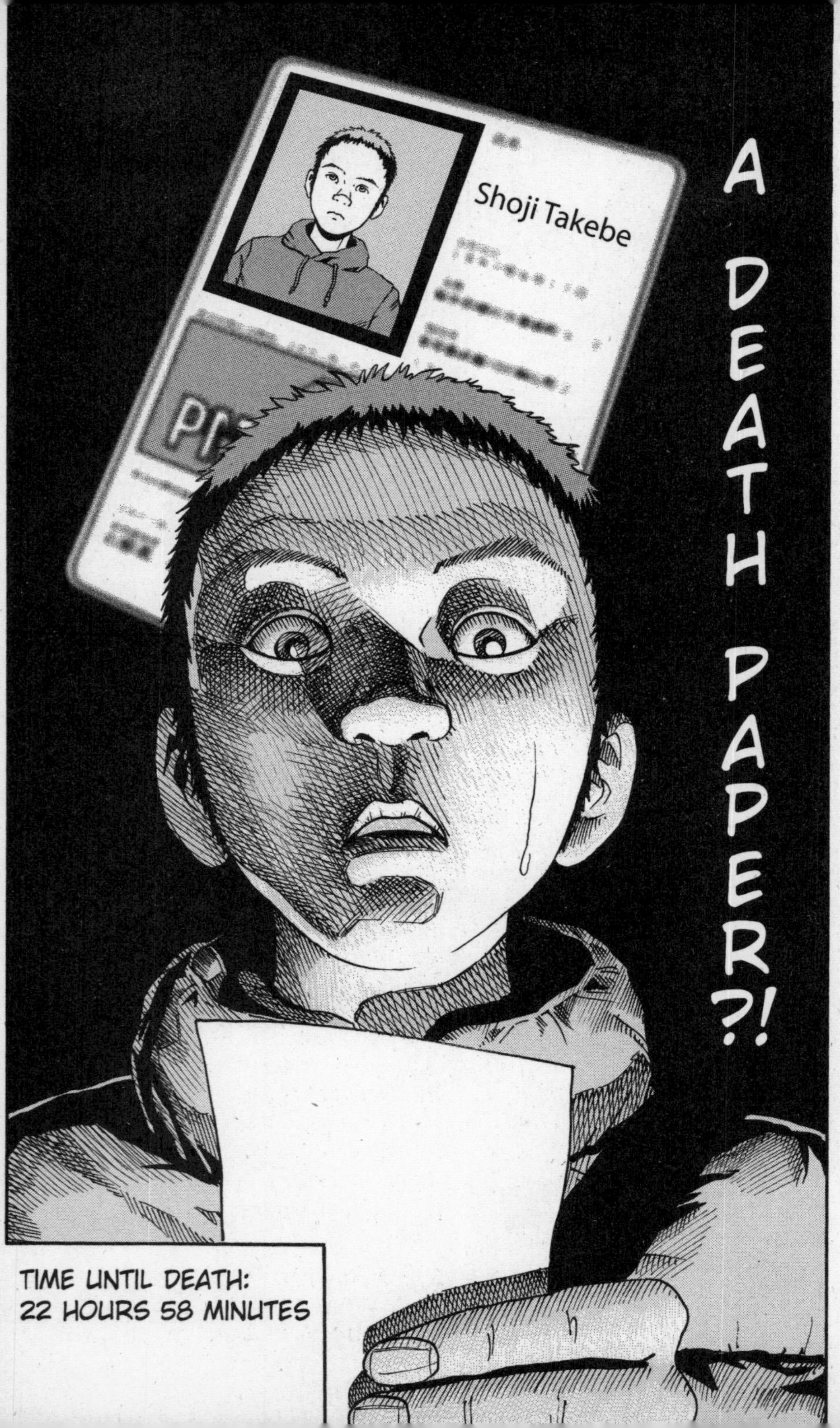
Shoji Takebe
A DEATH PAPER?!
TIME UNTIL DEATH:
22 HOURS 58 MINUTES

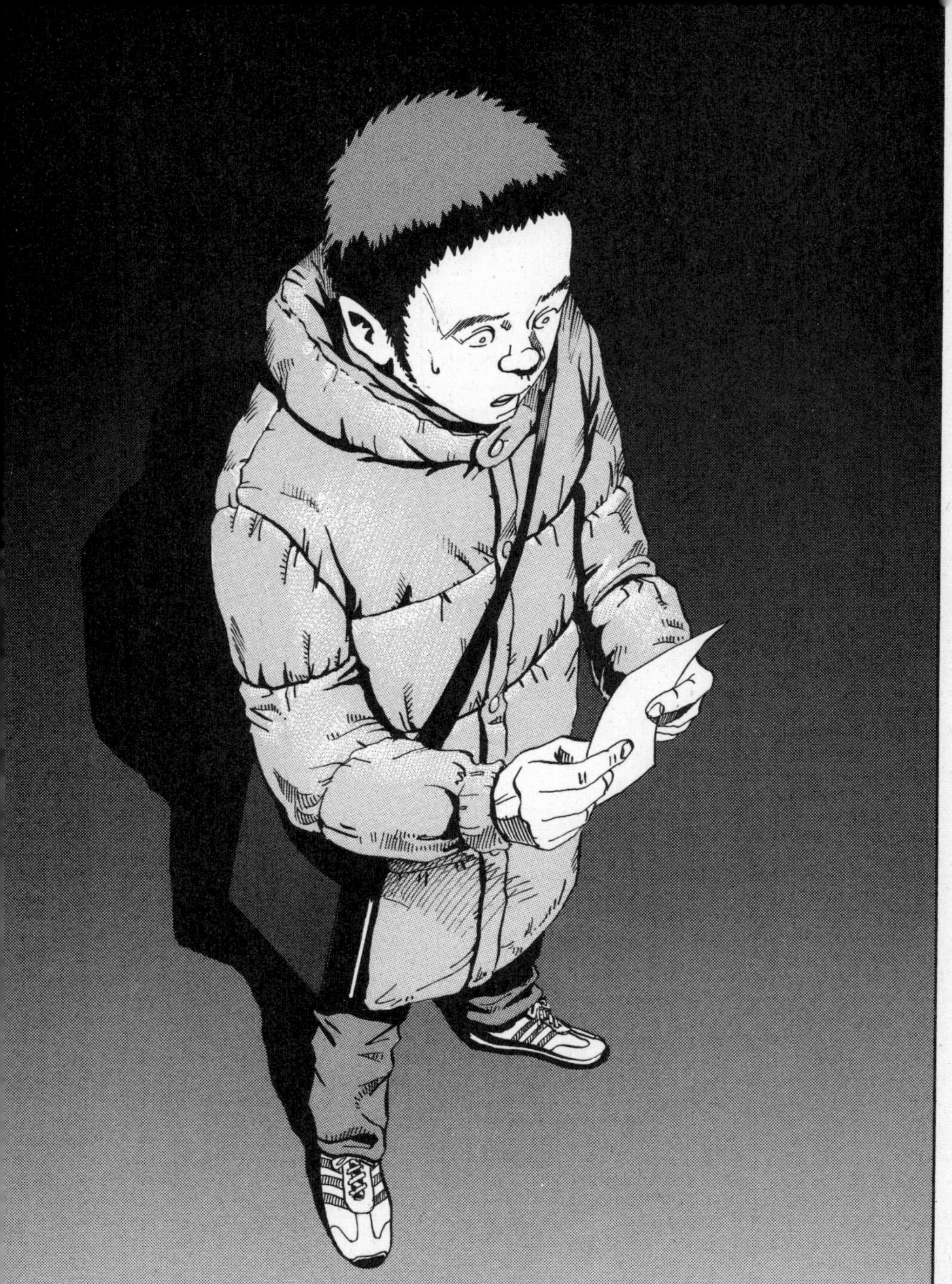

Episode 4 The Night He Left for War Act 2

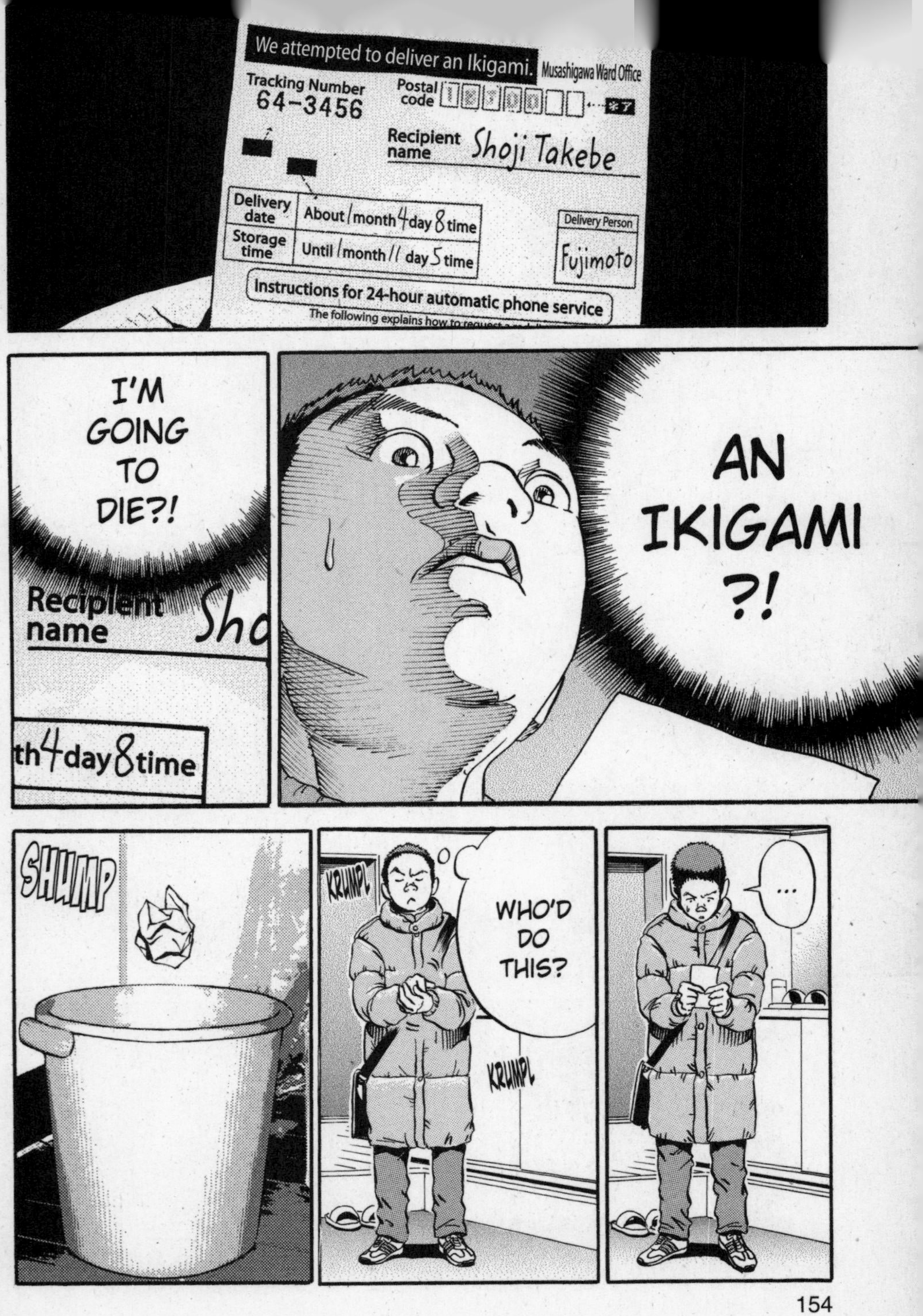
We attempted to deliver an Ikigami.
Musashigawa Ward Office
Tracking Number
64-3456
Postal code
Recipient name Shoji Takebe
Delivery date About 1 month 4 day 8 time
Storage time Until 1 month 11 day 5 time
Delivery Person
Fujimoto
Instructions for 24-hour automatic phone service
AN IKIGAMI ?!
I'M GOING TO DIE?!
Recipient name Sho
th 4 day 8 time
...
KRUMPL
WHO'D DO THIS?
KRUMPL
SHUMP

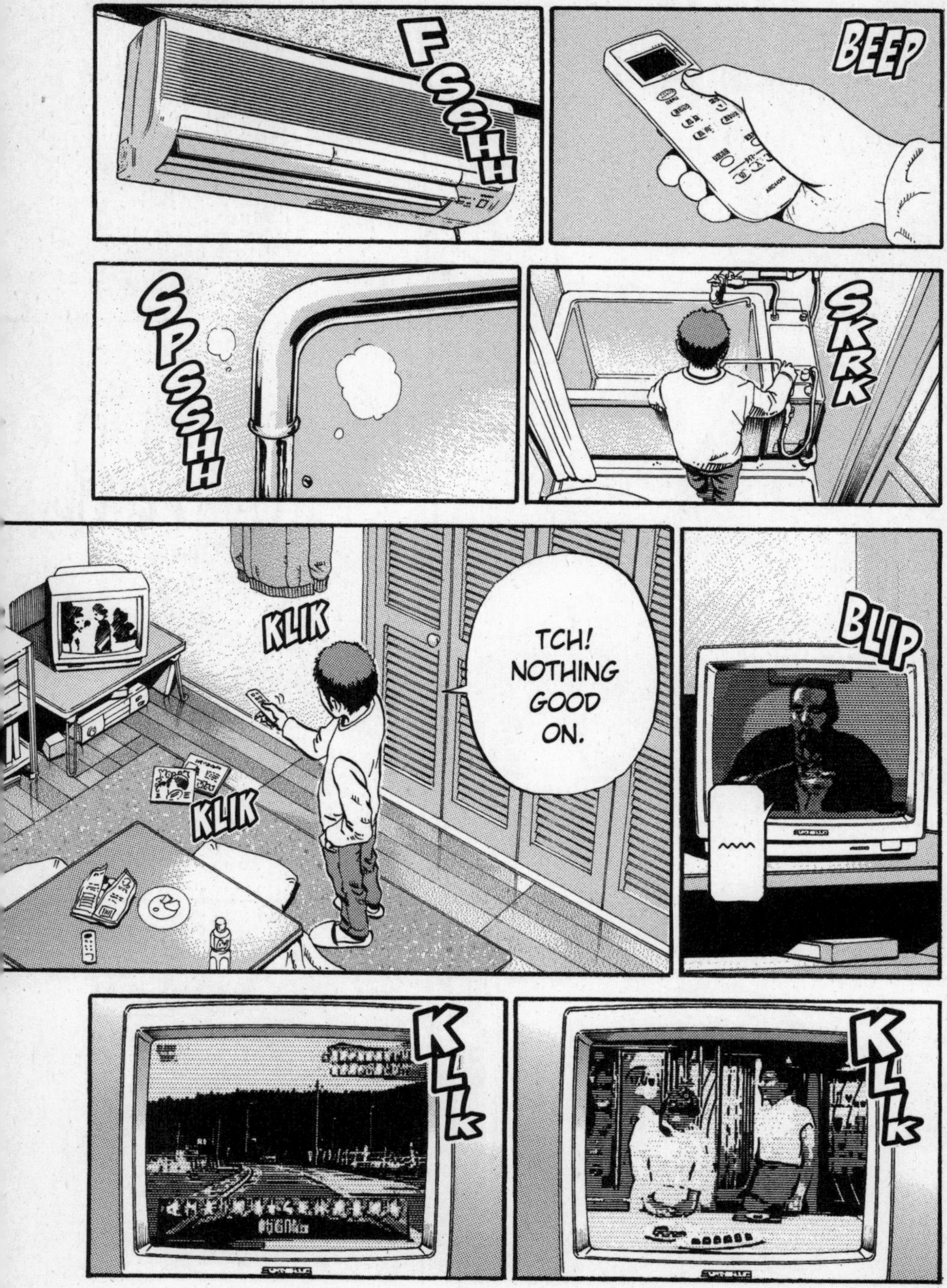
BEEP
FSSHH
SKRK
SPSSHH
BLIP
~~~
TCH! NOTHING GOOD ON.
KLIK
KLIK
KLIK
KLIK
~~~

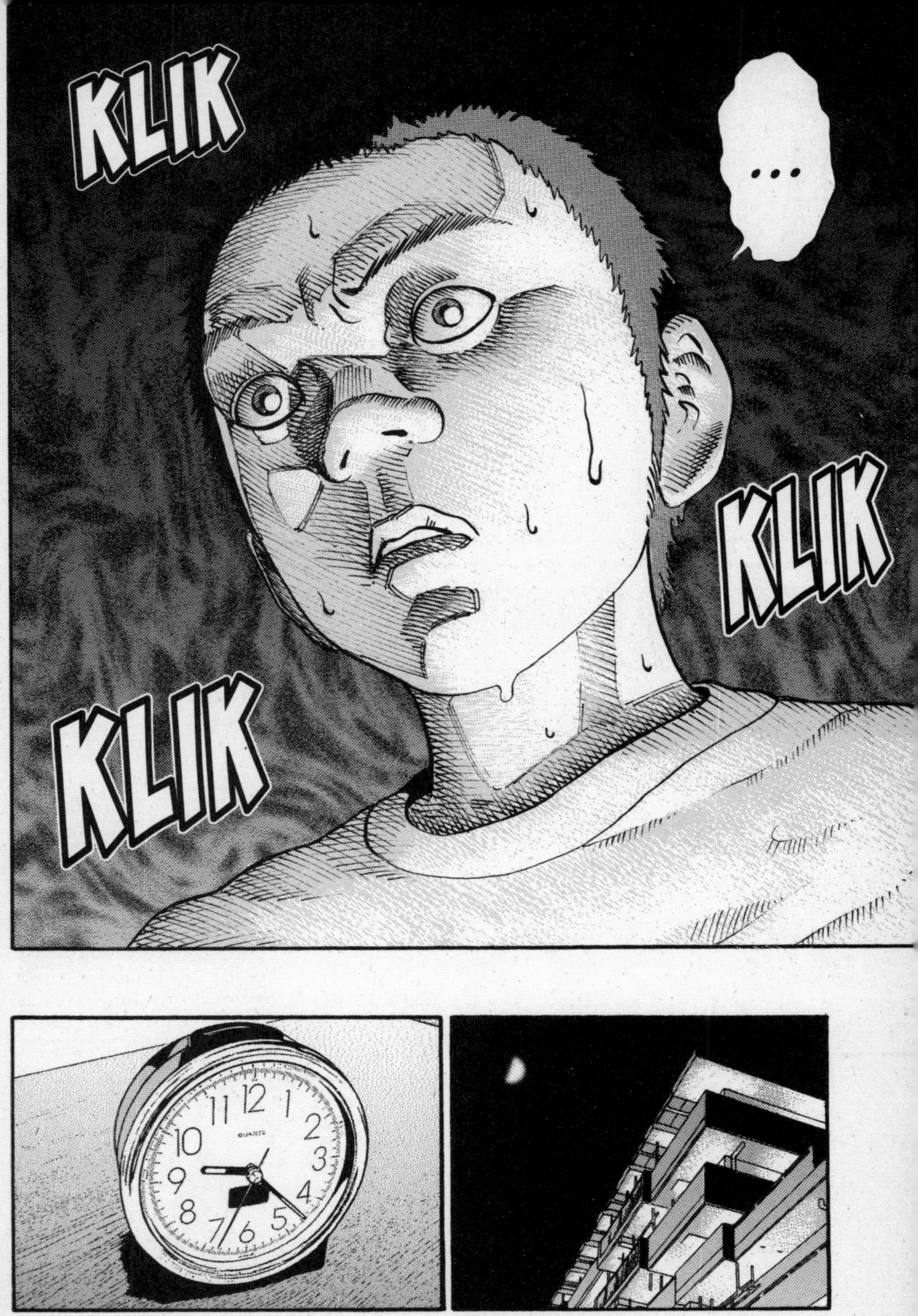
...
KLIK
KLIK
KLIK

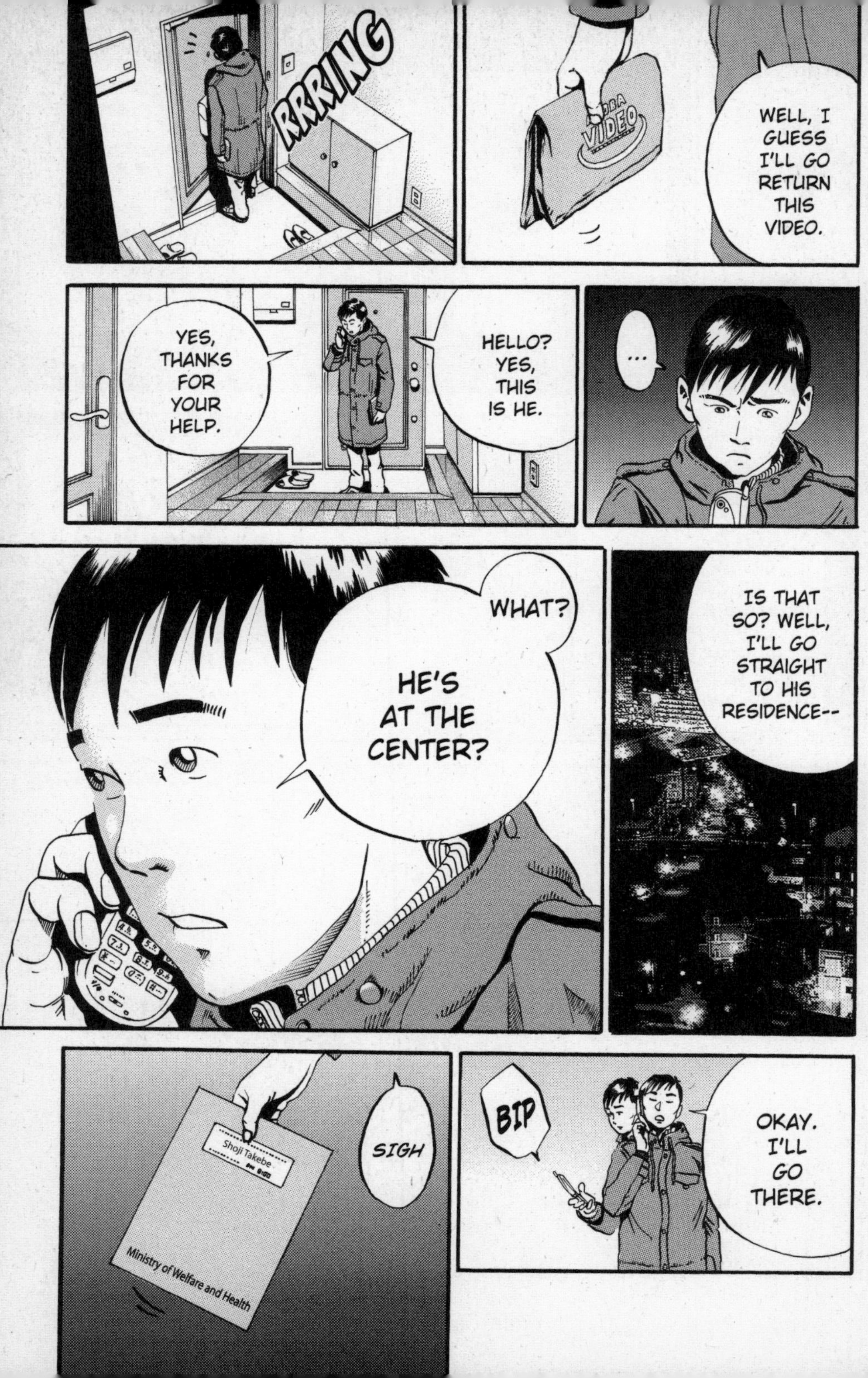
WELL, I GUESS I'LL GO RETURN THIS VIDEO.
VIDEO
RRRING
...
HELLO? YES, THIS IS HE.
YES, THANKS FOR YOUR HELP.
IS THAT SO? WELL, I'LL GO STRAIGHT TO HIS RESIDENCE--
WHAT?
HE'S AT THE CENTER?
OKAY. I'LL GO THERE.
BIP
SIGH
Shoji Takebe
Ministry of Welfare and Health

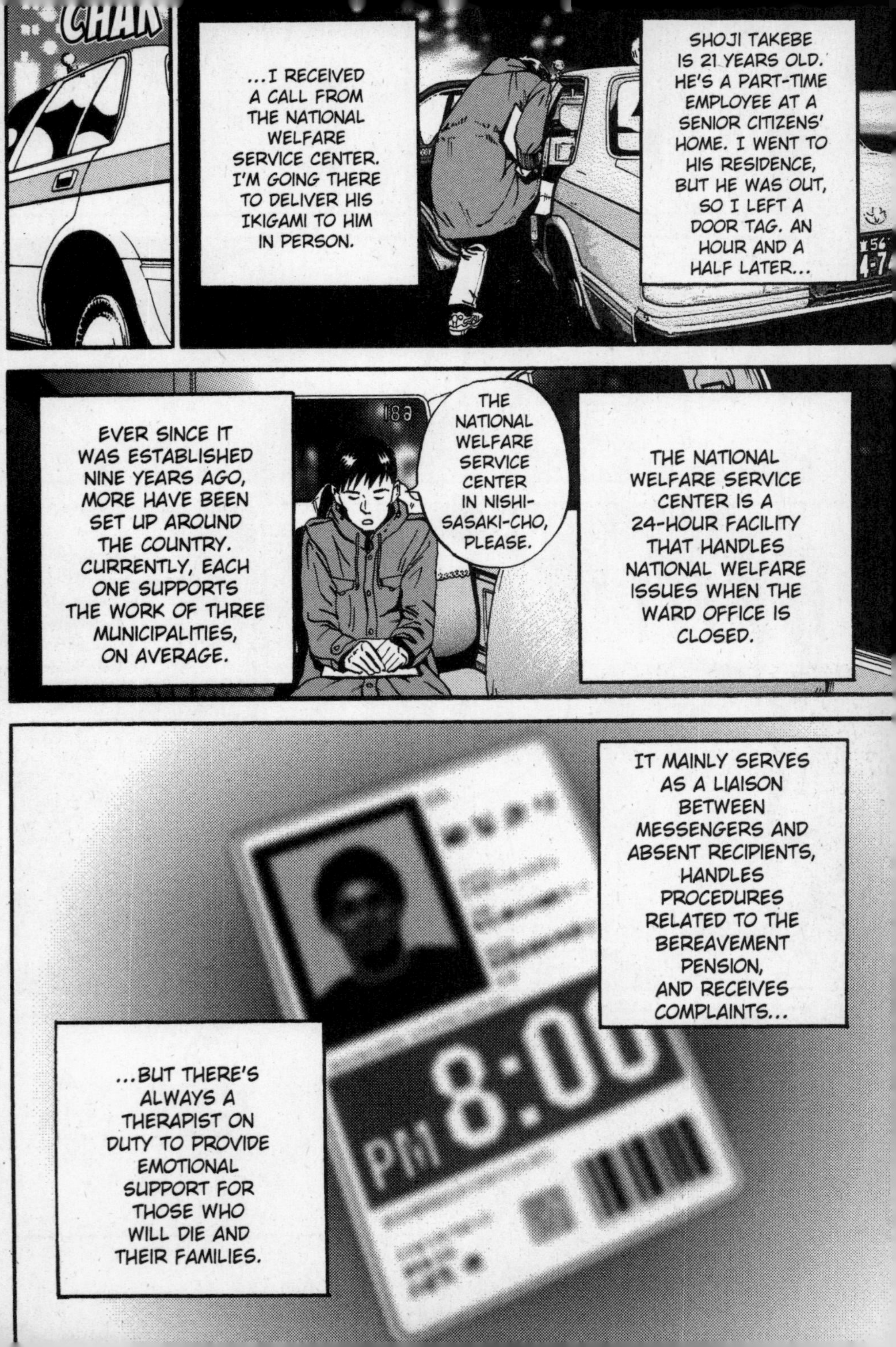
SHOJI TAKEBE IS 21 YEARS OLD. HE'S A PART-TIME EMPLOYEE AT A SENIOR CITIZENS' HOME. I WENT TO HIS RESIDENCE, BUT HE WAS OUT, SO I LEFT A DOOR TAG. AN HOUR AND A HALF LATER...
...I RECEIVED A CALL FROM THE NATIONAL WELFARE SERVICE CENTER. I'M GOING THERE TO DELIVER HIS IKIGAMI TO HIM IN PERSON.
CHAN
THE NATIONAL WELFARE SERVICE CENTER IS A 24-HOUR FACILITY THAT HANDLES NATIONAL WELFARE ISSUES WHEN THE WARD OFFICE IS CLOSED.
THE NATIONAL WELFARE SERVICE CENTER IN NISHI-SASAKI-CHO, PLEASE.
EVER SINCE IT WAS ESTABLISHED NINE YEARS AGO, MORE HAVE BEEN SET UP AROUND THE COUNTRY. CURRENTLY, EACH ONE SUPPORTS THE WORK OF THREE MUNICIPALITIES, ON AVERAGE.
IT MAINLY SERVES AS A LIAISON BETWEEN MESSENGERS AND ABSENT RECIPIENTS, HANDLES PROCEDURES RELATED TO THE BEREAVEMENT PENSION, AND RECEIVES COMPLAINTS...
...BUT THERE'S ALWAYS A THERAPIST ON DUTY TO PROVIDE EMOTIONAL SUPPORT FOR THOSE WHO WILL DIE AND THEIR FAMILIES.

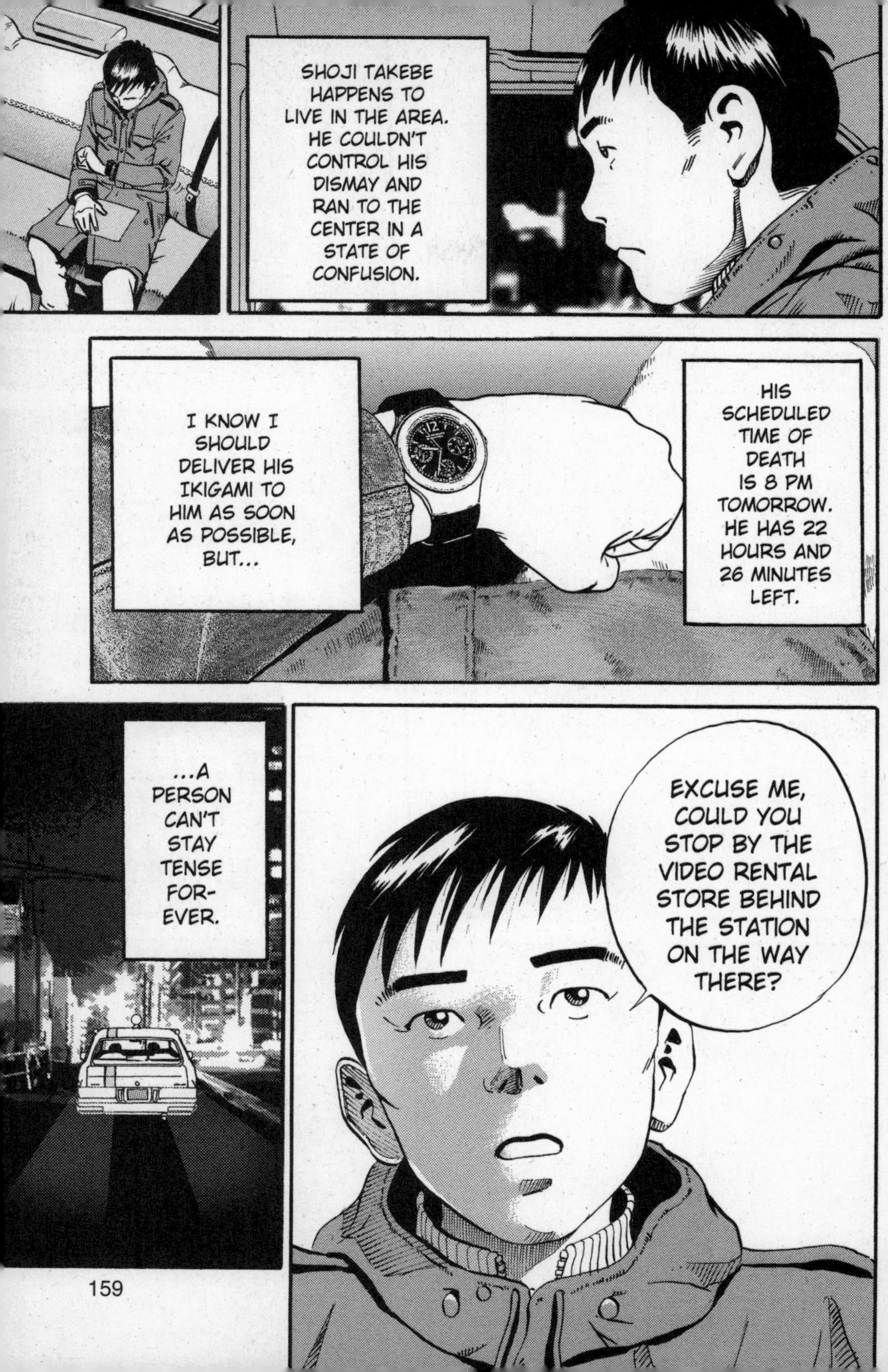
SHOJI TAKEBE HAPPENS TO LIVE IN THE AREA. HE COULDN'T CONTROL HIS DISMAY AND RAN TO THE CENTER IN A STATE OF CONFUSION.
HIS SCHEDULED TIME OF DEATH IS 8 PM TOMORROW. HE HAS 22 HOURS AND 26 MINUTES LEFT.
I KNOW I SHOULD DELIVER HIS IKIGAMI TO HIM AS SOON AS POSSIBLE, BUT...
EXCUSE ME, COULD YOU STOP BY THE VIDEO RENTAL STORE BEHIND THE STATION ON THE WAY THERE?
...A PERSON CAN'T STAY TENSE FOR-EVER.

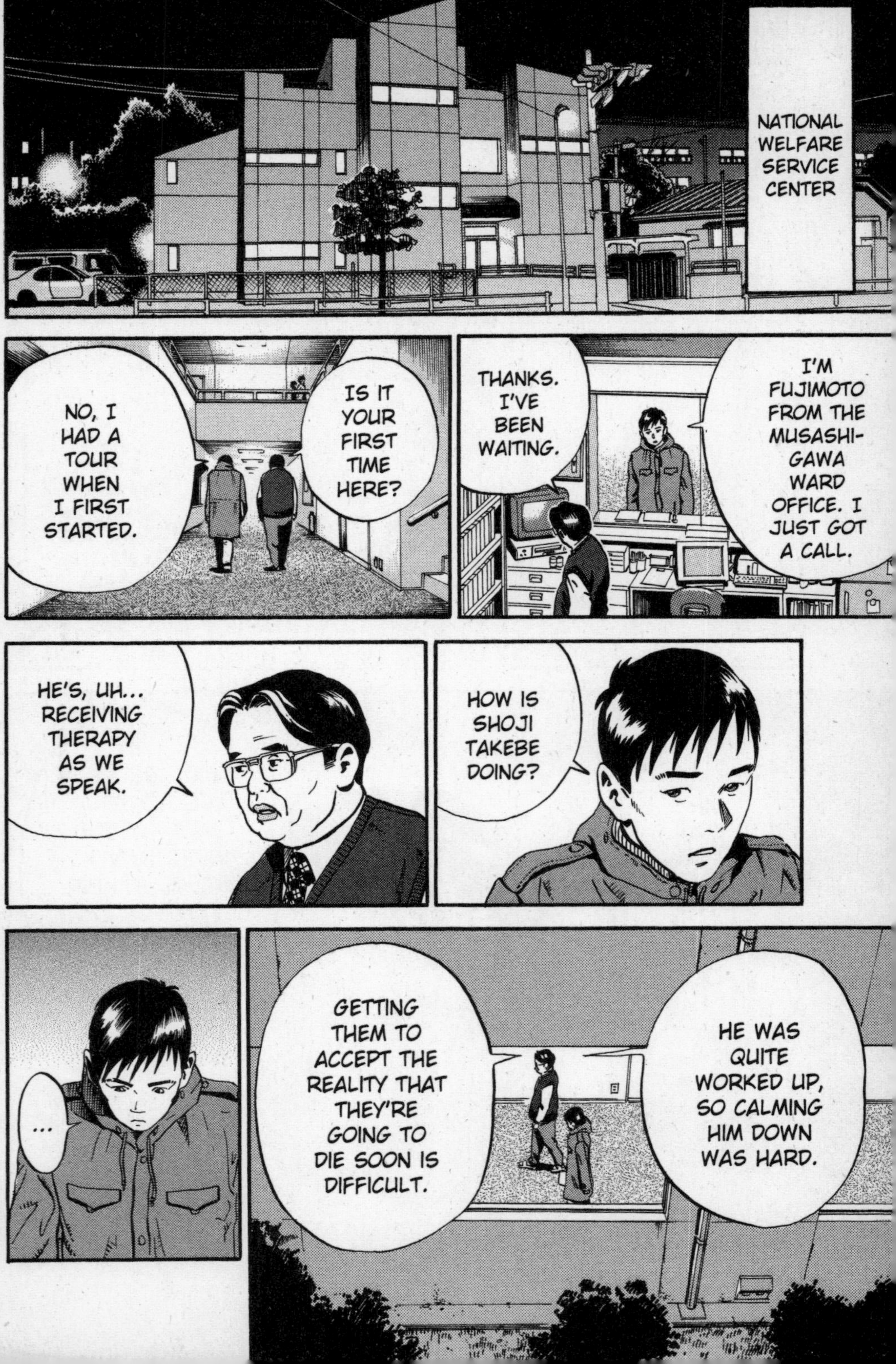
NATIONAL WELFARE SERVICE CENTER
I'M FUJIMOTO FROM THE MUSASHI-GAWA WARD OFFICE. I JUST GOT A CALL.
THANKS. I'VE BEEN WAITING.
IS IT YOUR FIRST TIME HERE?
NO, I HAD A TOUR WHEN I FIRST STARTED.
HOW IS SHOJI TAKEBE DOING?
HE'S, UH... RECEIVING THERAPY AS WE SPEAK.
HE WAS QUITE WORKED UP, SO CALMING HIM DOWN WAS HARD.
GETTING THEM TO ACCEPT THE REALITY THAT THEY'RE GOING TO DIE SOON IS DIFFICULT.
...

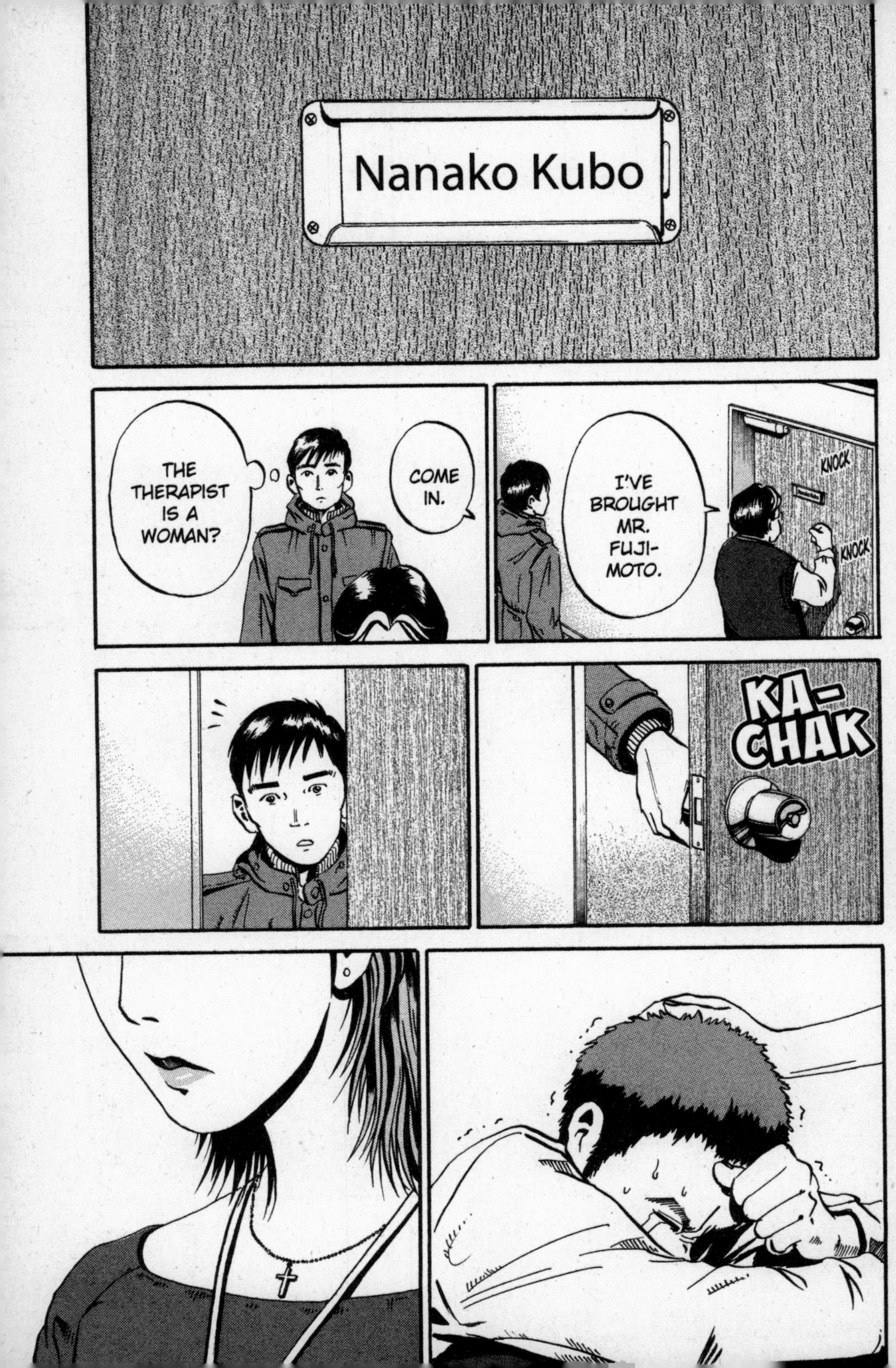
Nanako Kubo
KNOCK
KNOCK
I'VE BROUGHT MR. FUJI-MOTO.
COME IN.
THE THERAPIST IS A WOMAN?
KA-CHAK

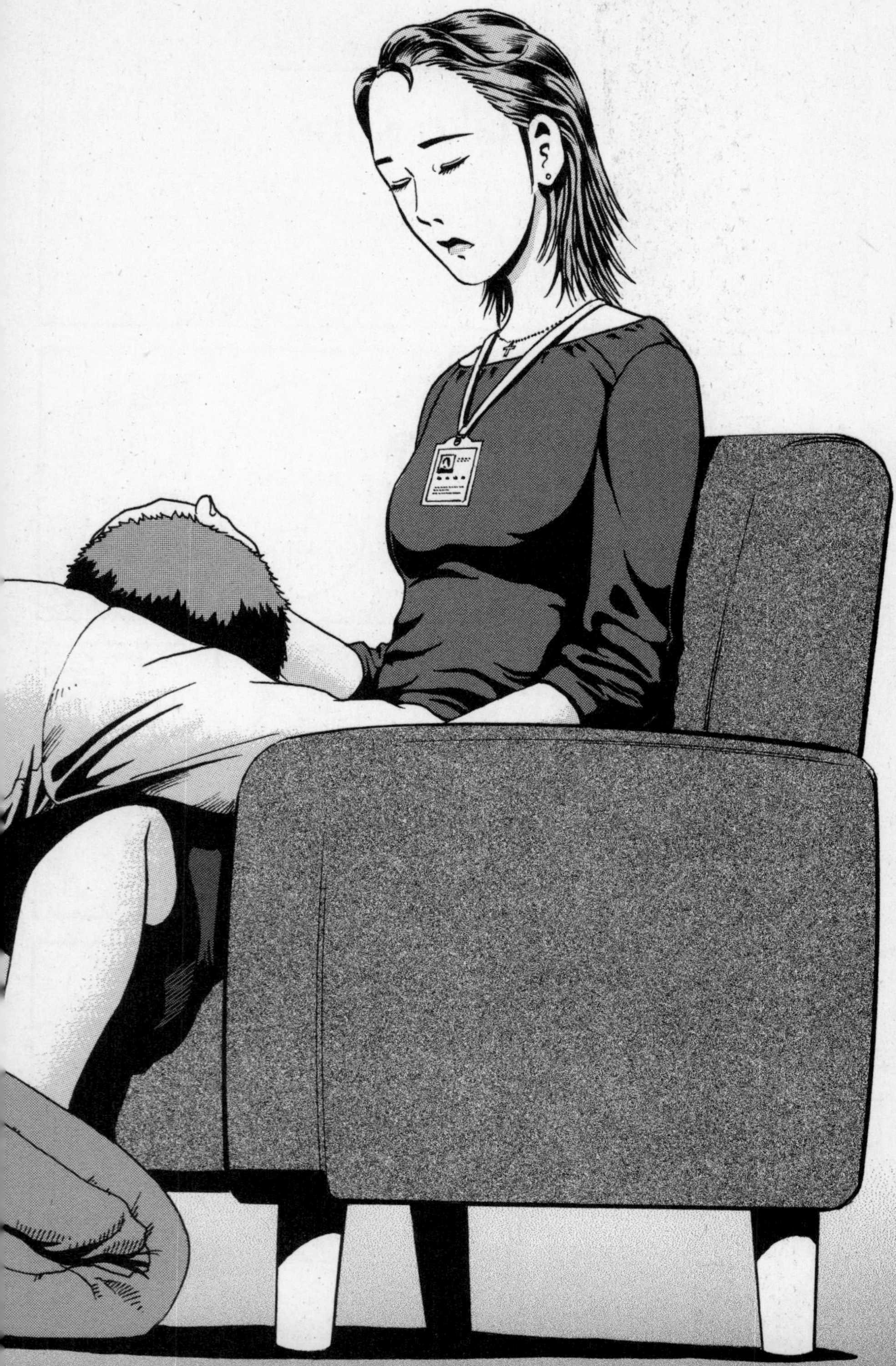

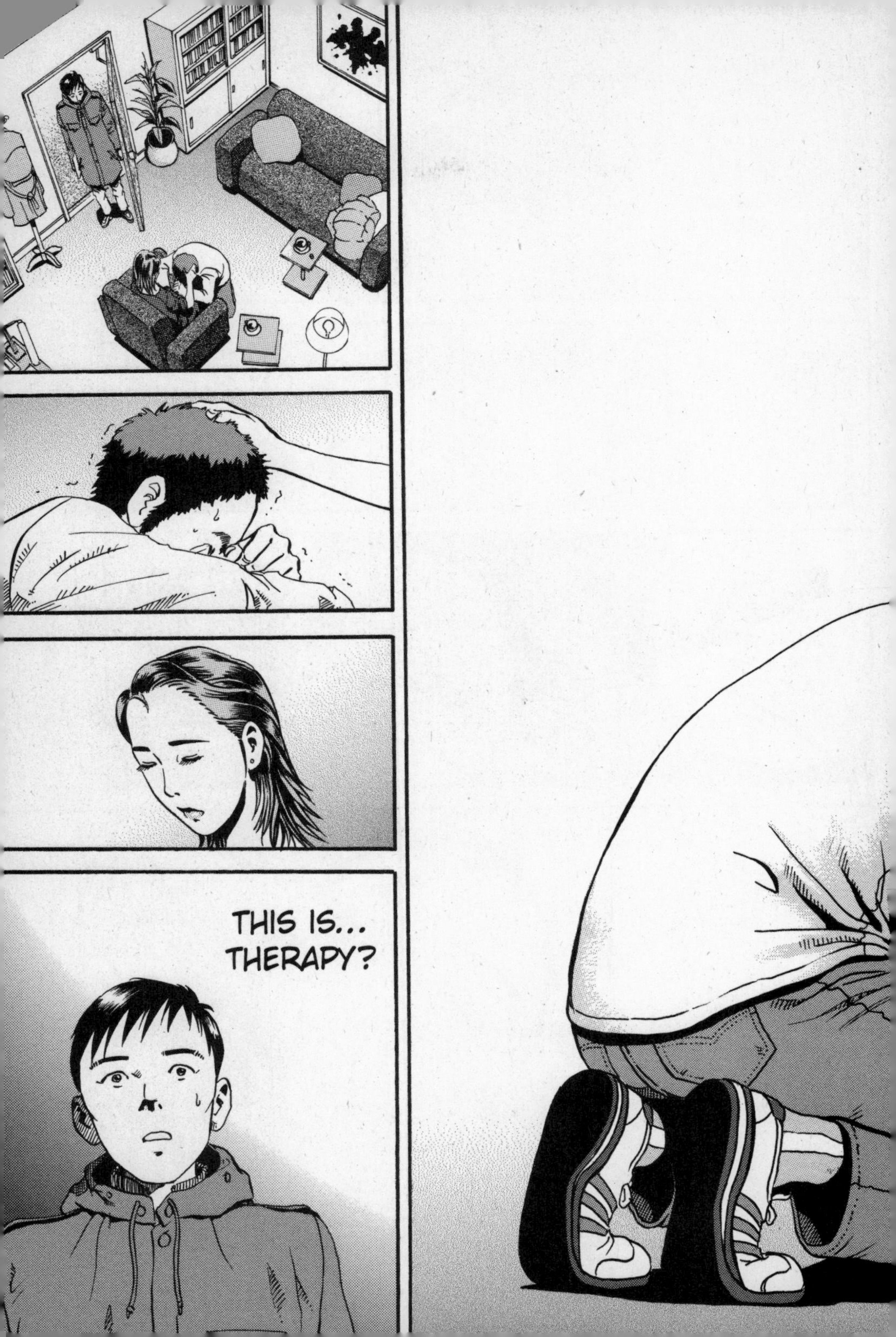
THIS IS... THERAPY?

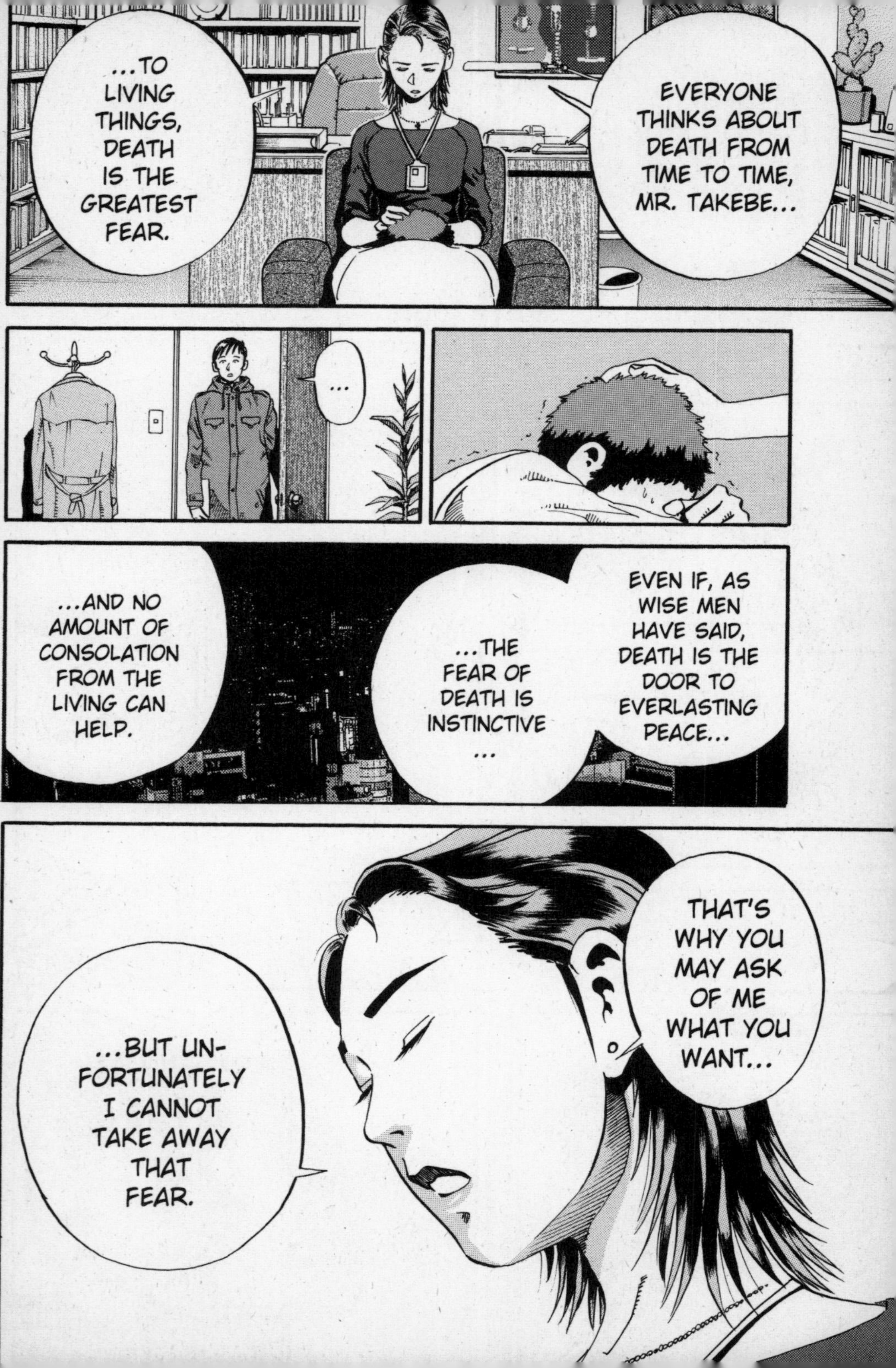
EVERYONE THINKS ABOUT DEATH FROM TIME TO TIME, MR. TAKEBE...
...TO LIVING THINGS, DEATH IS THE GREATEST FEAR.
...
EVEN IF, AS WISE MEN HAVE SAID, DEATH IS THE DOOR TO EVERLASTING PEACE...
...THE FEAR OF DEATH IS INSTINCTIVE ...
...AND NO AMOUNT OF CONSOLATION FROM THE LIVING CAN HELP.
THAT'S WHY YOU MAY ASK OF ME WHAT YOU WANT...
...BUT UN-FORTUNATELY I CANNOT TAKE AWAY THAT FEAR.

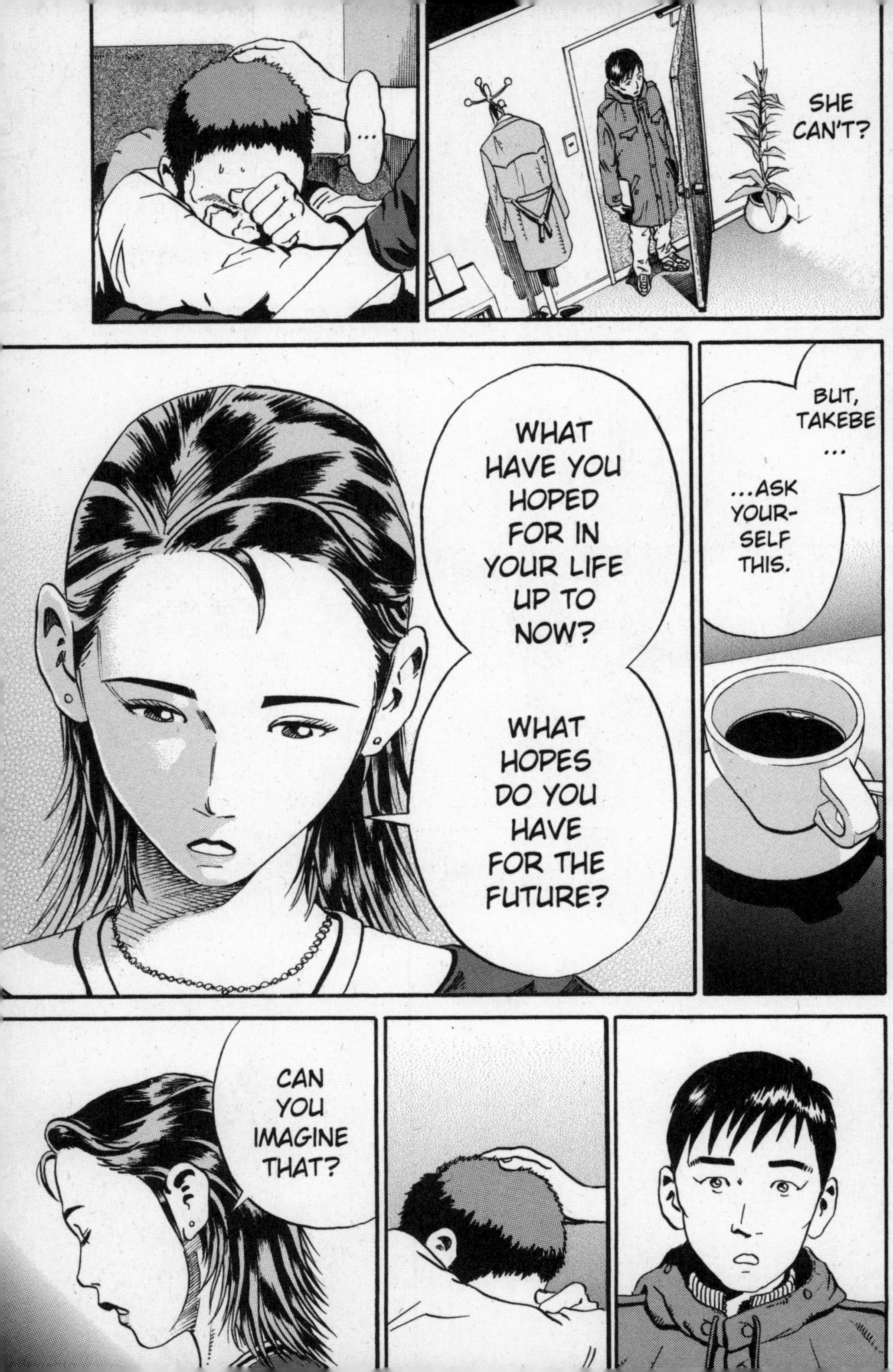
SHE CAN'T?
...
BUT, TAKEBE ...
...ASK YOURSELF THIS.
WHAT HAVE YOU HOPED FOR IN YOUR LIFE UP TO NOW?
WHAT HOPES DO YOU HAVE FOR THE FUTURE?
CAN YOU IMAGINE THAT?

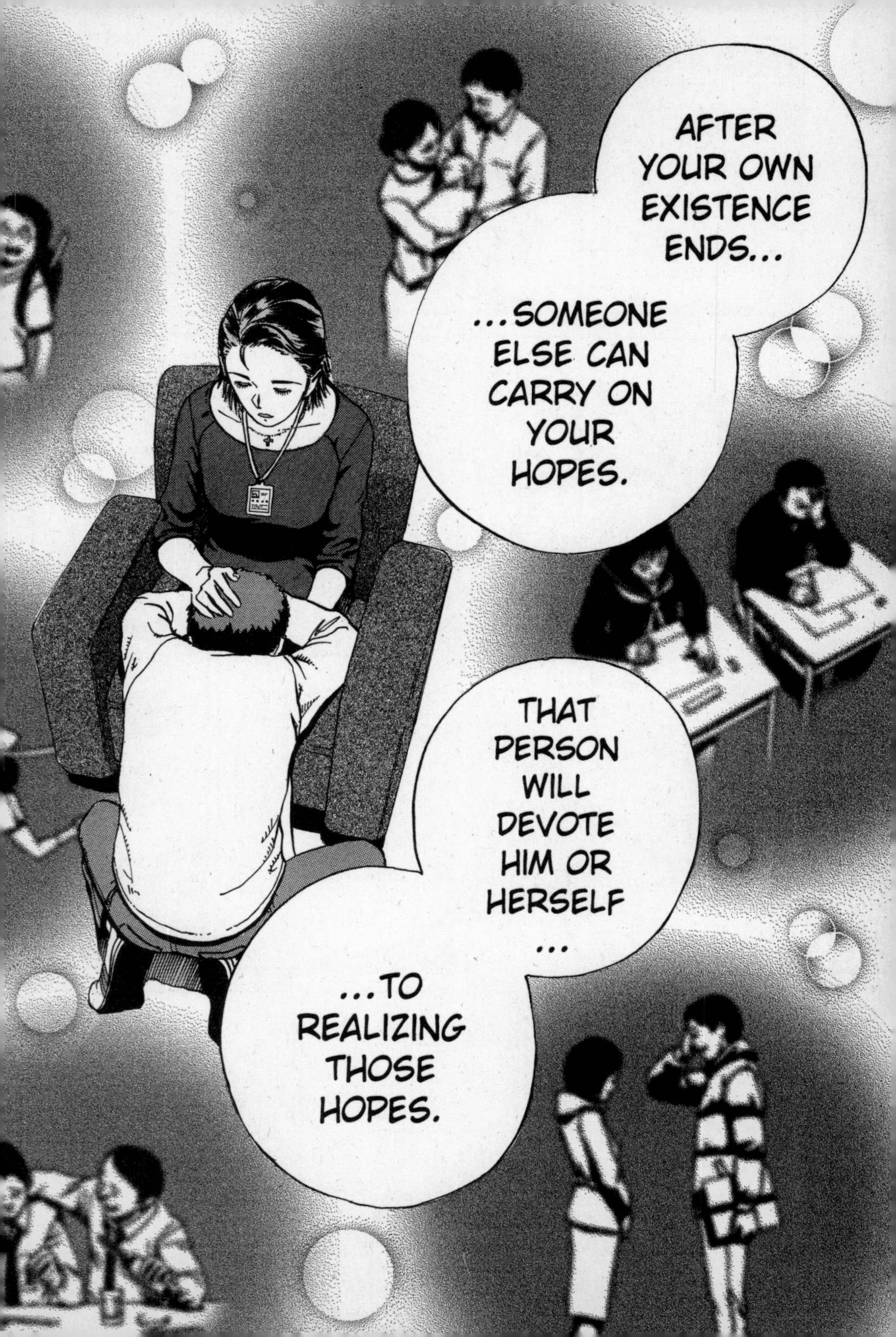
AFTER YOUR OWN EXISTENCE ENDS...
...SOMEONE ELSE CAN CARRY ON YOUR HOPES.
THAT PERSON WILL DEVOTE HIM OR HERSELF ...
...TO REALIZING THOSE HOPES.

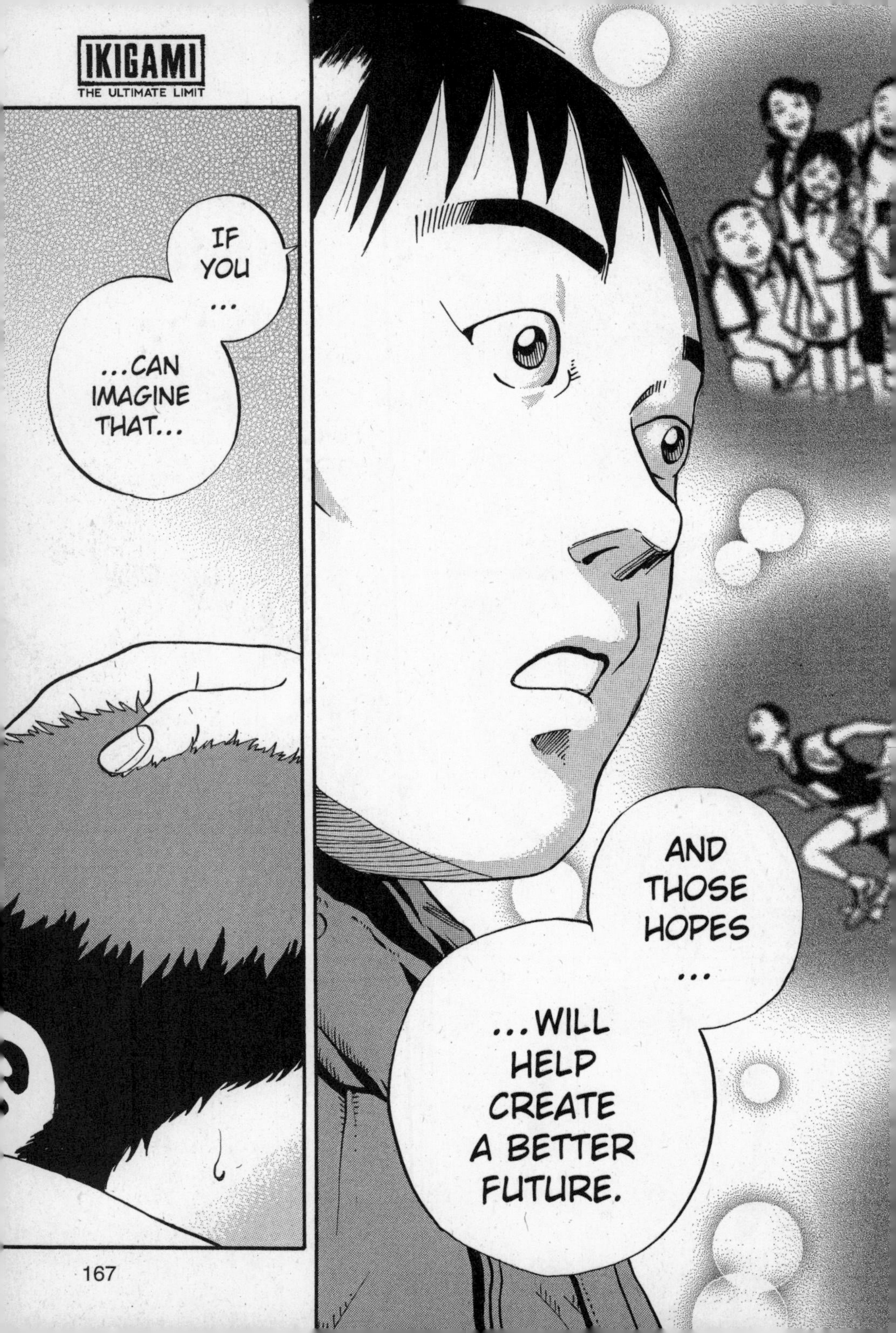
IF YOU ...
...CAN IMAGINE THAT...
AND THOSE HOPES ...
...WILL HELP CREATE A BETTER FUTURE.

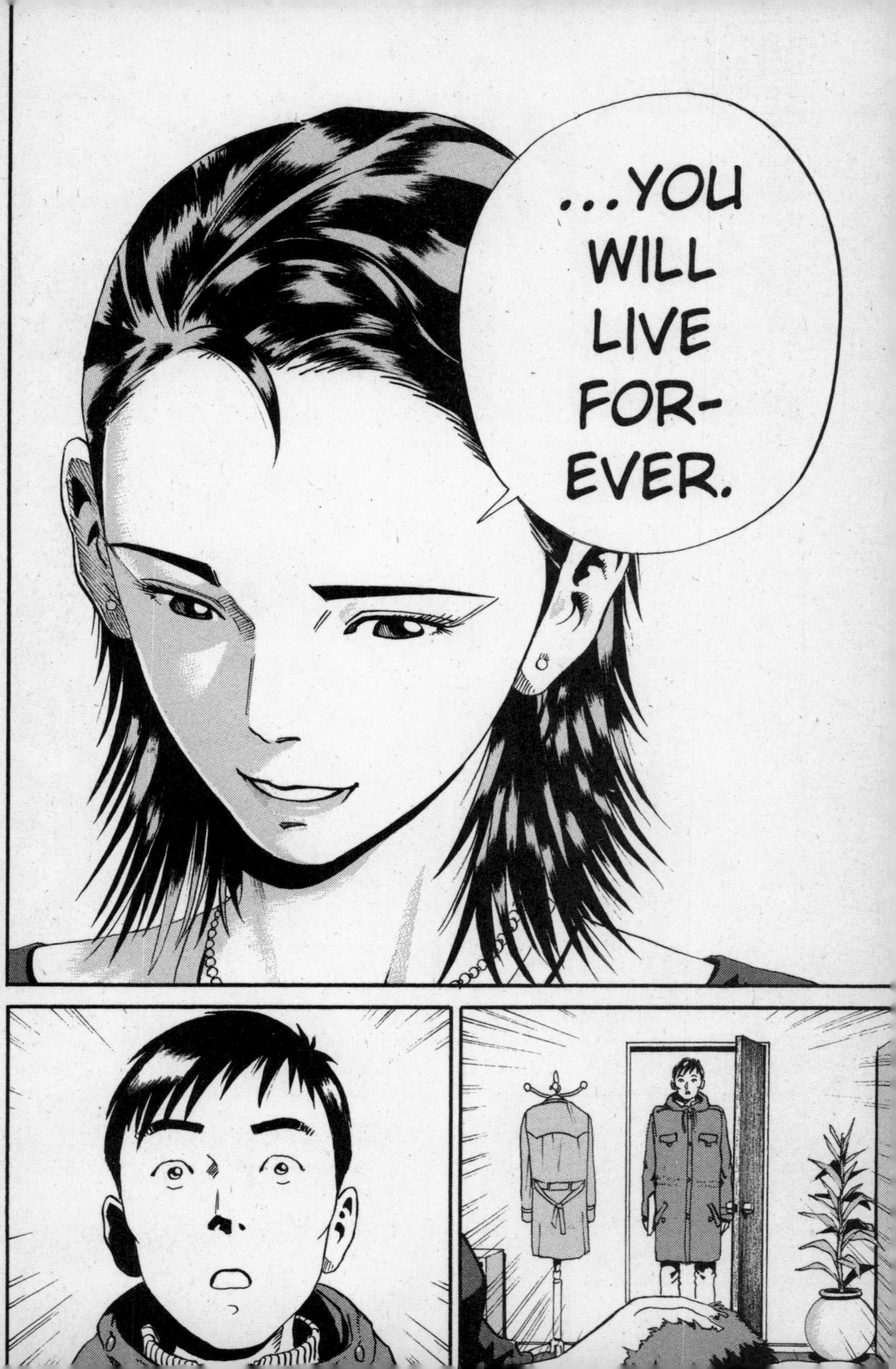
...YOU WILL LIVE FOR-EVER.

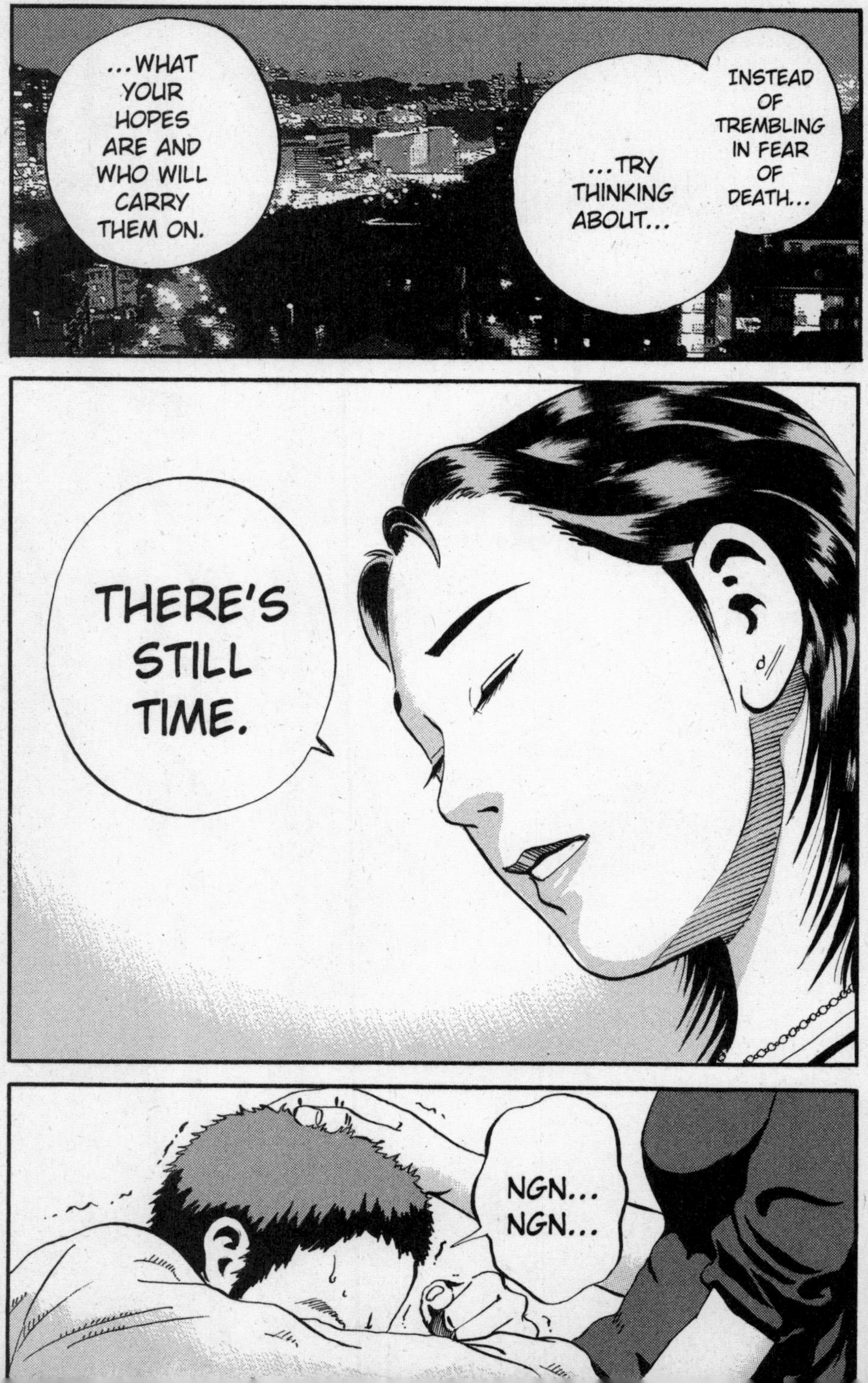
INSTEAD OF TREMBLING IN FEAR OF DEATH...
...TRY THINKING ABOUT...
...WHAT YOUR HOPES ARE AND WHO WILL CARRY THEM ON.
THERE'S STILL TIME.
NGN... NGN...

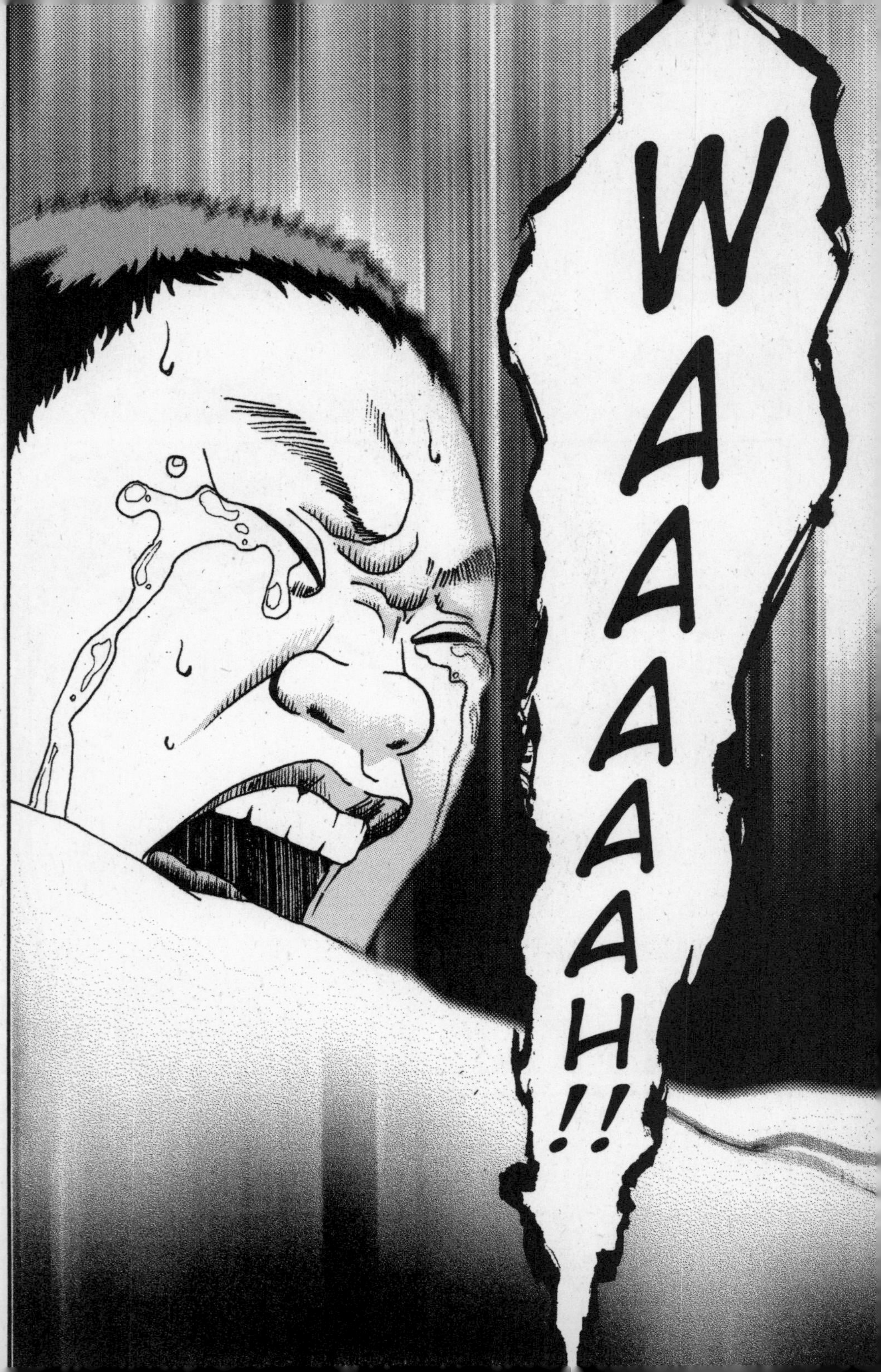
WAAAAAH!!

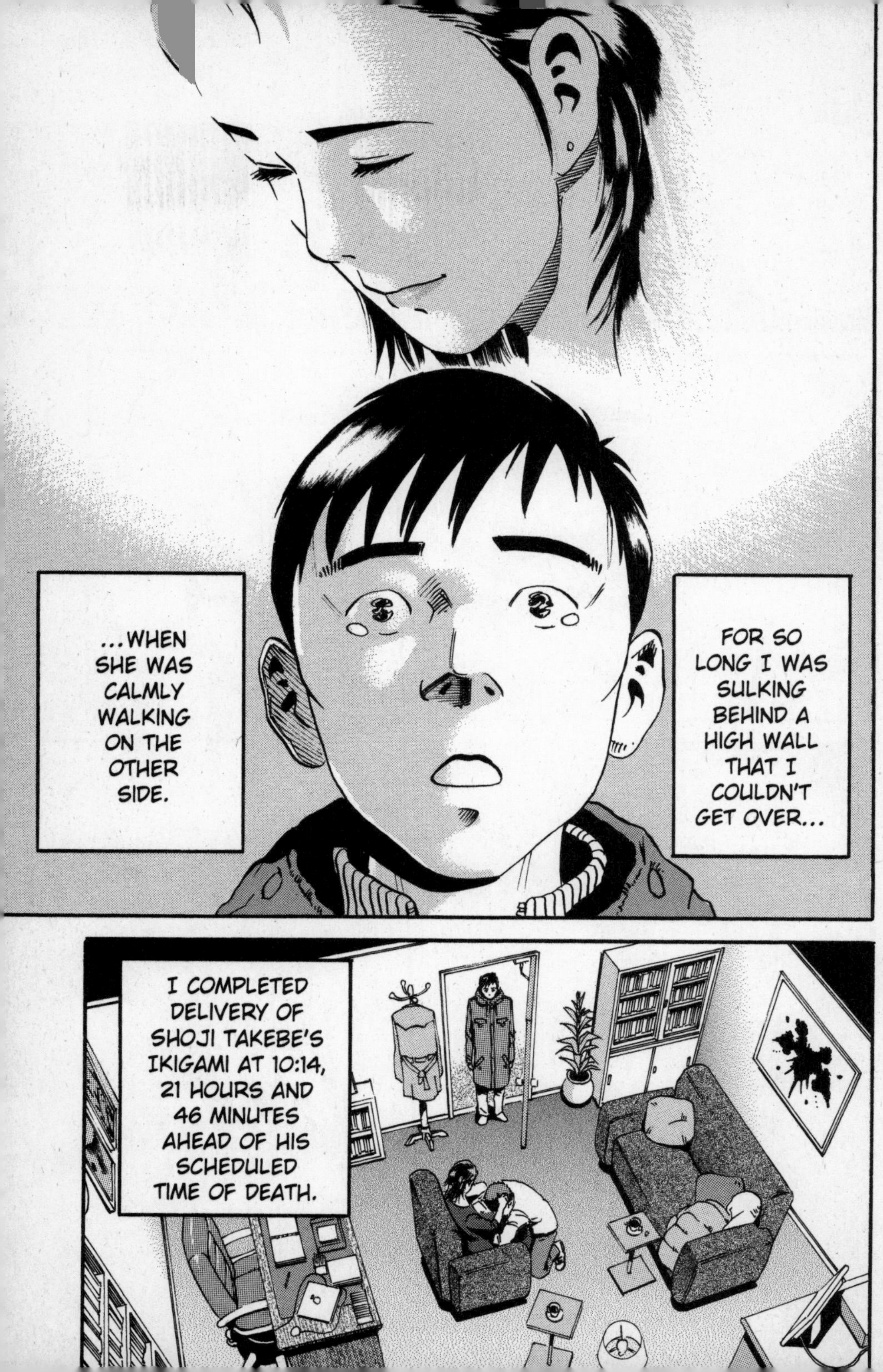
FOR SO LONG I WAS SULKING BEHIND A HIGH WALL THAT I COULDN'T GET OVER...
...WHEN SHE WAS CALMLY WALKING ON THE OTHER SIDE.
I COMPLETED DELIVERY OF SHOJI TAKEBE'S IKIGAMI AT 10:14, 21 HOURS AND 46 MINUTES AHEAD OF HIS SCHEDULED TIME OF DEATH.

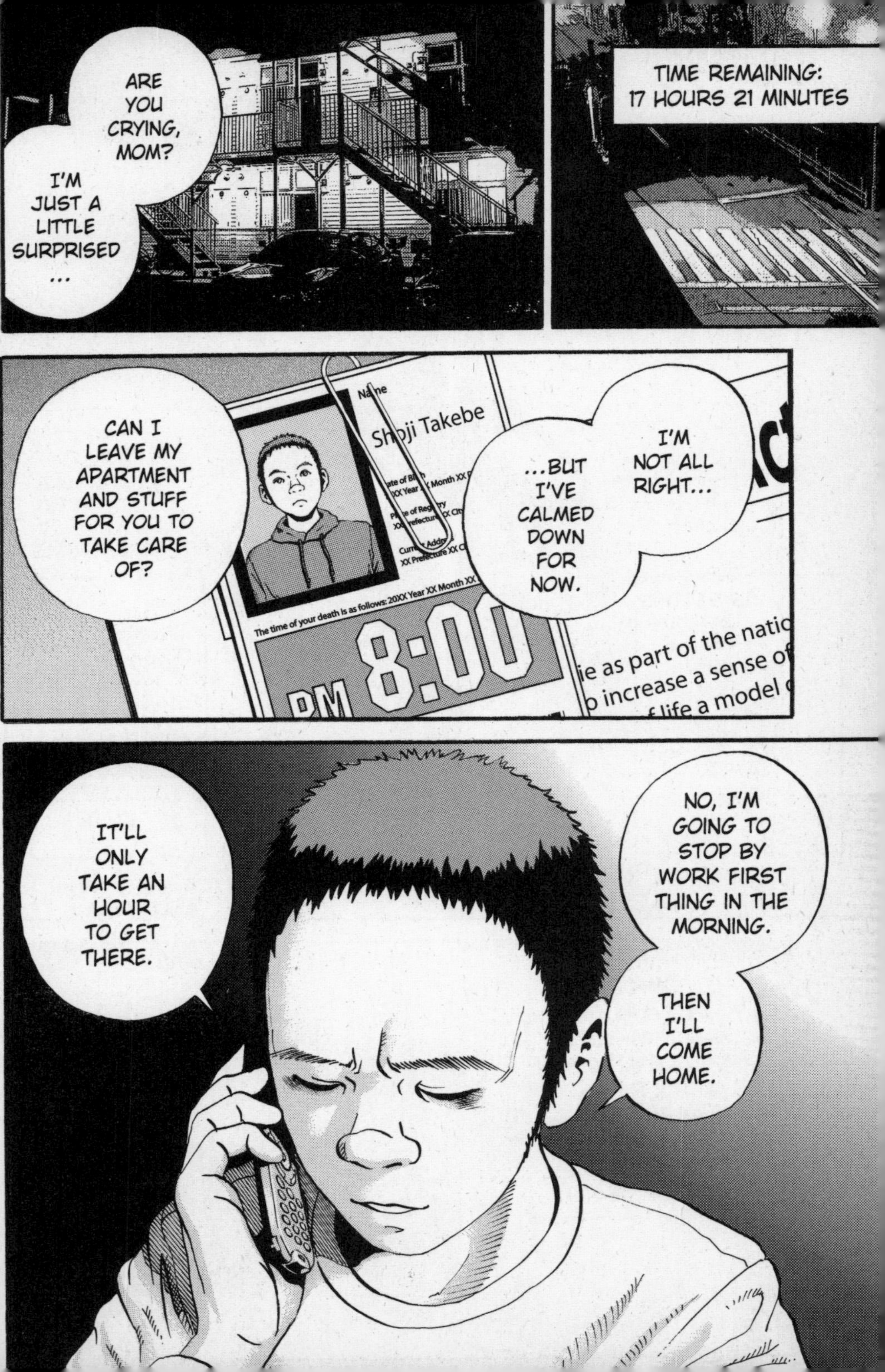
TIME REMAINING: 17 HOURS 21 MINUTES
ARE YOU CRYING, MOM?
I'M JUST A LITTLE SURPRISED...
Name
Shoji Takebe
The time of your death is as follows: 20XX Year XX Month XX
PM 8:00
I'M NOT ALL RIGHT...
...BUT I'VE CALMED DOWN FOR NOW.
CAN I LEAVE MY APARTMENT AND STUFF FOR YOU TO TAKE CARE OF?
NO, I'M GOING TO STOP BY WORK FIRST THING IN THE MORNING.
THEN I'LL COME HOME.
IT'LL ONLY TAKE AN HOUR TO GET THERE.

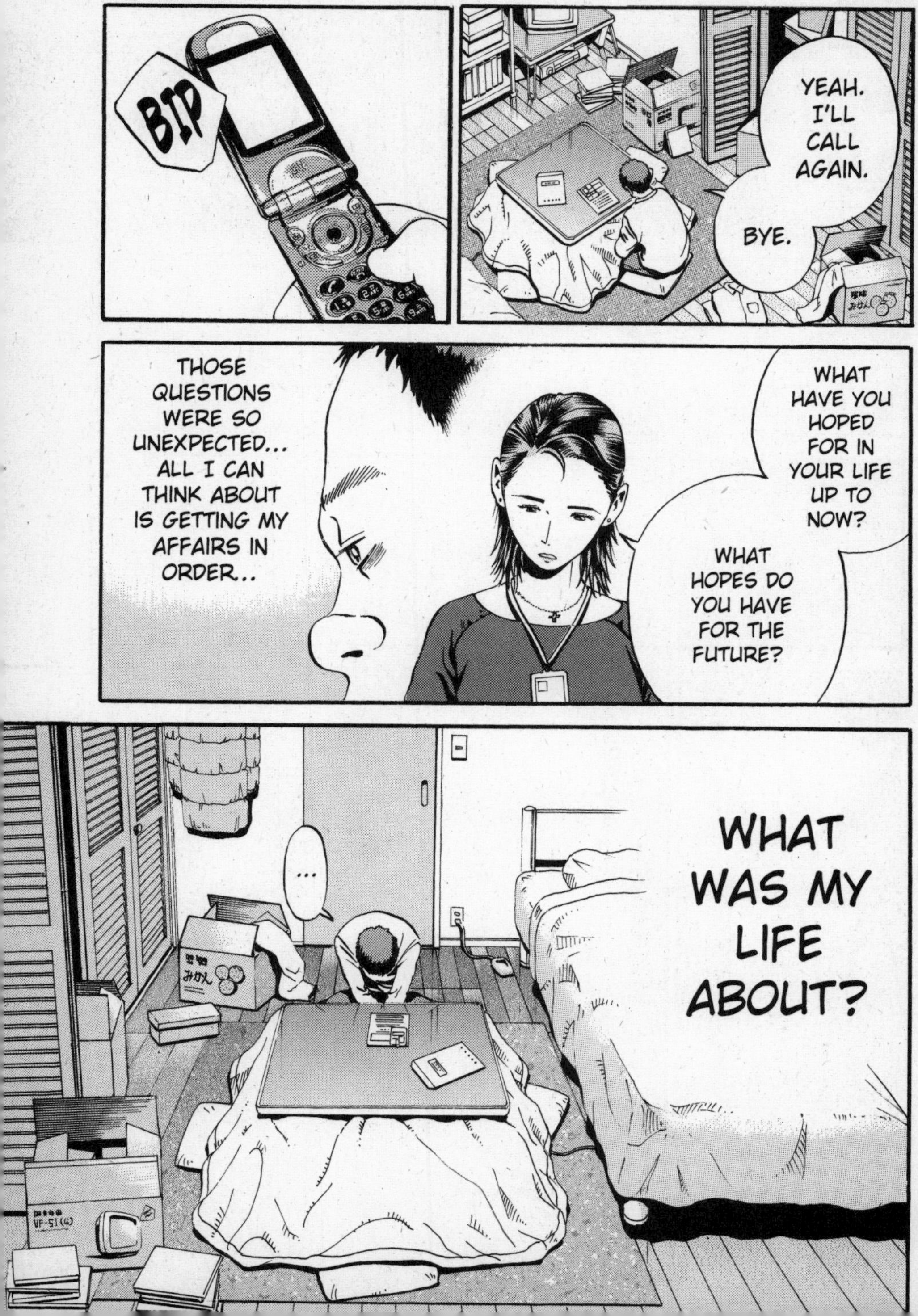
YEAH. I'LL CALL AGAIN.
BYE.
BIP
WHAT HAVE YOU HOPED FOR IN YOUR LIFE UP TO NOW?
WHAT HOPES DO YOU HAVE FOR THE FUTURE?
THOSE QUESTIONS WERE SO UNEXPECTED... ALL I CAN THINK ABOUT IS GETTING MY AFFAIRS IN ORDER...
WHAT WAS MY LIFE ABOUT?
...

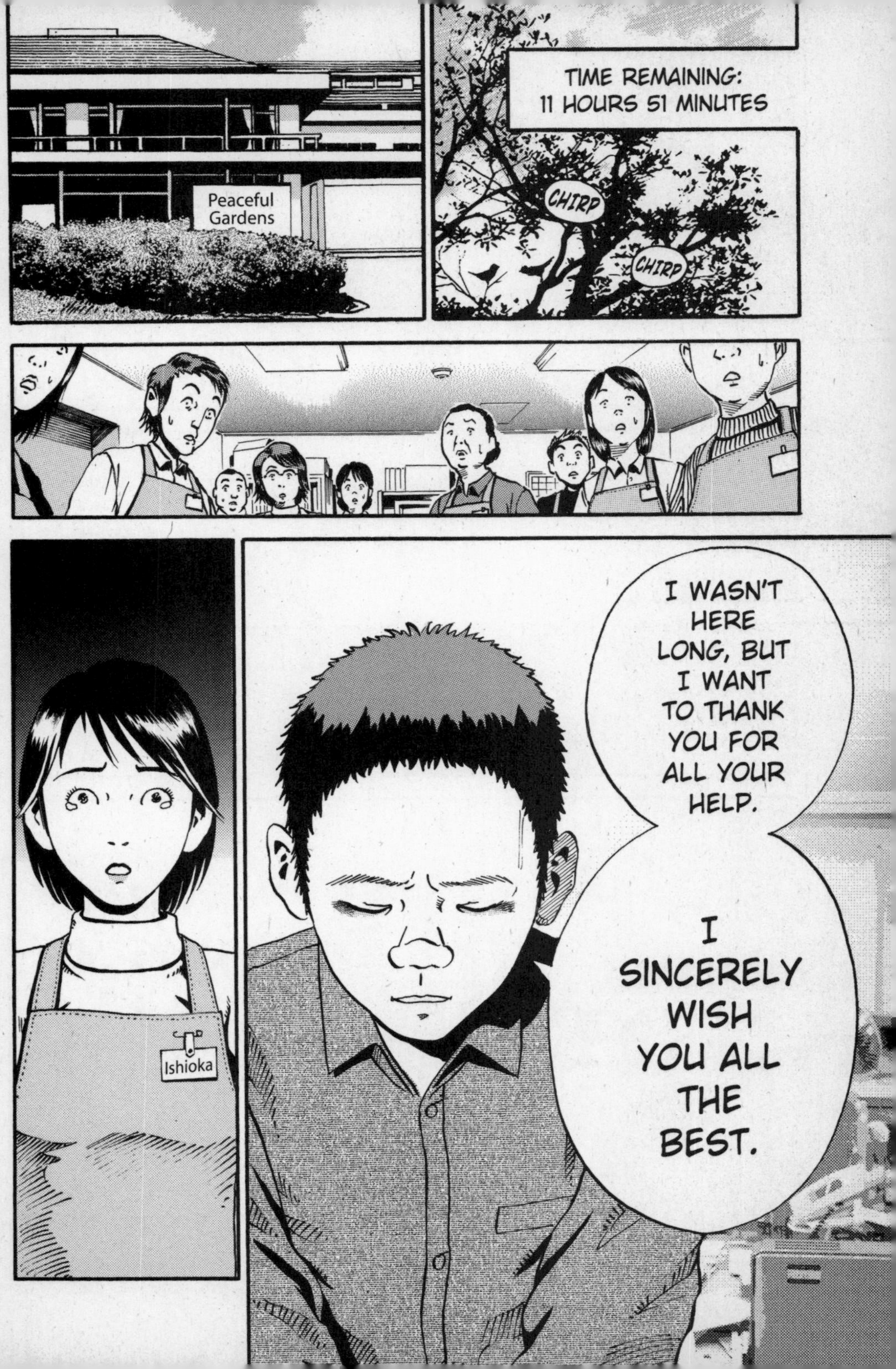
TIME REMAINING:
11 HOURS 51 MINUTES
CHIRP
CHIRP
Peaceful Gardens
I WASN'T HERE LONG, BUT I WANT TO THANK YOU FOR ALL YOUR HELP.
I SINCERELY WISH YOU ALL THE BEST.
Ishioka

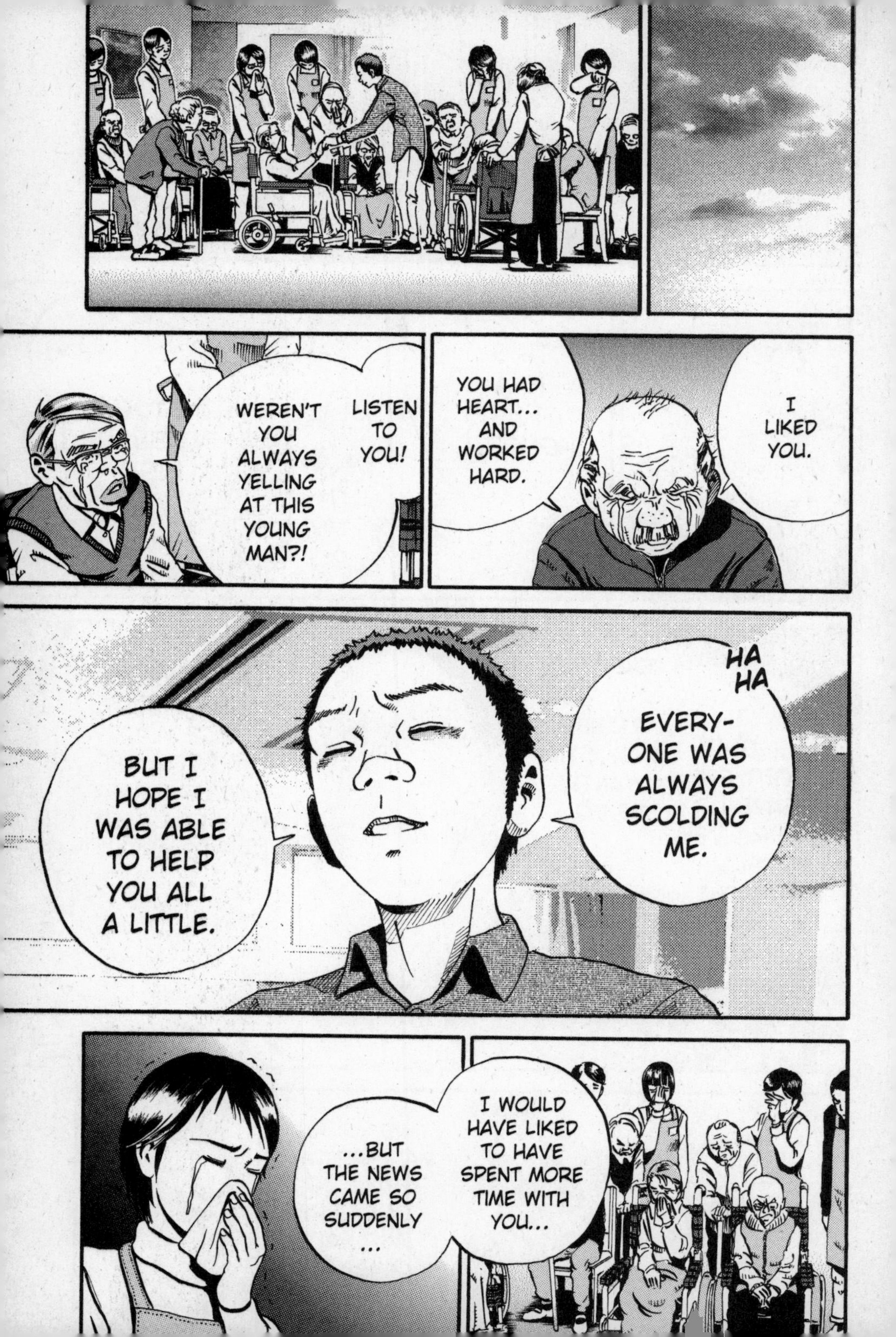
I LIKED YOU.
YOU HAD HEART... AND WORKED HARD.
LISTEN TO YOU!
WEREN'T YOU ALWAYS YELLING AT THIS YOUNG MAN?!
HA HA
EVERY-ONE WAS ALWAYS SCOLDING ME.
BUT I HOPE I WAS ABLE TO HELP YOU ALL A LITTLE.
I WOULD HAVE LIKED TO HAVE SPENT MORE TIME WITH YOU...
...BUT THE NEWS CAME SO SUDDENLY ...

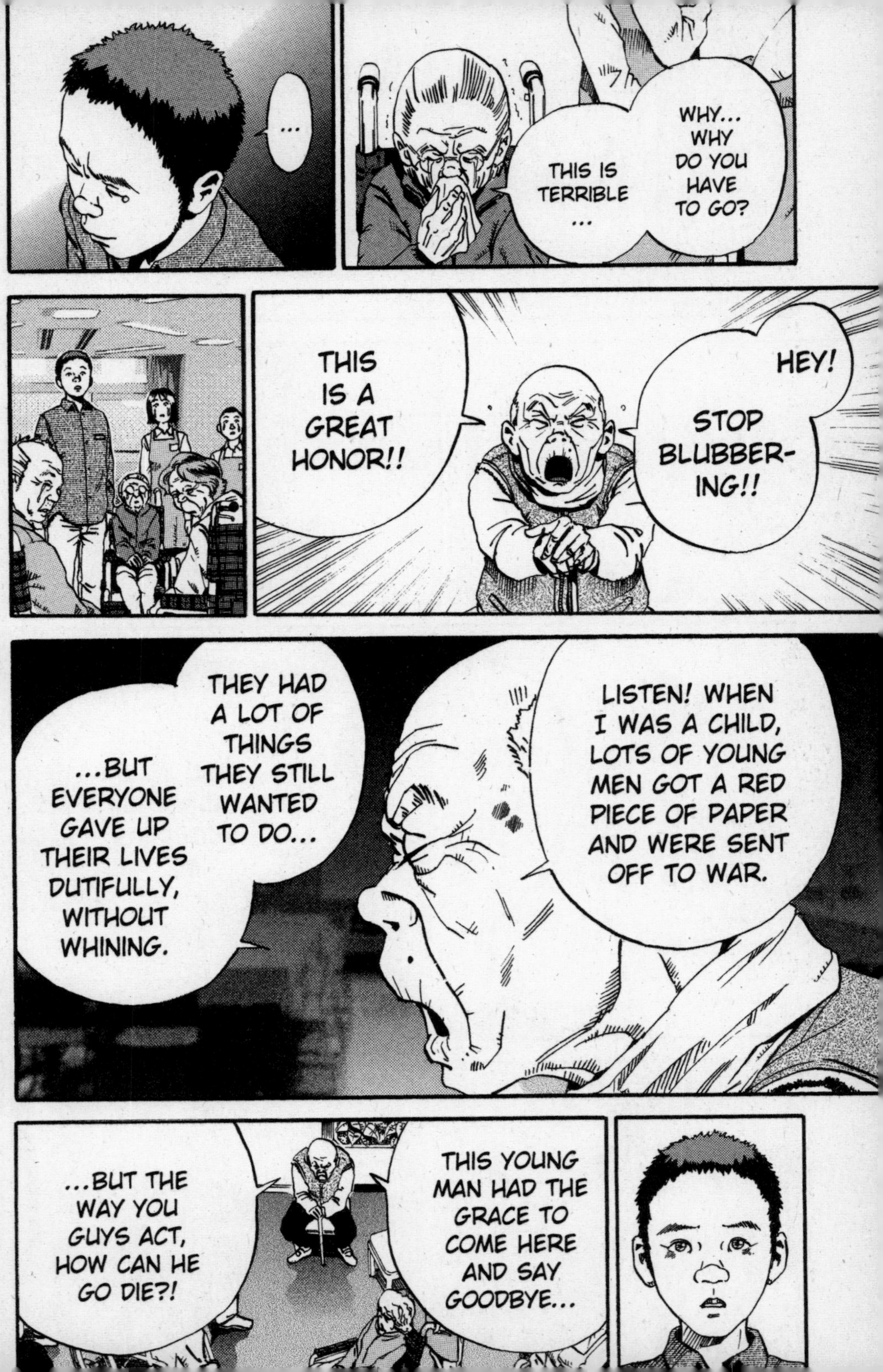
WHY... WHY DO YOU HAVE TO GO?
THIS IS TERRIBLE ...
...
HEY!
STOP BLUBBER-ING!!
THIS IS A GREAT HONOR!!
LISTEN! WHEN I WAS A CHILD, LOTS OF YOUNG MEN GOT A RED PIECE OF PAPER AND WERE SENT OFF TO WAR.
THEY HAD A LOT OF THINGS THEY STILL WANTED TO DO...
...BUT EVERYONE GAVE UP THEIR LIVES DUTIFULLY, WITHOUT WHINING.
THIS YOUNG MAN HAD THE GRACE TO COME HERE AND SAY GOODBYE...
...BUT THE WAY YOU GUYS ACT, HOW CAN HE GO DIE?!

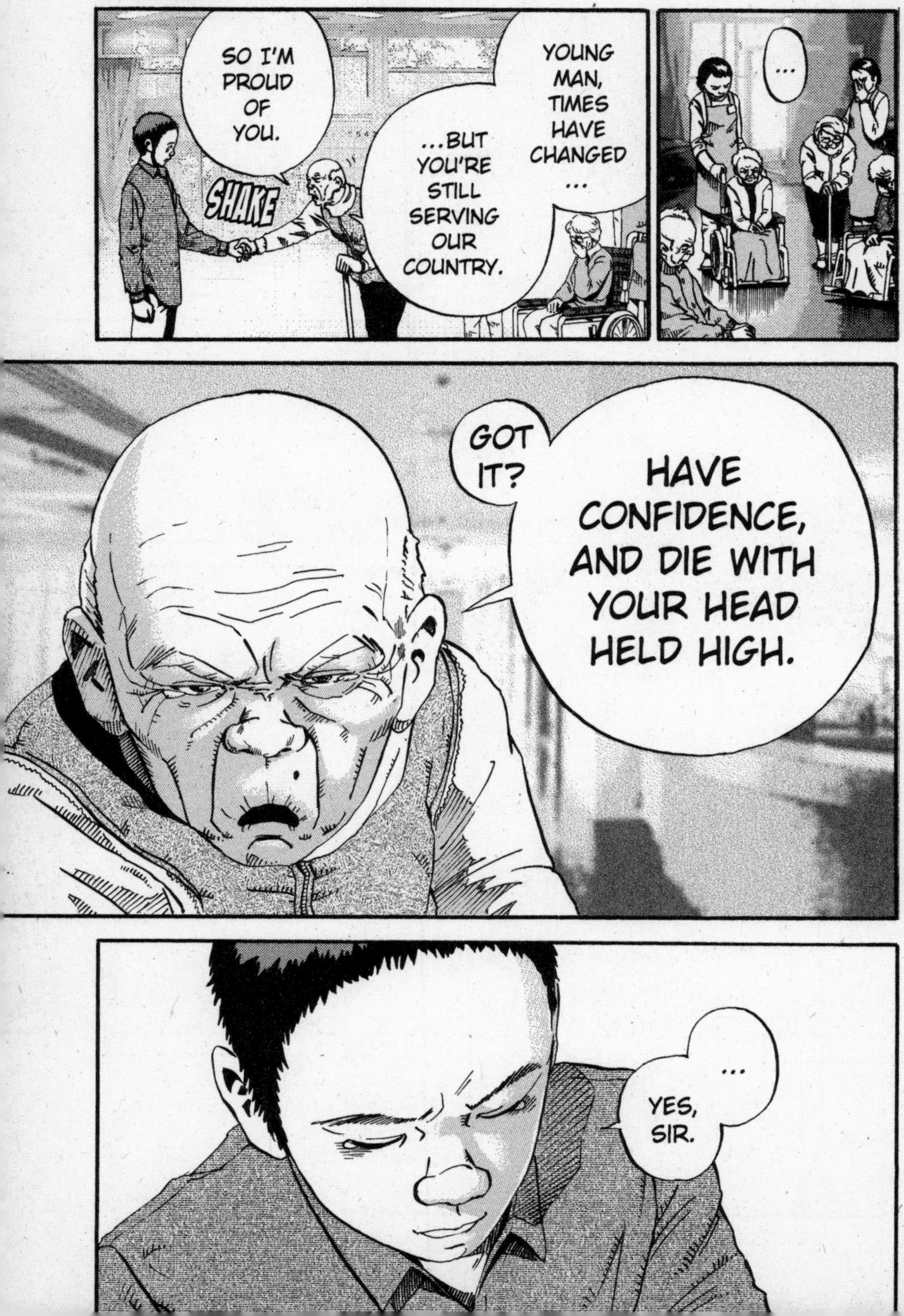
...
YOUNG MAN, TIMES HAVE CHANGED...
...BUT YOU'RE STILL SERVING OUR COUNTRY.
SO I'M PROUD OF YOU.
SHAKE
HAVE CONFIDENCE, AND DIE WITH YOUR HEAD HELD HIGH.
GOT IT?
...
YES, SIR.

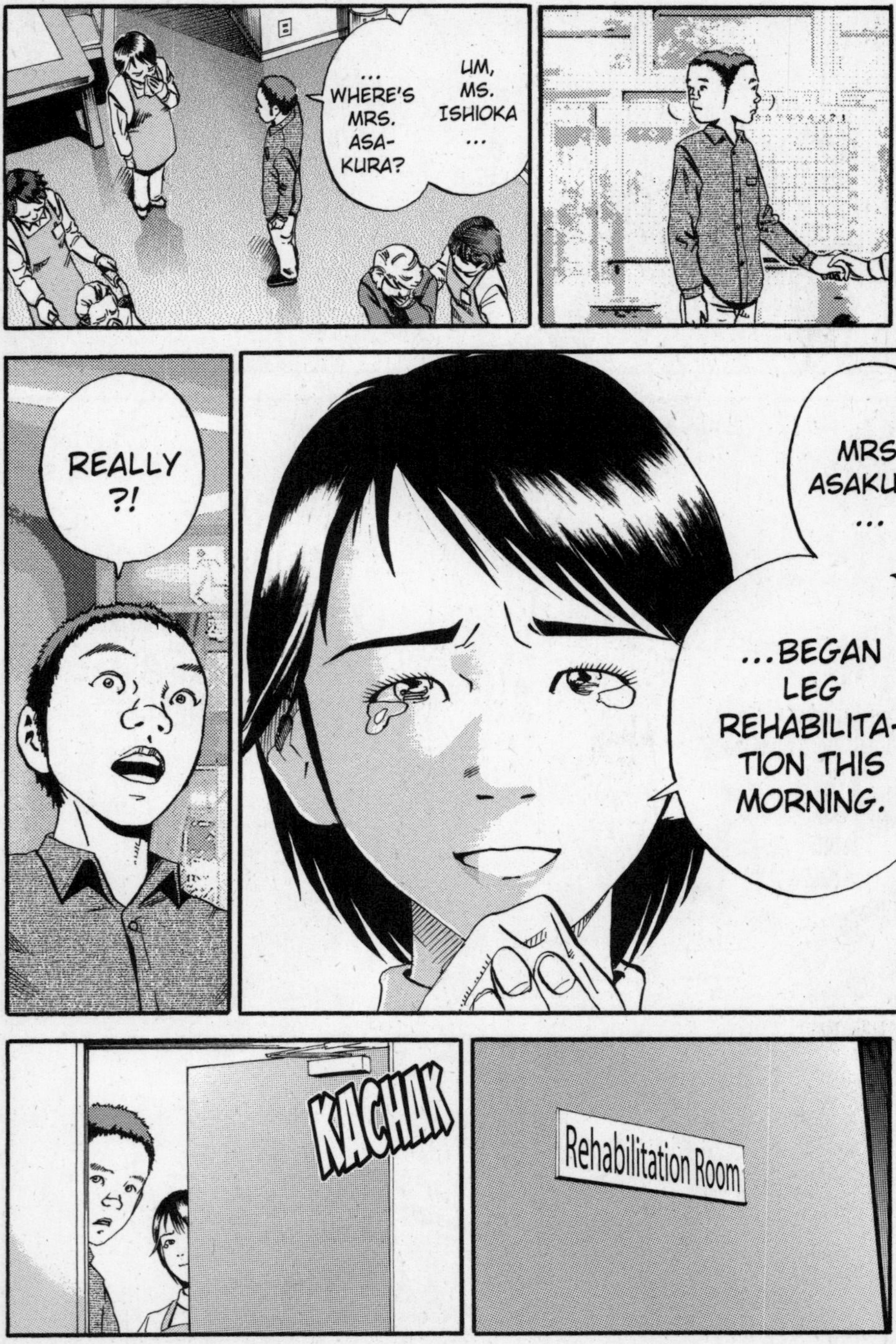
UM, MS. ISHIOKA ...
... WHERE'S MRS. ASA-KURA?
MRS. ASAKURA ...
...BEGAN LEG REHABILITA-TION THIS MORNING.
REALLY ?!
Rehabilitation Room
KACHAK

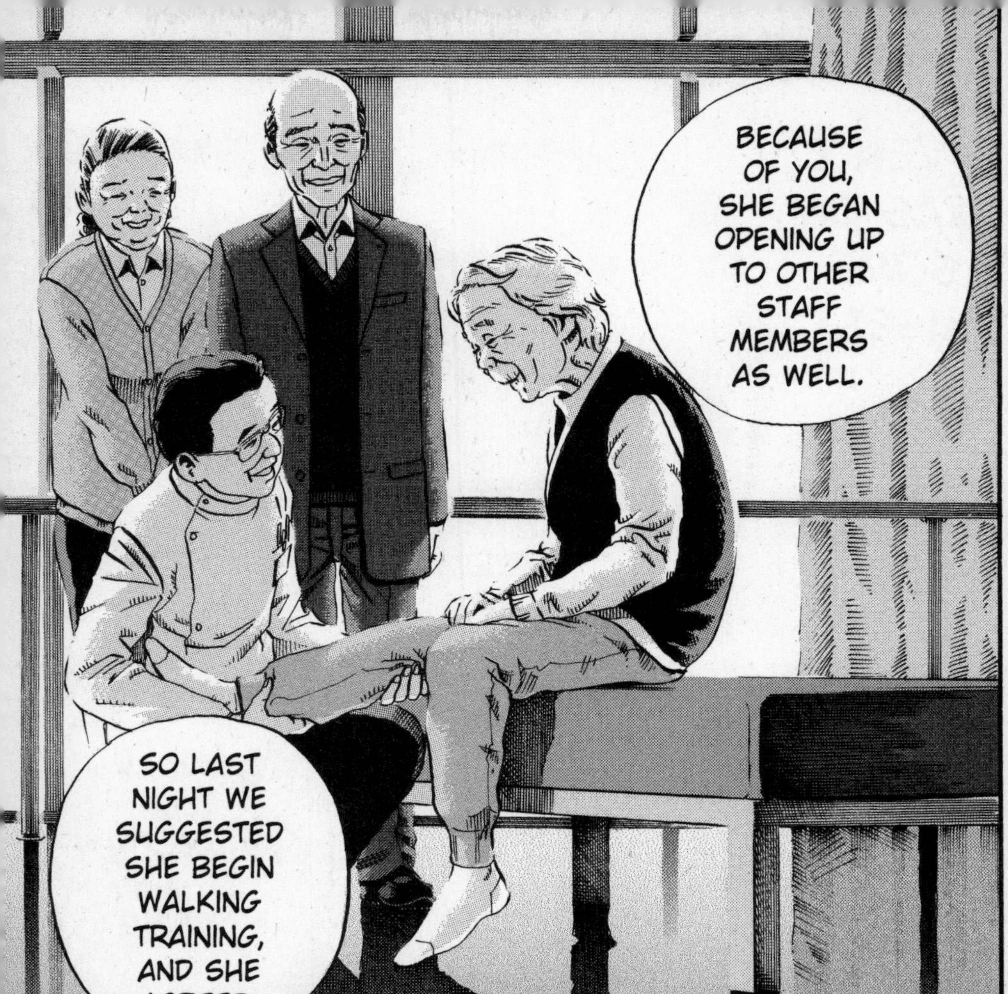
BECAUSE OF YOU, SHE BEGAN OPENING UP TO OTHER STAFF MEMBERS AS WELL.
SO LAST NIGHT WE SUGGESTED SHE BEGIN WALKING TRAINING, AND SHE AGREED.

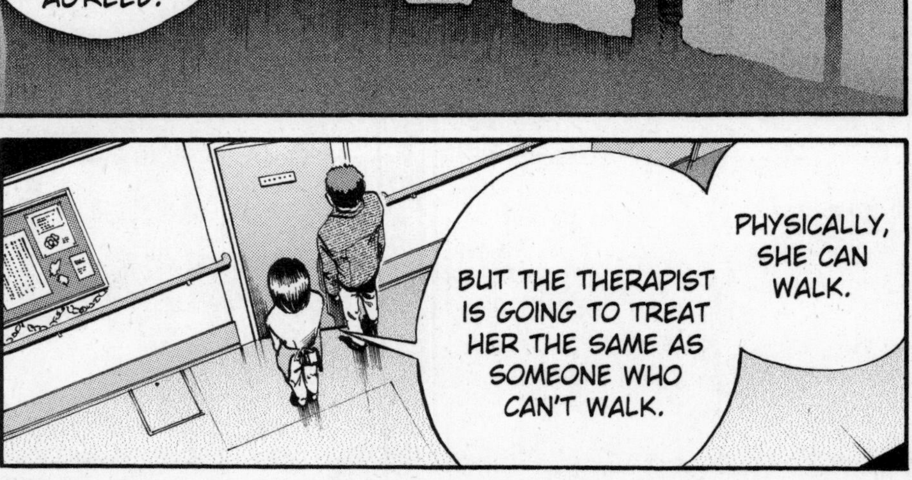
PHYSICALLY, SHE CAN WALK.
BUT THE THERAPIST IS GOING TO TREAT HER THE SAME AS SOMEONE WHO CAN'T WALK.

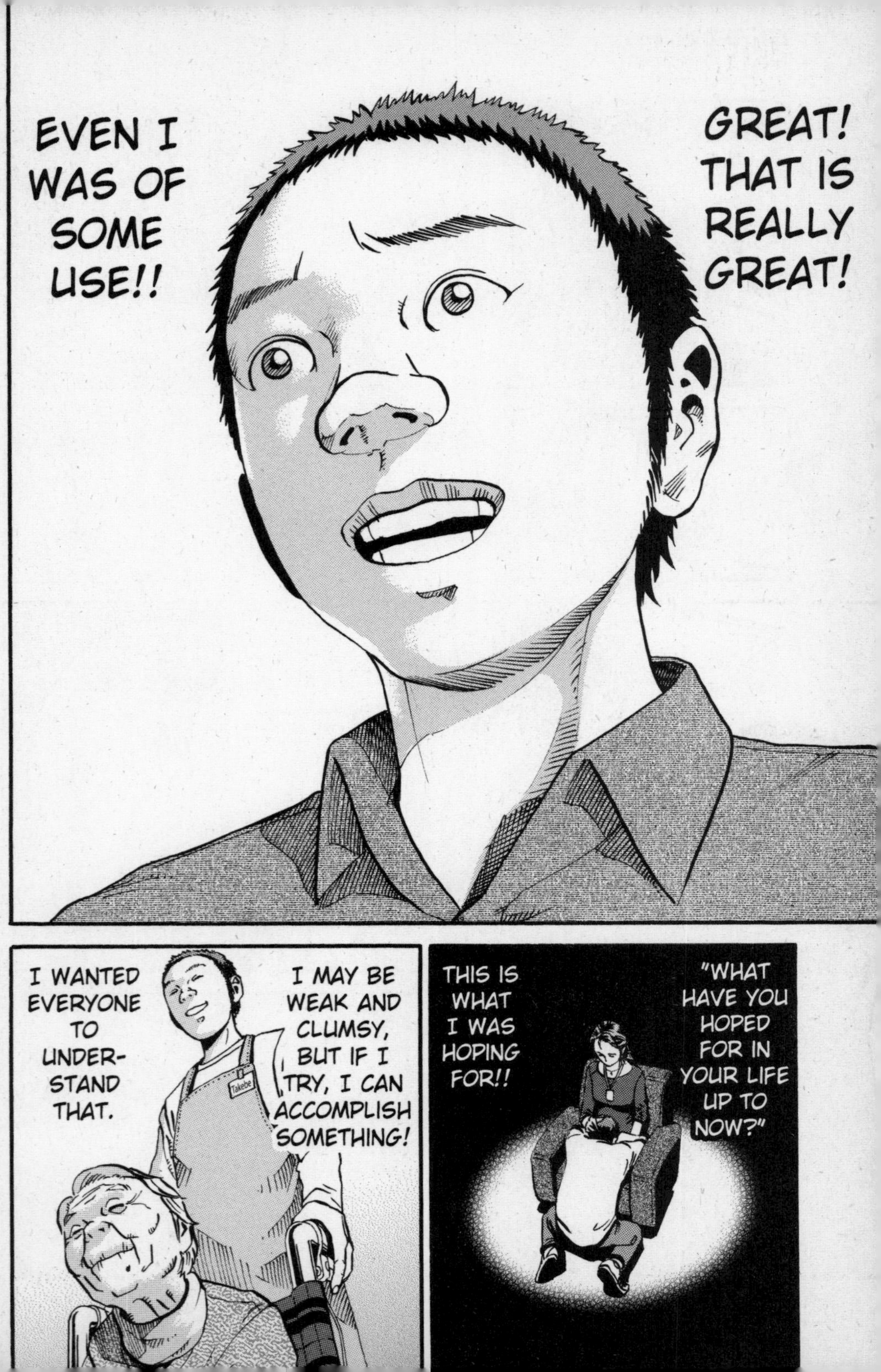
GREAT! THAT IS REALLY GREAT!
EVEN I WAS OF SOME USE!!
"WHAT HAVE YOU HOPED FOR IN YOUR LIFE UP TO NOW?"
THIS IS WHAT I WAS HOPING FOR!!
I MAY BE WEAK AND CLUMSY, BUT IF I TRY, I CAN ACCOMPLISH SOMETHING!
I WANTED EVERYONE TO UNDERSTAND THAT.
Takebe

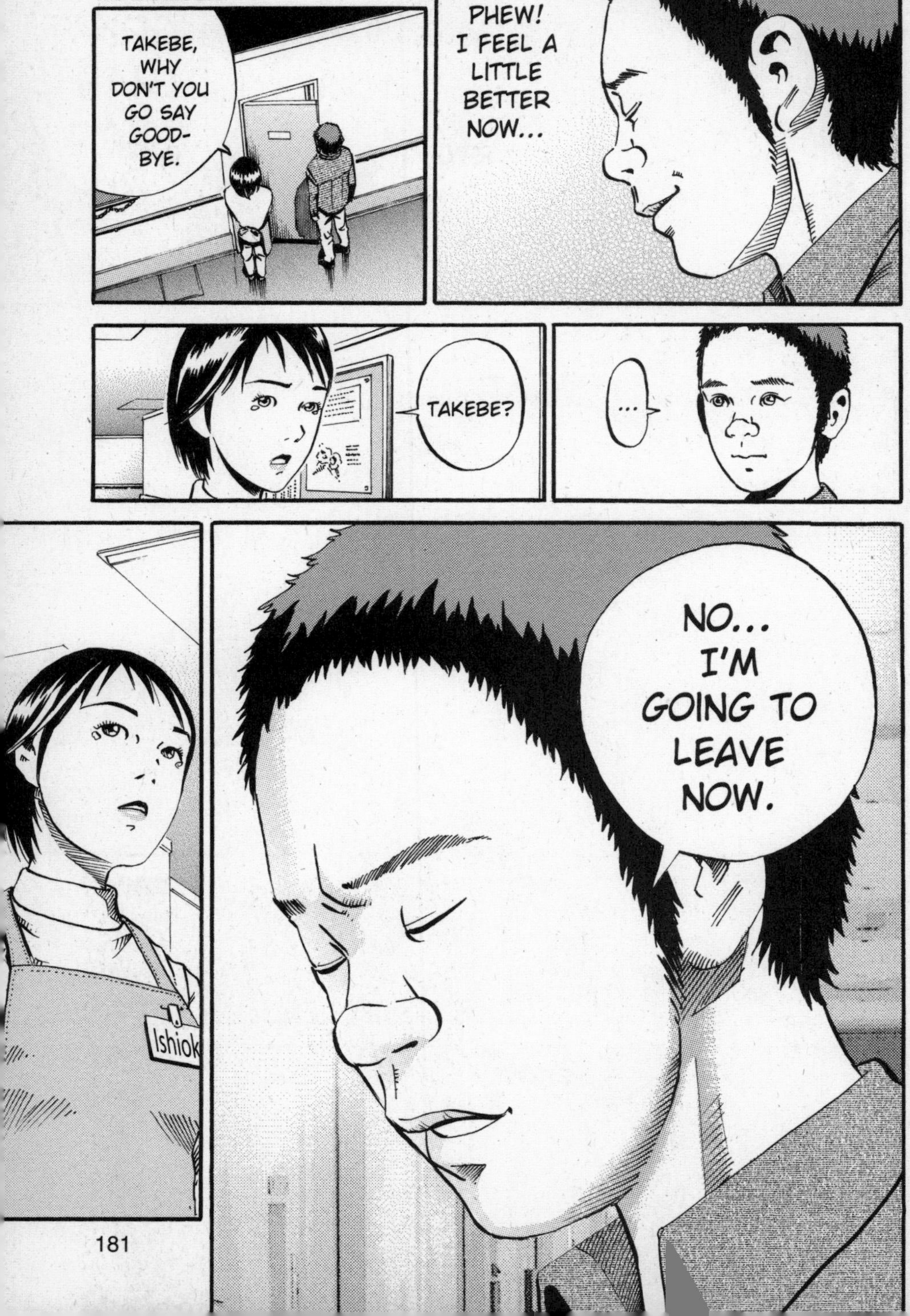
PHEW! I FEEL A LITTLE BETTER NOW...
TAKEBE, WHY DON'T YOU GO SAY GOOD-BYE.
...
TAKEBE?
NO... I'M GOING TO LEAVE NOW.
Ishiok

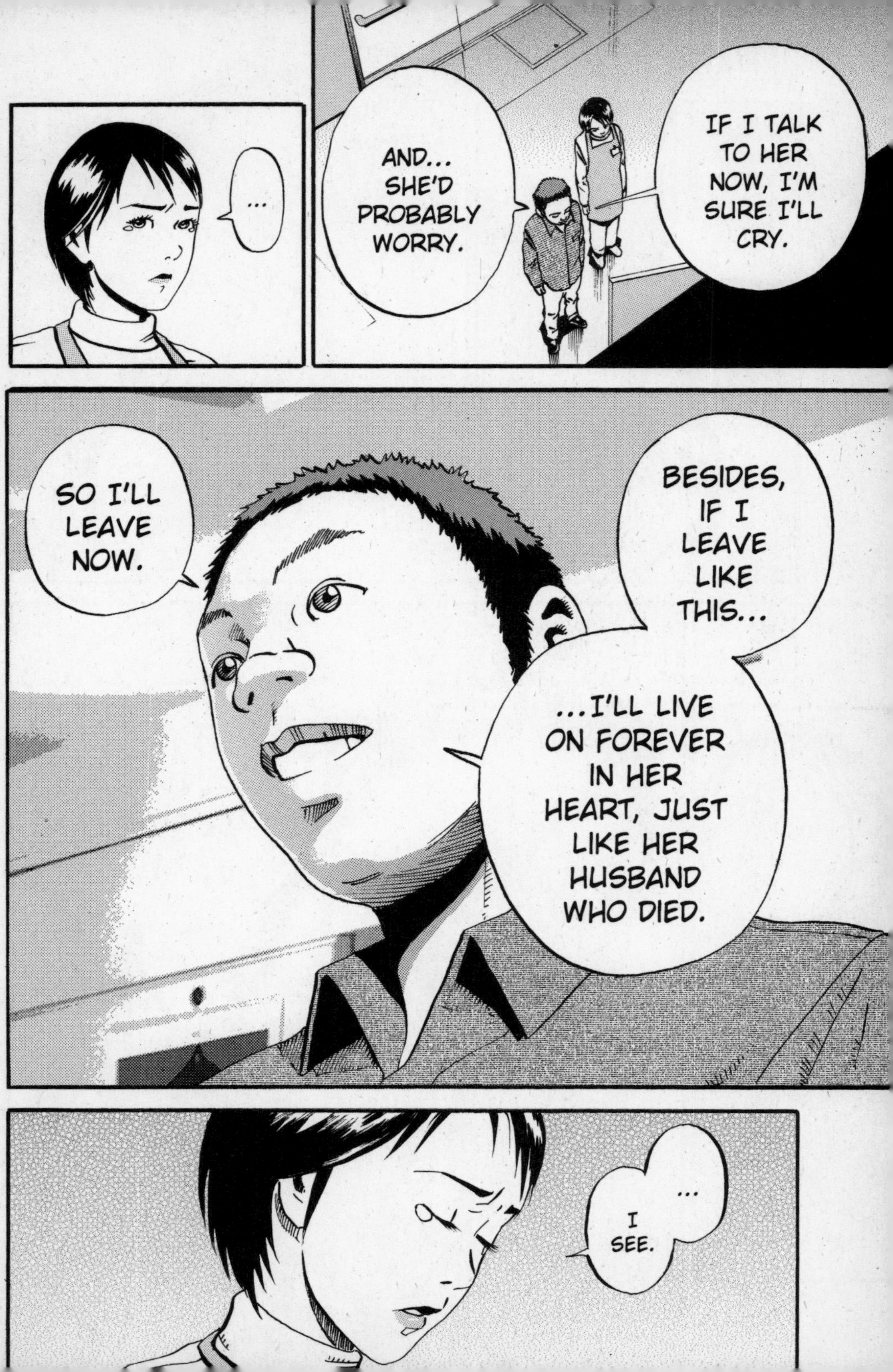
IF I TALK TO HER NOW, I'M SURE I'LL CRY.
AND... SHE'D PROBABLY WORRY.
...
BESIDES, IF I LEAVE LIKE THIS...
...I'LL LIVE ON FOREVER IN HER HEART, JUST LIKE HER HUSBAND WHO DIED.
SO I'LL LEAVE NOW.
... I SEE.

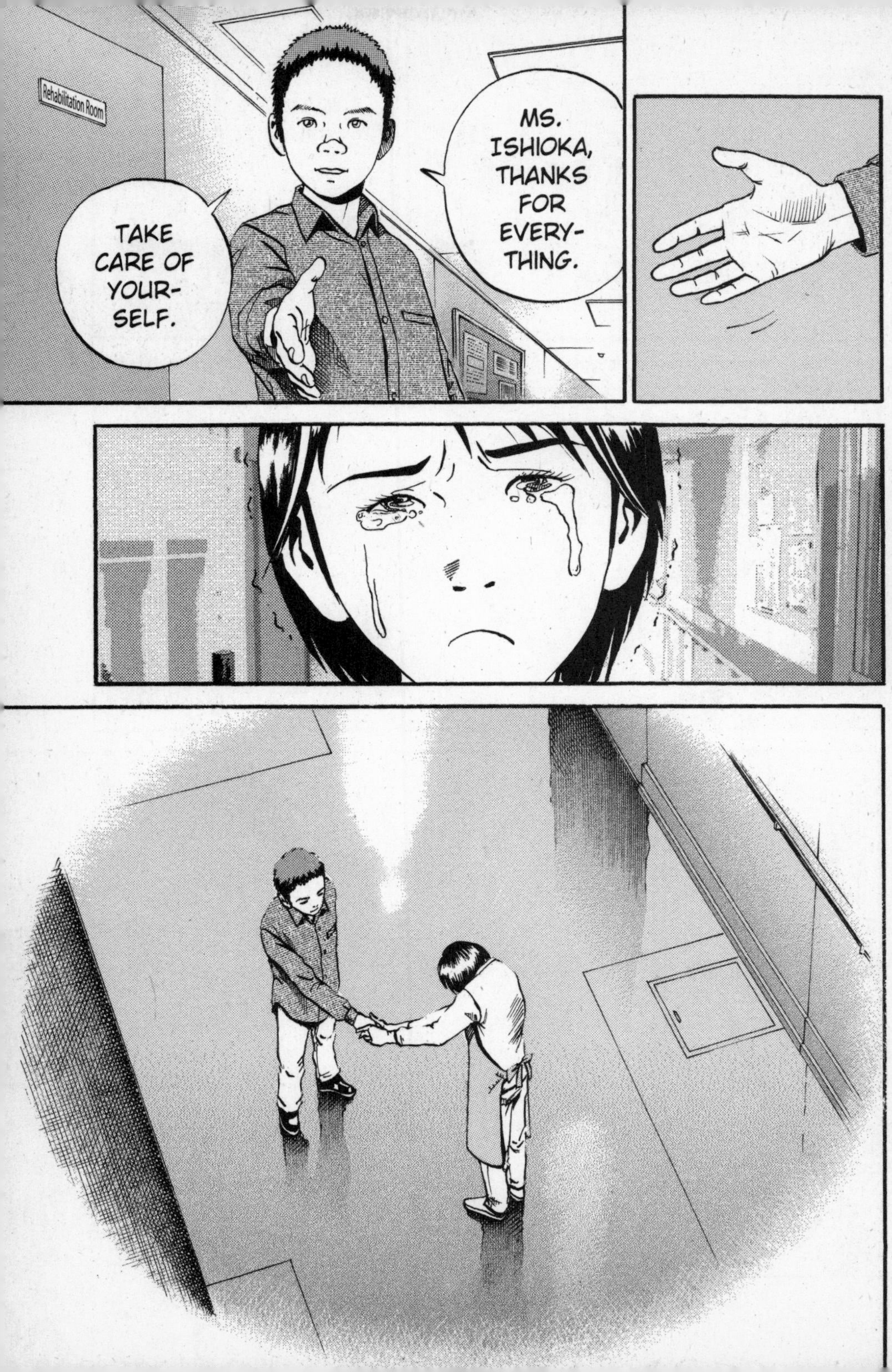
MS. ISHIOKA, THANKS FOR EVERY-THING.
Rehabilitation Room
TAKE CARE OF YOUR-SELF.

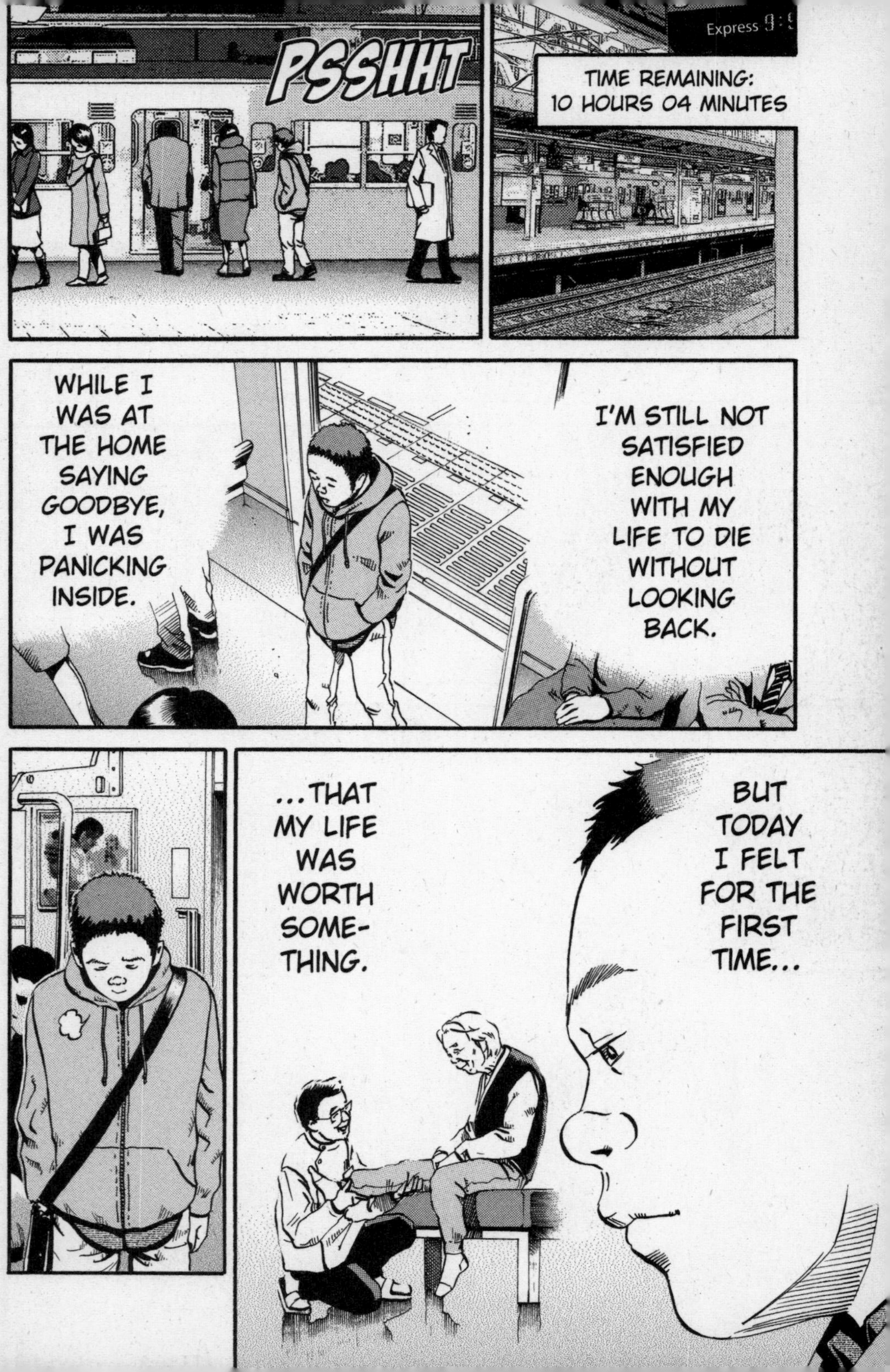
Express 9:
TIME REMAINING: 10 HOURS 04 MINUTES
PSSHHT
I'M STILL NOT SATISFIED ENOUGH WITH MY LIFE TO DIE WITHOUT LOOKING BACK.
WHILE I WAS AT THE HOME SAYING GOODBYE, I WAS PANICKING INSIDE.
BUT TODAY I FELT FOR THE FIRST TIME...
...THAT MY LIFE WAS WORTH SOME-THING.

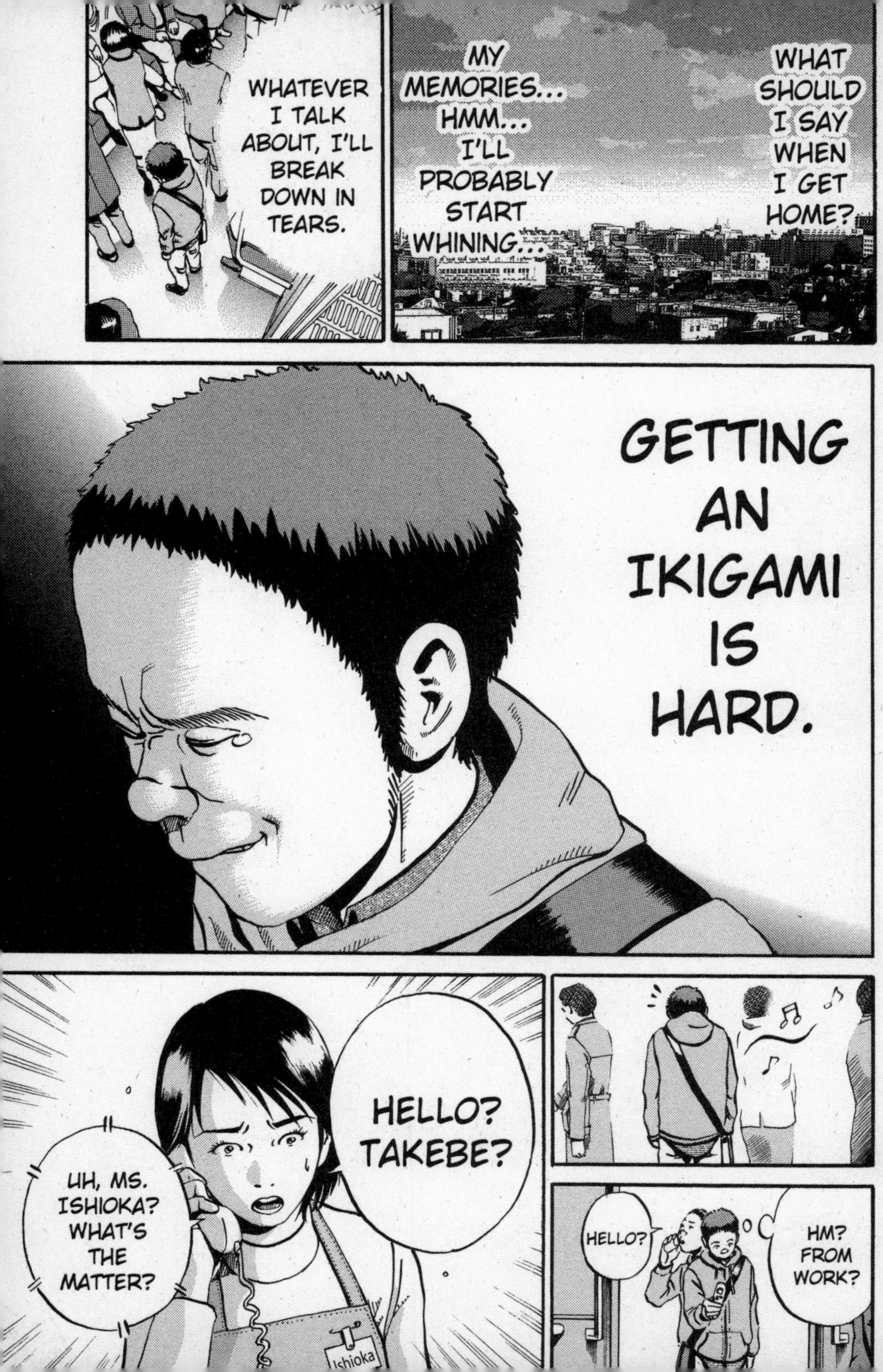
WHAT SHOULD I SAY WHEN I GET HOME?
MY MEMORIES... HMM... I'LL PROBABLY START WHINING...
WHATEVER I TALK ABOUT, I'LL BREAK DOWN IN TEARS.
GETTING AN IKIGAMI IS HARD.
HM? FROM WORK?
HELLO?
HELLO? TAKEBE?
UH, MS. ISHIOKA? WHAT'S THE MATTER?
Ishioka

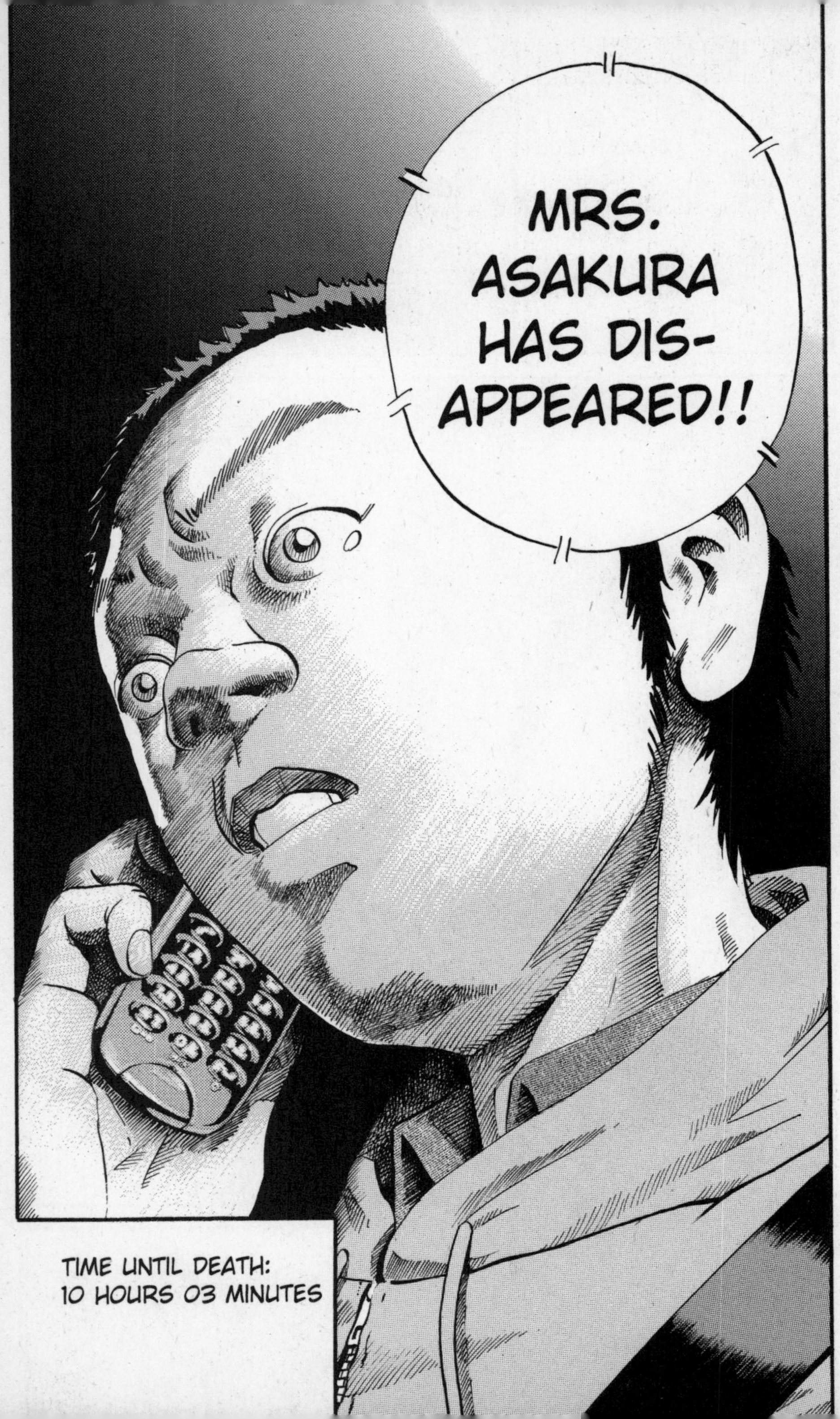
MRS. ASAKURA HAS DIS-APPEARED!!
TIME UNTIL DEATH: 10 HOURS 03 MINUTES

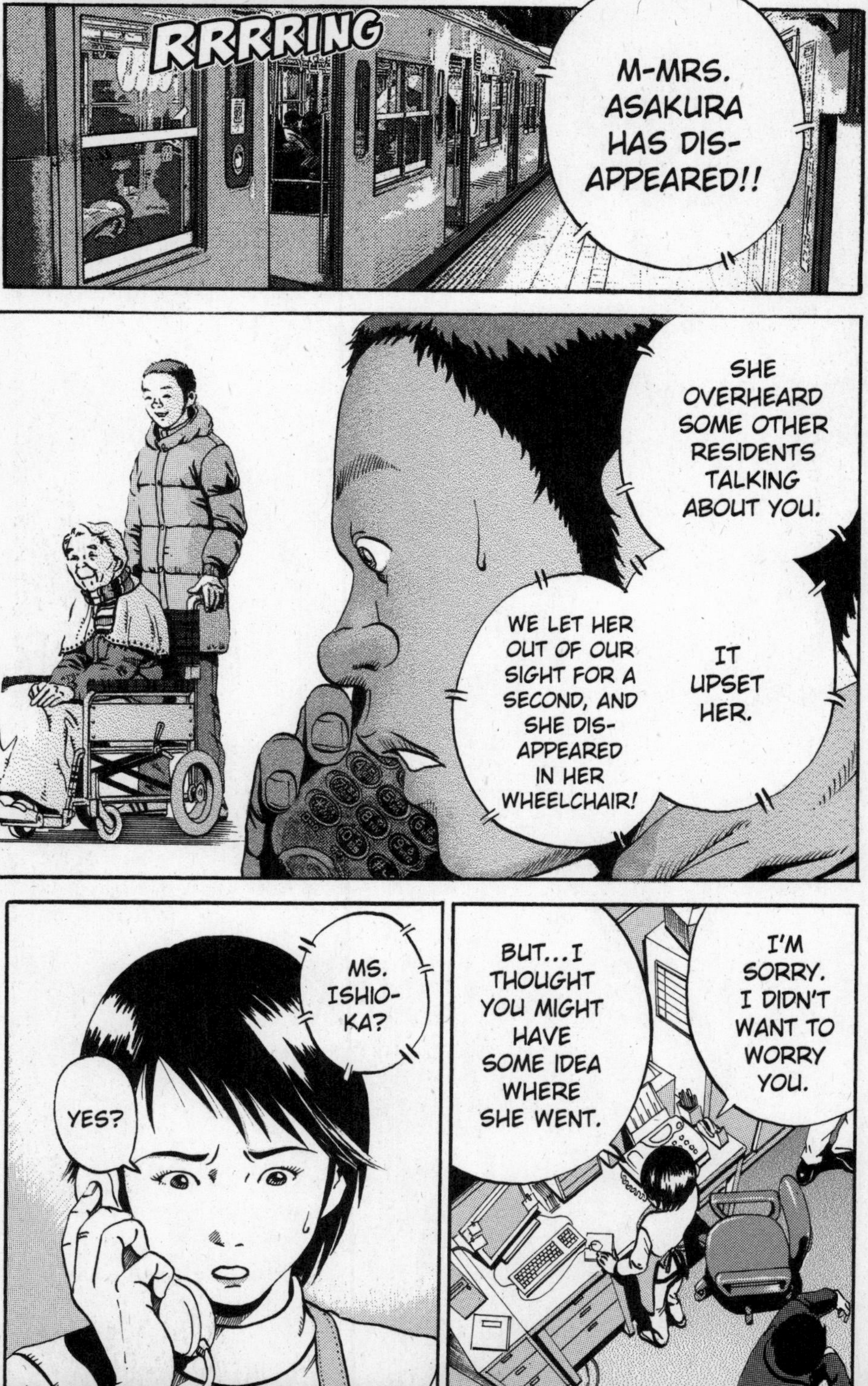
M-MRS. ASAKURA HAS DIS-APPEARED!!
RRRRING
SHE OVERHEARD SOME OTHER RESIDENTS TALKING ABOUT YOU.
IT UPSET HER.
WE LET HER OUT OF OUR SIGHT FOR A SECOND, AND SHE DIS-APPEARED IN HER WHEELCHAIR!
I'M SORRY. I DIDN'T WANT TO WORRY YOU.
BUT...I THOUGHT YOU MIGHT HAVE SOME IDEA WHERE SHE WENT.
MS. ISHIOKA?
YES?

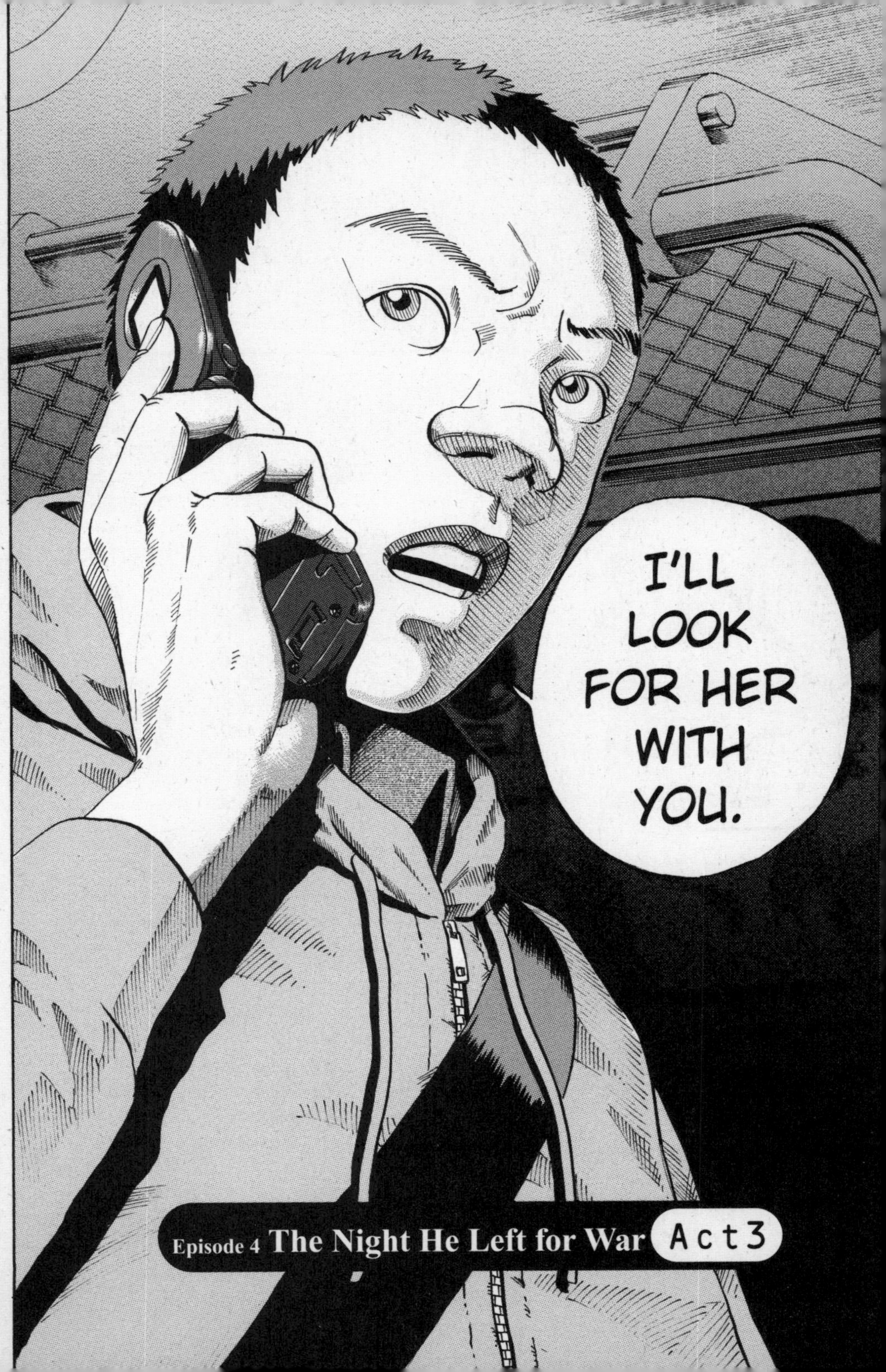
I'LL LOOK FOR HER WITH YOU.
Episode 4 The Night He Left for War Act 3

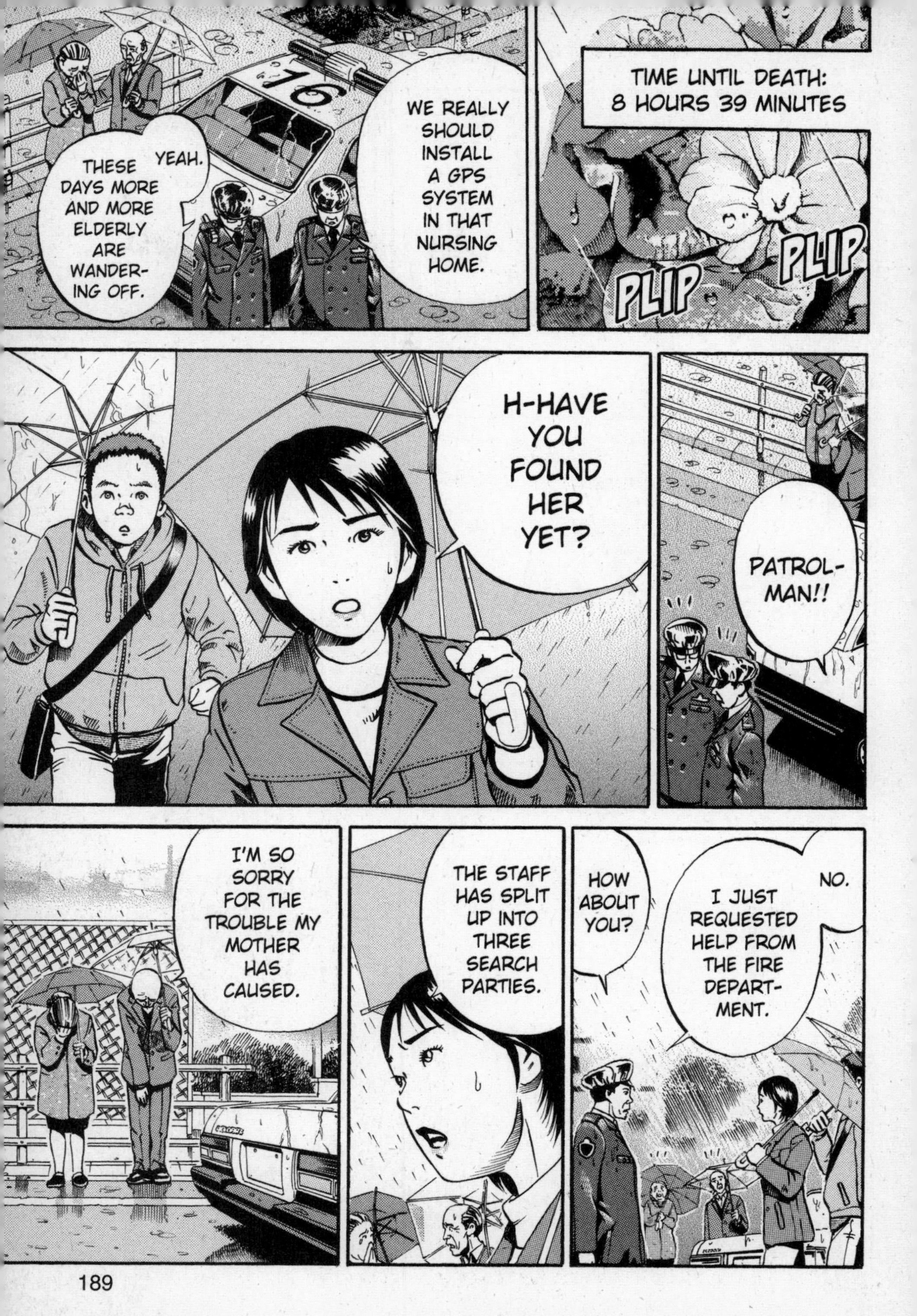
TIME UNTIL DEATH: 8 HOURS 39 MINUTES
PLIP
PLIP
WE REALLY SHOULD INSTALL A GPS SYSTEM IN THAT NURSING HOME.
YEAH.
THESE DAYS MORE AND MORE ELDERLY ARE WANDER-ING OFF.
PATROL-MAN!!
H-HAVE YOU FOUND HER YET?
NO.
I JUST REQUESTED HELP FROM THE FIRE DEPART-MENT.
HOW ABOUT YOU?
THE STAFF HAS SPLIT UP INTO THREE SEARCH PARTIES.
I'M SO SORRY FOR THE TROUBLE MY MOTHER HAS CAUSED.

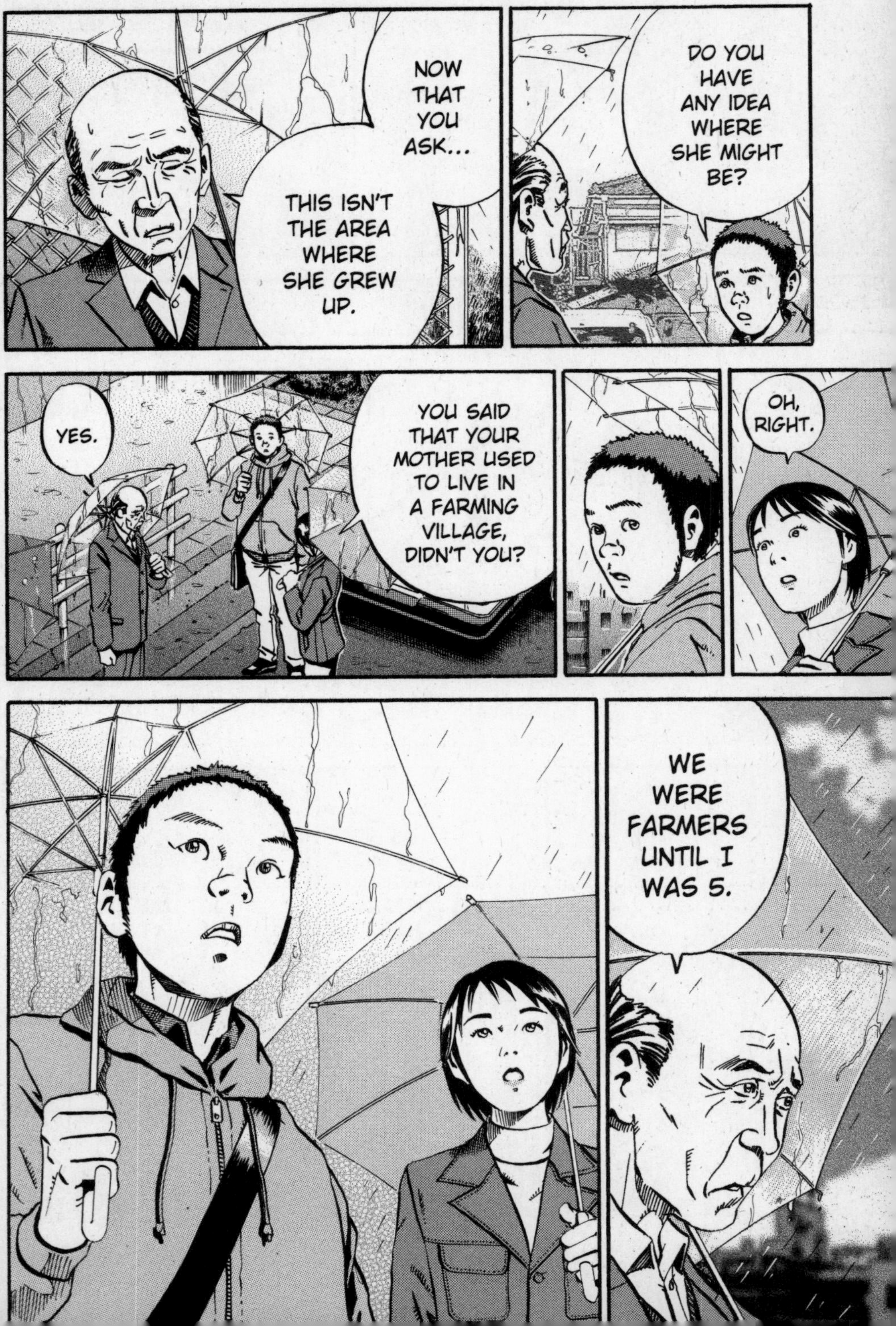
DO YOU HAVE ANY IDEA WHERE SHE MIGHT BE?
NOW THAT YOU ASK...
THIS ISN'T THE AREA WHERE SHE GREW UP.
OH, RIGHT.
YOU SAID THAT YOUR MOTHER USED TO LIVE IN A FARMING VILLAGE, DIDN'T YOU?
YES.
WE WERE FARMERS UNTIL I WAS 5.

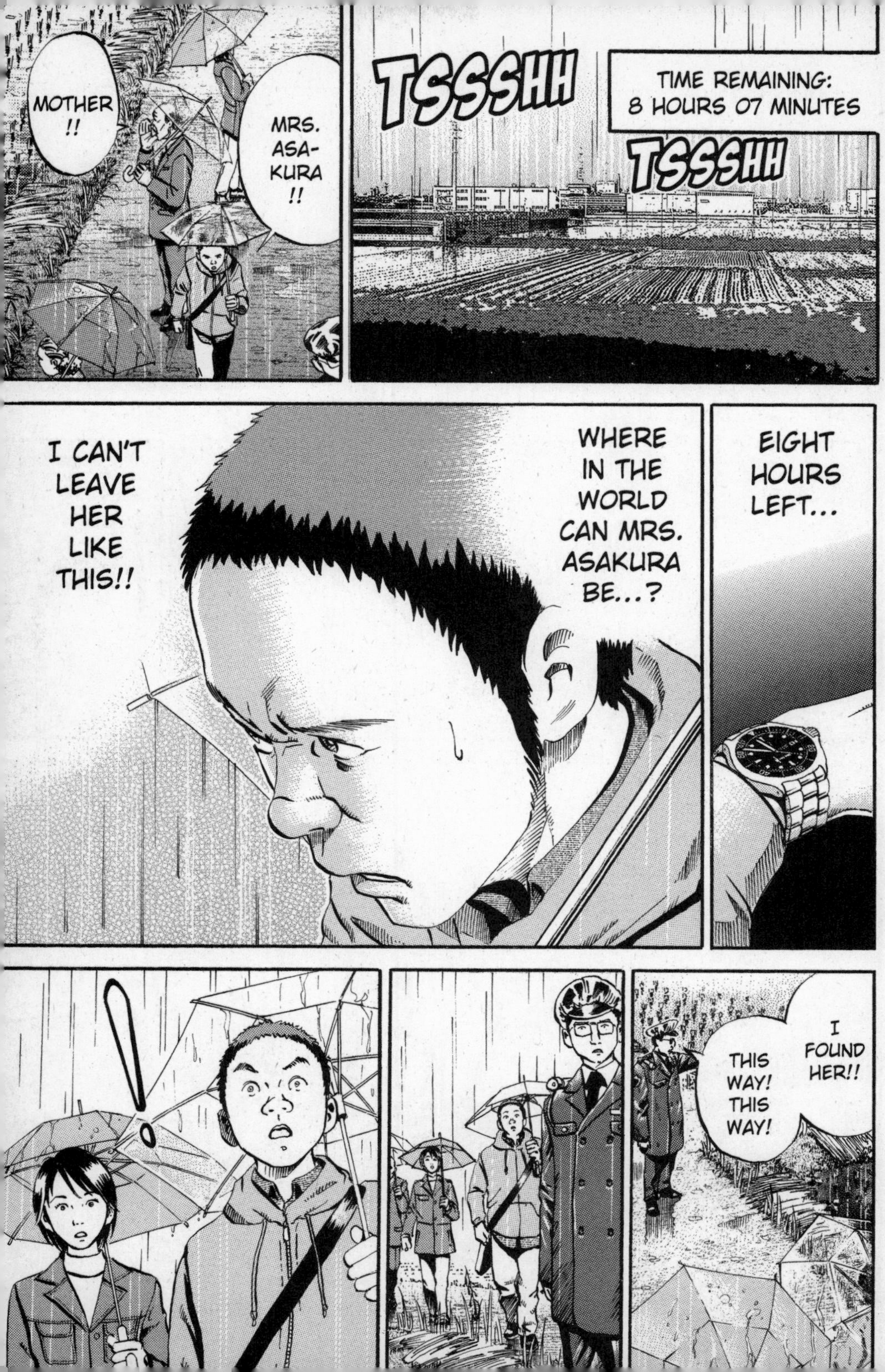
TIME REMAINING: 8 HOURS 07 MINUTES
TSSSHH
TSSSHH
MRS. ASAKURA!!
MOTHER!!
EIGHT HOURS LEFT...
WHERE IN THE WORLD CAN MRS. ASAKURA BE...?
I CAN'T LEAVE HER LIKE THIS!!
I FOUND HER!!
THIS WAY! THIS WAY!
!

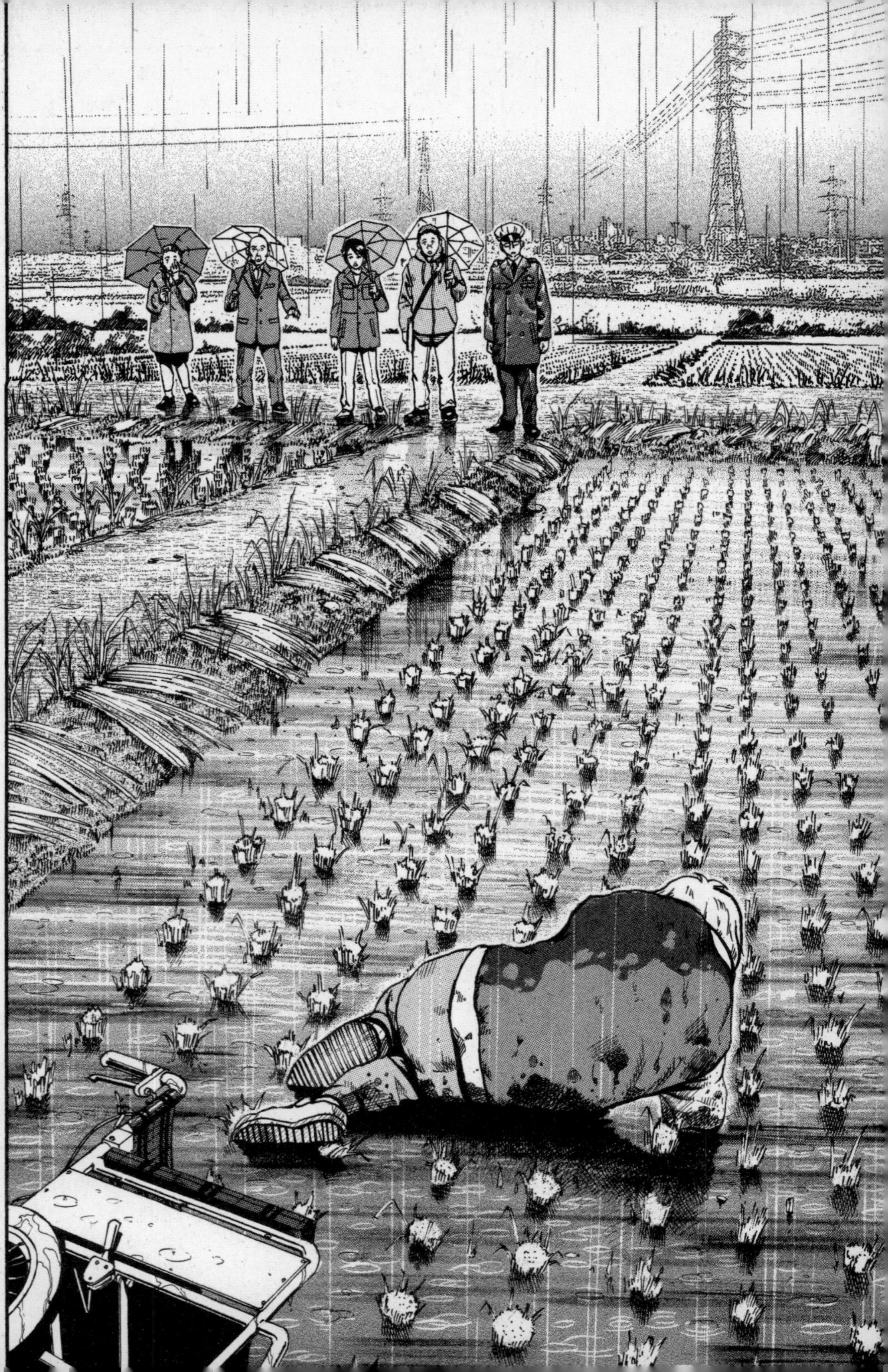

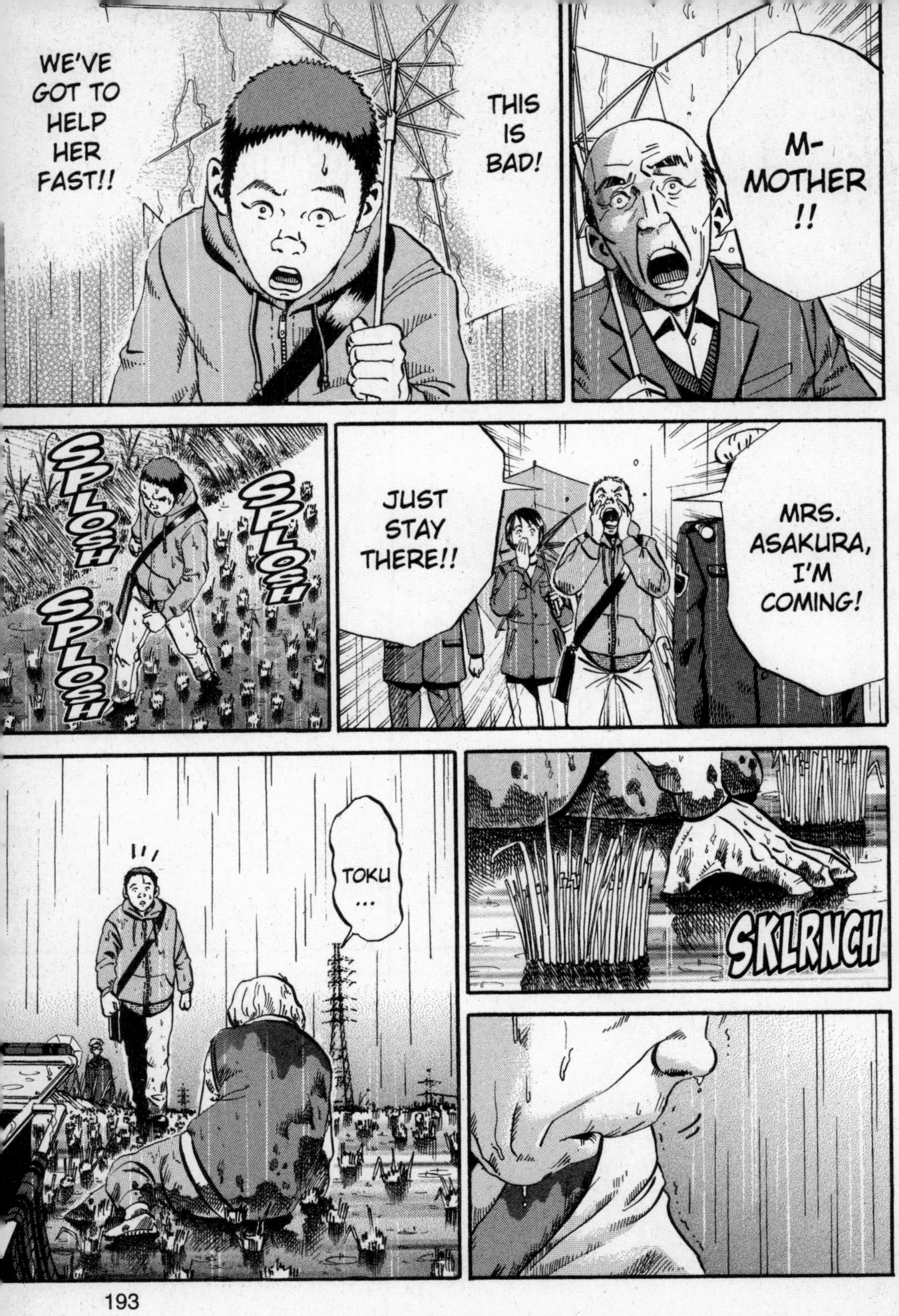
M-MOTHER!!
THIS IS BAD!
WE'VE GOT TO HELP HER FAST!!
MRS. ASAKURA, I'M COMING!
JUST STAY THERE!!
SPLOSH
SPLOSH
SPLOSH
SKLRNCH
TOKU ...

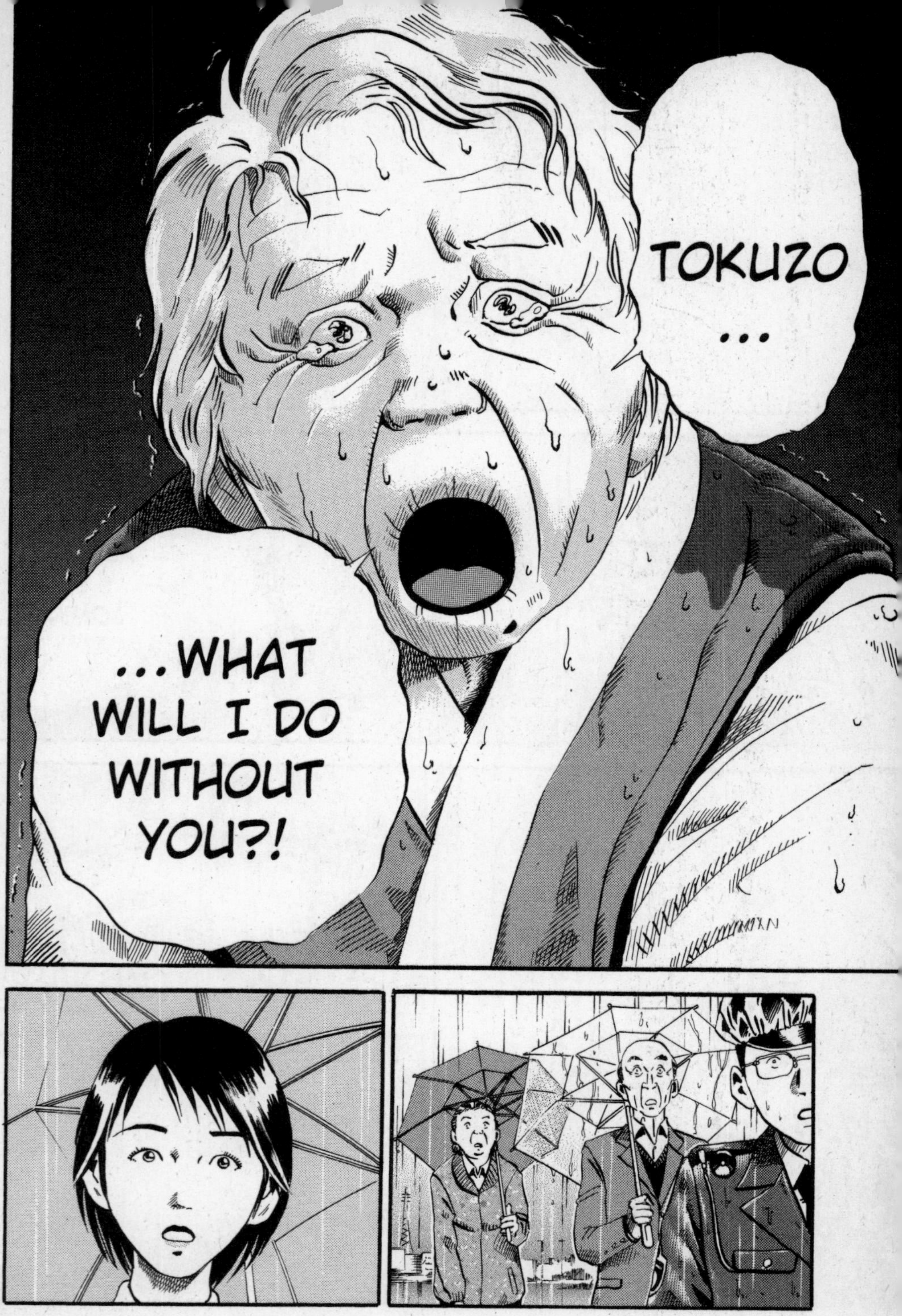
TOKUZO ...
...WHAT WILL I DO WITHOUT YOU?!

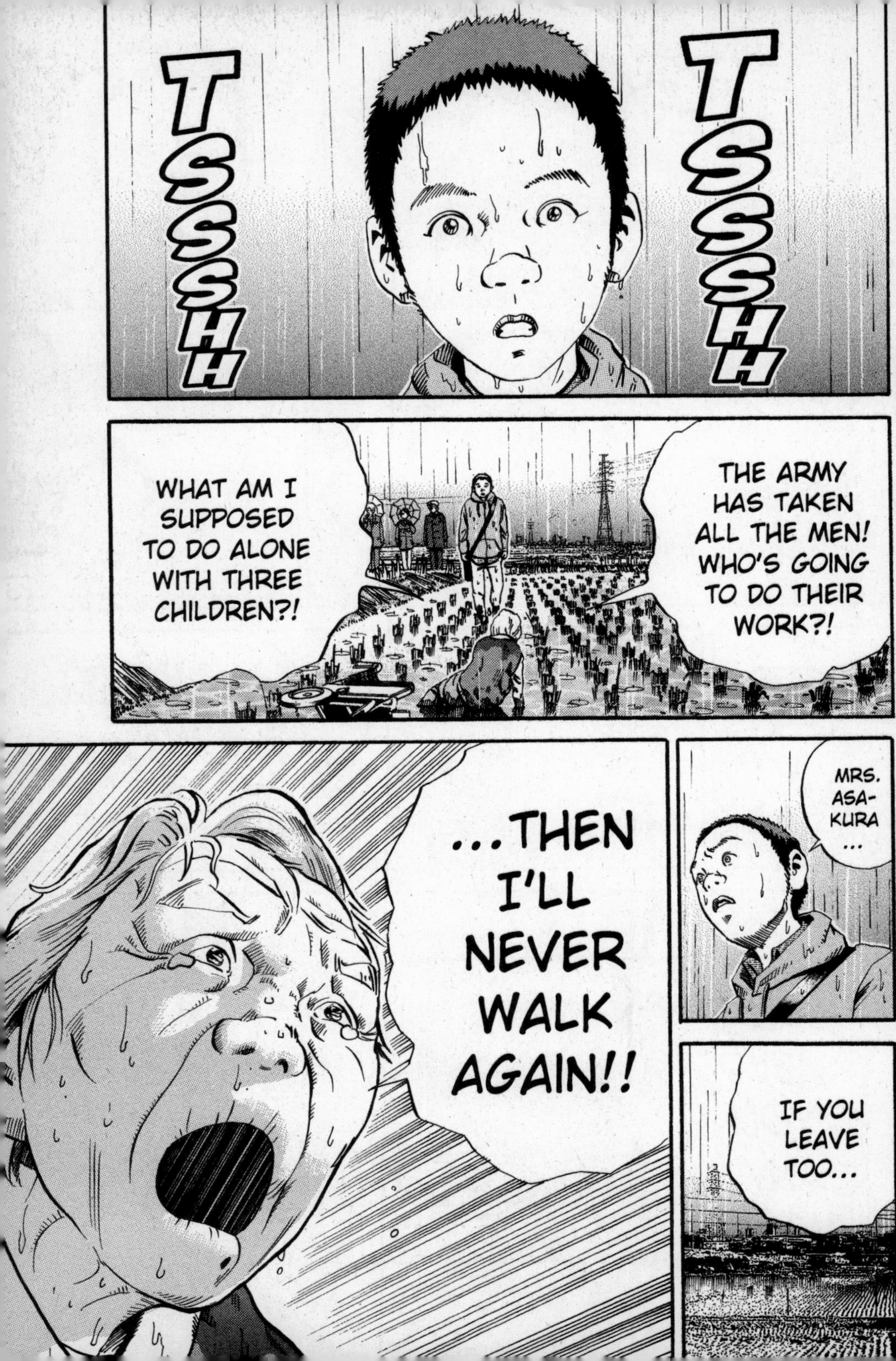
TSSSHH
TSSSHH
THE ARMY HAS TAKEN ALL THE MEN! WHO'S GOING TO DO THEIR WORK?!
WHAT AM I SUPPOSED TO DO ALONE WITH THREE CHILDREN?!
MRS. ASA-KURA ...
IF YOU LEAVE TOO...
...THEN I'LL NEVER WALK AGAIN!!

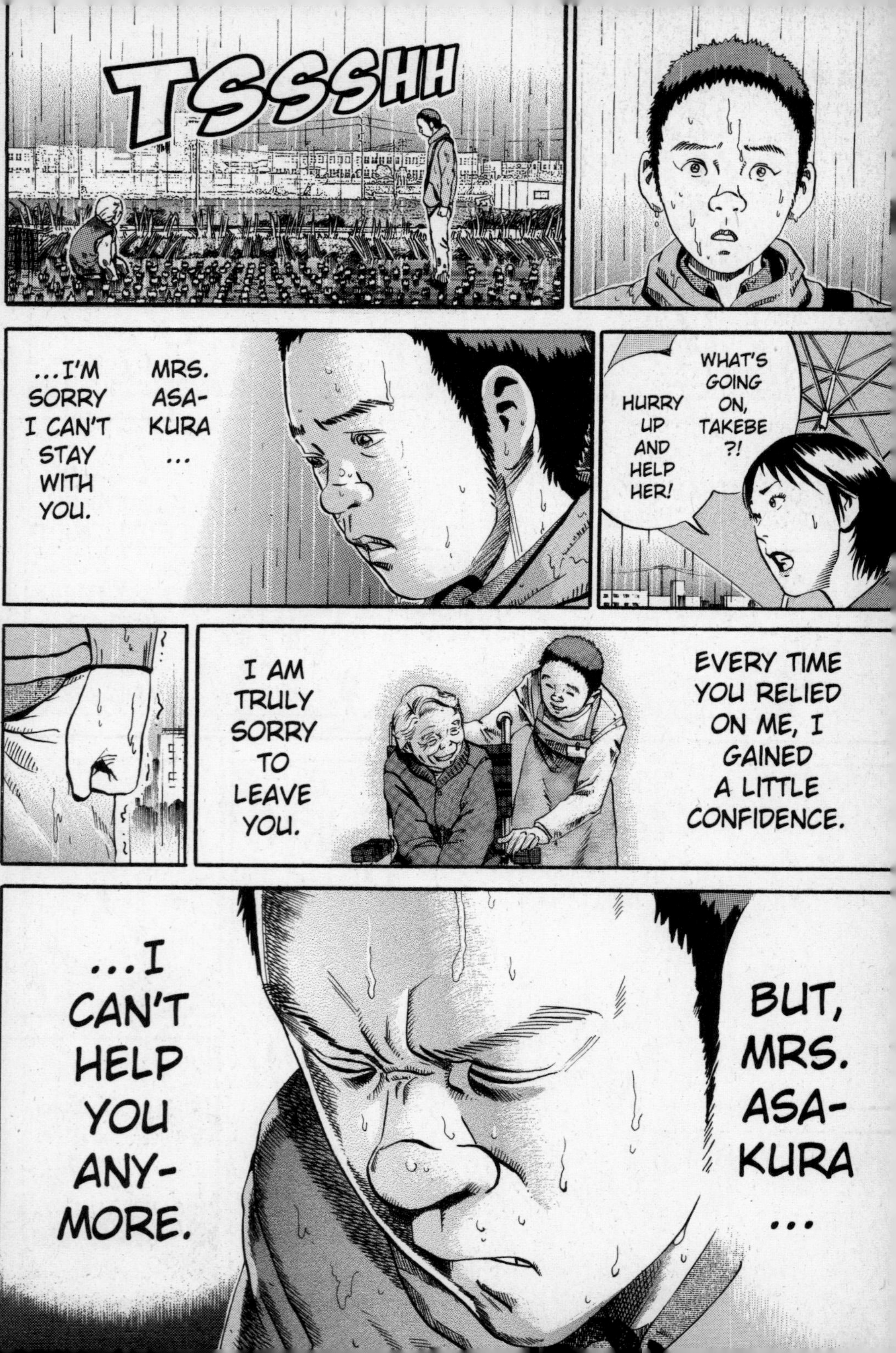
TSSSHH
WHAT'S GOING ON, TAKEBE?!
HURRY UP AND HELP HER!
MRS. ASA-KURA...
...I'M SORRY I CAN'T STAY WITH YOU.
EVERY TIME YOU RELIED ON ME, I GAINED A LITTLE CONFIDENCE.
I AM TRULY SORRY TO LEAVE YOU.
BUT, MRS. ASA-KURA...
...I CAN'T HELP YOU ANYMORE.

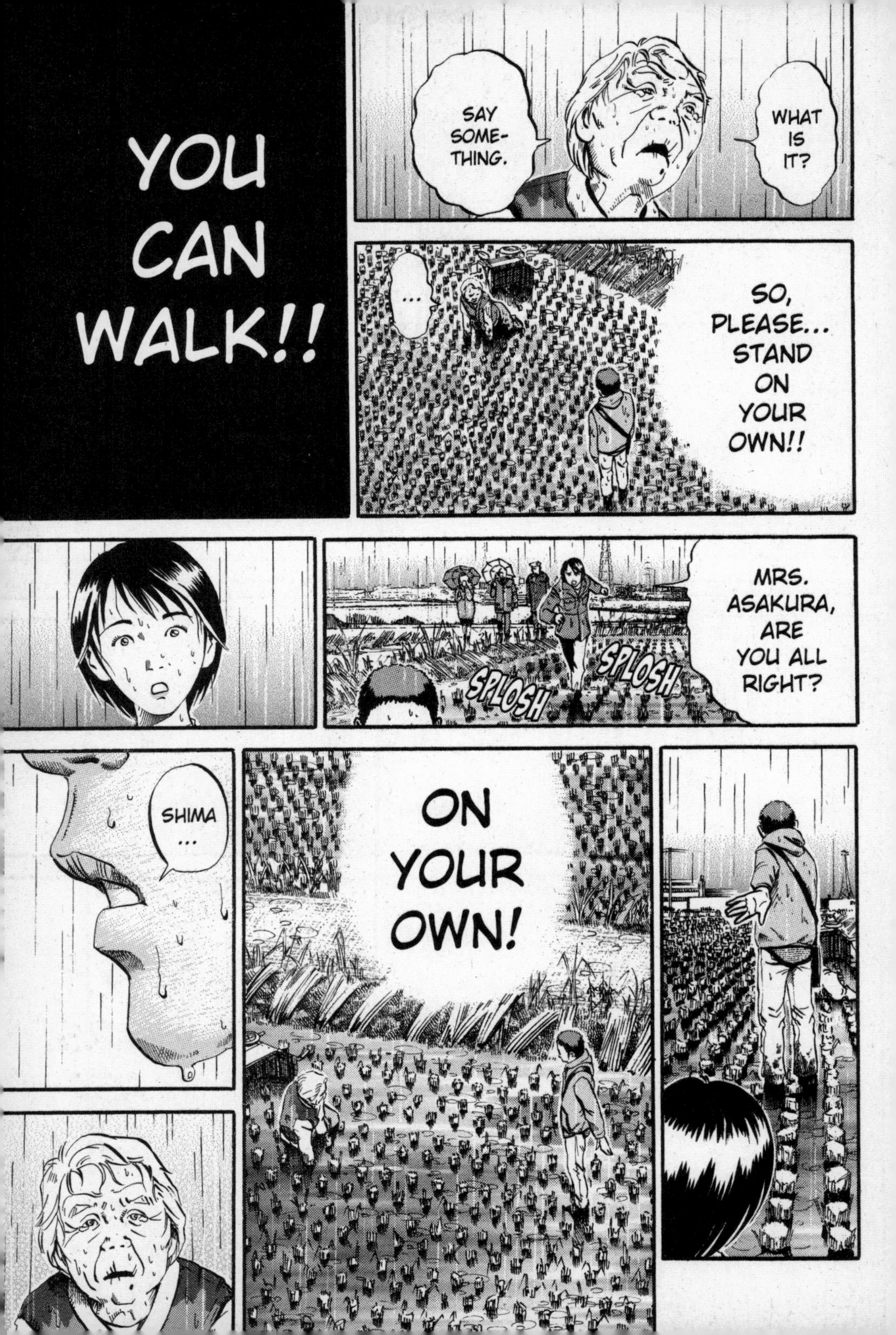
WHAT IS IT?
SAY SOME-THING.
SO, PLEASE... STAND ON YOUR OWN!!
...
YOU CAN WALK!!
MRS. ASAKURA, ARE YOU ALL RIGHT?
SPLOSH
SPLOSH
ON YOUR OWN!
SHIMA ...

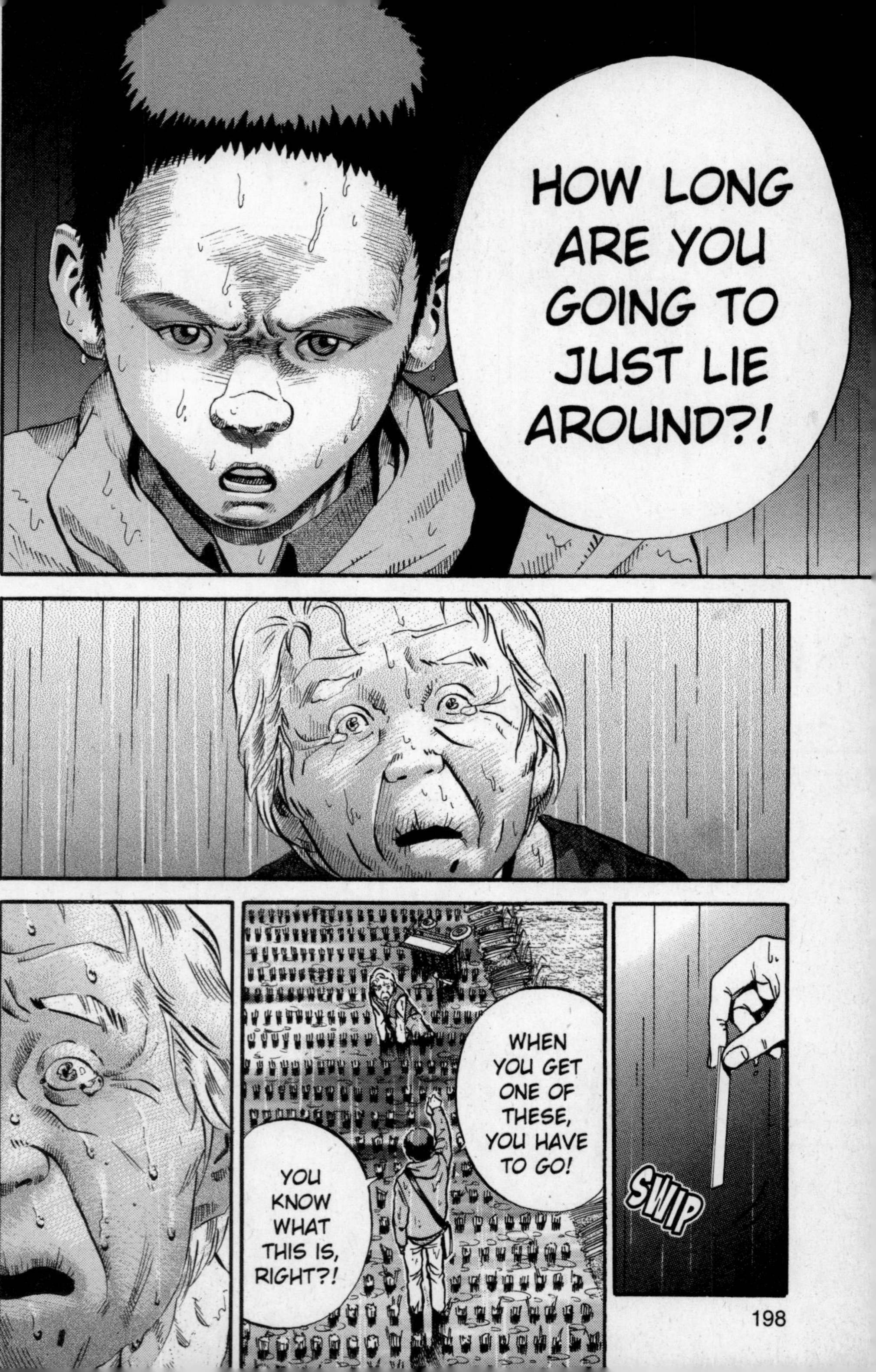
HOW LONG ARE YOU GOING TO JUST LIE AROUND?!
SWIP
WHEN YOU GET ONE OF THESE, YOU HAVE TO GO!
YOU KNOW WHAT THIS IS, RIGHT?!

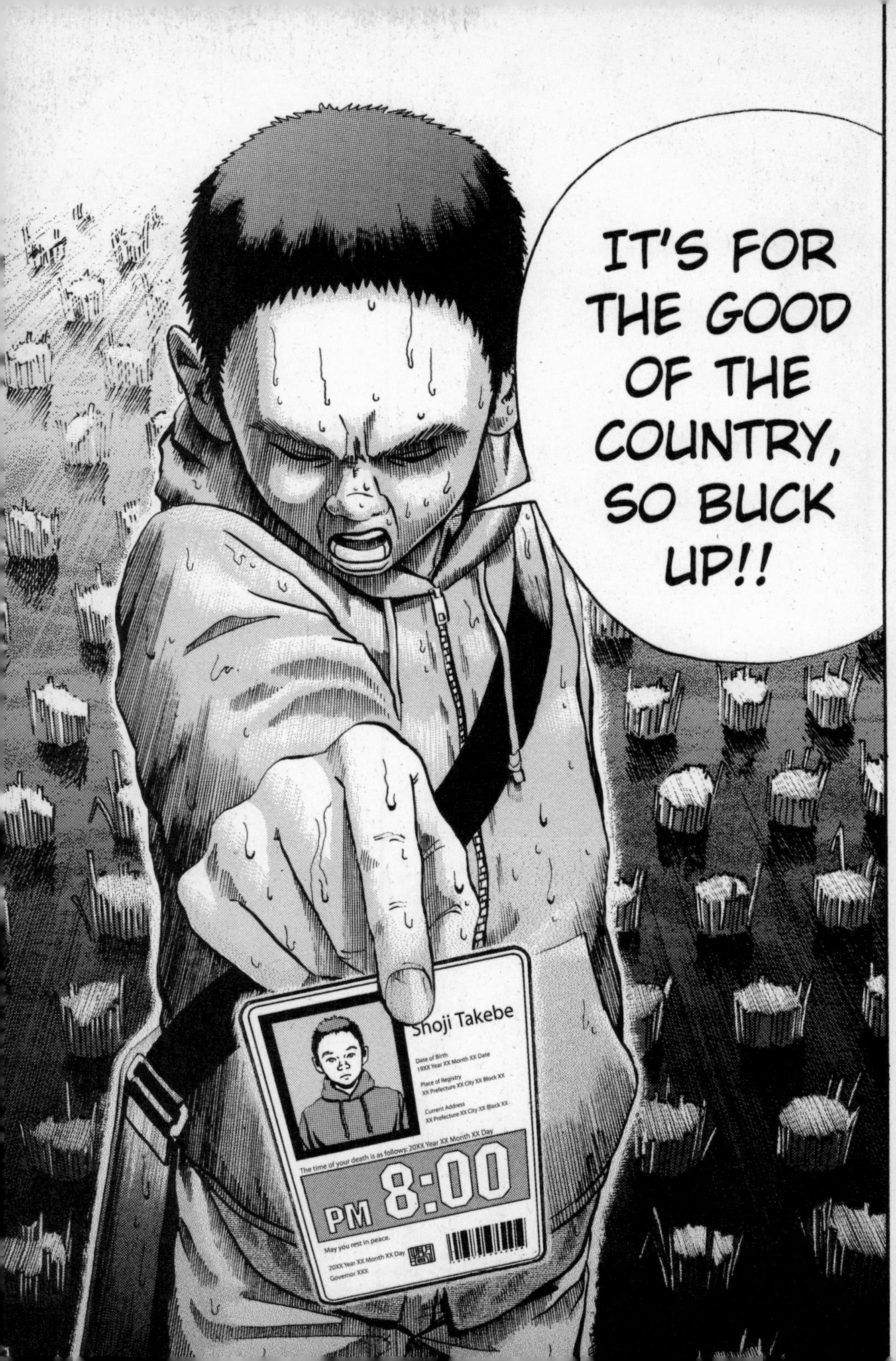
IT'S FOR THE GOOD OF THE COUNTRY, SO BUCK UP!!
Shoji Takebe
Date of Birth
19XX Year XX Month XX Date
Place of Registry
XX Prefecture XX City XX Block XX
Current Address
XX Prefecture XX City XX Block XX
The time of your death is as follows: 20XX Year XX Month XX Day
PM 8:00
May you rest in peace.
20XX Year XX Month XX Day
Governor XXX

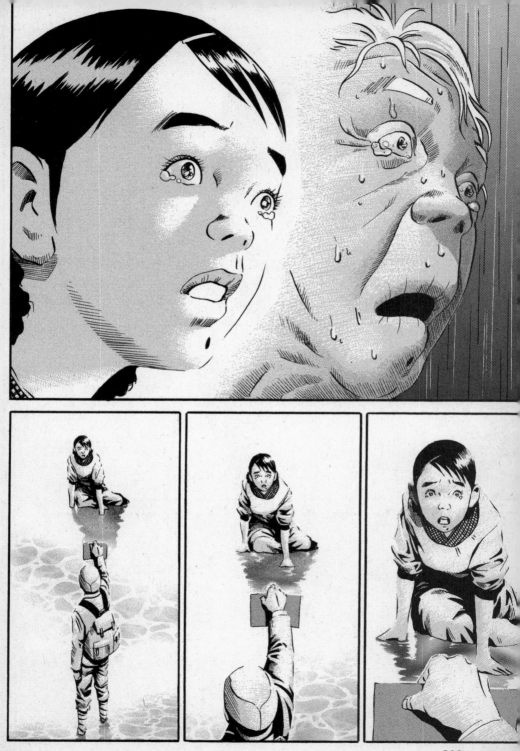

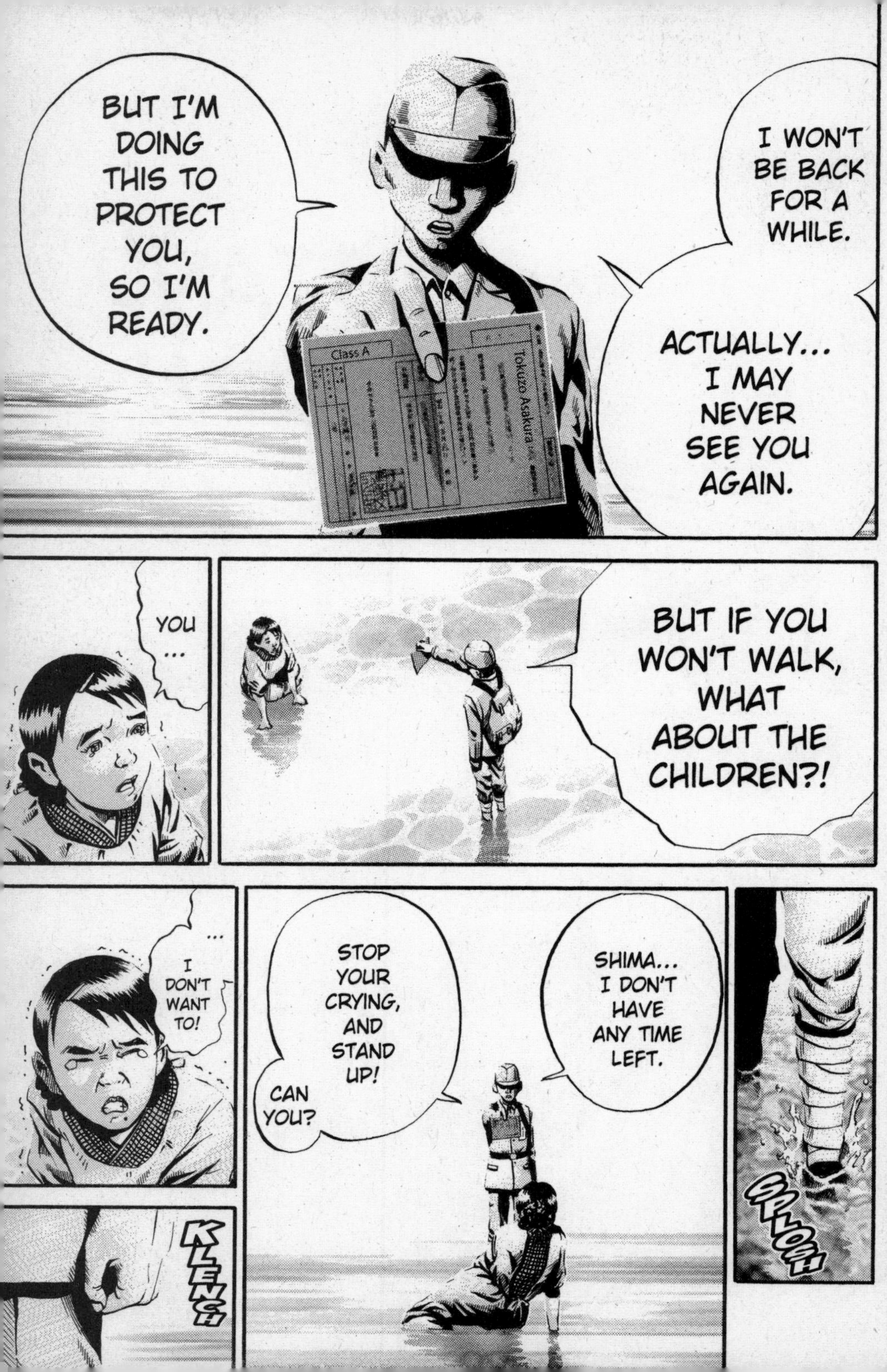
I WON'T BE BACK FOR A WHILE.
ACTUALLY... I MAY NEVER SEE YOU AGAIN.
Tokuzo Asakura
Class A
BUT I'M DOING THIS TO PROTECT YOU, SO I'M READY.
BUT IF YOU WON'T WALK, WHAT ABOUT THE CHILDREN?!
YOU ...
SPLOSH
SHIMA... I DON'T HAVE ANY TIME LEFT.
STOP YOUR CRYING, AND STAND UP!
CAN YOU?
... I DON'T WANT TO!
KLENCH

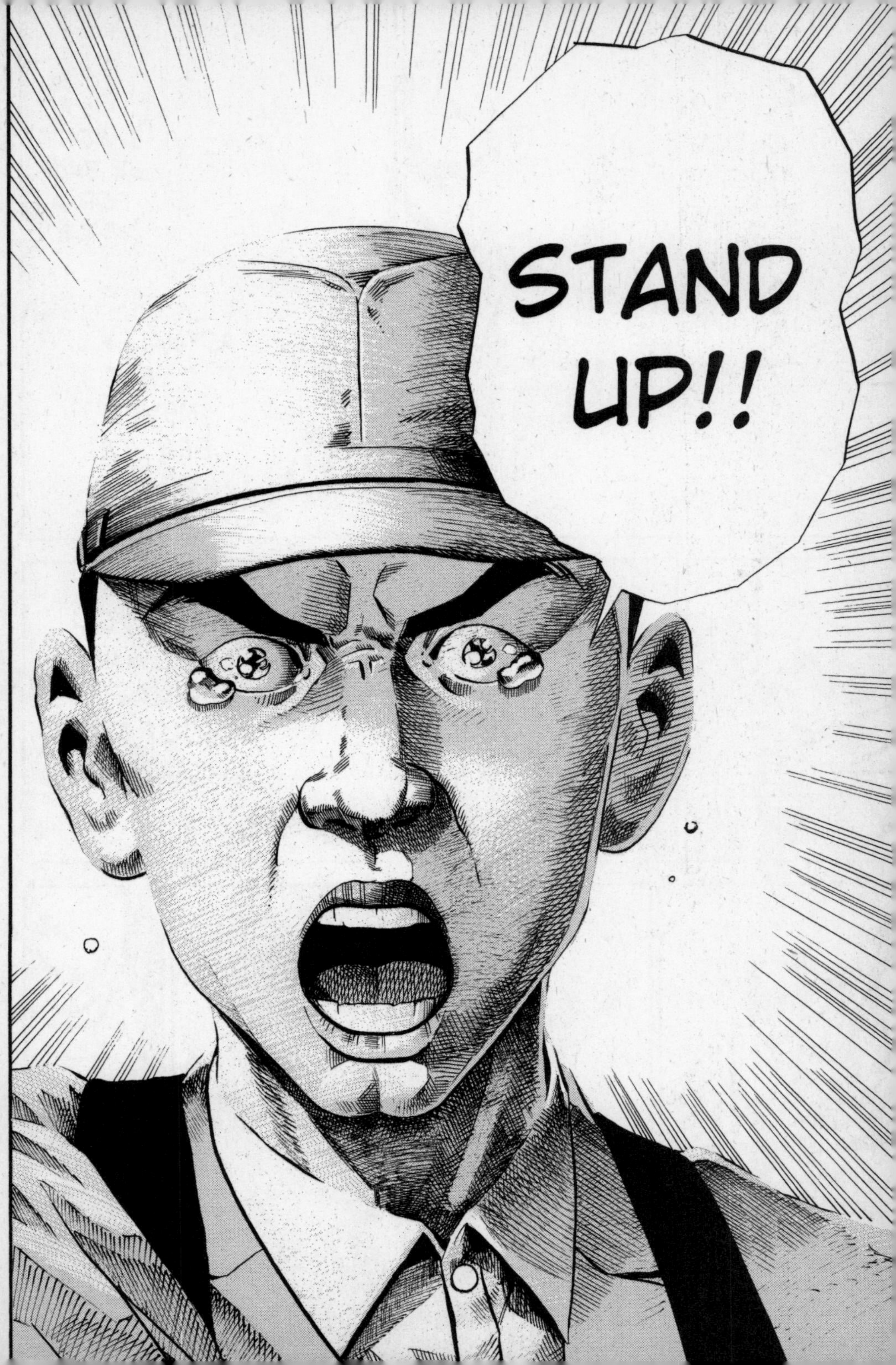
STAND UP!!

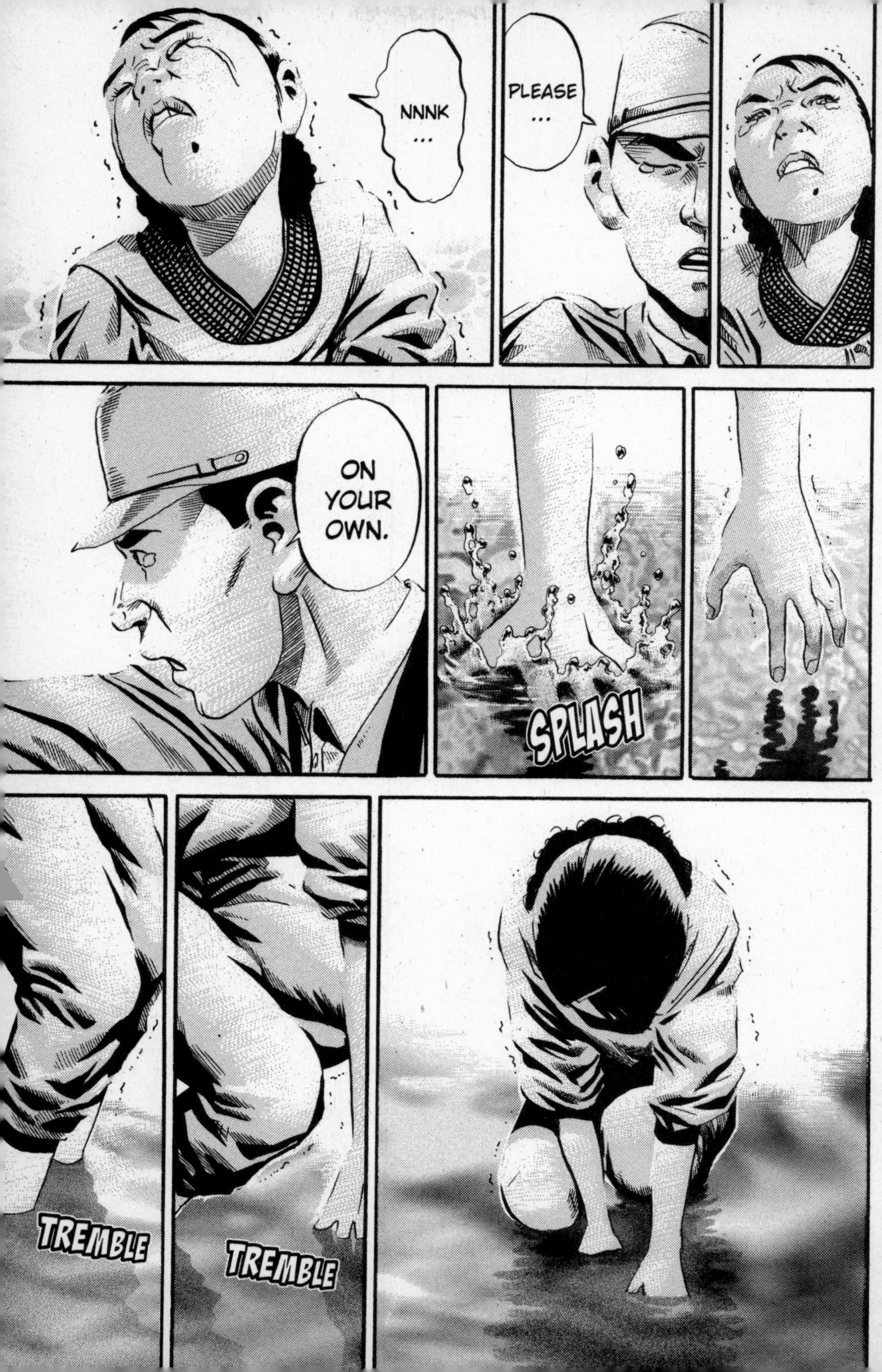
PLEASE ...
NNNK ...
SPLASH
ON YOUR OWN.
TREMBLE
TREMBLE

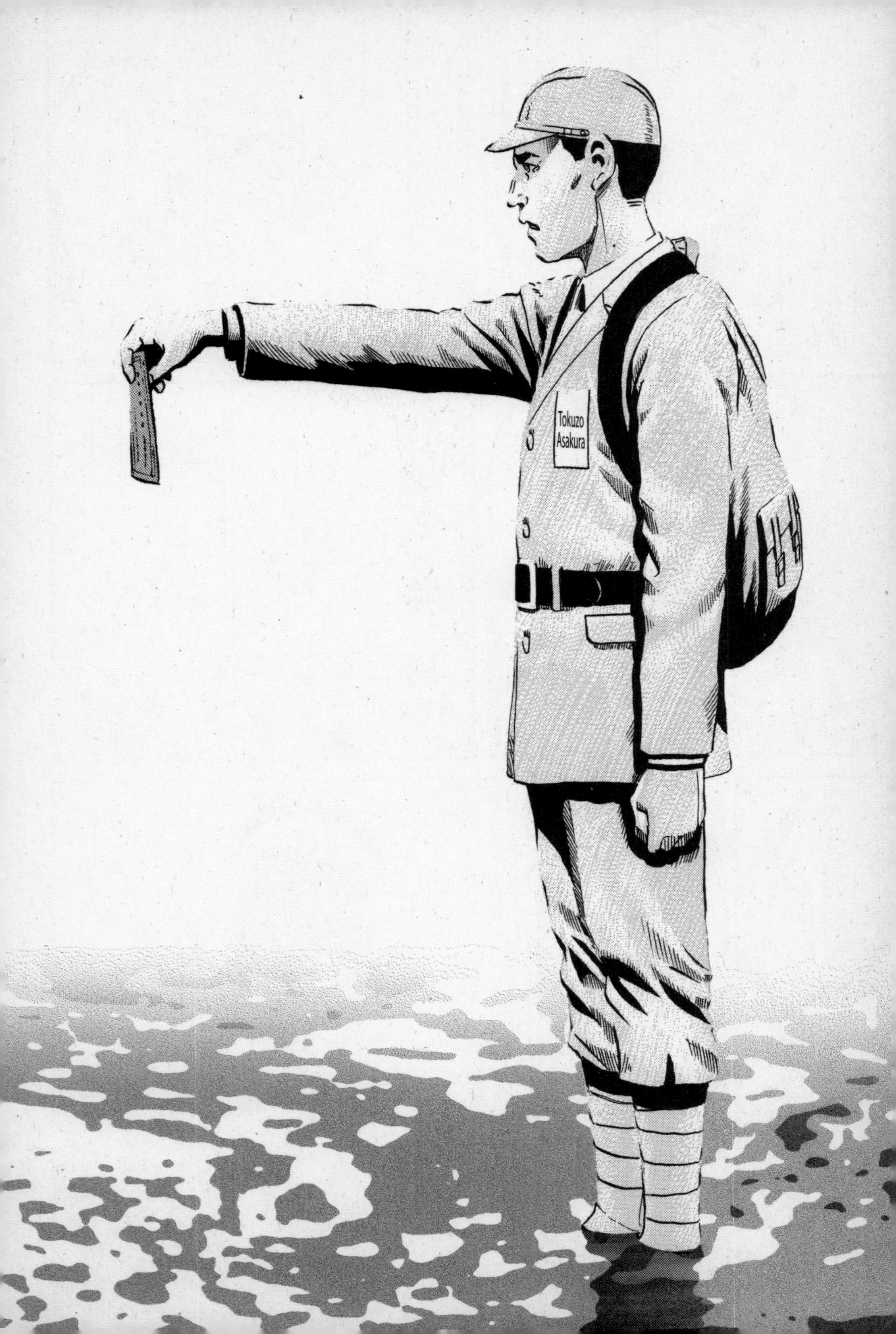
Tokuzo
Asakura

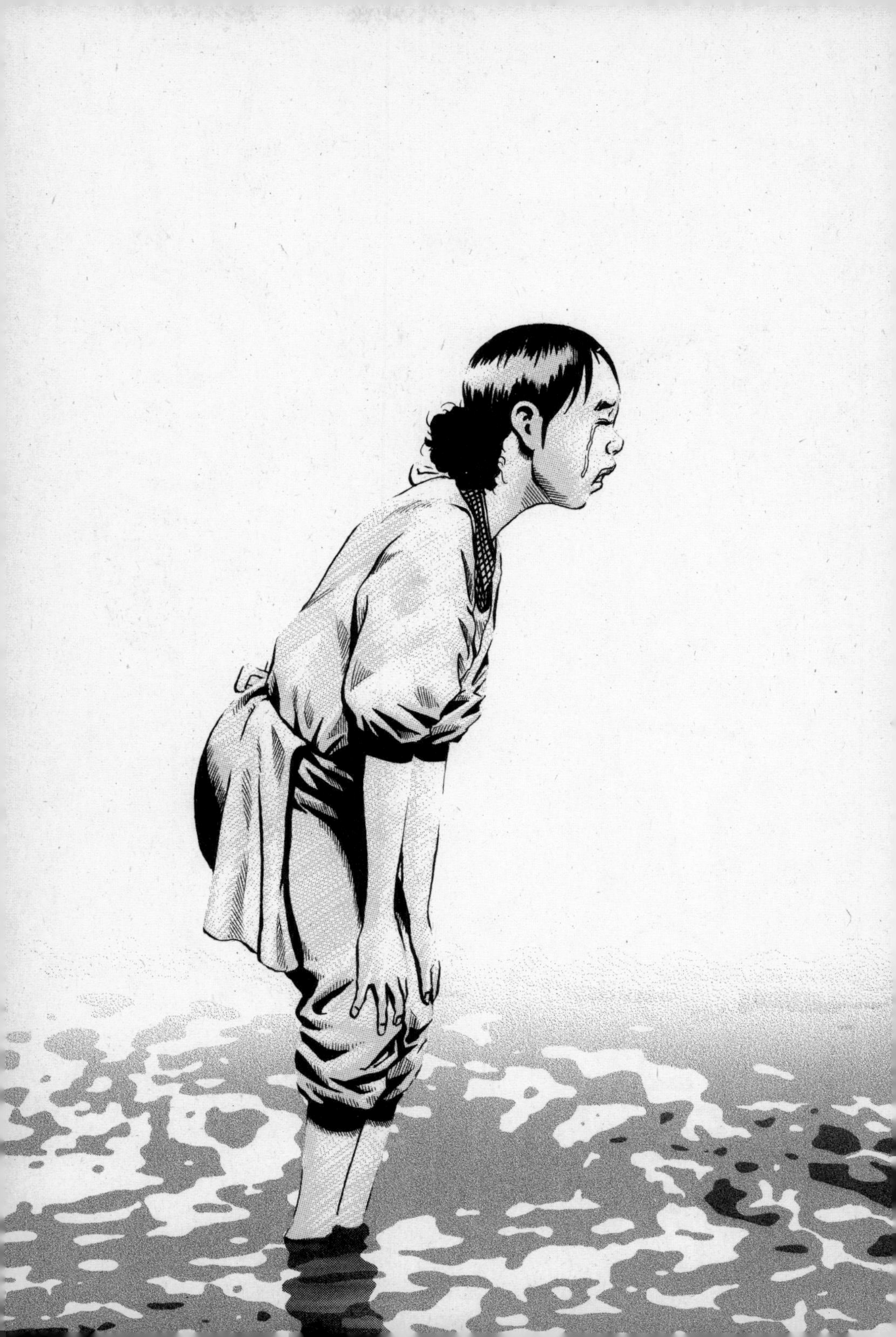

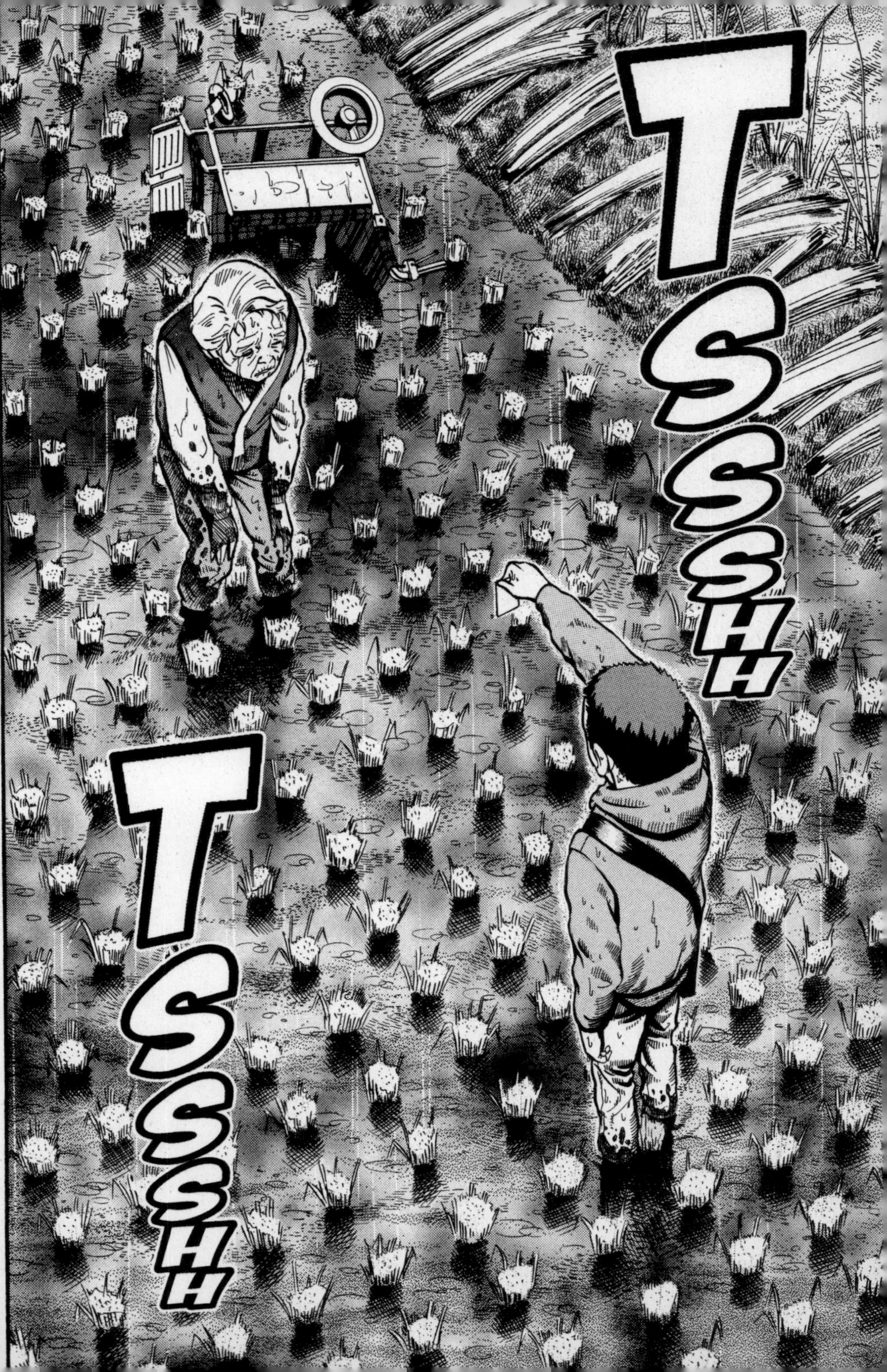
TSSSHH
TSSSHH

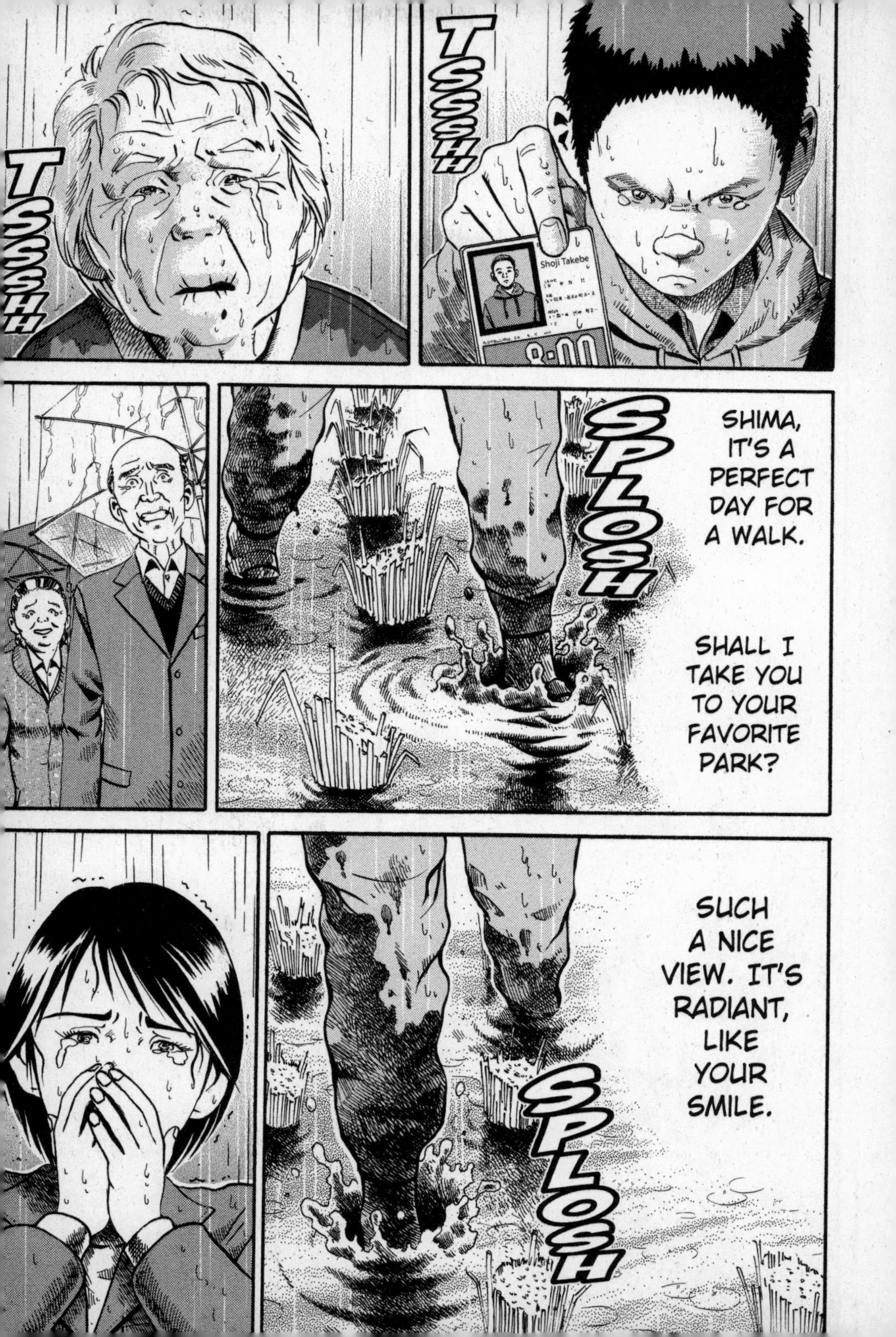
TSSSHH
Shoji Takebe
TSSSHH
SPLOSH
SHIMA, IT'S A PERFECT DAY FOR A WALK.
SHALL I TAKE YOU TO YOUR FAVORITE PARK?
SUCH A NICE VIEW. IT'S RADIANT, LIKE YOUR SMILE.
SPLOSH

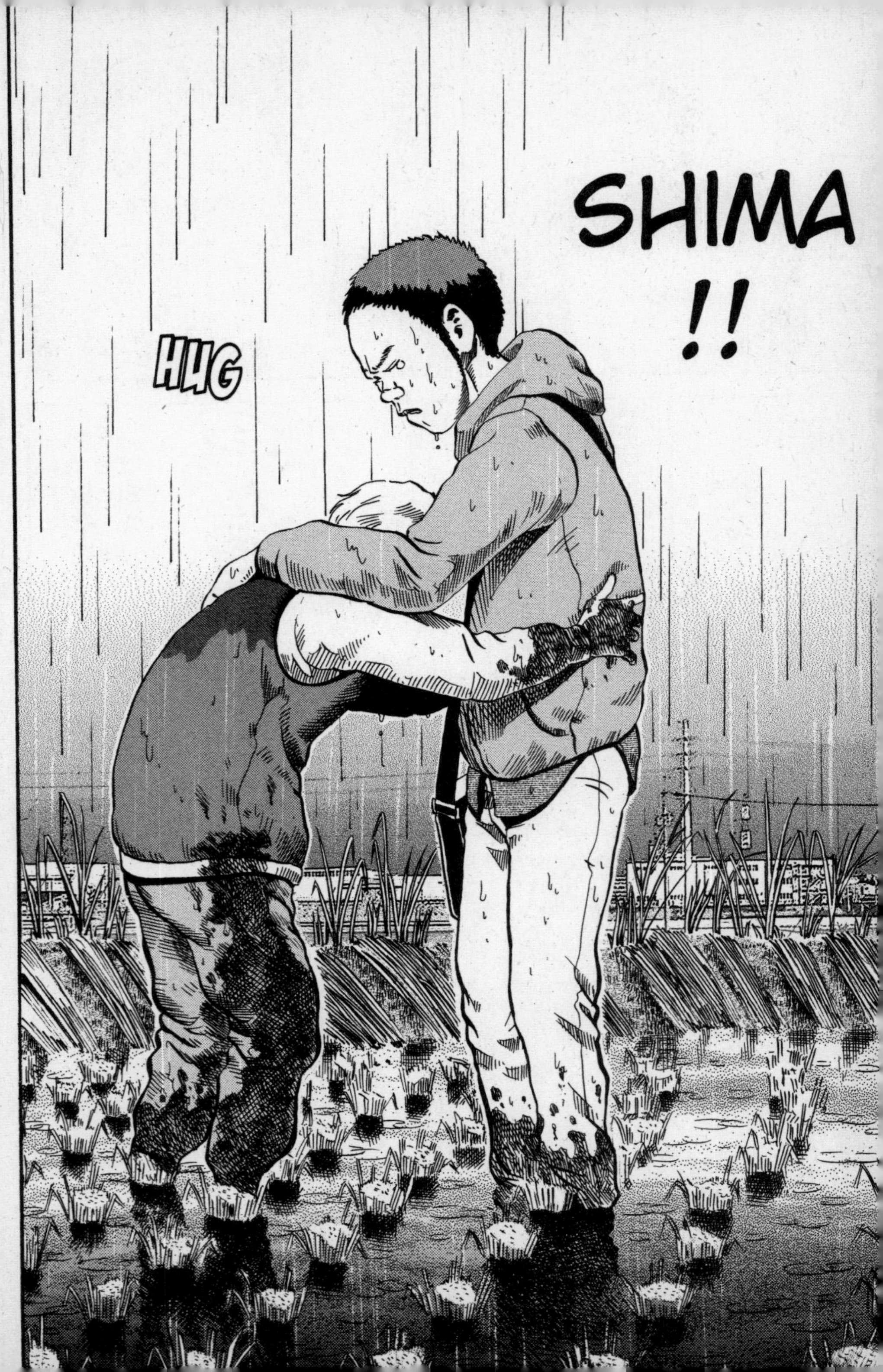
SHIMA !!
HUG

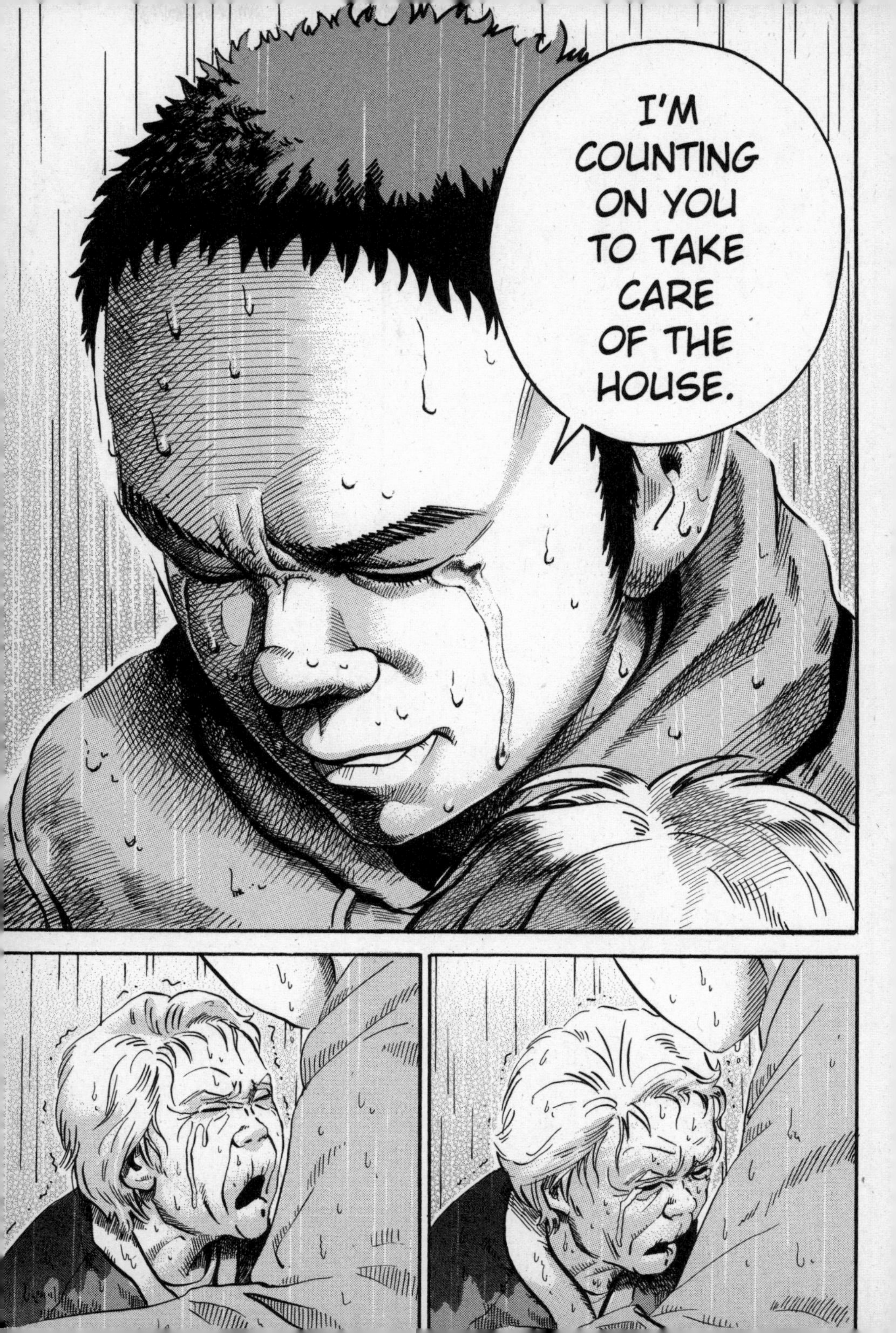
I'M COUNTING ON YOU TO TAKE CARE OF THE HOUSE.

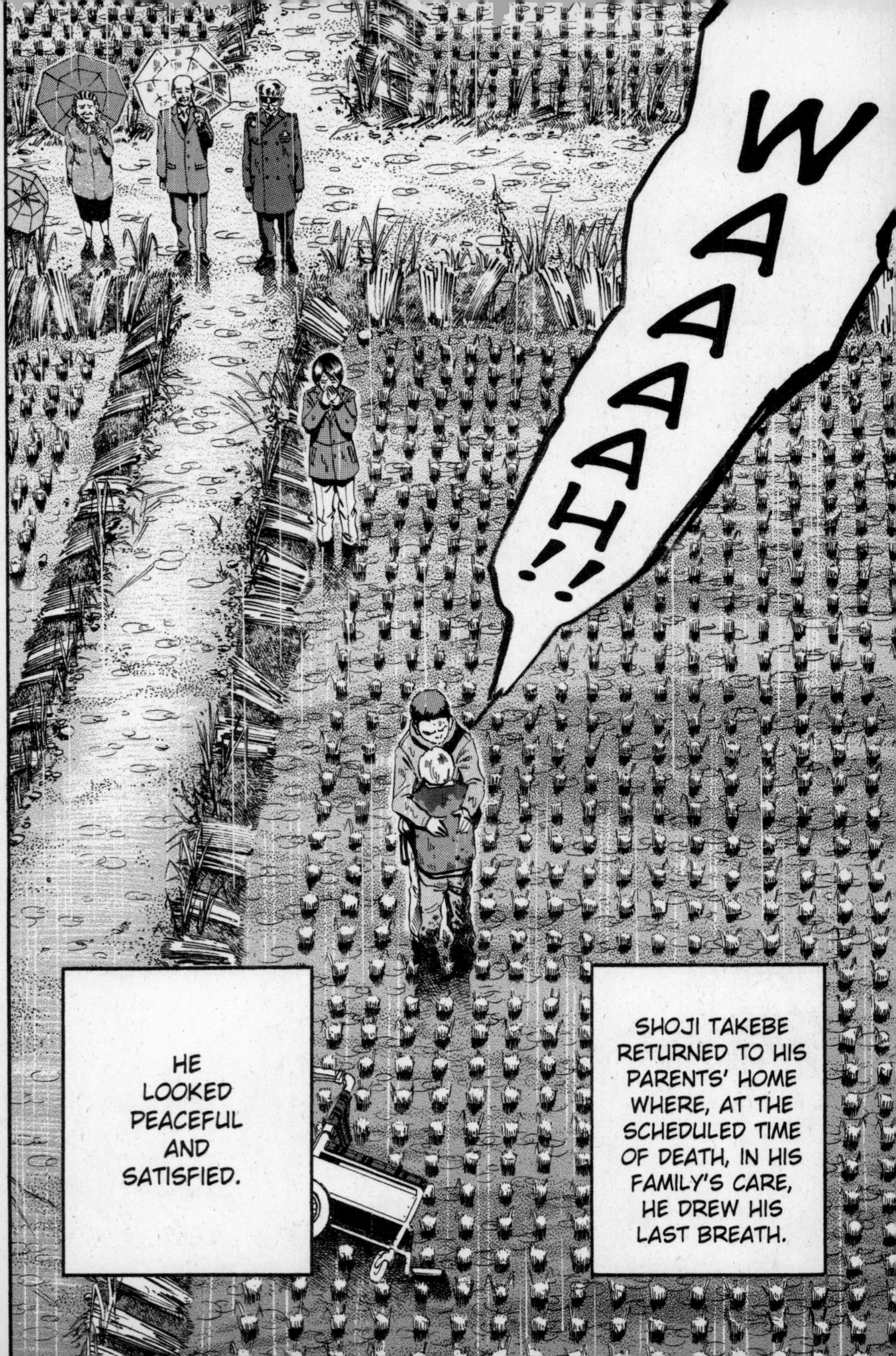
WAAAAH!!
SHOJI TAKEBE RETURNED TO HIS PARENTS' HOME WHERE, AT THE SCHEDULED TIME OF DEATH, IN HIS FAMILY'S CARE, HE DREW HIS LAST BREATH.
HE LOOKED PEACEFUL AND SATISFIED.

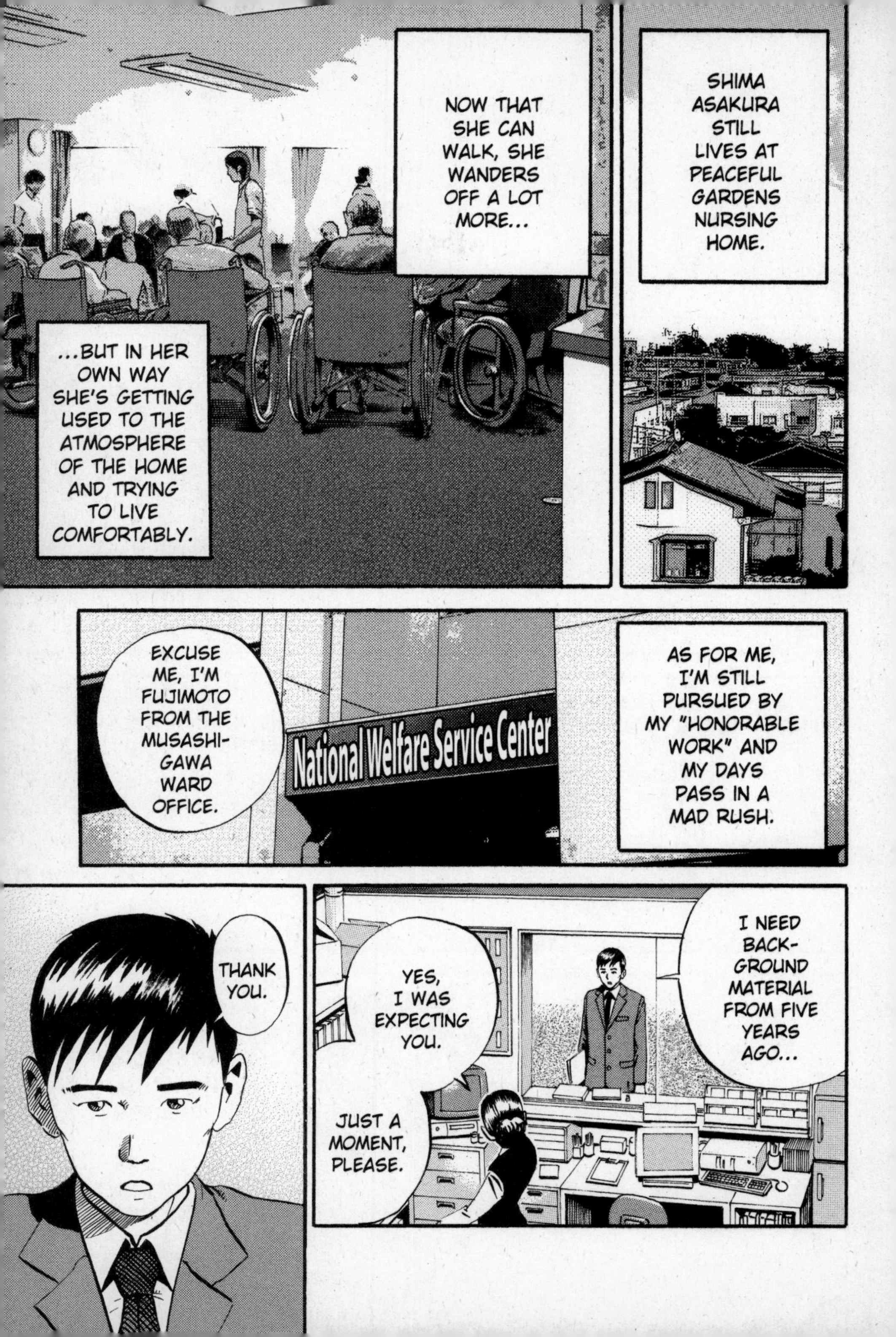
SHIMA ASAKURA STILL LIVES AT PEACEFUL GARDENS NURSING HOME.
NOW THAT SHE CAN WALK, SHE WANDERS OFF A LOT MORE...
...BUT IN HER OWN WAY SHE'S GETTING USED TO THE ATMOSPHERE OF THE HOME AND TRYING TO LIVE COMFORTABLY.
AS FOR ME, I'M STILL PURSUED BY MY "HONORABLE WORK" AND MY DAYS PASS IN A MAD RUSH.
National Welfare Service Center
EXCUSE ME, I'M FUJIMOTO FROM THE MUSASHI-GAWA WARD OFFICE.
I NEED BACK-GROUND MATERIAL FROM FIVE YEARS AGO...
YES, I WAS EXPECTING YOU.
JUST A MOMENT, PLEASE.
THANK YOU.

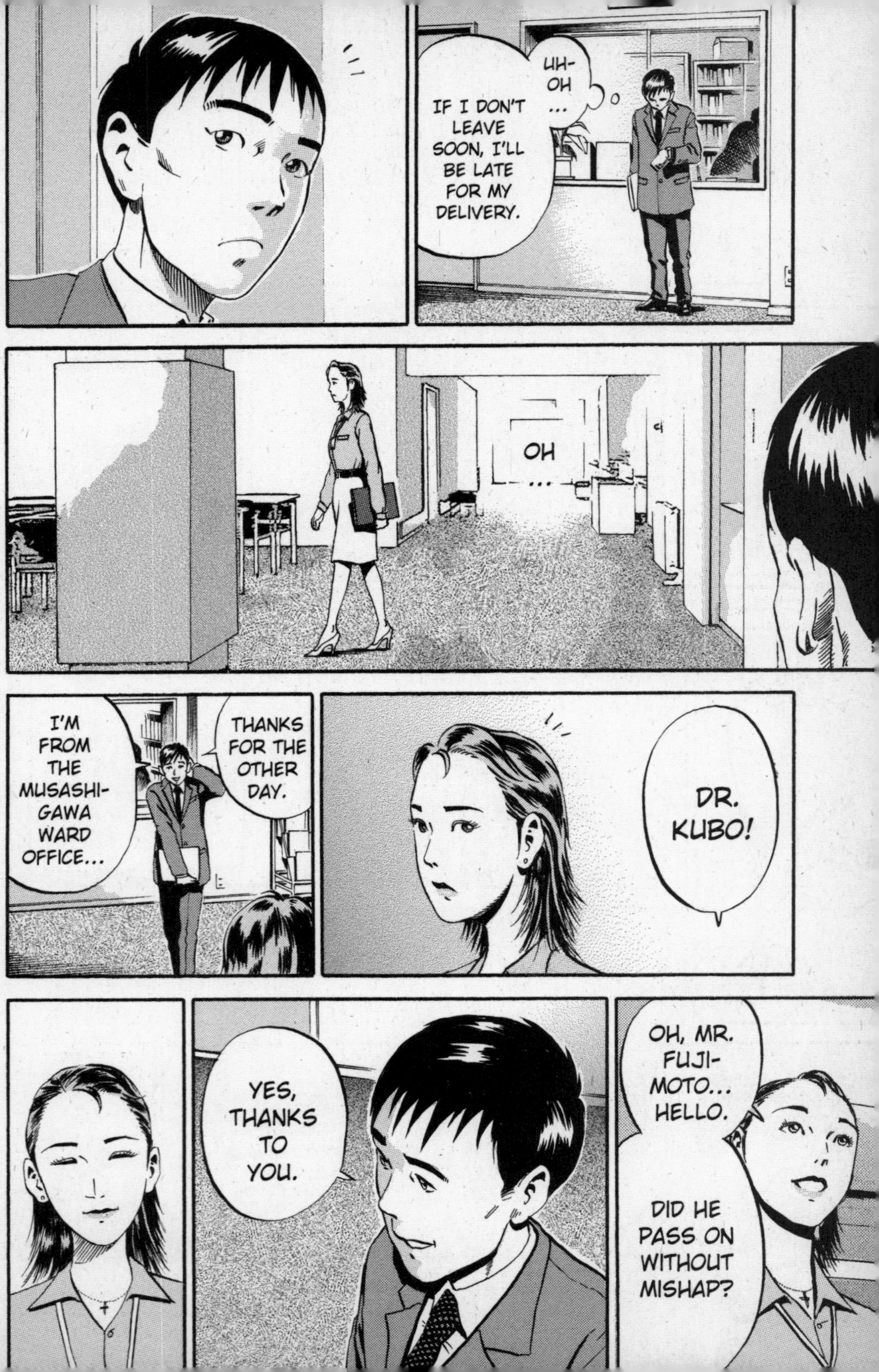
UH-OH ...
IF I DON'T LEAVE SOON, I'LL BE LATE FOR MY DELIVERY.
OH ...
DR. KUBO!
THANKS FOR THE OTHER DAY.
I'M FROM THE MUSASHI-GAWA WARD OFFICE...
OH, MR. FUJI-MOTO... HELLO.
DID HE PASS ON WITHOUT MISHAP?
YES, THANKS TO YOU.

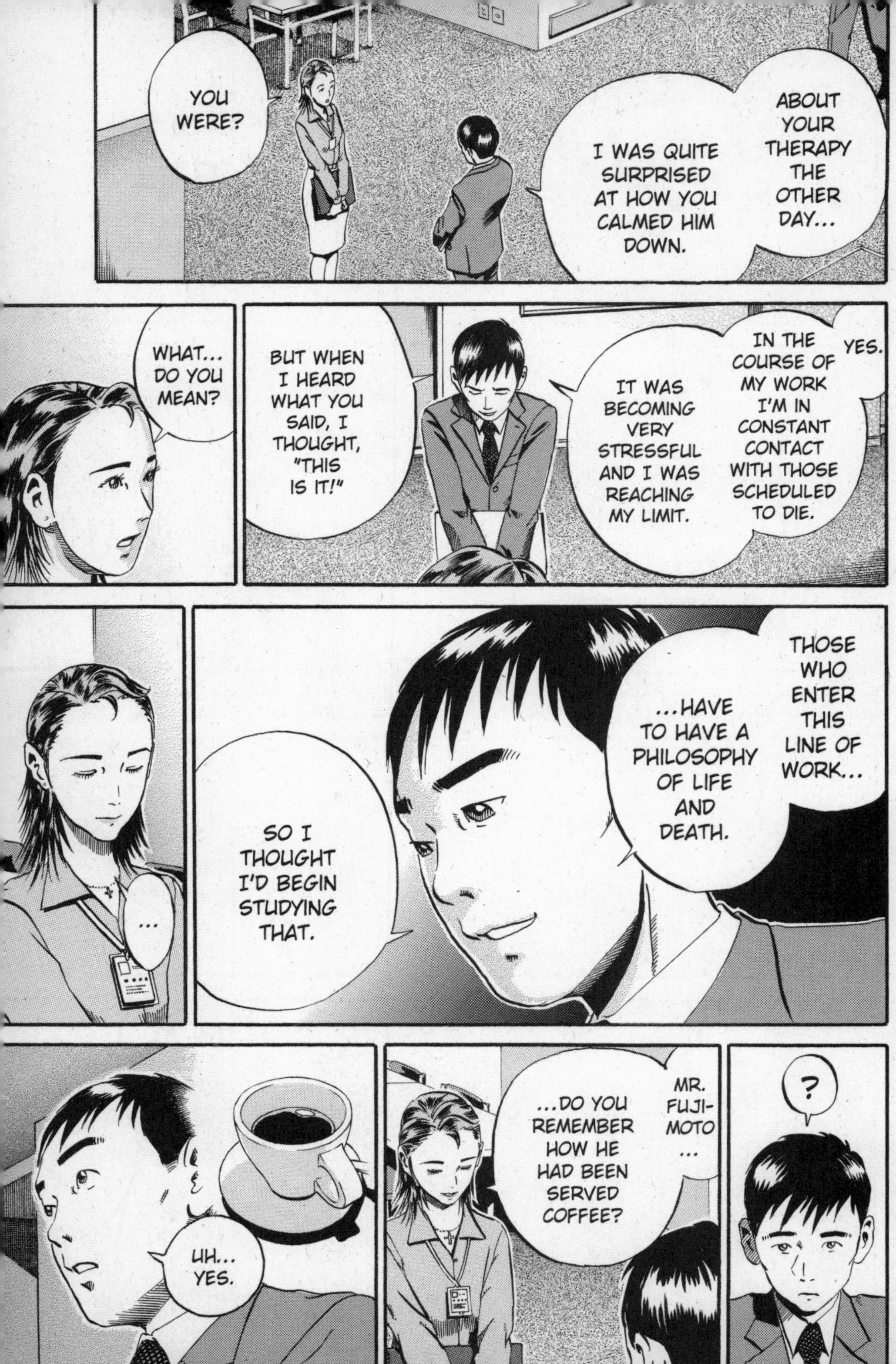
ABOUT YOUR THERAPY THE OTHER DAY...
I WAS QUITE SURPRISED AT HOW YOU CALMED HIM DOWN.
YOU WERE?
YES.
IN THE COURSE OF MY WORK I'M IN CONSTANT CONTACT WITH THOSE SCHEDULED TO DIE.
IT WAS BECOMING VERY STRESSFUL AND I WAS REACHING MY LIMIT.
BUT WHEN I HEARD WHAT YOU SAID, I THOUGHT, "THIS IS IT!"
WHAT... DO YOU MEAN?
THOSE WHO ENTER THIS LINE OF WORK...
...HAVE TO HAVE A PHILOSOPHY OF LIFE AND DEATH.
SO I THOUGHT I'D BEGIN STUDYING THAT.
...
?
MR. FUJI-MOTO...
...DO YOU REMEMBER HOW HE HAD BEEN SERVED COFFEE?
UH... YES.

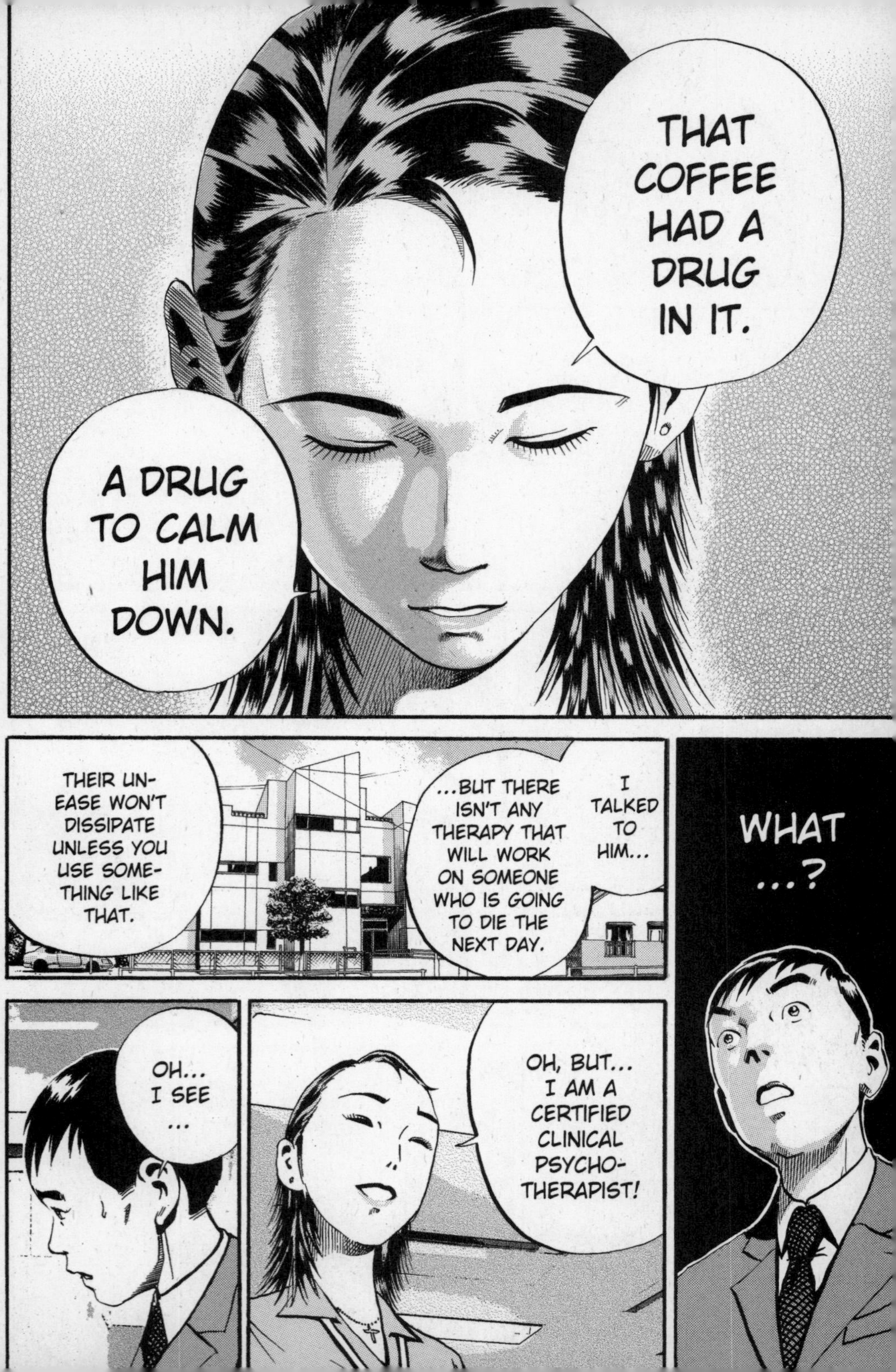
THAT COFFEE HAD A DRUG IN IT.
A DRUG TO CALM HIM DOWN.
WHAT ...?
I TALKED TO HIM...
...BUT THERE ISN'T ANY THERAPY THAT WILL WORK ON SOMEONE WHO IS GOING TO DIE THE NEXT DAY.
THEIR UN-EASE WON'T DISSIPATE UNLESS YOU USE SOME-THING LIKE THAT.
OH, BUT... I AM A CERTIFIED CLINICAL PSYCHO-THERAPIST!
OH... I SEE ...

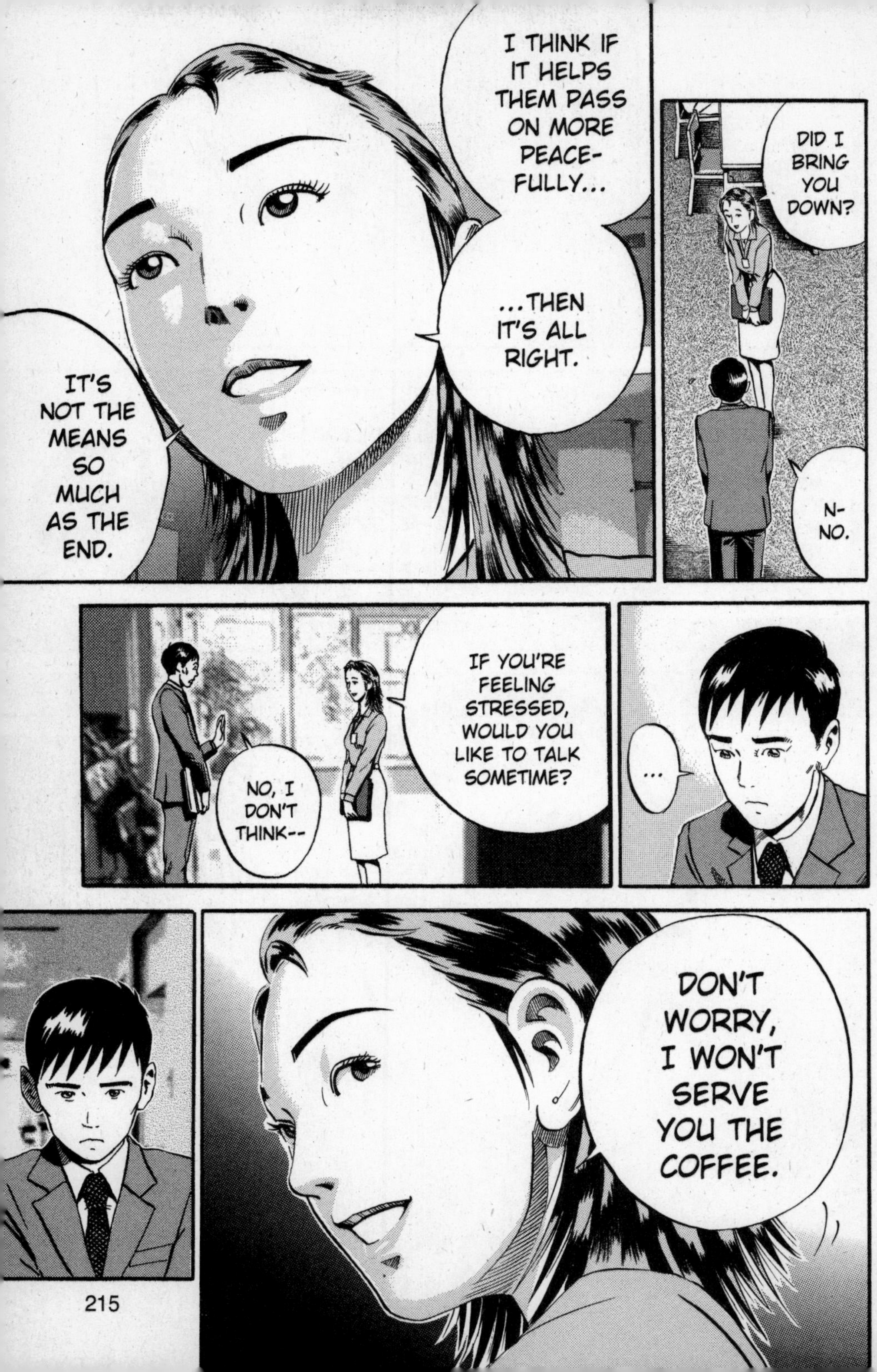
DID I BRING YOU DOWN?
N-NO.
I THINK IF IT HELPS THEM PASS ON MORE PEACE-FULLY...
...THEN IT'S ALL RIGHT.
IT'S NOT THE MEANS SO MUCH AS THE END.
...
IF YOU'RE FEELING STRESSED, WOULD YOU LIKE TO TALK SOMETIME?
NO, I DON'T THINK--
DON'T WORRY, I WON'T SERVE YOU THE COFFEE.

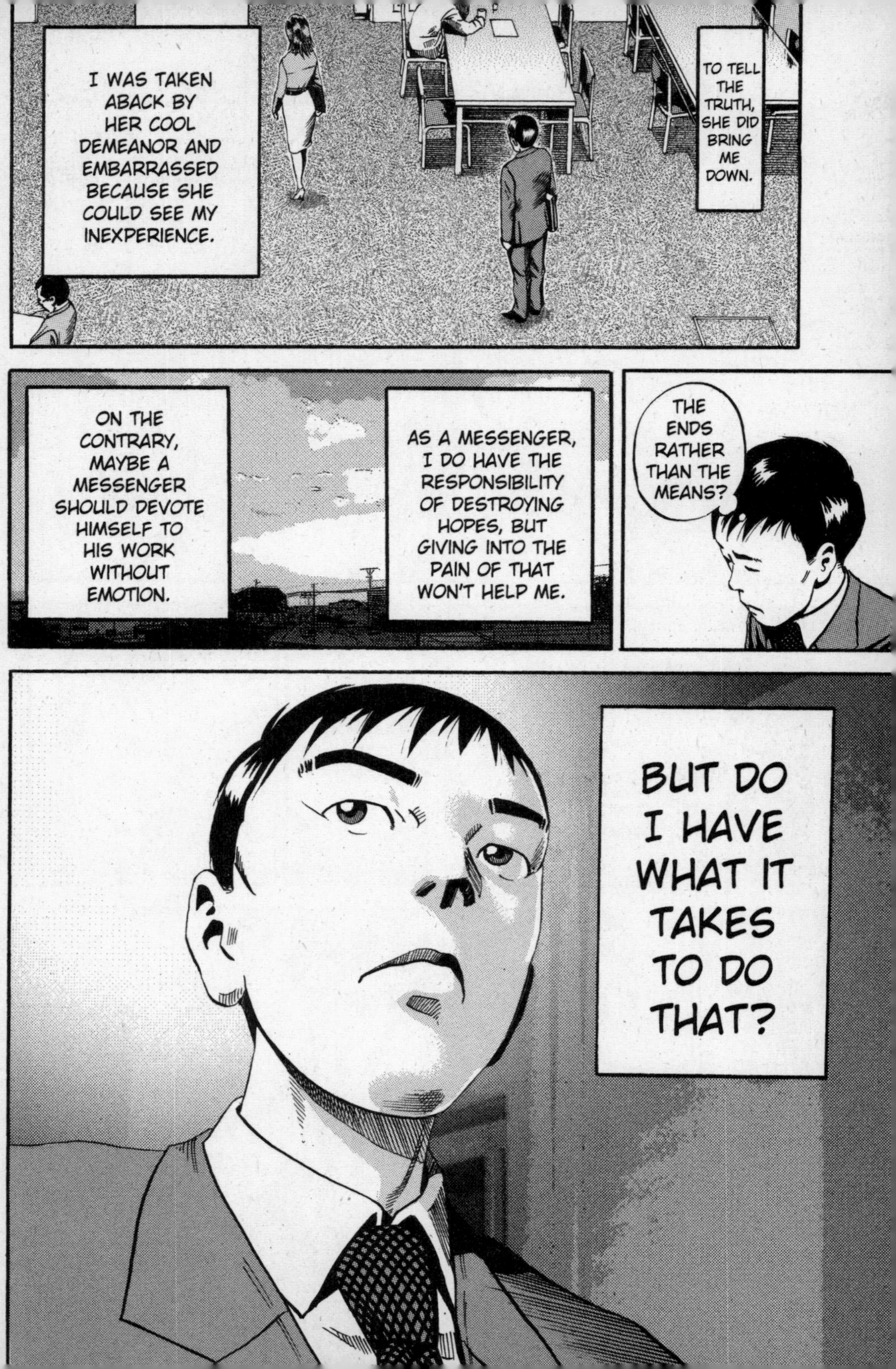
TO TELL THE TRUTH, SHE DID BRING ME DOWN.
I WAS TAKEN ABACK BY HER COOL DEMEANOR AND EMBARRASSED BECAUSE SHE COULD SEE MY INEXPERIENCE.
THE ENDS RATHER THAN THE MEANS?
AS A MESSENGER, I DO HAVE THE RESPONSIBILITY OF DESTROYING HOPES, BUT GIVING INTO THE PAIN OF THAT WON'T HELP ME.
ON THE CONTRARY, MAYBE A MESSENGER SHOULD DEVOTE HIMSELF TO HIS WORK WITHOUT EMOTION.
BUT DO I HAVE WHAT IT TAKES TO DO THAT?

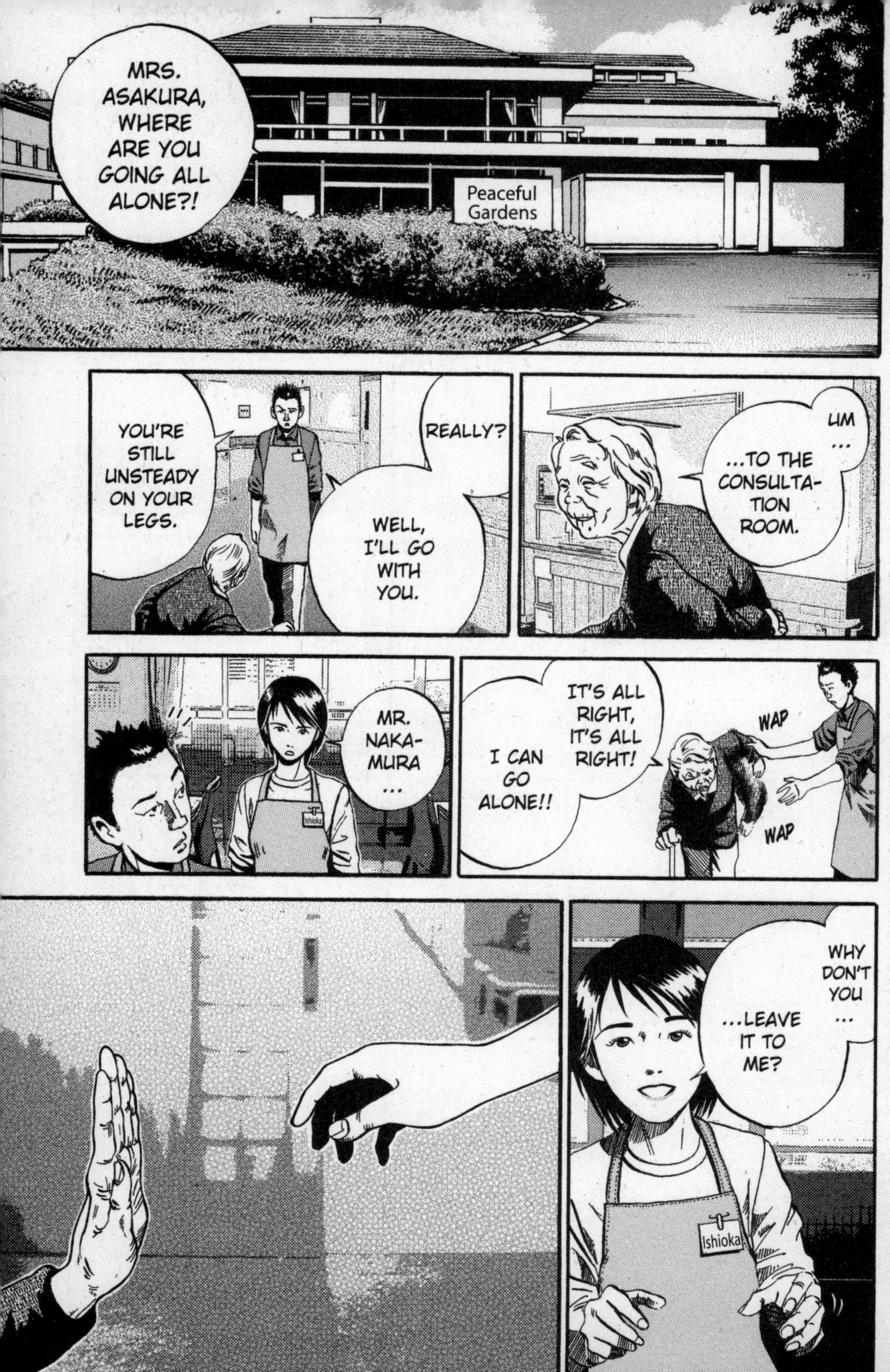
MRS. ASAKURA, WHERE ARE YOU GOING ALL ALONE?!
Peaceful Gardens
UM ...
...TO THE CONSULTATION ROOM.
REALLY?
WELL, I'LL GO WITH YOU.
YOU'RE STILL UNSTEADY ON YOUR LEGS.
IT'S ALL RIGHT, IT'S ALL RIGHT!
I CAN GO ALONE!!
WAP
WAP
MR. NAKAMURA ...
Ishioka
WHY DON'T YOU ...
...LEAVE IT TO ME?
Ishioka

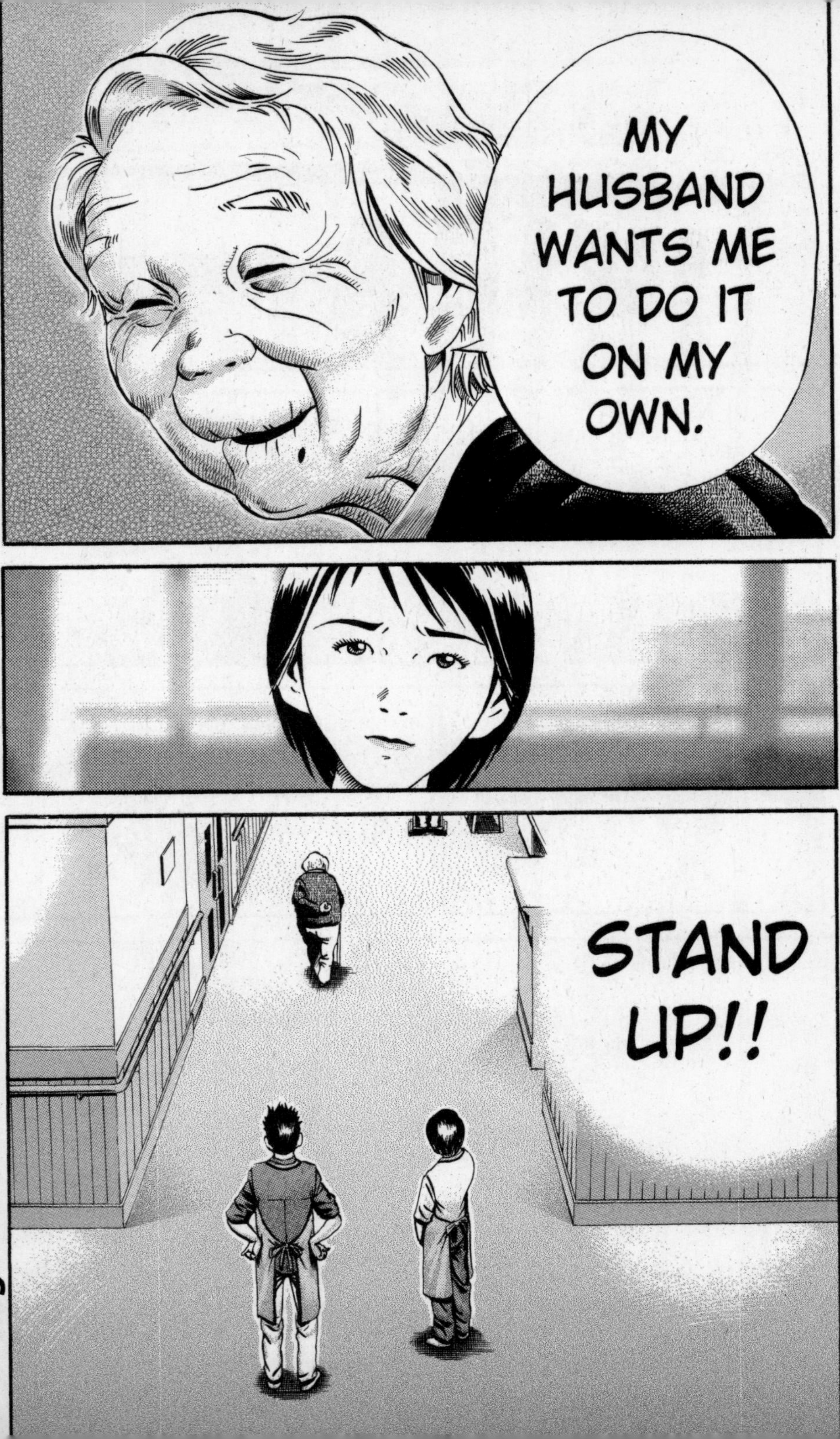
MY HUSBAND WANTS ME TO DO IT ON MY OWN.
STAND UP!!

Ikigami 2 / The end

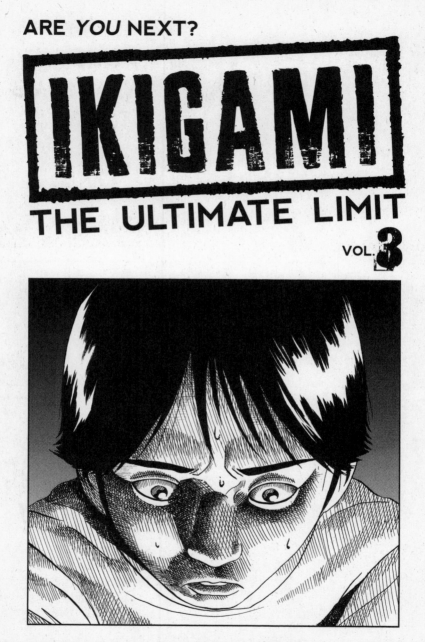

ARE *YOU* NEXT?

IKIGAMI
THE ULTIMATE LIMIT
VOL. 3

Featuring Episodes 5 *An Unpredictable Life* **& 6** *The Loveliest Lie!*

Motoro Mase was born in Aichi in Japan in 1969 and is also the artist of *Kyoichi* and, with Keigo Higashino, *HE∀DS*, which, like *Ikigami*, was serialized in *Young Sunday*. In 1998, Mase's *AREA* was nominated for Shogakukan's 43rd grand prize for a comic by a new artist.

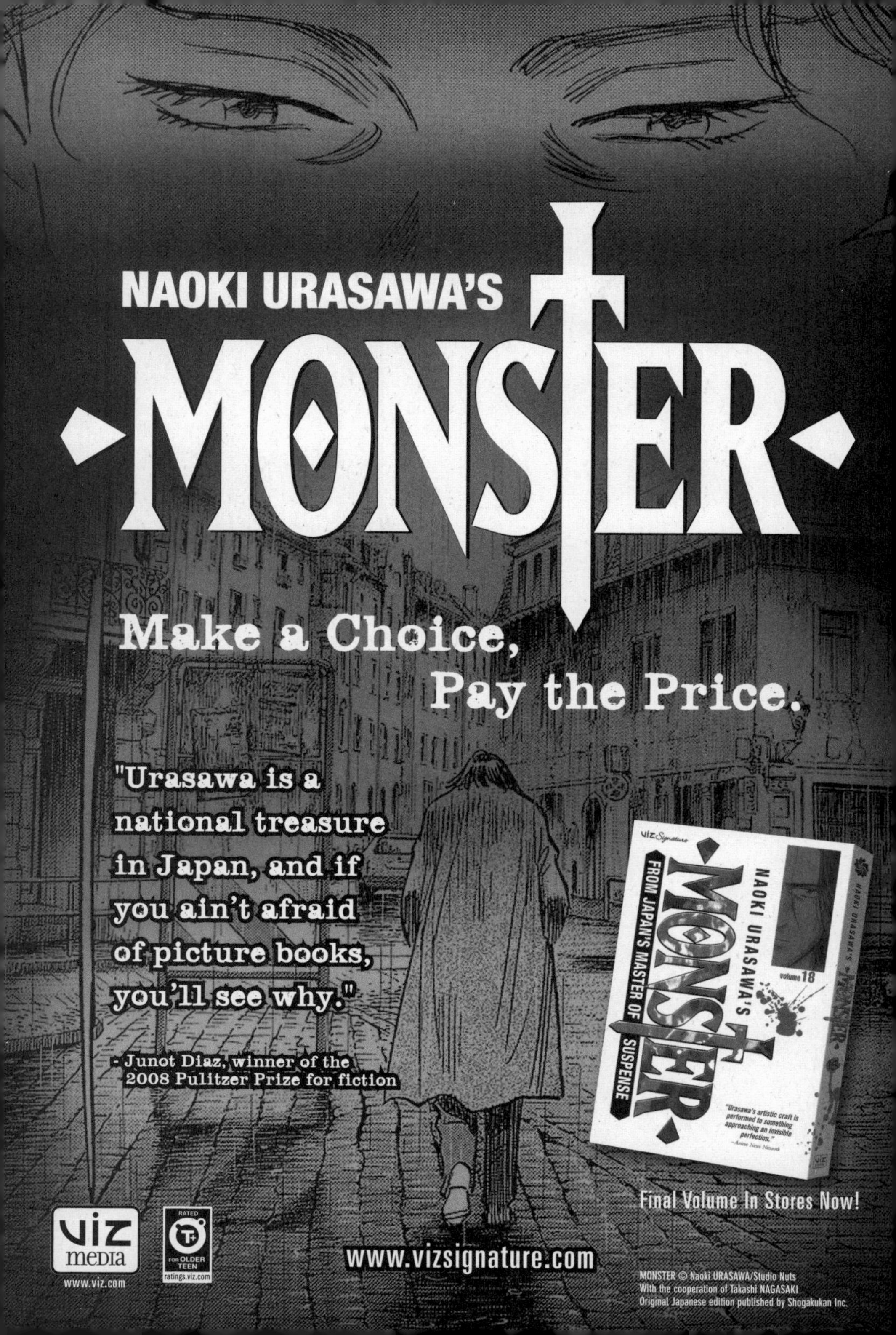

NAOKI URASAWA'S
MONSTER
Make a Choice,
Pay the Price.
"Urasawa is a national treasure in Japan, and if you ain't afraid of picture books, you'll see why."
- Junot Diaz, winner of the 2008 Pulitzer Prize for fiction
NAOKI URASAWA'S MONSTER
FROM JAPAN'S MASTER OF SUSPENSE
volume 18
Final Volume In Stores Now!
viz media
www.viz.com
RATED T+ FOR OLDER TEEN
ratings.viz.com
www.vizsignature.com
MONSTER © Naoki URASAWA/Studio Nuts
With the cooperation of Takashi NAGASAKI
Original Japanese edition published by Shogakukan Inc.

BLACK LAGOON

A GRAND ADVENTURE ON THE HIGH SEAS!

In a deadly world of outlawed heroes, brutal villains, and blazing gunfights, it's hard to know who to trust.

So when an average salaryman needs to make a very special delivery, can he count on the pirate crew of the infamous torpedo boat *Black Lagoon*?

Find out in the *Black Lagoon* manga series—buy yours today!

On sale at store.viz.com
Also available at your local bookstore and comic store.

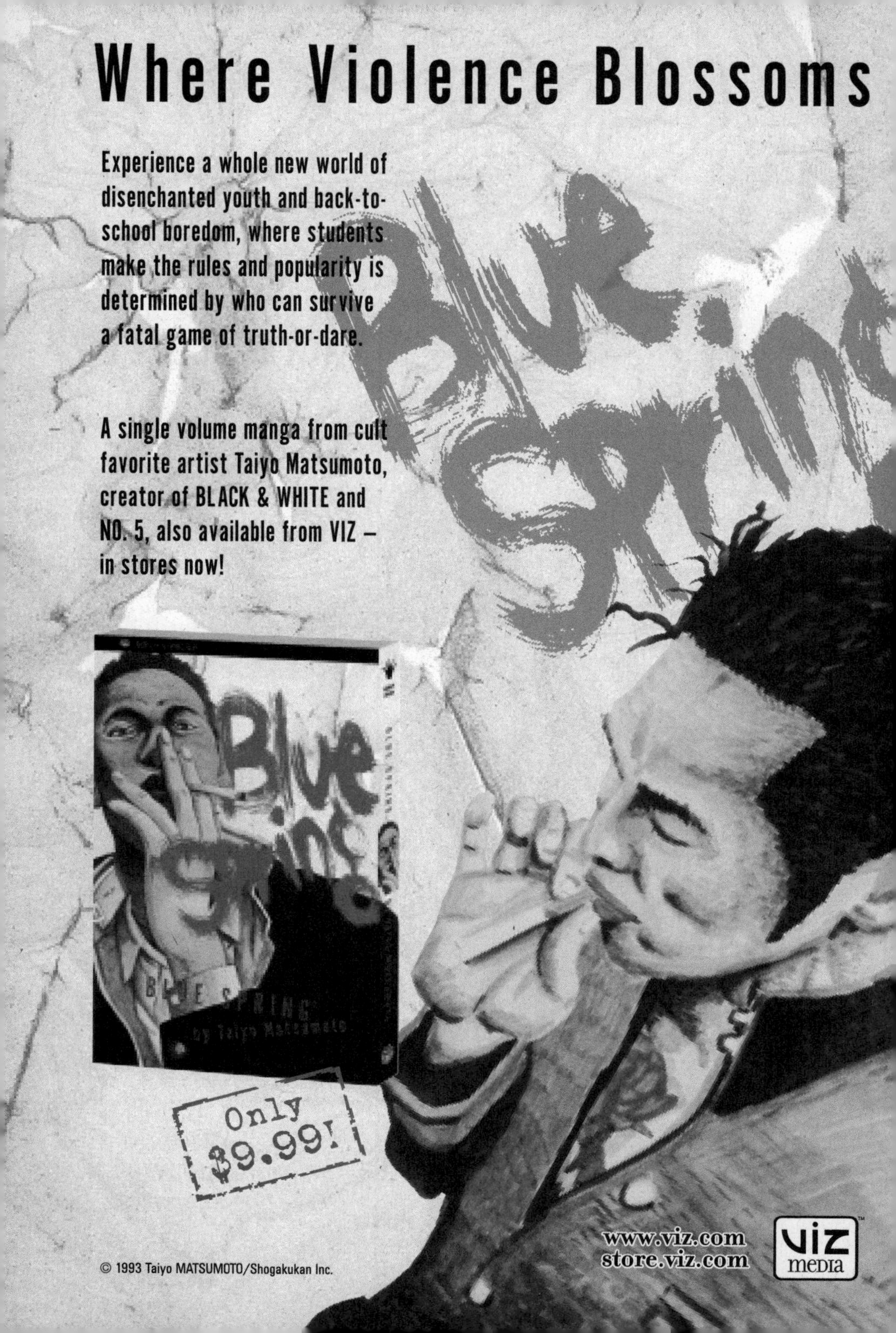
Where Violence Blossoms
Experience a whole new world of disenchanted youth and back-to-school boredom, where students make the rules and popularity is determined by who can survive a fatal game of truth-or-dare.
A single volume manga from cult favorite artist Taiyo Matsumoto, creator of BLACK & WHITE and NO. 5, also available from VIZ – in stores now!
Blue Spring
BLUE SPRING
by Taiyo Matsumoto
Only $9.99!
© 1993 Taiyo MATSUMOTO/Shogakukan Inc.
www.viz.com
store.viz.com
viz media